A White Paper
on
South-North Dialogue
in
Korea

A White Paper on South-North Dialogue
in Korea

Published on December 31, 1988
by
National Unification Board
Republic of Korea

C.P.O. Box 4161 Seoul, Korea

Table of Contents

Part III: Entry into Age of Inter-Korean Exchanges and Cooperation

Part One

Initiation of South-North Dialogue and the Search for an Approach

1. Changes in Inter-Korean Relations

a. Division

The Korean peninsula (area : 220,000 square kilometers), the home of the Korean people who retain a traditional culture and an uninterrupted national history of 4,300 years since the founding of their nation by Tangun, sits on a strategic location where the interests of the continental forces of China and Russia and the maritime forces of the United States and Japan have continuously converged.

Because of the geopolitical conditions of their land, the Koreans have had to wage countless struggles against alien peoples to safeguard their independence, often suffering trials and ordeals in the process.

Throughout their history, however, the Korean people have never resorted to arms for the purpose of expanding their land or for conquering other people. They have only indulged in cultivating their unique national culture and promoting freedom and peace based on the sense of nationhood as a homogenous people.

In the modern period, however, the Korean people suffered their worst tribulation when they lost their national sovereignty due to Japan's martial oppression. The Koreans were faced with an unprecedented crisis that shook the nation's survival from the very roots.

But the Korean people refused to yield to the wicked attempt of the Japanese imperialists to shatter Korea to pieces. They mounted relentless struggles at home and abroad against Japan to regain their national independence.

With the unconditional surrender of Japan on August 15, 1945, the Korean peninsula was liberated from the Japanese imperialists, and the Korean people experienced the joy of national liberation. This emotional rejoicing, however, did not last very long. A new tragedy was about to be experienced by the Korean people. The Korean peninsula, the Koreans' home for 4,300 years, was divided into the north and the south along the 38th Parallel by the victor countries, the United States and the Soviet Union.

In fact, it was at the Cairo conference of November 1943, that the world powers began to discuss seriously the future of the Korean peninsula. At a meeting attended by U.S. President Roosevelt, British Prime Minister Churchill and Chinese Generalissimo Chiang Kaishek, the leaders of the Allies agreed to "accord the Korean people freedom and independence through due process" after the war ends.

During the talks among the world powers, however, the seed of future misfortunes on the Korean peninsula was sown by agreements on a Korean trusteeship and division of the Korean peninsula into the north and the south. In April 1943, President Roosevelt and British Foreign Secretary Anthony Eden agreed in their meeting that Korea "would fall under international trusteeship" and that "the trustees might be the United States, the Soviet Union and China." Again in his meeting with Churchill and Stalin in Tehran on November 28, 1943, Roosevelt contended that the Koreans "need at least 40 years of apprenticeship before full independence might be attained," and obtained Stalin's concurrence.

Also, at the Yalta summit meeting of the United States, Britain and the Soviet Union in February 1945, President Roosevelt said there might be a trusteeship for Korea composed of Soviet, American and Chinese representatives for at least 20 to 30 years. Moreover, at Yalta they agreed to recognize Russia's pre-1905 territorial desires regarding Manchuria in return for the Soviets' entry into the war against Japan, thus paving the way to the North-South division of the Korean peninsula.

A working-level discussion followed on the issue of trusteeship, and it was agreed in principle that the trustees would be the United States, Britain, the Soviet Union and China. At the Potsdam summit meeting among the U.S., Britain and the Soviet Union in July 1945, which President Truman attended in place of the deceased Roosevelt, items agreed on at the Cairo meeting with respect to the Korean question were reaffirmed, thus emphasizing again the principle that Korea "should be made independent in due course."

As the war neared its end without any firm blueprint regarding the Korean question and when the Soviet Union entered the war against Japan on August 9, 1945, the United States came to face the question of where to draw the dividing line for the U.S. and Soviet occupation zones on the Korean peninsula.

Several American diplomats, who saw through the Soviet maneuver, recommended that their government speed up military actions in the Far East and that U.S.troops accept the surrender of the Japanese troops at least on the entire peninsula to prevent Soviet forces from entering into Korea. But when the Soviet troops promptly initiated direct military action against northern Korea after their entry into the war on August 9, the nearest American forces were on Okinawa.

Under these circumstances, the U.S. government, accepting the recommendation of Colonels C.H.Bonesteel (who later served as Commander-in-Chief of the United Nations Command in Korea) and Dean Rusk(later Secretary of State) of the General Staff of the War Department, decided on August 11 that the Soviet Union would be authorized to receive the Japanese surrender north of the 38th Parallel and the United States would receive it south of that line. The plan was transmitted to and accepted by the governments of Great Britain, the Soviet Union and China on August 13. It was also sent to the MacArthur Command on August 15 as General Order No. 1 for immediate implementation.

The order provided that after the U.S. and Soviet occupation commanders receive the surrender of Japanese troops in their respective areas of the Korean peninsula, the "civil administration functions should be integrated and turned over to a committee of commanders from those countries taking part in the occupation of the Korean peninsula to place the entire area of Korea under integrated control." But the order also said that during the receipt of the surrender period, the U.S. and Soviet occupation commanders would be responsible for the administration of civil affairs in their respective areas, thus providing the base on which the military division of the Korean peninsula could be developed into a political division.

The territorial division, imposed upon the Koreans unilaterally against their will, has hardened as time has passed. And from the very moment of division, south and north Korea were made to pursue unbridgeable and divergent roads.

11

In particular, the Soviet forces, who entered the northern area of Korea ahead of the American landing in the southern Korea, promptly embarked on a prepared scenario to build a Communist society in their occupation area of north Korea.

When the Soviets entered Pyongyang on August 24, 1945, there already existed an administration body, the Pyongannam-do branch of the Committee for the Preparation of Korean Independence. It was composed of 18 rightists and two Communists from the domestic Communist faction. The committee was chaired by Cho Man-shik, the president of the Christian Democratic Party.

On August 26, however, the Soviet occupation authorities transformed Cho's committee into the People's Political Committee, whose members were equally divided between rightists and Communists. By September 2, the same type of committees were set up in other northern provinces as well, which exercised perfunctory power under the close direction and supervision of the Soviet occupation authorities.

On October 28, 1945, the Soviet occupation authorities reorganized the People's Political Committees in five north Korean provinces into the Five-Provinces Administration Bureau. On February 8, 1946, they inaugurated the north Korean Interim People's Committee with a de facto government system with Kim Il-sung as chairman and most key posts filled by communists. The Communists thus expedited their scheme to set up a unilateral Communist regime in north Korea, regardless of the question of unifying divided Korea.

Earlier, in October 1945, the Soviet occupation authorities staged the "Conference of the North Korean Five Provinces Party Representatives and Enthusiasts" in Pyongyang to establish the north Korean Branch of the Korean Communist Party. It was here that Kim Il-sung was first introduced to the attending Communists. To most of them Kim Il-sung was a stranger. At the third expanded meeting of the north Korean Branch in December, the Branch was reorganized into the (north) Korean Communist Party with Kim Il-sung as its "responsible secretary" (party head). Kim Il-sung's absolute rule over the Party was thus secured.

It was around this time that the (north) Korean Communist Party, at

12

the instructions of the Soviet occupation authorities, began to act under the so-called "theory of north Korea as a base for democratic revolution," rejecting unification under conditions not conducive to the communization of the entire Korean peninsula and attempting to firm up the political fixation of territorial division and to establish a separate Communist regime in north Korea.

Meanwhile, confusion fed by fierce confrontations between the rightists and leftists reigned in south Korea in the early period of the U.S. military government. The unrest was attributable to the delayed arrival of the U.S. military in Korea and their lack of any advance preparation for military government.

The U.S. military government, totally unprepared for political developments in Korea, merely continued the futile efforts to arrange collaboration between the rightists and leftists on the premise of a plan for Korean trusteeship.

The meeting of the foreign ministers of the United States, Britain and the Soviet Union held in December 16-20, 1945, in Moscow, decided that 1) a trusteeship was to be established on the Korean peninsula by the U.S., Great Britain, China and the Soviet Union for five years, 2) a provisional Korean government was to be formed by Koreans, to have integrated administrative authority over the entire Korean peninsula, 3) a joint American-Soviet commission was to be established, its primary responsibility to assist in the formation of a provisional Korean government through consultation with the Korean "democratic" political parties and social organizations, and 4) the commission was to work out measures for helping and assisting the political, economic and social progress of the Korean people, and the development of an independent Korea, matters of which were to be referred to the four-power trustee council.

When the news of the Moscow agreement reached Korea on December 29, 1945, all the political forces in south Korea, right and left, opposed it. In a few days, however, the Communists and leftists, acting on instructions from Moscow, suddenly changed their position and declared their support of the trusteeship. Hence, a sharp antagonism developed between the right-wing forces rejecting the trusteeship and the pro-trusteeship Communists and left-wing elements.

In northern Korea, the north Korean Communist Party arrested Cho Man-shik, who opposed the trusteeship, and began purging other rightists and nationalist leaders opposed to trusteeship as "national traitors," "reactionaries" or "counter-revolutionaries." Faced with this and other oppressive actions, some 3,283,000 north Korean residents escaped the Communist tyranny and crossed the 38th Parallel, at the risk of their lives, into the south.

The Joint U.S.-USSR Commission formed under the Moscow protocol met twice, in March 20-May 12, 1946, and in May 21-October 18, 1947, in Seoul. But efforts to solve the Korean question through the Joint Commission ended in failure due to wide differences in the two countries' basic positions. The Soviets argued that "the Commission should not even hold discussion with those organizations and individuals that opposed the tsusteeship, much less let them be included in an interim government," thus revealing their intent to consult only with the leftists that supported the trusteeship idea.

The Soviet occupation authorities, disregarding the Joint U.S.-USSR Commission, accelerated their efforts to establish a separate Communist regime in northern Korea. On November 3, 1946, the first local elections were held in northern Korea to choose the members of province, city, county and township people's committees. On February 17, 1947, the north Korean Supreme People's Assembly was inaugurated as the highest legislative body in the north. Concomitantly, the Central People's Committee, consisting of various ministries and bureaus, was established in a complete government form.

Moreover, the Communists effected an agrarian reform, redistributed all farm implements and animals, and nationalized all industrial facilities, banks, private industries, transportation, communications and other public facilities. This was soon followed by such state-level measures as the "1st Economic Development Plan." In effect, all these mea—sures amounted to the emergence of a de facto Communist regime in north Korea as early as before the end of 1946.

South Korea, under the U.S. military government, could not merely sit idle when faced by such measures in the north. The U.S. military government, which established the Korean Democratic Council in February 1946 as an advisory body, reorganized it into the south Korean Interim Legislative Assembly in December 1946, and thus began, albeit belatedly, to take measures to counter events taking place in the north.

The U.S. military government continued to defend the proposed Korean trusteeship until it reconsidered in early 1947 after the south Korean Interim Legislative Assembly passed a resolution on January 20, 1947 opposing the trusteeship. After the second and final conference of the Joint U.S.-USSR Commission broke up in October of that year, the U.S. military government and Washington, by now abandoning the trusteeship plan, resolved to promote the establishment of an independent government of the Korean people as soon as possible.

The United States then decided to refer the Korean question to the newly inaugurated United Nations. On September 17, 1947, the U.S. delegation to the United Nations formally asked that the question of the independence of Korea be included in the General Assembly agenda. Despite opposition from the Soviet Union, the Assembly decided, by a vote of 41 to 6 with 7 abstentions, to adopt the General Committee recommendation that the Korean question be included in the Assembly's agenda and referred it to the Political Committee. On November 14, the General Assembly adopted, by a vote of 43 to 9 with 6 abstentions, a resolution stipulating that 1) general elections are to be held on the entire Korean peninsula not later than March 31, 1948, through general, equal, direct and secret voting, to elect representatives to a national assembly with the authority to establish an independent and unified government, 2) all alien forces are to be withdrawn upon the establishment of a government, and 3) a Temporary Commission on Korea is to be formed with the responsibility of observing the general elections.

The U.N. Temporary Commission on Korea, arriving in Seoul on January 8, 1948, sent a message to the commander of the Soviet occupation forces on January 12 informing him that it would visit Pyongyang to meet him to discuss the procedures of the south-north general elections set under the United Nations resolution. The Soviet occupation authorities refused even to accept the message and returned it to the Temporary Commission on January 23, thus blocking the entry of the U.N. Commission into north Korea.

Here, the Interim Committee of the U.N. General Assembly resolved that "the U.N. Temporary Commission on Korea should observe elections in all areas on the Korean peninsula, but if this is impossible, it should observe elections in those areas where it can have access," thus paving the way to general elections confined to south Korea.

Accordingly, general elections were held in south Korea on May 10, 1948. In the elections, 75 percent of all eligible voters took part in the voting to elect a total of 198 representatives, who formed the Constitutional National Assembly. Under the Constitution adopted by the Assembly, the Republic of Korea government with Syngman Rhee as the first President was formally inaugurated on August 15, 1948. The military government of the United States was terminated on the same date.

In north Korea, on the other hand, last-minute preparations were under way for the establishment of a separate Communist regime. As early as June 14, 1947, Kim Il-sung, in a report made before a meeting of the North Korean Democratic People's Front, disclosed a plan to establish a separate Communist regime in north Korea under the name of the "Democratic People's Republic of Korea." Under this time-table, the North Korean Supreme People's Assembly set out to draft a constitution as early as November 1947, and formally adopted a draft constitution in April 1948. Finally on September 9 the same year, the establishment of the north Korean regime was promulgated.

The Korean peninsula was thus politically divided. However, upon receipt of a report from the U.N. Temporary Commission on Korea, the U.N. General Assembly on December 12, 1948, confirmed the sole legitimacy of the Republic of Korea government by adopting "General Assembly Resolution No. 195-III" which declared, "there has been established a lawful government having effective control and jurisdiction over the part of Korea where the Temporary Commission was able to observe and consult and in which the great majority of the people of all Korea reside," and that "this government was based on an election which was a valid expression of the free will of the electorate of that part of Korea." It added that "this is the only such government in Korea."

b. Fixation of Division

Since 1948, the south and the north of divided Korea have thus existed as independent entities with different political systems. But from well before 1948, the Communists in the north, having succeeded in communizing north Korea, set out to prepare, as a next step, for a war to communize the entire peninsula. Soon after the Communists seized control of north Korea in 1945 under the aegis of the Soviet occupation authorities, they began to organize military forces with an eye at "liberating south Korea by force of arms," creating the (north) Korean People's Army, a de facto regular force, in February 1948.

Following the inauguration of the north Korean regime in September 1948, large numbers of the Korean veterans who had joined the Chinese Communist forces in battles against the Japanese and the Nationalist Chinese during World War II began transfering to north Korea where they were integrated into the People's Army to swell its strength to a point where it far outpaced that of the south Korean forces.

By March 1950, north Korea could line up impressive, battle-ready forces : ten infantry divisions (30 regiments), a tank brigade, an air division and various other special units plus the navy and the air division. All told, the manpower of the People's Army totaled 198,000. Their equipment by the time the war began included 242 tanks, 176 self-propelled guns, 560 armed sidecars, 380 vehicles, a large number of artillery pieces, 211 various airplanes and about 30 naval vessels. With the People's Army having thus been built up, the Soviet Union on December 27, 1948, announced the complete with-

17

drawal of their forces from north Korea, and, together with north Korea, launched an extensive propaganda campaign to demand U.S. military withdrawal from south Korea.

In south Korea, meanwhile, efforts to create an independent army continued to face difficulties partly due to a passive attitude from the United States and partly to obstructive maneuvering by the leftist forces. When the Korean War broke out, the manpower strength of the south Korean forces was no more than 105,000 including eight army divisions. The south lagged far behind the north in terms of military equipment, too. They had no tanks, self-propelled guns and anti-aircraft guns at all. The military airplanes the two sides had showed a 9.6 to 1 ratio in favor of the north.

Alarmed by the tremendous military buildup going on in north Korea, the Republic of Korea government asked the United States to postpone the scheduled U.S. military withdrawal at least until the south Korean military forces were bolstered to a desirable extent, and to provide equipment necessary to strengthening the south Korean forces. But the United States withdrew its forces from south Korea in June 1949, leaving behind about 500 military advisors. As to military assistance, the U.S. left behind only some light equipment, mostly small fire arms.

Moreover, in a speech, "Crisis in Asia," made before the National Press Club in Washington D.C. on January 12, 1950, Dean Acheson, the then U.S. Secretary of State, strongly hinted that the United States would not intervene in armed conflicts on the Korean peninsula, a speech which served in consequence to boost the aggressive scheme of the north Korean Communists against the south.

Immediately prior to the unleashing of their armed aggression against the south, north Korea launched a series of deceptive peace offensives by, for instance appealing for peaceful unification or proposing the exchange of Cho Man-shik, a great national leader in captivity in the north, with Lee Chu-ha and Kim Sam-yong, high-ranking Communist agents in prison in the south. The disguised peace offensive was designed to distract the south's attention away from their last-minute preparation for invasion and secure the grounds for justify-

18

ing their position at the outbreak of a war.

Finally at 4 a.m. June 25, 1950, the north Korean forces launched an unprovoked attack all along the 38th Parallel to commit the crime of firming up national division. The north Korean forces, spearheaded by tanks, took the south's capital city of Seoul in three days on June 28, and continued advancing. The south Korean Army columns fell and were retreating in utter confusion. Unexpectedly, however, the United States took speedy military actions to repel the aggressors. On a U.S. initiative, the United Nations Security Council adopted a resolution on June 27 in the Soviet delegate's absence, in which the world organization, branding the north Korean incursion as an express act of aggression counter to the United Nations Charter, called upon the members of the United Nations to furnish such assistance to the Republic of Korea as might be necessary to repel the armed attack.

In response, a total of 16 countries sped their Army, Navy and Air Force contingents to Korea. They were the United States, Great Britain, Australia, New Zealand, France, Canada, South Africa, Turkey, Thailand, Greece, the Netherlands, Colombia, Ethiopia, the Philippines, Belgium and Luxembourg. Four other countries including India and Denmark extended varied economic and humanitarian assistance to the Republic of Korea.

In a massive counter-offensive by the United Nations forces led by General Douglas MacArthur, especially the highly successful Inchon landing on September 15, the north Korean forces retreated beyond the 38th Parallel. It thus seemed that the time to achieve the unification of the Korean people was within sight.

However, as more than one million Chinese Communist troops were thrown into the war after the end of October, the situation began to change. For about two years and a half since, a war of attrition raged, during which ceasefire negotiations were under way beginning July 10, 1951. The armistice was signed on July 27, 1953, by United Nations Commander General Mark Clark, north Korean Commander Kim Il-sung and Chinese commander Peng Tehuai.

The war wreaked unparalleled havoc. The war, during which all sorts of modern weaponry were employed over a protracted period in a limited land area, had swept almost the entire Korean peninsula, leaving massive casualties and turning Korea into huge piles of debries. The combat casualty toll numbered 229,000 south Korean troops, 38,000 United Nations troops, 520,000 north Korean troops and 900,000 Chiness soldiers, while the wounded included 717,000 south Korean soldiers, 115,000 United Nations troops and 406,000 north Korean troops. In addition, 43,000 south Korean soldiers and 500 U.N. troops were listed as missing. Non-military casualties in the south reached 245,000 killed, 230,000 injured and 330,000 missing (presumably killed), 130,000 massacred by Communist troops, 85,000 forcibly taken to north Korea and 18,000 policemen killed.)

Moreover, the war produced 300,000 war widows and 100,000 war orphans, and caused 330,000 persons to be physically handicapped and 1,000,000 others to be affected by tuberculosis. Some 440,000 south Korean youths were forcibly taken into the north Korean forces as "volunteers." On the other hand, more than one million north Korean residents fled their homes in search of freedom in the south during the U.N. forces' retreat from the north at the intervention of the Chinese forces. The north Korean war refugees brought to some five million the number of north Korean residents fleeing to the south since national liberation, thereby becoming the very victims of the "tragedy of division."

The ceasefire did not unify divided Korea nor did it result in the punishment of the north Korean Communists who had caused such an untold fratricidal national tragedy. Above all, it still contains the seeds of another war because the truce – the product of international opinion that feared the Korean war might develop into the powder keg of a third world war – was a mere temporizing step to end the hostilities. For this very reason the Republic of Korea refused to agree to the ceasefire, boycotting the signing of the Armistice Agreement.

The Armistice Agreement provided, among other things, that the two sides in the Korean War would hold a high-level political conference within three months after signing the truce agreement. Pursuant to this provision, the representatives of the Republic of Korea and the

16 participants on the side of the United Nations Command and the delegates from the Soviet Union, Red China and north Korea met in Geneva on April 26, 1954. However, the meeting broke up on June 15, 1954, due to the Communist side's refusal to accept the competence and authority of the United Nations, and its absurd insistence on the prior withdrawal of all alien forces as well as on a formula to unify the Korean peninsula under communism. On the day the Geneva Conference broke-up, the allied side issued a "Sixteen-Nation Declaration on Korea," formally acknowledging that the Geneva Conference had been in vain due to the Communist side's unreasonable demands. The allied side requested that the United Nations deal with the issue of political solutions to the Korean question and declared that the United Nations forces would remain in Korea until the danger of a recurring war could be removed through a political solution to the Korean issue.

The division of Korea had cost the high price of war. But what remains today is truce line that has replaced the 38th Parallel. The original form of the Korean community that had lasted for about 5,000 years retaining the single blood line and the same language, culture and customs, had thus begun to be defaced. It is incumbent upon contemporary Koreans to restore and re-create the community of all Koreans.

c. Changes in South and North Korea

The division of Korea, which a majority of the Koreans thought only as temporary at the time of the split in 1945, had grown firmer with the lapse of time influenced by the hardening of the Cold War mechanism. Moreover, the state of confrontation and hostility picked up speed as the peninsula entered the stage of national split following the establishment of two conflicting ideological and socio-economic systems in south and north Korea in 1948 and the fratricidal Korean War of 1950–1953. Social heterogeneity had deepened between the two societies of south and north Korea, doing considerable damage to the life mode of the Koreans as a homogeneous people. Whereas the Republic of Korea has developed as a free and open society based on

21

the basic political order of free democracy while genuinely inheriting and developing time-honored national history, culture and traditions, north Korea has become a closed society completely isolated from the rest of the world, a uniform society where national history had been rewritten based on the "materialistic class concept of history" and where the absolute authority of a single deified man has been established.

The paramount task facing the Republic of Korea was to safeguard its survival from the tenacious attempts of the north Korean Communists to unify Korea under communism by overthrowing the Republic through either a violent revolution or a military defeat. Politically, the Republic of Korea adopted as its basic political ideology liberal democracy guaranteeing the basic freedom and rights of the people as well as a conduit through which the people can take part in political process through elections.

North Korea, on the other hand, promptly started to arm their entire populace with the monolithic Kim Il-sung thought with a view to creating a totalitarian society where a single ideology rigidly controls and regulates all areas of the society. As early as before the establishment of the Communist regime in 1948, the north Korean Communists eliminated nationalist leaders, and immediately after the ceasefire of the Korean War those who belonged to the south Korean Workers' Party. Through the late 1960s, the Pyongyang regime purged one politically rival faction after another, which included the Yenan, USSR and Kapsan factions and even some military leaders opposed to the Kim Il-sung system.

At the same time, the north rearranged residential areas and occupation for all based on family loyalty to the regime, and cemented the foundation for Kim Il-sung's one-man system through rigid political indoctrination and surveillance networks.

As part of the ideological control program, the north conducted the so-called "concentrated guidance program of the Central Party" in one year beginning the end of 1958 and a supplementary "residents registration program" in 1962. In the "concentrated guidance program of the Central Party," all north Korean residents were classified into three categories – 1) nucleus forces, 2) intermediate forces and 3) "counter-revolutionary" forces – depending on their family loyalty and the trend of each individual's political ideology. Those branded "counter-revolutionaries" had their residence restricted and were sent to concentration camps. The "counter-revolutionaries" included 1) the families of those who had gone to south Korea and those who cooperated with south Korea during the Korean War, and their families, 2) former religiously active persons, land owners, entrepreneurs and businessmen and their families, 3) returned prisoners of war and their families, 4) former public officials under the Japanese rule and their families, 5) prisoners and ex-convicts and their families, and 6) those Communists who were purged for their "sectarian activities" (actually those who belonged to the crushed domestic, Yenan and Soviet factions) and their families.

In the power structure, too, north Korea has instituted a one-party dictatorial system. The Workers' Party guides and controls all government offices and political organizations, and extends its influence to all sectors of social activities. All social organizations, too, have been turned into front organizations of the Workers' Party as north Korea itself argues, "The social organizations of our country are the voluntary and revolutionary popular political organizations and, at the same time, the 'outer setups' of the party founded by our Great Leader Comrade Kim Il-sung. The basic mission of social organizations as positive helpers for our party is, under the guidance of the party, to protect Comrade Kim Il-sung with one's own life and organize and mobilize all workers for a thorough implementation of the teachings of the Leader, by arming them thoroughly with the great revolutionary ideas of Comrade Kim Il-sung and establishing the monolithic ideological system of the party."

North Korea has thus been transformed into a society saturated with Kimilsungism through ideological indoctrination and political surveillance and oppression of an unprecedented magnitude. The people of north Korea have become the "loyal, suicide guards of the Leader. They absolutize, defend and safeguard the Leader ideologically, they carry out the Leader's teachings unconditionally to the last, and they dedicate their entire being to the Leader to ease the worries of the Leader."

In particular, Kim Il-sung's personality cult campaign has been waged so extensively and thoroughly that it is unrivaled in terms of extent, intensity and tenacity.

Meanwhile, the different political systems in the two sides of Korea have led to substantial differences in their respective economic development aspects. Before national division, both sides were basically agrarian pre-industrial societies. In a relative sense, the north had more industrial facilities than the south which had more farm lands than the north.

Since national division, however, south Korea has pursued industrialization and urbanization based on the principle of a free market economy while ensuring the people's individual freedoms to the most extent possible under the ideology of a liberal democracy, while in the north all industries were nationalized and industrialization was promoted under the strong centrally controlled method under the system of socialism.

Between national liberation and the year 1961, south Korea had to subsist on foreign grants, unable even to produce enough grain for domestic needs. Worse yet, the Korean War reduced to debries virtually all the meager industry south Korea had, dealing a crushing blow to its economy.

However, with the 1961 Military Revolution and the subsequent birth of the Third Republic in 1963, south Korea managed to lay a base for political stability and achieved on that base the momentum for rapid economic development. Through the successful implementation of five-year economic development plans begun in 1962, the south registered spectacular economic growth – an 8 percent annual growth during the first plan period (1962-66) and a 10.5 percent expansion during the second plan period (1967-71).

At the same time, the Republic of Korea expanded key industries and other major industrial sectors, creating favorable conditions for private investment and expanding the social overhead capital. It also encouraged the introduction of foreign capital to ensure smooth fund raising for investment as well as promoting exports through expanded international economic cooperation and pursuit of an open-trade system. In this way the country has succeeded in achieving high economic growth which has astonished the whole world.

In north Korea, on the other hand, economic development has been pursued within the restricted framework of the concept of value, a concept that the economy is merely a means of attaining the political objective of laying a material base for the perfection of a Communist dictatorial system based on Kim Il-sung's absolutism, as well as for the communization of the entire Korean peninsula. This political manipulation of the economy has inevitably resulted in the backwardness of the technological sector, the sacrifice of light industries and the people's welfare, and an imbalance among industries. Under these circumstances, north Korea could not retain its absolute economic edge over the south shown at the time of national division. Beginning in the latter half of the 1960s, the tide has reversed and the gap has been widening as time passes.

In north Korea, economic policies have been determined by such political objectives as the communization of north Korean society, the unification of the Korean peninsula under communism and Kim Il-sung's personality cult. In this course, there have arisen numerous problems because of their disregard of the general rules of economic development.

Moreover, in their consistent attachment to the armed conquest of south Korea even after the Korean War, the north pushed through a rigid, heavy-industry-first policy with top priority on the munitions industries, causing a serious imbalance between heavy and light industries. As a result, north Korea failed to achieve the goals of the 1961-67 seven-year economic development plan despite the extension of the plan period by three years.

Because of the heavy political nature inherent in the economy, the north Korean economy has shunned external exchanges, adhering only to a base of extremely primitive self-supply in total isolation from the rest of the world. This has brought about a reduced will to production among the people, the backwardness of knowhow, and the paralysis of the sense of international competitiveness.

Such a stiff economic policy of north Korea has not only become a vital factor behind the widening economic gap between the south and the north but also has resulted in determining the relative standing of the open and closed systems, the free entrepreneurship and planned Communist economic systems, and the competitive and controlled societies.

Table 1

Comparison of Major Economic Indicators
of South and North Korea
(1960–1975)

Classification	Unit	South Korea				North Korea			
		1960	1965	1970	1975	1960	1965	1970	1975
Population	10,000	2,499	2,867	3,224	3,528	1,079	1,225	1,400	1,577
Population growth rate	%	2.84	2.62	2.20	1.70	3.82	2.70	2.50	2.50
GNP	US$ 100mil.	19.5	30.1	79.9	208.5	15.2	23.4	39.8	93.5
Per-capita GNP	US$	94	105	248	591	137	192	286	579
Total trade volume	US$ 1 mil.	376	591	2,819	12,355	320	450	805	1,912
Exports	US$ 1 mil.	33	175	835	5,081	154	219	366	819
Imports	US$1mil	343	416	1,948	7,274	166	231	439	1,093
Financial burden rate of national economy	%	17.0	11.6	16.1	15.2	50.4	57.7	58.7	59.3
Electric capacity	10,000 KVA	19	77	251	472	176	222	339	427
Steel-manufacturing capacity	10,000 TON	15	32	85	285	66	205	217	240

Source : National Unification Board, 1987

26

The disruption between south and north Korea has brought about a considerable extent of heterogeneity between the two sides not only in the aspects of the political and economic systems but also in the aspects of value and culture such as social customs, the family system and social activities. The basic difference between the socio-cultural systems of the south and the north derives from the fact that whereas the south inherits and develops the historical continuity of the nation pursuing a society where individual people can enjoy free lives and activities, north Korea, in a rigid and uniform observance of the principle of collectivism, sees to it that individual needs are met only through the organizations to which individual citizens belong.

Under the motto of "creatively adapting Marxism-Leninism to the realities of our country," north Korea distorts national tradition and cultural legacies, forcing the people to display unbounded loyalty to Kim Il-sung and the party. Moreover, they insist that "socialistic patriotism" and "socialistic humanism" are the positive ethics and morals people should abide by, and invoked the people's hatred by inventing the symbol of the "people's enemy" for use as an important mechanism for social integration.

The north also rejects the traditional morals and etiquette of the Korean people as a "norm created by the feudal ruling class for the exploitation of the ruled class." They retain only those which they believe serve their political purpose, that is, to maintain their system. Under these circumstances, there appeared more socio-cultural dissimilarities than similarities between south and north Korea despite their being a single community sharing the same history, language and customs.

Moreover, north Korea, adhering to their basic goal to construct a Communist society on the whole area of the Korean peninsula, has endlessly perpetrated southward provocations to further raise the barrier of distrust between the two sides.

At the fifth plenary session of the fourth Central Committee of the Workers' Party in December 1962, by which time post-war rehabilitation could be completed to a certain extent in the north, north Korea adopted the so-called "Four-Point Military Lines" calling for the arming of the entire population, turning the entire land into a fortification, cardinalizing all members of the armed forces and the modernization of military equipment. With this resolution as a catalyst, north Korea inaugurated the Workers' Party Military Committee chaired by Kim Il-sung and embarked on a full-fledged military buildup with emphasis on the all-out development of the munitions industries.

North Korea launched a seven-year economic plan in 1961. But at the instructions of Kim Il-sung that "our military strength should be beefed up even if it requires the revision of economic plans in view of the current situation facing us" (at the second representatives' meeting of the Workers' Party held in October 1966), north Korea forced through a revision of the economic plan to place greater emphasis on their heavy industry-first policy and to launch full-fledged arms build-up programs.

In the north, military outlays began to swell sharply from 1964. The ratio of defense expenditures to the total state budget increased from 5.8 percent in 1964 to 8 percent in 1965, 10 percent in 1966, 30.4 percent in 1967, 32.4 percent in 1968, 31 percent in 1969, 31 percent in 1970 and 30 percent in 1971 (See Table 2, below). The figures given here are based on the defense expenditures north Korea publicly announced, and, therefore, do not include those concealed in the budget of the "people's economy" sector. It is believed that if such hidden amounts were taken into account, the ratios of the north's defense expenditures to the overall state budget would be much higher than the figures given in the table below.

Parallel with such extensive military buildup, north Korea significantly strengthened their irregular special warfare force for infiltration into and surprise attacks at the south, committing incessant acts of military provocation against the south. The special warfare troops total more than 80,000, including the members of the 695th Unit under the Liaison Department of the Workers' Party, 25,000 in 40 battalions of five brigades in the Special 8th Corps under the Reconnaissance Bureau of the People's Armed Forces Ministry (Defense Ministry), and 53,000 assigned to the 88 battalions of the 11 light infantry brigades under the three army groups deployed in the for-

28

ward area. The north's acts of provocation reached a peak in the years 1967 and 1968.

Typical of such provocative acts were the reckless attempt to raid the Chong Wa Dae(the ROK President's residence) by some members of the north Korean 124th Unit on January 21, 1968, the seizure of the USS Pueblo on January 23 the same year, and the landing of 120 guerrillas on the east coast area (Uljin and Samchok) in October 1968.

Table 2

Trends of Military Expenditures in North Korea

(Unit : 10,000 won in north Korean currency)

Year	Total Budget	Defense Outlays	Ratio(%)
1953	49,597	7,539	15.2
1954	72,956	5,836	8.0
1955	98,800	6,126	6.2
1956	95,598	5,640	5.9
1957	102,244	5,419	5.3
1958	118,300	5,678	4.8
1959	164,960	6,104	3.7
1960	196,787	6,100	3.1
1961	233,800	6,079	2.6
1962	272,876	7,095	2.6
1963	302,821	5,754	1.9
1964	341,824	19,826	5.8
1965	347,613	27,809	8.0
1966	357,140	35,714	10.0
1967	394,823	120,026	30.4
1968	481,289	155,938	32.4
1969	504,857	156,506	31.0
1970	618,662	191,785	31.0
1971	727,727	218,320	30.0

Source : National Unification Board

The inter-Korean relationship of the 1960s was thus characterized by persisting military tensions and mutual distrust due to the north's unveiled agitation of a violent revolution in and guerrilla infiltration into the south. No clue had ever been found for the realization of dialogue to discuss peaceful unification. As heterogeneity has deepened and the sense of confrontation has been hardened between the two sides contrary to the national wish for the restoration of the national community, unification is now thought to be something beyond reach.

2. Background of South-North Dialogue in the 1970s

It was only a quarter century after national division that south and north Korea, with conflicting political ideologies and in a hostile relationship, came to the conference table. Until then, the two sides of Korea had no way but to remain in the state of hostile confrontation under the U.S. — USSR Cold War mechanism or under the system of military confrontation between the United States and mainland China.

Since the end of the 1960s, however, tremendous changes began to take place in both the internal and external situations affecting the Korean peninsula.

Internally, south Korea registered rapid economic growth since the 1960s thanks to the concentrated promotion of modernization with emphasis on industrialization. North Korean, on the other hand, placed greater stress on an arms buildup than on economic construction under the Four-Point Military Lines. Also, symptoms of the inefficiency of a centrally-controlled economic system started to appear in the north.

As a result, the south began to outpace the north in terms of both GNP and per-capita GNP. In 1960, the per-capita GNP of the south amounted to 94 dollars whereas in the north it stood at 137 dollars. In 1975, however, the situation was reversed with the south's per-capita GNP reaching 591 dollars compared with the north's 579 dollars. The south Koreans thus started to entertain confidence against the north.

Here, in the late 1960s, scholarly views began to appear in the south, that called for efforts to resolve the Korean question in a manner that recognizes the reality of national division.

Though the south outperformed the north in terms of economic construction, it lagged far behind the north in the area of military strength. This, coupled with the growing pressure for the pullout of U.S. forces from Korea under the Nixon Doctrine, obliged the south to seek self-rescue measures to ensure its own survival. Under these circumstances, south Korea carefully considered promoting a south-north dialogue, faced with the need to reconsider its policy of "construction first and unification later."

North Korea, too, had a reason of its own for coming to the conference table. First, as the U.S. intervention in the Indochina war seemed to fail after the close of the 1960s, the north came to harbor the wishful thinking that before long the United States, faced with surging neo-isolationism domestically, would militarily disengage from the Korean peninsula and the rest of Asia. To Kim Il-sung, who carefully watched the tide of the Vietnam War, the question was how to foment conditions ripe for such a "national liberation war" on the Korean peninsula. In his eyes, the biggest obstacle to such conditions was the presence of the U.S. forces in Korea. Kim Il-sung believed that though the U.S. military in Korea was the "target" of expulsion by means of "struggles" in the past, they would now leave by themselves if only some conditions, such as the alleviation of tensions, were provided to warrant their departure.

Second, at that time north Korea made a big miscalculation concerning the political situation in south Korea. The north's strategy against the south was based on the "united front tactics" which ultimately aim to overthrow the government of south Korea in collusion with dissident forces in the south whom they call "patriotic democratic forces." When the unification issue emerged as a serious campaign issue during the presidential election period of 1971 in the south, north Korea sought to use such a new development in their southward strategy. In other words, they sought to form a "united front" in the south in a legal manner by way of a south-north dialogue. Their intent can be perceived in the remarks made by one of the north Korean delegates to a south-north Red Cross meeting held in Seoul in September 1972 about the crowds along Seoul streets welcoming them :"The south Korean people greeted not merely as Red Cross delegates but as 'unification emissaries' of Great Leader Kim Il-sung."

Third, north Korea believed that they could use the inter-Korean dialogue in surmounting the difficulties with which their economy was faced. Because of their over-emphasis on arms buildup in line with the Four-Point Military Lines throughout the 1960s, the north was in a serious economic crisis. For instance, the north failed to accomplish its seven-year economic plan begun in 1961 despite the fact that they toned down plan goals halfway and even extended the target year by three years. They found it unavoidable to switch a considerable portion of their military outlays, which exceeded 30 percent of their whole national budgetary expenditures, to economic programs. Here the north thought that the south-north dialogue would serve to apply a brake to the south's forces modernization plan and freeze the status quo of the south and north Korean military strength. They hoped that the funds thus saved could be used for economic purposes.

In the international situation, the United States and the Soviet Union, which hotly contested for hegemony since the turn of the 1960s, began to develop relationship of mutual coexistence and detente. The polarized system centered on the United States and the USSR had gradually given way to a system of multi-polarization additionally involving China, Japan and West Europe. In Northeast Asia, the power balance between the Free World involving south Korea, the United States and Japan and the Communist-bloc comprising the Soviet Union, China and north Korea started to be shaken.

Beginning 1971, there was a rapid approach between the United States and China. U.S. President Richard Nixon visited Beijing in

February 1972. Subsequently, China was admitted to the United Nations, and full diplomatic relations were concluded between the U.S. and China and between Japan and China.

China's approach to the U.S. and Japan had led to the reorganization of the power equilibrium among the powers surrounding the Korean peninsula. In consequence, the trend toward valuing national interests overshadowed the tendency of blind ideological unity. At the same time, the Nixon Doctrine calling for a reduced American role in Asia premised a greater arming and role of Japan. Thus, the reorganized power structure in Northeast Asia necessitated a new adaptation by the Koreans.

The position of the world powers surrounding the Korean peninsula had changed from the policy of supporting a unification achieved under the initiative of their allies with the same ideology with theirs, to the support for an "independent, peaceful unification of the Korean peninsula." This policy change can be taken to mean that the world powers won't actively interfere in the issue of Korean unification nor do they want to see the status quo of the Korean peninsula shattered by an armed provocation.

This rapid development caused a tremendous shock to both the south and the north, an area where the interests of the world powers converged historically, obliging the two sides of Korea to reconsider their mechanism of confrontation.

These changes in both the internal and external situations of the peninsula were behind the initiation of a dialogue between the two feuding sides.

But it was by no means coincidental that the south took the initiative in promoting the dialogue. This was due to the fact that south Korea, being a free society having a free access to international information, was better capable of accommodating changes in surrounding situations than the north, and also was subject to much lesser shock of the mutual opening of the two societies.

Finally, in. his Liberation Day message on August 15, 1970, President Park Chung-hee said the south "is willing to set forth epochal and realistic devices to remove step by step the artificial barriers lying across south and north Korea." In his "Idea for Peaceful Unification," President Park challenged the north to embark on a "competition of development, construction and creation" to determine which system, democracy or communism, can facilitate better lives for the people.

The Idea for Peaceful Unification suggested that under the premise that the two sides of Korea stop the arms race and renounce the use of arms as a means of unification, south and north Korea can therefore transform their relationship into that of a good-intentioned competition of systems toward development, construction and creation. It further provided that based thereon, the two sides could remove the artificial barriers between them step by step and thereby reduce the pains, misfortune and inconveniences stemming from division. On the other hand, in his political report at the fifth Workers' Party Congress in November the same year, Kim Il-sung boasted, "Now all the people of north Korea know how to handle guns. The whole land has been fortified and the entire military is able to perform the duty of their next higher ranks. Also, equipment has been modernized. Now that the Four-Point Military Lines have thus been accomphshed successfully, we can liberate south Korea on our own without any assistance from China and the Soviet Union."

North Korea, which initially showed a cool reaction to the south's Idea for Peaceful Unification, could not turn a deaf ear to public opinion which desired a direct dialogue between the south and the north. It was significant that with regard to the scope of participants in a south- north political conference the north proposed on August 6, 1971, Kim Il-sung toned down his obstinacy and chose the south's ruling party as the first in a list of invitees. This was a prelude to their agreement to the Seoul-side proposal for the South-North Red Cross Conference.

3. Start of South -North Dialogue

a. South-North Red Cross Conference

(1) ROKNRC Proposal for Talks and NKRC Acceptance

In a special statement on August 12, 1971, Choi Doo-sun, president of the Republic of Korea National Red Cross (ROKNRC), proposed to the North Korean Red Cross (NKRC) that a South and North Korean Red Cross Conference be held to discuss ways to ease the sufferings of dispersed families in the South and the North of Korea and ultimately arrange their reunions. The special statement of the ROKNRC president was in substance as follows:

The quarter-century barrier between the south and the north is the source of all national tragedies, especially, the tragedy of families separated in the south and the north are symbolic of the mankind's tragedy in this century.

In view of our professed mission of humanitarian causes and selfless services for relief work, it is indeed a heart-breaking sorrow to see this situation perpetuated.

The fates of separated families can of course be terminated when the artificial wall dividing the south and the north is removed. Under the present circumstances, however, it is hard to imagine that this invisible wall will crumble in a short space of time.

In this context, we seek to initiate a "Campaign to search for lost families" to confirm the present condition of the 10 million separated family members, arrange exchange of letters between them and realize their reunions.

I, on behalf of the ROKNRC and in accordance with the spirit of inherent Red Cross wish to make the following proposal with the purposes of settling the purely humanitarian problem of the Korean people:

First, Red Cross representatives from the south and the north shall hold talks soon with regard to the above-mentioned campaign for a search for separated families.

Second, a preliminary meeting shall be held in Geneva, Switzerland, before the end of coming October to discuss procedural matters for the talks.

It is our ardent hope that the above proposals will be met with a due reply from the North Korean Red Cross. The reply may be made through radio broadcasts, communication net works, the International Red Cross or any other means available to them... .

Two days later on August 14, Radio Pyongyang of north Korea broadcast a message of Son Sung-pil, chairman of the Central Committee of the north Korean Red Cross, addressed to ROKNRC President Choi Doo-sun. The gist of the message was as follows :

On August 12, you proposed to the Red Cross Society of the Democratic People's Republic of Korea that the North and South Korean Red Cross Societies start a campaign to search for separated families and hold a preliminary meeting in Geneva before the end of next October to discuss matters related to the campaign.

As to the subjects of the North and South Korean Red Cross representatives' talks, we believe the search for families alone cannot satisfy the ardent wishes of separated families, relatives and friends in the north and the south.

Therefore, in view of the common wishes of all the people in North and South Korea and of the humanitarian principle, we hereby cordially propose that the following matters be discussed :

First, the question of realizing free travel and mutual visits between families, relatives and friends separated in the north and the south ;

Second, the question of freely exchanging letters between separated families, relatives and friends in the north and the south ; and

Third, the question of searching for separated families and arranging their reunions.

We will send two messengers carrying a letter from our Red Cross Society to Panmunjom at 12 noon August 20. We would like to have your messengers receive our letter at that time at the place.

In their response the North Korean Red Cross demanded the handling of "political problems" beyond the realm of the humanitarian "family search project" which the ROKNRC proposed, and insisted that the scope of search for missing families should be expanded to include even missing friends, thus implying that they were agreeing to

Red Cross talks simply to reap political gains rather than to achieve humanitarian objectives.

The north Korean response, though hardly motivated by humane considerations, was to accept the ROKNRC proposal at least on the surface, which opened a new chapter in the history of national division. An inter-Korean dialogue began, the first talks ever to take place between the two halves of Korea during a quarter century of division.

As was discussed in the preceding chapter, millions of family members were dispersed in the south and the north of Korea after the national division in 1945.

The separation of families on the Korean peninsula is more tragic than in other countries. They have lived in an agonizing period of more than a quarter century in the complete severance of mutual contact, lacking even the exchange of letters or news of their missing ones by other means, not to mention reunion.

There were in fact some efforts in the ceasefire's wake to solve the issue of dispersed families from a humanitarian standpoint.

The first of such efforts took place from December 11, 1953 to March 1, 1954, through the "Committee for Assisting the Return of Displaced Civilians" established pursuant to the provisions of Paragraph 59, Article 3 of the Armistice Agreement. In South Korea, a total of 76 former North Korean residents applied for their repatriation, 39 of whom withdrew their applications at the final stage of their return, and the remaining 37 were turned over to North Korea through Panmunjom on March 1, 1954. North Korea, however, returned no South Korean residents. It only returned 19 foreigners – 11 Turks and 8 White Russians.

With the initial effort having failed to materialize any return of South Koreans from the north, the Republic of Korea tried again soon thereafter, this time through the International Committee of the Red Cross (ICRC). In late 1954, South Korea requested the ICRC in Geneva immediate arrangements of a solution to the dispersed family issue in Korea in accordance with Resolution No. 20, "Problem of the Reunion of Displaced Families," adopted at the 18th Conference of the ICRC held in Canada in 1952.

Accepting the request, the ICRC in November 1955 proposed fact-finding tours of both south and north Korea by ICRC representatives. South Korea, readily responding to the ICRC offer, specifically suggested that a three-stage project be launched under ICRC management to 1) find out the fate and whereabouts of dispersed families, 2) provide information about surviving families and allow exchange of communications, and 3) facilitate ruturn to their original places of residence.

At first, North Korea simply ignored the ICRC suggestion. In January 1957, however, the North Korean Red Cross turned down fact-finding visits by the ICRC and instead proposed direct talks between the South and North Korean Red Cross Societies, suggesting that letters be exchanged between dispersed families through the good offices of the two Red Cross Societies. This proposition, disregarding such necessary basis procedures as confirmation of the fate and whereabouts of the dispersed families, was intended only to serve propaganda purposes.

At this point, the ROKNRC questioned the NKRC, through the ICRC, about the fate and whereabouts of the 7,034 persons who were formally reported in South Korea to have been forcibly taken to the north. In a counter-action, the NKRC questioned the ROKNRC about a total of 14,132 North Koreans who came to south Korea. In November 1957, the NKRC informed the ROKNRC of 337 survivors out of the 7.034 persons sought. The ROKNRC, meanwhile, notified the NKRC that of the 14,132 it asked about, 14,112 were not taken to the South against their will as North Korea alleged, but had come to the south of their own accord.

At 12 noon, on August 20, 1971, the first contact between messengers from the Red Cross Societies of South and North Korea occurred at the Neutral Nations Supervisory Commission conference room. The ROKNRC was represented by Lee Chang-yol, director of the Administration Department, and Mrs. Yoon Yeohoon, a staff officer in the

Public Relations Department, and the NKRC by So Song-chol, deputy director of the Culture and Information Department, and Ryom Jong-ryon, a guidance officer. The ROKNRC messengers delivered the text of the August 12 proposal from ROKNRC President Choi to the NKRC, while the NKRC handed to ROKNRC messengers of NKRC chairman Son's message addressed to the ROKNRC president.

The messengers made their second contact on August 26, when the ROKNRC handed the NKRC a message from ROKNRC President Choi which contained a "proposal for procedural steps for preliminary talks." The contents of the ROKNRC president's proposition were as follows :

1. The preliminary talks between the south and north Korean Red Cross shall open at 11 a.m. September 28 at the conference room of the Neutral Nations Supervisory Commission.

2. Each side will be represented by five delegates.

3. The lists of delegates to the preliminary talks shall be exchanged at 12 noon September 24 at the conference room of the Neutral Nations Supervisory Commission.

4. As to the agenda of the humanitarian south-north Red Cross talks, I would like to remind you that, as I explained in my August 12 proposal, the "family search campaign" means all humanitarian activities to alleviate the sufferings of separated families in the south and the north, including arrangement of the exchange of letters and visits between them. Therefore, agenda items shall be decided through discussions at the preliminary talks and shall not be restricted beforehand.

5. The venue of the full-fledged talks, procedural and all other matters related to the talks shall be discussed by the preliminary talks delegates.

At the third messengers' contact on August 30, the NKRC counter-proposed that the first preliminay meeting be held on September 20. At the fourth contact on September 3, the ROKNRC informed the NKRC of its acceptance of the counter-offer, thus completing all preparation for the convening of the South-North Red Cross preliminary talks. At the final messengers' contact on September 16, the two sides exchanged the lists of delegates to the preliminary talks as follows :

ROKNRC Delegation

Chief Delegate :   **Kim Yon-joo,** chief of the ROKNRC Health & Social Service and concurrently chief of the Public Relations

Alternate Chief :   **Park Son-kyu** president of the ROKNRC Chungchong Namdo Chapter

Delegate :   **Chong Hong-jin,** chief of the Conference Management Department

Delegate :   **Chong Hee-kyong,** guidance member of the ROKNRC Junior Red Cross Services and principal of Ehwa Girl's High School

Delegate :   **Chong Choo-nyon,** spokesman for the ROKNRC Conference Secretariat

NKRC Delegation

Chief of Delegate :   **Kim Tae-hui,** NKRC secretary-general

Deputy Chief :   **Kim Dok-hyon,** chief of NKRC Public Information Department

Delegate :   **Cho Myung-il,** chief of NKRC Culture and Information Department

Delegate :   **Li Jong-hak,** NKRC chief councilor

Delegate :   **So Song-chol,** deputy chief of NKRC Culture & Information Department

(2) Preliminary Talks

(a) Installation of South-North Direct Telephone Line

The first preliminary meeting between the South and North Korean Red Cross Societies was held in open session at 11 a.m. September 20, 1971, at the conference room of the Neutral Nations Supervisory Commission. At the meeting, the ROKNRC suggested that to effectively operate the talks, there should be permanent liaison offices in each side's sector at Panmunjom and a direct telephone link between the two. The NKRC agreed and, as a result, a telephone line between the south and the north could be installed, though for limited use, for the first time in 26 years since all telephone circuits between the two sides were cut in 1945.

Under the agreement, the ROKNRC and NKRC established their liaison offices in the Freedom House and Panmungak, respectively, in the joint security area of Panmunjom and installed two telephone circuits there on September 22.

(b) Agreement on Agenda and Procedures of Preliminary Talks

From the outset, however, the preliminary talks encountered rough sailing due to the conflicting stands of the two sides. The ROKNRC tried to conduct the meetings in an orderly way befitting working-level talks, whereas the NKRC sought propaganda gains by producing a politically-motivated package proposal in disregard of conference procedures.

At the first preliminary meeting on September 20, the ROKNRC proposed that prior to the adoption of the agenda of preliminary talks, the two sides first discuss and agree on a seven–point procedure for operating the preliminary talks, including 1) place of preliminary talks and facilities, 2) number of attendants and their seating arrangement, 3) recording of talks and confirmation of contents, 4) order of speeches, 5) the question of opening proceedings of talks, 6) announcement of agreements, and 7) establishment of permanent liaison offices.

On the contrary, the NKRC, laying down an agenda and procedure for full-dress talks in disregard of the issue of procedural matters at the preliminary talks, demanded that they be discussed and agreed on

41

immediately. The NKRC insisted that the venue of the full-dress talks should be Panmunjom, that the agenda of the full-dress talks should include "friends" beyond the scope of a "family search campaign," and that chief delegates to the full-dress talks should be the chiefs of the two Red Cross Societies.

The ROKNRC pointed out that it was unreasonable to take up the agenda and procedures for the full-dress talks even those of the preliminary talks were yet to be discussed and settled. Consequently, the NKRC was obliged to accept the ROKNRC position. At the second preliminary meeting held on September 29, the two sides agreed on the procedures and agenda for the preliminary talks as follows.

1. Place of Preliminary Talks

(1) The place of preliminary talks shall be the conference room of the Neutral Nations Supervisory Commission at Panmunjom (NNSC).

(2) Conference room facilities shall be installed through consultation between working-level officials of the two delegations.

2. Operation of Permanent Liaison Offices

(1) The ROKNRC shall set up its permanent liaison office at Freedom House and the NKRC shall have its liaison office at Panmungak.

(2) The two sides shall install two-way telephone lines linking the two liaison offices.

(3) In case either of the two sides needs to deliver a document to the other side, prior notification shall be made by phone and duty officers of the two sides shall meet at the NNSC conference room for the delivery.

(4) Each side shall assign two officials to the permanent liaison office which will open from 9 a.m. to 4 p.m. Monday through Friday, and from 9 a.m. to 12 noon on Saturdays. They will be closed on Sundays.

3. Attendants and Their Seating Arrangement

The number of attendants for the preliminary talks shall be limited to no more than 10 because of the space situation of the conference room. They shall be seated behind their respective delegates.

4. Recording of Talks and Confirmation of Contents

42

Each side shall record the talks separately and render maximum convenience for the other side to confirm the contents.

5. Method of Speeches

Chief delegates shall be the primary speakers at the talks, and other delegates can also speak upon asked so by the chief delegates.

6. Opening of Talks

(1) The Preliminary talks shall be open to the public in principle, but can also be held behind closed doors when so agreed between the two sides.

(2) For the convenience of press coverage, newsmen will be allowed inside the conference room until the opening of the conference, and loudspeakers will be installed in press rooms to relay delegates' speeches.

7. Determination of the Dates of Next Meetings

The dates of next meetings shall be decided at the close of each session or can be decided later through the liaison offices.

8. Announcement of Agreements

At each session of the talks, both sides will document agreements respectively, exchange notes between them, confirm whether the contents are identical and then make announcements separately.

9. Agenda Items and Their Order

(1) Venue of full-dress talks.

(2) Date of first full-dress talks.

(3) Agenda of full-dress talks.

(4) Formation of delegations to full dress talks.

(5) Other procedural matters of full dress talks.

(c) Determination of Venues of Full-Dress Talks

At the second preliminary meeting held on September 29, the ROKNRC proposed that the full-dress talks be held in Seoul and in Pyongyang by turn, stressing that the convening of full-dress talks was in part to meet the wish of the 50 million Korean people for early unification of the divided fatherland.

The NKRC, however, insisted that Panmunjom should be the site of the full-dress talks. It argued that there were transportation and communication problems and that no guarantee could be made for delegates' safety or their freedom of conduct. At the third preliminary meeting held on October 5, however, the NKRC suddenly changed its position and agreed to the ROKNRC offer for alternating the venues of the full-dress talks between Seoul and Pyongyang.

(d) Rough Going of Negotiations for Agenda of Full-Dress Talks

At the sixth preliminary meeting, the two sides began discussing the issue of the agenda for the full-dress talks. But over this issue of full-dress talks agenda the preliminary·talks were deadlocked and entered a protracted stalemate. The NKRC did not conceal its blatant attempt to exploit the humanitarian talks for political gains, while the ROKNRC wanted to ensure that the Red Cross talks would be faithful to their original objective, namely to remove the sufferings of·dispersed families. Because of these conflicting stands, no fewer than 15 rounds of preliminary meetings and 13 closed-door working-level meetings had to be held over a period of eight months before complete agreement was reached on the agenda of the full-dress talks at the 20th prelimiary meeting held on June 16, 1972.

At the sixth preliminary meeting, the ROKNRC suggested the following five items as the agenda of the full dress talks :

(1) The question of confirming the fate and whereabouts of dispersed families in the south and the north and providing them with such information.

(2) The question of exchanging letters between dispersed families in the south and the north.

(3) The question of arranging reunion and mutual visits for dispersed families in the south and the north.

(4) The question of permanent reuniting of dispersed families in the south and the north, and

(5) Other questions to be solved supplementarily.

The agenda offered by the ROKNRC, highly objective and justifiable, was based on the procedure commonly adopted in international Red Cross searches for missing persons.

Nonetheless the NKRC insisted on the inclusion of "dispersed friends" in the scope of the dispersed family search project. Moreover, the north Koreans demanded that the project be carried out with emphasis on "friends" rather than on "families." The NKRC, dismissing reasonable procedures, argued that the fate and whereabouts of dispersed families should be discovered through "free travels back and forth and mutual visits" between the families concerned. After consistent persuasion by the ROKNRC, however, the NKRC withheld its insistence on "friends." Still, confirmation of the agenda for full-dress talks required six more months due to the NKRC's adherence to the phrase of "free travels back and forth between families and relatives" in the wording of the agenda.

There was a reason for their adamant demand for "free travels back and forth." By insisting on "free travels" that literally called for travel in the other side freely, without any controls whatsoever, North Korea sought to infiltrate all of South Korea with a large number of political agitators posing as "separated families" or "separated relatives."

As no sign was seen of an early settlement of the issue, the ROKNRC proposed at the 18th preliminary meeting on February 10, 1972 to hold "closed-door working-level talks to straighten out the wording of the agenda of the full-dress talks." The NKRC agreed and there ensued a total of 13 closed-door meetings from February 21 to June 16, 1972, before the two sides could finally agree on a five-part agenda for the full-dress talks. The following agenda was formally adopted at the 20th preliminary meeting on June 16, 1972 :

(1) The question of ascertaining, and notifying thereof, the whereabouts and fate of the dispersed families and relatives in the south and the north.

(2) The question of facilitating free mutual visits and free meetings among the dispersed families and relatives in the south and the north.

45

(3) The question of facilitating free exchange of mails among the dispersed families and relatives in the south and the north.

(4) The question of facilitating reunion of the dispersed families according to their free individual wishes.

(5) And other humanitarian problems to be settled.

(e) Formation of Delegations to Ful-Dress Talks

Beginning at the 21st preliminary meeting on July 10, 1972, the two sides discussed the issue of forming delegations to the full dress talks. The ROKNRC first suggested that each delegation be composed of seven delegates, and carry 20 attendants and an adequate number of necessary support personnel. The NKRC's idea was that the delegations be led by the chiefs of the two Red Cross Societies, and be composed of five to seven delegates each. Here it was agreed to set the number of delegates at seven.

At the 22nd preliminary meeting on July 14, the two sides agreed their delegations would be headed by either the chiefs of the deputy chiefs of their Red Cross Societies. But, it was at this meeting that the NKRC came up from nowhere with the issue of "advisors" to stiffen the conference atmosphere. The NKRC asserted that the delegations should be accompanied by "groups of advisors" so that "they can help the delegations settle problems on the spot." It then said that such advisors should include the representatives of the Supreme People's Assembly, political parties and social organizations of north Korea for the NKRC, and those of corresponding organizations for the ROKNRC. The attempt of the NKRC here was to turn the Red Cross talks into a sort of political conference.

But, for the early conclusion of the long-dragged-out preliminary talks, the ROKNRC had to make another concession. At the 23rd preliminary meeting on July 19, the ROKNRC produced a compromise offer that "the two sides would appoint no more than seven advisors depending on their need." The NKRC accepted it, and the issue of the formation of delegations was thus settled. It was agreed that the two delegations would each carry about 70 attendants and support personnel.

(f) Agreement on Procedural Matters of Full-Dress Talks

Upon the solution of the issue of forming delegations at the 23rd preliminary meeting, the two sides started to discuss procedural matters of the full-dress talks. This discussion, too, encountered difficulties due to obstinacy from the north Koreans.

The NKRC first insisted that the first full-dress meeting be held in Pyongyang and that the number of attendants and support personnel, which was already fixed at around 70, should be cut back drastically. The NKRC also rejected the ROKNRC suggestion that foreign correspondents be allowed to accompany delegations. Originally the two sides, at the suggestion of the NKRC, had agreed to hold the first full-dress meeting on August 5, 1972. But the meeting failed to take place on that day due to the additional problems posed by the north Koreans.

It was only after three rounds of "working-level meetings for adjustment of wording of procedural matters of full-dress talks" held on July 27, August 3 and August 9 that the two sides could agree on the following "Note of Agreement on Procedural Matters and Date of Full-Dress Talks." This agreement was formally adopted at the 25th and final preliminary meeting on August 11 to wind up preliminary talks and complete preparations for the full-dress talks. The substance of the agreement was as follows:

1. First Meeting of Full-Dress Talks
The first full-dress meeting will be held in Pyongyang and the second full-dress meeting in Seoul.
2. Guarantee of Personal Safety
(1) The host side shall guarantee the inviolability of such articles as documents, photographs, films, tapes, reporters' notes, and press release belonging to the invited side during their travel and stay in the

area of the inviting side.

(2) Each side shall see to it that the authorities concerned of its side will make an announcement guaranteeing the safety of the delegation and the press corps of the other side during their stay in its area and their safe return at least one week before their visit and shall deliver the text of the announcement to the other side.

3. Procedure for Visits

(1) Each side shall furnish the other side with a list of the members of its delegation and press corps at least three days before their visit, and if there is any change in the list, it will be notified to the other side through the direct telephone line beween the South and the North and a copy of the verbal notification will be delivered to the other side later through the Panmunjom liaison offices. (The list should include names, sex and positions.)

The list should be signed by the chief of each Red Cross organization before it is delivered to the other side. Change in the original list may be signed by the head of the liaison office with the authorization by the chief of the Red Cross organization.

(2) Delegates should carry credentials and identification cards issued by the chief of their Red Cross organization, while advisors, attendants and reporters should carry only ID cards.

(3) Each delegation and press corps shall enter the area of the other side through Panmunjom. The time of the passage and reception shall be fixed through consulations between the two sides.

(4) Precedure for Panmunjom Passage

-Matters related to passage through Panmunjom shall be handled by officials assigned to the Panmunjom liaison offices and a list of these officials shall be notified to the other side.

-All procedures for passage through Panmunjom shall be carried out exclusively by the Red Cross organization of each side.

-All checkpoints on both sides shall not check the travelling personnel and their vehicles.

-Each side shall receive the visitors from the other side at a designated place in the area where the Panmunjom liaison offices are located, confirming their identities with the list provided earlier and the ID cards the visitors are carrying.

The host side shall hand over the list of visitors it received, signed by the chief of its Panmunjom liaison office, to the other side. At the time of their return both sides shall check the returning personnel with this list.

4. Period of Stay and Schedule of Talks

(1) Each visiting group can stay in the area of the other side for four to six days. Detailed itineraries and conference schedules will be decided on through mutual agreement.

(2) The delegation and press corps shall respect order in the other side and follow the guidance of the other side.

5. Emblems

(1) Both delegations shall wear the badges of their respective Red Cross organizations.

(2) Members of the press corps shall wear the badges of their respective Red Cross organizations and armbands of single-colored material with the word "Press" on them in whatever design is deemed convenient.

(3) The transportation means of both sides shall display only the Red Cross flag.

6. Equipment and Belongings

(1) Both sides can carry equipment for communications (except for wireless transmitters and receivers), recording of talks, drafting of documents and news coverage; medicine for emergency use; simple medical equipment; stationery goods and other articles necessary for the talks and their reporting.

(2) Personnel of both sides can carry personal belongings, publications and other articles necessary for life in the area of the other side.

(3) Neither side shall carry arms, explosives or other dangerous arti-

cles.

7. Transportation

Each side shall guarantee convenient and safe passage routes and transportation means for the members of the delegation and press corps visiting its area.

8. Communications

(1) Both sides shall install a total of 20 telegraph and telephone circuits between the south and the north for the convenience of the delegation and press corps.

(2) Both sides shall keep open two direct telephone circuits between the central offices of the southern and northern Red Cross organizations for convenient communications in connection with the talks and, during the period of each round of talks, secure two direct telephone circuits for communications between the delegation staying in the area of the other side and its Red Cross central office. (One of the two circuits will be linked to the conference site and the other to the lodging place.)

(3) Both sides shall connect the south-north telegraph and telephone circuits at a convenient point in Panmunjom.

(4) The allocation of telegraph and telephone circuits between the south and the north for different purposes, and the procedures of their operation will be consulted on between working-level officials.

(5) The permanent Panmunjom liaison offices shall be operated continuously.

9. Activities Outside Conference Site

Each side can take personnel from the other side to various sight-seeing programs.

10. Facilities at Conference Site

(1) The host side shall provide all necessary facilities for the management of the conference and install communication means at the conference site for the delegation and press corps to be able to reach their own area instantly.

(2) The host side shall place Red Cross flags at both ends of the conference table every time the talks are in session.

11. Recording of Talks

(1) Both sides shall record the contents of the talks by tape recording and stenography.

(2) Each side shall install two relay circuits for the delegation of the other side to be able to relay the talks directly from the conference room to its own Red Cross central office.

12. Whether to Open the Talks to the Public

(1) Conference shall be held behind closed doors in principle, but can be opened to the public if both sides so agree.

(2) The first-day sessions of the first and the second round talks be open to the public.

13. Press Coverage

(1) Each side shall limit the number of domestic newsmen covering the talks to 20.

(2) The first-day sessions of the first and the second round talks shall be open to the public.

(3) The two sides shall not slander each other in reporting the talks in the spirit of the South-North Joint Communique, try to promote mutual trust and understanding and observe the principle of accuracy.

14. Method of Operating Talks

(1) Conference shall be attended by delegates, advisors and attendants.

(2) Chief delegates shall be the principal speakers at the talks, but other delegates also can speak when necessary.

(3) The two sides discussed the issue of whether advisors should be allowed to speak, but this question was shelved because no agreement could be reached.

15. Drafting and Announcement of Agreement

Both sides shall draft the text of the agreement jointly, sign it together and announce it simultaneously.

16. Provision of conveniences

The host side shall provide the delegation and press corps of the other side with lodging, meals, transportation, communications service, medical care, press conveniences and other necessary facilities during their stay in its area and bear the expenses for those facilities.

17. Number of Persons Traveling to South and North for Talks

The number of persons traveling to the south and the north for the talks shall be seven delegates, seven advisors, 20 attendants and 20 domestic reporters.

18. Times of Full-Dress Talks

The first round of the full-fress talks will open at 10 a.m. August 30, 1972 in Pyongyang and the second round at 10 a.m. September 12, 1972 in Seoul.

In accordance with the procedural steps agreed on, the NKRC and the ROKNRC made public the lists of their delegates and advisors as follows on August 13 and August 17, respectively:

ROKNRC

-Delegates-

Chief Delegate :	**Lee Bom-sok,** ROKNRC vice president
Alternate Chief :	**Kim Yon-joo,** chief of the ROKNRC Health & Social Service Department
Delegate :	**Kim Dal-sul,** director of the ROKNRC Conference Secretariat
Delegate :	**Park Son-kyu,** president of the ROKNRC Chungchong Namdo Chapter
Delegate :	**Chong Hee-Kyong,** guidance member of the ROKNRC Junior Red Cross Services and principal of Ewha Girl's High School
Delegate (Spokesman) :	**Chong Choo-nyon,** spokesman for the ROKNRC Confrence Secretariat
Delegate :	**Soh Yong-hun,** chief of the ROKNRC Youth Department

-Advisors-

Kim Jun-yop,	professor of Korea University
Cho Dok-song,	editorial writer of the Chosun Ilbo

Yang Hung-mo,	editorial writer of the Joong-ang Daily News
Park Jun-kyu,	professor of Seoul National University
Ku Bom-mo,	professor of Seoul National University
Song Kon-ho,	editorial writer of the Dong-a Ilbo
Lee Sang-yol,	senior staff member of the South-North Red Cross Talks Supporting Committee

NKRC

-Delegates-

Chief Delegate :	**Kim Tae-hui,** vice chairman of the NKRC
Deputy chief :	**Ju Chang-joon,** secretary of the NKRC
Delegate :	**Cho Myung-il,** NKRC Executive Committee member and conference spokesman
Delegate :	**Gung Sang-ho,** NKRC senior staff member
Delegate :	**Li Chong-il,** NKRC Executive Committee member
Delegate :	**Han Si-hyok,** chief of the NKRC Culture & Publicity Department
Delegate :	**Kim Su-chol,** deputy chief of the NKRC organization and Planning Department

-Advisors-

Yun Ki-bok,	vice chairman of the Workers' Party External Relations Committee
Kim Sung-ryul,	vice chairman of the north Korean Democration Party
Kang Jang-su,	vice chairman of the Chondogyo-chongwu Party
Kim Kil-hyon,	deputy secretary-general of the Democratic Front for the Reunification of the Fatherland
Paek Nam-jun,	vice chairman of the League of All Vocations
O Kwang-taek,	vice chairman of the League of Socialist Working Youth
Kim Byong-shik,	first vice chairman of Chochongryon

On August 16, the two sides, in a meeting of working-level communications officials at Panmunjom, concluded the Agreed Minute on Installation and Operation of Telegraph and Telephone between the south and the North, calling for installing a total of 20 direct telephone and telegraph circuits between the two sides. In accordance with this agreement, the two sides installed direct south-north telegraph circuits on August 17.

On August 22, the South and the North issued statements guaranteeing the personal safety of the other side's Red Cross delegates and other persons. The statements were signed by Lee Hu-rak, SNCC Seoul-side co-chairman, on behalf of the Seoul side, and the Ministry of Social Security of the Pyongyang regime. On August 26, a direct telephone line was opened between the central Red Cross organizations in Seoul and Pyongyang.

b. Issuance of South-North Joint Communique

When the Red Cross preliminary talks were progressing at Panmunjom, the South and the North of Korea were working on an historic project that would soon electrify the whole world. It was a back-stage negotiation for the south-North Joint Communique. At 10 a.m. July 4, the South-North Joint Cummunique was simultaneously announced in Seoul and Pyongyang. It was made public by Lee Hu-rak, the then director of the Central Intelligence Agency, in Seoul and by Park Sung-chul, the then second vice premier, on behalf of Kim Young-joo, director of the Workers' Party organization and Guidance Department, in Pyongyang. The full text of the Joint Communique was as follows :

South-North Joint Communique

Recently there were talks held both in Pyongyang and Seoul to discuss problems of improving South-North relations and unifying the divided fatherland.

Director Lee Hu Rak of the Central Intelligence Agency of Seoul visited Pyongyang from May 2 to 5, 1972, to hold talks with Director Kim Young Joo of the Organization and Guidance Department of Pyongyang. Second Vice Pre-

mier Park Sung-chul , acting on behalf of Director Kim Young Joo, also visited Seoul from May 29 to June 1 1972 to hold further talks with Director Lee Hu Rak.

With the common desire to achieve peaceful unification of the fatherland as early as possible, the two sides in these talks had a frank and openhearted exchange of views and made great progress in promoting mutual understanding.

In the course of the talks, the two sides, in an effort to remove misunderstanding and mistrust, and to mitigate increased tensions that have arisen between the south and the north as a result of the long separation, and further to expedite unification of the fatherland, have reached full agreement on the following points

1) *The two sides have agreed to the following principles for unification of the fatherland :*

First, unification shall be achieved through independent efforts without being subject to external imposition or interference.

Second, unification shall be achieved through peaceful means, and not through use of force against one another.

Third, a great national unity, as a homogeneous people, shall be sought first, transcending differences in ideas, ideologies and systems.

2) *In order to ease tensions and foster an atmosphere of mutual trust between the south and the north, the two sides have agreed not to defame and slander one another, not to undertake armed provocations against one another, whether on a large or a small scale, and to take positive measures to prevent inadvertent military incidents.*

3) *The two sides, in order to restore severed national ties, promote mutual understanding and to expedite an independent peaceful unification, have agreed to carry out various exchanges in many areas.*

4) *The two sides have agreed to cooperate positively with one another to seek an early success of the South-North Red Cross Conference, which is currently in progress amidst the fervent expectations of the entire people of Korea.*

5) *The two sides, in order to prevent unexpected military incidents and to cope*

with problems arising in the ·relations between the south and the north directly, promptly and accurately, have agreed to install and operate a direct telephone line between Seoul and Pyongyang.

6) *The two sides, in order to implement aforementioned agreements, settle all the problems that exist in the relations between the South and the North and to solve the question of unifying the country, based on the agreed principles, have agreed to create and operate a South-North Coordinating Commitee, jointly chaired by Director Lee Hu Rak and Director Kim Young Joo.*

7) *The two sides, firmly convinced that the aforementioned agreements correspond with the common aspirations of the entire people eager to see early unification of their fatherland, hereby solemnly pledge before the entire Korean people that they will faithfully carry out the agreements.*

July 4, 1972

Upholding the desires of their respective superiors

Lee Hu Rak   **Kim Young Joo**

(1) Secret Contacts between Working-Level Officials and Mutual Visits

The secret and backstage negotiations between south and north Korea that gave birth to the July 4 South-North Joint Communique, were begun in November 1971 between the two sides' working-level officials carrying letters of credentials signed by Lee Hu-rak, director of the south's Central Intelligence Agency, and Kim Young-joo, director of the north Korean Workers' Party Organization and Guidance Department. The backstage contacts took place separately from the Red Cross preliminary talks that began at Panmunjom on September 20 of the same year. On November 20, 1971, one day ofter the 9th Red Cross preliminary meeting, Chong Hong-jin, a member of the ROKNRC delegation of the Red Cross talks, proposed a secret, exclusive meeting with a North Korean representative, and the contact began that same day. Representing North Korea was Kim Dok-hyon of the NKRC.

The Republic of Korea offered such additional contacts in hopes of preparing a political channel for inter-Korean dialogue in addition to the Red Cross talks intended to discuss and solve humanitarian questions. This initiative from the Republic of Korea was motivated by two factors.

First, there arose the need to prepare a political channel of dialogue if only to prompt the Red Cross talks to indulge in the solution of humanitarian issues, in the face of growing attempts by north Korea to degrade the Red Cross meetings into political talks.

Second, despite the universal trend of detente since the mid-1960s, tensions remained high on the Korean peninsula due to intensifying north Korean armed provocations against the South beginning in the latter half of the 1960s. Against this backdrop came President Park's declaration of an "idea of laying a ground work for peaceful unification" on August 15, 1970 and south Korea, with this declaration as impetus, began to seek peaceful coexistence between the south and north on an interim basis and to institute a system of good-natured competition between the two sides on the basis of such peaceful relations. The Republic of Korea hoped to provide momentum for such a policy of durable peace on the Korean peninsula through direct dialogue with north Korea by arranging a political channel of talks between the south and the north.

A total of 11 rounds of Chong-Kim secret contacts were held at Panmunjom from November 20, 1971 to March 22, 1972, during which they agreed to a meeting between Lee Hu-rak and Kim Young-joo to pave the way for a political dialogue. Lee Hu-rak, assigned by President Park to the duty of promoting inter-Korean political talks, chose as his north Korean counterpart Kim Young-joo, the younger brother of Kim Il sung and director of the powerful Workers' Party Organization and Guidance Department, who was then considered second only to Kim Il-sung in the north Korean hierarchy. North Korea agreed to the nomination. South Korea first suggested that these two persons meet in a third country venue such as Geneva or Paris. But north Korea wanted Lee Hu-rak to visit Pyongyang first. Consequently, it was agreed that Lee Hu-rak and Kim Young-joo would exchange visits to Pyongyang and Seoul, with Lee visiting Pyongyang first.

Prior to Lee Hu-rak's visit to Pyongyang, Chong Hong-jin, the south's representative at the secret contacts, visited Pyongyang March 28-31, 1972, and the north's Kim Dok-hyon visited Seoul April 19-21 the same year to prepare for the planned visits of Lee Hu-rak and Kim Young-joo. For communications between Seoul and Pyongyang during the projected visits, the two sides decided to install a direct telephone line linking the Central Intelligence Agency office of Lee Hu-rak in Seoul and Kim Young-joo's office at the Workers' Party Organization and Guidance Department in Pyongyang. The hotline was opened on April 29.

(2) *Exchange of Visits*

After these preparatory steps, Lee Hu-rak, accompanied by three aides, embarked on a top-secret visit to Pyongyang on May 2, 1972, by way of Panmunjom.

During his four-day stay in Pyongyang May 2-5, Lee Hu-rak met Kim Il-sung twice and had two rounds of meetings with Kim Young-joo.

In his discussions with Kim Il-sung, Lee Hu-rak explained the basic policy of the Republic of Korea toward the Korean question as instructed by President Park. The two exchanged views on various issues with emphasis on the questions of easing tensions between the two sides and of expediting the peaceful solution of the unification question. Kim and Lee shared the opinion that the most immediate question pending between the two sides was to remove mutual misunderstanding and distrust.

Lee Hu-rak pointed out in the meetings that the source of mutual misunderstanding and distrust lay in the different ideas and systems of the two sides, as well as the deep-rooted distrust of north Korea among the south Korean people, which he said was prompted by the Korean War and unending armed provocations and subversive schemes perpetrated by north Korea. In response, Kim Il-sung conceded the attempted raid on Chong Wa Dae by commandos of the north Korean Army's 124th Unit on January 21, 1968, offering a sincere apology.

The contents of the negotiations between Lee Hu-rak and Kim Il-sung were embodied in two of the three principles for unification contained in the South-North Joint Communique – "Unification shall be achieved through independent efforts without being subject to external imposition or interference" and "unification shall be achieved through peaceful means, and not through the use of force against each other." The two sides agreed that on the basis of these understandings they would pursue "national unity" through the implementation of concrete projects aimed at easing tensions and removing misunderstanding and distrust in favor of mutual understanding and trust. Lee Hu-rak suggested that to this end, the two sides 1) would not slander or defame each other, 2) would not make unilateral unification formulas for propaganda purposes, and 3) would not harass each other militarily. More specifically, Lee proposed that the search campaign for dispersed families be successfully implemented through the ongoing South-North Red Cross Conference, that personal, material and communication exchanges be promoted between the two sides, and that based on these achievements, the two sides enter political talks. Kim Il-sung then suggested that to implement these programs, a "South-North Coordinating Committee" be organized and put into operation. Kim also raised the issue of mutual military reduction.

In the wake of Lee Hu-rak's visit to Pyongyang, Park Sung-chul visited Seoul on a similarly secret four-day tour from May 29 to June 1. Lee Hu-rak's north Korean counterpart was Kim Young-joo. But, Kim Il-sung dispatched Park Sung-chul as "Kim Young-joo's substitute" on the grounds that Kim Young-joo was sick. (From this time on, Kim Young-joo did not show up at the scenes of south-north talks. His role was assumed by Park Sung-chul.)

During his stay in Seoul, Park, accompanied by three aides, conferred with Lee Hu-rak twice and made a courtesy call on President Park. In the Seoul meetings between Lee Hu-rak and Park Sung-chul, the two sides generally reaffirmed what Lee discussed with Kim Il-sung and Kim Young-joo in Pyongyang. In particular, the two sides agreed to organize and operate a South-North Coordinating Committee co-chaired by Lee Hu-rak representing the Seoul side and Kim Young-joo from the Pyongyang side, and composed of three-to-five members from each side. They also decided to set up various subcommittees by area of interest to promote manysided exchanges and cooperations.

While receiving Park Sung-chul at Chong Wa Dae, the Presidential residence, on May 31, President Park, stressing that success of the south-north dialogue hinges on the creation of the base for mutual understanding and trust, called for the solution of practicable and easy problems first on a step-by-step basis. As a first step toward such endeavors, the President said, the two sides should make the South-North Red Cross Conference bear fruit at an early date.

Further pointing out that the people of south Korea harbour a deep-rooted distrust of the Communist system in north Korea because of its aggression during the Korean War and continuing armed, violent provocations such as infiltration of agents and guerrillas ever since the ceasefire, President Park also said that such distrust cannot be removed overnight. He added that in a state where this distrust remains unremoved, the time of unification cannot be approached, even if unification efforts were made in haste. Therefore, the President emphasized, the two sides should first concentrate their efforts upon restoring the national homogeneity, transcending the difference in systems.

(3) Agreement on Direct Telephone Line

The mutual visits to Seoul and Pyongyng by Lee Hu-rak and Park Sung-chul and the consequent high-level talks gave birth to the historic

South-North Joint Communique. The two sides agreed to make public at home and abroad in the form of a joint communique what was discussed and agreed on in the above-mentioned secret visits. The South-North Joint Communique was signed by Lee Hu-rak and Kim Young-joo on June 29 before it was fomally announced at 10 a.m. July 4.

The two sides decided to put an official seal to the direct south-north telephone line in use since April 28 prior to Lee Hu-rak's visit to Pyongyang, and accordingly made public the Agreement on Installation and Operation of South-North Dirct Telephone Line on July 4 along with the issuance of the South-North Joint Communique. The agreement on the direct telephone line is as follows :

Agreement on Installation and Operation of
South-North Direct Telephone Line

1. Purpose
A direct telephone line shall be installed and operated between Seoul and Pyongyang in order that the two sides cope, directly, promptly and acurately, with the task of achieving unification of the fatherland peacefully and independently, with problems arising in the relations between the South and the North and with unexpected incidents between them.

2. Places of Installation
The direct telephone line shall connect the offices of Director Lee Hu-rak of the Central Intelligence Agency in Seoul and Director Kim Young-joo of the Organization and Guidance Department in Pyongyang, with the telephone sets installed in the two offices, respectively.

3. Operation
The two sides shall operate the direct telephone line from 9 a.m. to noon and from 4 to 8 p.m. every day except Sundays and holidays. However, in case the two sides deem it necessary, they may operate the direct telephone line in extra hours as well as on Sundays and

holidays by making arrangements to that effect through mutual agreement in advance.

4. Users

The two sides shall name three persons each, appointed respectively by Director Lee Hu-rak of the Central Intelligence Agency in Seoul and Director Kim Young-joo of the Organization and Guidance Department in Pyongyang, to have the direct telephone line operated exclusively under their charge.

5. Tests

The two sides shall test the direct telephone line at 10 a.m. everyday, except Sundays and holidays, in order to check the mechanical conditions of the line.

6. Repair Works

The two sides shall be responsible for repair works within areas under their respective jurisdictions, should the direct telephone line develops mechanical troubles.

7. Confidentiality of Conversations

The two sides shall keep the contents of conversations by the direct telephone strictly confidential.

8. Amendments and Supplements

The contents of this Agreement shall be amended and/or supplemented only through mutual agreement.

9. Date of Expiration

This Agreement shall go into effect as soon as the two sides respectively share a copy of the Agreement, with their signatures affixed to them, and shall remain in effect unless abolished through mutual agreement.

July 4, 1972

Lee Hu Rak   Kim Young Joo
Director   Director
Central Intelligence Agency Organization & Guidance Dept.
Seoul   Pyongyang

4. Progress of Dialogue

a. South-North Coordinating Committee

(1) Co-Chairmen's Meetings

Following the issuance of the South-North Joint Communique, three rounds of co-chairmen's meetings were held between the two sides ; the first co-chairmen's meeting at the Freedom House at Panmunjom on October 12, the second meeting in Pyongyang on November 2-3 and their meeting in Seoul on November 30, 1972.

The co-chairmen's meetings were disigned to discuss and settle various procedural steps necessary for the formation and operation of the proposed South-North Coordinating Committee, as well as to review new developments in inter-Korean relations in the wake of the Joint Communique. At the second co-chairmen's meeting held in Pyongyang on November 4, 1972, the two sides adopted the Agreed Minute on Formation and Operation on South-North Coordinating Committee.

Agreed Minute on Formation & Operation of South-North Coordinating Committee

The two sides have agreed on formation and operation of the South-North Coordinating Committee (SNCC) as follows :

1. The SNCC shall make it its aim to implement the agreements spelled out in the South-North Joint Communique of July 4, 1972, improve the relations between the South and the North, undertake cooperative activities in various fields and, thus, to settle the question of unifying the country on the basis of the agreed principles for unification of the fatherland.

2. The functions of the SNCC shall be as follows :

a. To deliberate and settle the question of unifying the country independently and peacefully based on the agreed principles for unification of the fatherland and to secure its implementation.

b. To deliberate and settle the question of effecting a wide range of political exchanges among political parties, social organizations and individuals of the south and the north and to secure its implementation.

c. To deliberate and settle the question of facilitating economic, cultural and social exchanges and cooperation between the south and the north and to secure its implementation.

d. To deliberate and settle the question of relaxing tensions, preventing armed incidents and dissolving the state of military confrontations between the south and the north and to secure its implementation.

e. To deliberate and settle the question of enhancing the national pride as a single homogeneous nation by taking joint steps in overseas activities and to secure its implementation.

3. The SNCC shall be organized as follows :

a. The SNCC shall be composed of one Co-chairman, one Vice Chairman, one Executive Member and two Members, respectively, from each side. The number of the Committee Members may be increased when deemed necessary. Director Lee Hu-rak of the Central Intelligence Agency and Director Kim Young-joo of the Organization and Guidance Department are hereby named as Cochairmen. Vice chairmen, Executive Members and Members shall be of ministerial or vice ministerial ranks and shall be appointed respectively by the Co-chairmen through prior consultations.

b. An Executive Council shall be created within the SNCC. The Executive Council shall be charged with the mission of deliberating and settling all the problems arising while the SNCC is in recess and of securing implementation of the decisions, when the authority is delegated to that effect by the Co-chairmen. The Executive Council shall be composed of two Secretaries, in addition to the SNCC Executive Member, respectively from each side.

c. The SNCC shall have five Subcommittees – Political, Military, Foreign Affairs, Economic and Cultural – with each of them to be created according to progresses made in the SNCC. The functions and formations of the Subcommittees shall be regulated separately through mutual agreement.

d. The SNCC shall have a Joint Secretariat to be located in Panmunjom. The two sides shall respectively appoint one Co-director of the Joint Secretariat each and respectively have a necessary number of personnel placed under them to staff the Joint Secretariat.

4. The SNCC shall be operated as follows :

a. The SNCC shall make it a principle to hold its meetings in Seoul and Pyongyang, in turns. It may hold meetings at Panmunjom through mutual agreement, if necessary.

b. The SNCC shall hold its plenary meetings once every two to three months and the Executive Council meetings once every month. Extraordinary meetings may be called into session through mutual agreement.

c. The SNCC meetings shall be held either in public or behind the closed door.

d. Necessary numbers of specialists and Joint Secretariat staffs may be allowed to attend the SNCC and Executive Council meetings, through mutual agreement.

e. The final agreements at the SNCC shall take effect as soon as the Co-chairmen of the two sides affix their signatures to them. The agreements shall be announced simultaneously through the Joint Secretariat; through mutual agreement.

f. The SNCC shall have other regulations relative to its operation worked out separately,

5. This Agreed Minute may be amended and supplemented through mutual agreement.

6. This Agreed Minute goes into effect as soon as the two sides share a document each with their signatures affixed to them.

November 4, 1972

Director Lee Hu Rak
Co-chairman(Seoul side)
SNCC

Park Sung Chul
For Director Kim Young Joo
Co-chairman (Pyongyang side)
SNCC

(a) *First Meeting*

The first co-chairmen's meeting of the South-North Coordinating Committee was held in the Freedom House at Panmunjom on October 12, 1972. It was attended by Lee Hu-rak, Kim Chi-yol and Chong Hong-jin from the Seoul side, and from the Pyongyang side by Park Sung-chul, Ryu Jang-shik and Kim Dok-hyon. At the meeting, a wide discrepancy was revealed between the two sides' respective interpretations of the matters agreed to in the Joint Communique, especially the three principles for national unification. Because of the differences, heated debates raged throughout the meeting that lasted two and a half hours.

The Seoul side emphasized that to realize independent and peaceful unification and the promotion of national unity, conditions conducive to facilitating them should be created. In this respect, the Seoul side suggested that the two sides first inaugurate the projected South-North Coordinating Committee, and then translate the agreements embodied in the Joint Communique (Articles 2-6) into action through the Coordinating Committee, promoting step by step the restoration of national homogeneity through removal of the misunderstanding and the distrust existing between the two sides. The Seoul side stated that in order to implement this series of steps to improve inter-Korean relations, the two sides should engage in mutual exchanges and cooperation, and open their societies to each other without interfering in the internal order of the other side's system.

On the contrary, the Pyongyang side insisted now that the two sides had agreed on the three principles for national unification in the Joint Communique, 1) south Korea should abandon its anti-Communist policy, 2) south Korea should no longer defend the free-democratic system in connection with unification, 3) the United Nations, being an "external force," should not intervene in the Korean question in any form, 4) the U.S. forces in Korea should withdraw immediately, and 5) south Korea should stop building up its armed forces and conducting military maneuvers. Thus north Korea revealed its intention to create an atmosphere favorable to the execution of a "people"s revolution in south Korea" by applying the three principles for unification only to south Korea, true to the logic of Communst-style negotiations that dictates "mine is mine and yours is mine, also."

After the meeting, the two sides jointly announced that 1) they discussed various issues that arose between the South and the North after the issuance of the Joint Communique, and reaffirmed the spirit of the Joint Communique, and 2) sincerely discussed the issue of removing misundestanding and distrust between the two sides, promoting a great national unity, and expediting independent and peaceful unification of the fatherland through the sincere implementation of the agreed matters in the Joint Communique. It was also reported that the two sides agreed to hold the second co-chairmen's meeting toward the end of October.

(b) Second Meeting

The second co-chairmen's meeting of the South-North Coordinating Committee was held in Pyongyang November 2-3, 1972. Besides the co-chairmen, the meeting was attended by "consultants" to the co-chairman Chang Key-yong, former Deputy Prime Minister, Choi Kyu-hah, Special Assistant to the President, Kang In-dok, director of the ROKCIA 9th Bureau, and Chong Hong-jin, director of Consultation and Coordination Bureau of ROKCIA, from the Seoul side. The Pyongyangside "consultants" were Ryu Jang-shik, deputy director of the Workers' Party organization and Guidance Department and concurrently director of the Party's External Project Department, Ri

Kyung-suk, a cabinet councilor, and Han Ung-shik, and Kim Uok-hyon, an instructor of the Political Committee of the Worker's Party Central Committee. In addition, ten correspondents and another ten attendants from each side took part in the meeting.

At this meeting, the two sides concluded the Agreed Minute on Formation and Operation. of South-North Coordinating Committee, and agreed on 1) cessation of propaganda radio broadcasts against each other, 2) cessation of propaganda broadcasts through public address systems along the Military Demarcation Line, and 3) cessation of the scattering of propaganda leaflets in each other's area. These steps were just put into force effective November 11, 1972.

On the other hand, the Pyongyang side, adhering to its unilateral interpretation of the three principles for unification contained in the Joint Communique, attempted to interfere in the internal and exter-nal affairs of south Korea, taking advantage of the three principles and stiffening the conference atmosphere. Insisting that "a dialogue based on the Joint Communique cannot be compatible with the anti-Communist policy of south Korea," Park Sung-cul challenged the Re-public of Korea to 1) stop giving anti-Communist education to the people and making anti-Communist propaganda, 2) release those being criminally punished for their violation of the Anti-Communist Law and the National Security Law, 3) punish those who persecute the Communists, 4) cause the American forces in Korea to be with-drawn, and 5) sever friendly and cooperative relations with Japan.

In response, Lee Hu-rak urged that the two sides should carry on the dialogue transcending the difference in ideas and systems without interfering in the internal affairs of the other side while maintaining their own systems, as stipulated by the Joint Communique. He stressed that since the inter-Korean talk is a dialogue between two extremely different systems, the dialogue cannot be carried on if either of the parties attempts to interfere in the internal problems of the other's system.

During their stay in Pyongyang, Co-chairman Lee Hu-rak and his "consultants," escorted by Park Sung-chul and his "consultants," called on Kim Il-sung in his "cabinet building" office for four hours and 30 minutes from 10:15 a.m. November 3. The occasion was also attended by Kim Il, vice premier, and Kim Chung-rin, secretary in charge of north Korea's south Korean revolutionary operations of the Workers' Party Political Committee. During the meeting, Kim Il-sung, who until then showed considerable interest in the dialogue, instructed Pyongyang delegates to ensure the drafted Agreed Minute on Formation and Operation of South-North Coordinating Committee, whose adoption had been delayed due to a dispute over some working, be agreed on without fail. Kim Il-sung also called for political, economic and cultural "collaboration" between the two sides, and defended mutual military reduction and the so-called "confederation" system between the South and the North.

(c) Third Meeting

The third co-chairmen's meeting was held at the conference room of the "Yungbin Kwan" in Seoul at 4 p.m. November 30, 1972. It was attended by Lee Hu-rak, Park Sung-chul and the "consultants" from the two sides. The "consultants" were the same as those who attended the second co-chairmen's meeting, except that Pyongyang's Ri Kyung-suk was replaced by Ri Wan-ki (a cabinet councilor) due to the former's death. At the third meeting, the two sides took all necessary steps to inaugurate the South-North Coordinating Committee, winding up the co-chairmen's meeting. They agreed to form the Coordinating Committee as follows:

Seoul Side	
Co-chairman :	**Lee Hu-rak**
Vice-chairman :	**Chang Key-yong**
Member :	**Choi Kyu-hah**
Member :	**Kang In-dok**
Executive Member :	**Chong Hong-jin**
Pyongyang Side	
Co-chairman :	**Kim Young-joo** (with **Park Sung-chol** acting for **Kim Young-joo**)

Vice-chairman :	Ryu Jang-shik
Member :	Ri Wan-ki(a cabinet councilor)
Member :	Han Ung-shik
Executive Member :	Kim Dok -hyon

(2) SNCC Plenary Meetings

Three rounds of plenary meetings of the South-North Coordinating Committee were held – the first round in Seoul on November 30 and December 1, 1972, the second in Pyongyang on March 15, 1973 and the third in Seoul on June 12 and 13, 1973 – before the normal operation of the Coordinating Committee was halted by north Korea's statement of unilateral suspension of the dialogue on August 28, 1973. The evolutions of the SNCC plenary meetings :

Following the example of the second Co-chairmen's meeting held in Pyongyang, the two sides agreed that the plenary meetings, to be held in Seoul and Pyongyang by turn, would be attended by 10 attendants and another 10 domestic correspondents in addition to the five members from each side.

(a) First Meeting

The first plenary meeting of the South-North Coordinating Committee convened twice at the "Yungbin Kwan" in Seoul, at 5 : 30 p.m. November 30 and 10 a.m. December 1, 1972. Upon completion of the first plenary meeting, the two sides said in a joint announcement that 1) they exchanged opinions on the questions of carrying out exchanges and cooperations in various fields, and 2) they agreed to inaugurate the Executive Council, establish the Joint Secretariat and prepare necessary operational regulations soon with a view to setting in motion the working-level function of the Coordinating Committee at an early date.

At this first formal get-together of the South-North Coordinating Committee born of the South-North Joint Communique, the two sides failed to narrow their views on basic matters.

70

Seoul side Co-chairman Lee Hu-rak said that in view of the subst-ance of the talks prior to the inauguration of the Coordinating Com-mittee, the two sides maintained different stands regarding inter-pretation of the three principles for unification, causing the danger that the working-level talks of the dialogue might encounter rough going. To cope with the situation, Lee suggested the two sides put into operation the various working-level functions of the Coordinating Committee on a priority basis, and to facilitate smooth progress of the dialogue, both sides during the period of the dialogue should, 1) de-sist from rejecting each other's system, 2) understand each other's sys-tem, 3) desist from interfering in or denouncing the internal affairs of each other's system, 4) not attempt to impose one's own system upon the other, 5) endeavor to promote people's welfare based on one's own system, 6) promote cooperative relations in such a way as to strengthen national homogeneity, transcending the difference in sys-tems, and 7) establish new inter-Korean relations based on the princi-ple that the south-north talk is a dialogue between one system and another. The Seoul side further proposed that in view of the reality of national division, the Coordinating Committee should first under-take projects in those non-political and non-military areas where the least factors of friction and resistance from the difference in systems and ideas were anticipated, and then move to the political and milit-ary areas on the basis of the understanding and trust built up through initial efforts.

However, the Pyongyang side was not interested in setting in mo-tion the working-level functions of the Coordinating Committee. Park Sung-chul simply demanded that the two sides 1) discuss ways to re-move the state of military confrontation by convening a meeting of military representatives and 2) inaugurate the five subcommittees of politics, military, foreign policy, economy and culture at the same time, arguing that "now that the Joint Communique has been issued, the South and the North should trust each other."

(b) Second Meeting

The Seoul-side members of the South-North Coordinating Committee, along with attendants and correspondents, drove to Pyongyang by way of Panmunjom on March 14, 1973 to attend the second meeting of the Coordinating Committee. At this time, however, a significant change appeared in the attitude of the north Koreans, a signal that they were beginning to lose interest in the dialogue. The first sign of the change was seen when they deviated from prior practice by not offering helicopters to ferry the Seoul-side members and other attendees from Kaesung to Pyongyang. The second sign was that Kim Il-sung, who previously met with Seoul-side delegates, refused to this time on the grounds of "his tour of provincial areas for on-the-scene guidance."

The altered attitude of the Pyongyang side was more visible at the conference table.

The Seoul side, as it did at the first meeting, emphasized that the most exigent concern the Coordinating Committee had to insure its successful operation was to straighten out the working functions of the Coordinating Committee. In this regard, the Seoul side proposed that 1) the operational regulations of the Coordinating Committee, the Executive Council and the provisions of establishment of the Joint Secretariat be worked out at an early date, and 2) the two sides jointly construct the building for the proposed Joint Secretariat in the Joint Security Area of Panmunjom. At the same time, the Seoul side, agreeing to the inauguration of two of the five subcommittees envisaged for the Coordinating Committee – economy and socio-culture suggested that detailed problems related to their establishment be refered to executive members' meeting.

However, the Pyongyang side had no interest in straightening out the working functions of the Coordinating Committee. Contending that "unless the state of military confrontation between the two sides is removed first, no genuinely trustworthy dialogue can not take place, problems related to the issue of unification can not be settled and the inter-Korean relations can not be improved." Park Sung-chul set forth a five-point military-related proposal, demanding that his proposition be discussed before any other questions. The five-point overture provided that 1) the South and the North would desist from building their military strength and from engaging in an arms race, 2) the two sides would reduce their armed forces to 100,000 or less and drastically reduce their military equipment, 3) the two sides would stop introducing any weapons, operational equipment and all other military materials from abroad, 4) all foreign troops including U.S. forces would be taken out of the country, and 5) a peace agreement would be signed between the two sides as a mutual pledge to solve these issues and to refrain from using the force of arms against each other. Park Sung-chul demanded that to handle these questions, the South-North Coordinating Committee be reorganized to allow the participation of military leaders or a military subcommittee be inaugurated on a priority basis. Park Sung-chul further demanded the activation of the proposed five subcommittees of the Coordinating Committee — politics, military, foreign policy, economy and culture — on a package basis. In this demand, the Pyongyang side turned down the Seoul-side offer for the preferential establishment of the two subcommittees of economy and socio-culture, and showed an attitude that was contradictory even to its own call for the prior activation of the military subcommittee. Going a step farther, the Pyongyang side laid down a new demand that a "joint conference of political parties and social organizations in both sides of Korea" be held separately from the South-North Coordinating Committee.

From their attitude at the second meeting, the north Koreans had made their intention clear. By producing a seemingly comprehensive and positive proposal, which in effect lacked any practicality, the Pyongyang side attempted to deadlock the talks and shift the responsibility to the other side.

Because of this stiffened north Korean attitude, the second meeting ended without any joint announcement on the results of the meeting. However, Park Sung-chul, breaking the custom of not making public anything that was not agreed on, openly discussed what he offered at the meeting, beginning to use the Coordinating Committee for propaganda purposes.

(c) Third Meeting

The third meeting of the South-North Coordinating Committee was held on June 12–15, 1973, in Seoul. But the Pyongyang side simply reiterated the demands of the second meeting, again obliging a meeting to end without any agreement. The renewed north Korean demand was 1) prior discussion of its five-point military proposal, 2) convening of a "joint conference of political parties and social organizations in both sides of Korea," and 3) establishment of the five subcommittees envisioned for the Coordinating Committee on a package basis.

Lee Hu-rak, the Seoul-side co-chairman, on the other hand, called upon the north Koreans to show a more sincere attitude toward preparing the operational regulations of the Coordinating Committee and its subordinate organizations, as well as toward inaugurating the projected Joint Secretariat. Lee also protested that despite the south-north agreement to desist from slandering each other effective November 11, 1972, north Korea continued to defame the Republic of Korea and infiltrate its agents into the south. The Seoul-side co-chairman specifically noted that north Korea continued to operate.the so-called "Voice of Unification and Revolutionary Party," a propaganda radio exclusively directed against the south, which north Korea ridiculously claims is an "underground radio operated somewhere in the south."

The Seoul-side suggested inauguration of the envisaged economic and socio-cultural sub-committees to : 1) exchange businessmen, 2) exchange materials, 3) exchange science and technology, 4) jointly explore resources, 5) exchange commodity fairs, and 6) allow the opening of company branches in the other side. In the socio-culture area, the Seoul-side proposed the two sides 1) exchange science and cultural programs, 2) exchange sports and enter international sports events under a single ticket, 3) exchange films and stage arts, 4) jointly explore and study archaeology and history, 5) jointly study the task of preserving indigenous words, 6) conduct broad personnel exchanges in various walks of society and social organizations, 7) exchange journalists and permanent press bureaus, 8) exchange such communications as correspondence, telephone and telegraph, and 9) exchange tourism programs.

(3) Executive Council Meetings

The South and the North in March 1973 formed the Executive Council as a working-level steering body of the Coordinating Committee in accordance with the Agreed Minute on Formation and Operation of South-North Coordinating Committee. The Executive Council had three rounds of meetings at Panmunjom, on March 10, April 24 and May 23, 1973. The Seoul-side was represented at the meeting by Chong Hong-jin, executive member, Lee Dong-bok, spokesman, and Paik Chun-il, and the Pyongyang side by Kim Dok-hyon, executive member, Chun Gum-chul, spokesman, and Huh Pil-kook.

At the three rounds the two sides endeavored to straighten out the wording of three draft agreement : Operational Regulations of South-North Coordinating Committee, Operational Regulations of Executive Council, and Agreed Minute on Establishment of Joint Secretariat. But the meetings failed to make any further headway due to the Pyongyang-side's insistence that a clause "representatives of political parties, social organizations and individuals may be invited as observers to the meetings of the South-North Coordinating Committee" should be included in the operational regulations of the Coordinating Committee. After the third plenary meeting of the Coordinating Committee held in Scoul June 12-14, 1973, the Pyongyang-side even refused to receive telephone calls over the direct south-north line, causing the operation of the Executive Council to be suspended after its third meeting.

b. South-North Red Cross Conference

(1) Summary

Seven rounds of the full-dress meetings of the South-North Red Cross Conference, the first full-fledged dialogue between the two divided halves in a quarter century, were held in Seoul and Pyongyang by turn.

Full-Dress Meetings Held

Classification	Place	Time
1st	Pyongyang	August 29-September 2, 1972
2nd	Seoul	September 12-16, 1972
3rd	Pyongyang	October 23-26, 1972
4th	Seoul	November 22-24, 1972
5th	Pyongyang	March 20-23, 1973
6th	Seoul	May 8-11, 1973
7th	Pyongyang	July 10-13, 1973

The first round in Pyongyang and the second round in Seoul were held in a festive mood because of the emotions arising from the fact that for the first time since the territorial division, large delegations from the South and the North crossed the boundary line. Various congratulatory events prevailed over the conference itself.

However, the attitudes of the southern and northern delegations toward the talks were poles apart. The southern side's sincerity and adherence to humanitarianism contrasted with the North Korean maneuverings to turn the Red Cross talks into a forum for political propaganda. At the first full-dress meeting in Pyongyang, the North Korea Red Cross brought eight "representatives of political parties and social organizations" to the rostrum and then at the second full-dress meeting in Seoul, it had two of its "advisors" – Yun Ki-bok and Kim Byung-shik – make political speeches eulogizing "Kim Il-sung

76

thoughts" rather than showing any interest in the solution of the Red Cross humanitarian project. The northerners at times said "Unification is the best humanitarian settlement" and chanted, "Let's get rid of foreign influence." They were acting as if they were holding a unification conference or political talks, not humanitarian discussions aimed at finding ways to lessen the sufferings of 10 million divided family members. This north Korean Red Cross attitude cast a dark shadow on the future of the Red Cross talks.

Substantive discussions were made beginning at the third full-dress meeting after the festive mood died down. At this meeting, the ROKNRC presented the following six principles to ensure the success of the family search project:

(1) The campaign for search for families and relatives should be carried out exclusively by the two Red Cross Societies in the south and the north under their full responsibility.

(2) All elements hampering the humanitarian nature of this project should be discarded.

(3) The free will of the concerned people should be respected.

(4) Private secret of the concerned people should be protected.

(5) When an agreement is reached on any specific project, it should be put into action immediately.

(6) The confirmation of present conditions and whereabouts should be made most accurately and speedily.

The NKRC, however, insisted that some legal and social preconditions should be met before the talks entered into substantive discussions on agenda items. As one of such preconditions, they demanded that "legal conditions should be improved and favorable social circumstances should be created in south Korea." Conflicting positions from the start prevented the talks from making any substantial progress on item No.1. Deadlock in the Red Cross talks in fact began to emerge at this third session.

At the third full-dress meeting, the NKRC proposed that:

(1) Statutory conditions and social circumstances in the south be improved,

(2) Red Cross "expounders" be dispatched to areas of the other side.

(3) The scope and method of the family search project be decided by the desire of the concerned persons, and

(4) As Red Cross project organs, a joint committee of the South and North Korean Red Cross Societies and Red Cross representatives' offices be established.

The demand for legal and social improvements was their excuse for shunning substantive discussions at the Red Cross talks. Increase in the number of the reporters allowed to cover the talks by five on each side was the only item agreed on at the third full-dress meeting.

As the talks hit a snag, the ROKNRC, playing host for the fourth full-dress meeting in Seoul, proposed that a joint committee be set up for the day-to-day running of the Red Cross project and that the two Red Cross Societies open their representatives' offices in Seoul and Pyongyang, respectively. The ROKNRC suggested that for detailed discussion of this proposition, working-level meetings be held.

The NKRC rejected the idea of Red Cross representatives' offices in each other's area, and insisted instead on forming a joint committee and a "joint project office" at Panmunjom. To avoid a hitch, the ROKNRC agreed to the revised NKRC proposal.

The north Korean demand for improved legal and social conditions in south Korea was more clearly phrased at the sixth full-dress meeting. At this meeting, the NKRC demanded that south Korea 1) abrogate such anti-Communist legislation as the Anti-Communist Law and the National Security Law, 2) disband anti-Communist agencies and organizations, 3) ban all anti-Communist activities, and 4) guarantee the freedom of speech, publication, assembly and movement for people coming from the north to the south to meet their separated families and relatives, provide all kinds of facilities for them and take legal and administrative measures to respect the inviolability of their safety and their belongings.

In addition, the NKRC insisted that Red Cross expounders should be sent to every "ri" or "dong," the lowest administrative unit, of the other area, with the expounders guaranteed the same freedom and facilities as other visitors so as to enable them to engage in publicity acitivities.

The "publicity activities" suggested by the north were to have the expounders guaranteed freedom of all kinds of activities, travel in the area of the other side and explain how the mistrust and mis-understanding between the South and the North should be removed, and also provide information on the conditions of separated families. The North Koreans argued this was "the most effective way to facili-tate family reunions."

The NKRC proposal on the "publicity activities" was an out right denial of the basic principle that the family reunion campaign should be carried out under the exclusive management of the Red Cross.

In case the publicity personnels were dispatched to each village in the south and the north it would mean that some 36,000 northern personnel would swarm into the south, while 4,300 would visit the North from the South. It was apparent that the dispatch of such large numbers of people to the area of the other side was only intended for political activites. If such "publicity activities"were really necessary, the North Koreans should have asked to use the Red Cross joint com-mittee and joint project office, whose establishment was agreed upon at the fourth full-dress meeting, for that purpose.

The North Koreans further argued that the Red Cross should not intervene in the process of confirming the present conditions and whereabouts of separated families. According to their idea, such con-firmation should be left to the separated families themselves who would travel in the area of the other side, looking for their dividied families and relatives.

To this, the ROKNRC said it was more reasonable for the Red Cross to carry out the confirmation service as the tracing by the di-vided families themselves would involve extreme difficulties because administrative designations had been revised and addresses had been changed during the long period of national division.

It was apparent that the northern demand for "free travel" by the separated families in the north and the south was not for the search for families but for the launching of Communist political activities in every corner of the south Korean society.

Lee Bom-sok, chief ROKNRC delegate, told the north Koreans that their "unreasonable and unrealistic" proposal concerning what they called "prerequisites" was outright interference in the internal affairs of the Republic of Korea. He emphatically said that humanitarian activities based on the Red Cross spirit and principles which forego laws, politics and systems, should not be impeded by any existing legal and social conditions. He stressed that this had been the tradition of the ROKNRC and the International Red Cross and the expressed position of the ROK government, which had vowed positive support for the Red Cross project. "For this very reason, the ROKNRC has never mentioned the legal and social conditions now existing in north Korea," he said, calling on the North to withdraw its unreasonable demands and come up to orderly discussion of agenda items as already agreed upon, instead of sticking to unreasonable "preconditions."

However, the NKRC kept asking for the repeal of anti-Communist statutes in the Republic of Korea and refused to carry on the Red Cross project purely as a humanitarian task. It contended that "the only way to realize humanitarianism in our country is to achieve the unification of the fatherland.... No humanitarian project can be detached from the unification problem.... Therefore, anti-Communist laws in south Korea should be scrapped first."

This NKRC attitude did not change at the seventh full-dress meeting, driving the talks to the brink of collapse. In an effort to find a breakthrough, the ROKNRC made a new proposal for the exchange of groups of visitors to ancestral tombs between the two sides on the occasion of the 1973 *Chusok* holiday(Korean Thanks-giving Day). It was suggested that the south and the north send and receive the same number of tomb visitors around *Chusok*, the fifteenth day of the eighth month by lunar calendar.

The NKRC rejected the proposal. In its view, the ROKNRC proposal was "not a solution to the whole question" and would rather "hinder the progress of the talks."

Finally on August 28, 1973, shortly before the scheduled opening of the eighth full-dress meeting set to be held in Seoul, north Korea issued a statement in the name of Kim Young-joo, Pyongyang-side Co-chairman of the South-North CoordinatingCommittee, in which it denounced South Korea in connection with some of its internal affairs and announced its unilateral boycott of the South-North dialogue. The full-dress talks of the South-North Red Cross Conference was thus suspended.

(2) First Full-Dress Meeting

The inaugural session of the Red Cross full-dress meeting between the South and the North opened at the "Taedongang Hall" in Pyongyang at 10 a.m. August 30, 1972. The first round of the full-dress talks was largely ceremonial with the delegates hearing "congratulatory speeches" by representatives of social organizations and political parties and formally adopting the agenda of the full-dress talks. But the fact that the 54-man south Korean Red Cross delegation visited Pyongyang and held a meeting with the North Koreans there had immense historical significance.

In his opening address, ROKNRC chief delegate Lee Bom-sok said that the ROKNRC delegation would "carry on the Red Cross talks with full consciousness of the national cause, and endeavor to fulfill the ardent wish of the separated families while sitting together with the North Korean Red Cross delegates under the mandate of national reunification."

North Korean Red Cross chief delegate Kim Tae-hui said that the Red Cross talks "provided an opening in the quarter-century barrier," adding that "the mission of the Red Cross delegates is highly important because these talks are directly related to the unification of the country."

The two chief delegates signed an agreement on the procedural matters of the full-dress talks, reconfirmed the adoption of the five agenda topics agreed upon at the preliminary meetings, and ascertained that the two Red Cross delegations would try to alleviate the suffering of the divided families, adhering to the humanitarian principles of the Red Cross.

At the opening session on August 30, "congratulatory speeches" were given by the representatives of eight organizations – the Workers' Party, the Democratic Party, Chochongryon in Japan, the Chondogyo Chongwu Party, the League of All Vocations, the League of Agricultural Workers, the League of Socialist Working Youth and the League of Democratic Women. Congratulatory cables from other organizations were also read at the session. The "congratulatory speeches" by the north Koreans, discussing little of the task of helping the separated families, were all political speeches propagandizing chiefly on "juche (self-reliance) thought." The speakers then invariably called for "multifarious exchanges and contacts" and participation of political parties, social organizations and all walks of life in the Red Cross talks.

The following agreement was reached at the first full-dress meeting.

Agreement at First Full-Dress Meeting of
South-North Red Cross Conference

1. Both delegations to the Red Cross talks confirmed the following agenda, which had been adopted at the 20th Red Cross preliminary meeting on June 16, 1972, as the agenda of the full-dress meetings.

(1) The question of ascertaining, and informing thereof, the fate and whereabouts of dispersed families and relatives in the south and the north.

82

(2) The question of realizing free visits and free reunions between dispersed families and relatives in the south and the north.

(3) The question of arranging free exchange of letters between dispersed families and relatives in the south and the north.

(4) The question of reuniting dispersed families as they wish, and

(5) Other questions to be solved in humanitarian way.

2. Based on the South-North Joint Communique providing for the three principles of independence, peaceful unification and a grand national unity, as well as on the humanitarian principles of the Red Cross, the two sides will make all efforts to discuss and solve productively all problems envisaged in the agenda items of the Red Cross full-dress talks, thereby dissipating the sufferings of divided people in the north and the south and then preparing a stepping stone for the reunification of the fatherland.

(3) Second Full-Dress Meeting

The second full-dress meeting of the South-North Red Cross Conference opened at 10 : 20 a.m. September 13, 1972 in the Grand Ballroom of the Chosun Hotel in Seoul.

Begun with an opening address by ROKNRC Chief Delegate Lee Bom-sok, the meeting proceeded with an address by NKRC Chief Delegate Kim Tae-hui, and congratulatory speeches by ROKNRC President Kim Yong-woo, Ewha University President Kim Ok-gil, who was representing the divided families in the south, ROKNRC advisor Professor Kim Jun-yop, and NKRC advisors Yun Ki-bok and Kim Byung-shik.

ROKNRC Chief Delegate Lee first expressed a warm welcome to the northern delegation's visit to Seoul and then laid down three principles which he said should be observed in the course of carrying out the Red Cross projects. They were : 1) respect for the free will of the divided families and relatives in the south and the north, 2) devoted service by the southern and northern Red Cross Societies, which should take full control of, and full rsponsibility for, the project, and 3) accuracy and promptness in project management based on the traditional method of the International Red Cross projects for tracing missing persons.

"There is only one barrier in this would which bars the flow of letters correctly addressed and stamped. That is the wall between the south and the north in this country," Lee said. He expressed the belief that travelling between Seoul and Pyongyang by Red Cross officials would surely help tear down this wall of division, adding :

"If the Red Cross workers from the South and the North lay a track for the Red Cross project smoothly with mutual trust and sincere efforts, this track will certainly connect us to another one leading to the historical task of reunification."

"No matter whatever difficulties may lie ahead of us, we can accomplish our mission, if we serve with pride as Red Cross workers and cooperate with sincerity and patience."

ROKNRC President Kim Yong-woo urged in his congratulatory speech that "both sides should try to find what is common between them instead of what is different between them." He went on to say: "The world activity slogan of the Red Cross this year is 'bridge of humanitarianism' and we should bury all mistrust from the unhappy past involving brotherly love and a sense of mission, and walk on this bridge of humanitarianism."

Ewha Women's University President Kim Ok-gil, speaking for the divided families, said that "people exist before ideology and systems and they are bound by paternal and brotherly love. There's no individual or organization that can change the direction of history and we all must follow the national imperative only with the spirit of service."

Meanwhile, NKRC chief delegate Kim Tae-hui and two advisors, Yun Ki-bok and Kim Byung-shik, filled their speeches with political propaganda as they did at the first-round talks. They disappointed the people in the south and surprised the world.

In his address, Kim Tae-hui said : "The unification of the fatherland will be the realization of humanitarianism because it will dissipate the sufferings of the people from the division most fundamentally." Putting the family reunion task aside, he called for the immediate start of debate on unification problems. The speech of Yun Ki-bok was interspersed with such phrases as "the nation's glorious capital Pyongyang." and "our nation's respected leader Kim Il-sung..." and continued no blessing of the Red Cross conference itself.

A two-point agreement was signed by the two chief delegates at the Tower Hotel, where the north Koreans were staying, at 6:45 p.m. in the presence of all the delegates and advisors. The signing of the document was held summarily in a hotel room and took only five minutes.

Agreement at the Second Full-Dress Meeting of South-North Red Cross Conference

1. The two sides shall thoroughly adhere to the principles of democracy and freedom, the spirit of the South-North Joint Communique, brotherly love and the Red Cross humanitarianism in solving all problems envisaged in the agenda topics of the Red Cross meetings in accordance with the wishes and desires of all the people.

2. Based on the atmosphere of understanding and trust enhanced by the first and second full-dress meetings, the two sides shall start discussions of agenda items at the third full-dress meeting. The third full-dress meeting shall be held on October 24, 1972 in Pyongyang and the fourth meeting on November 22, 1972, in Seoul.

(4) Third Full–Dress Meeting

The third full–dress meeting of the south–north Red Cross talks opened on October 24, 1972 in Pyongyang to begin substantive discussions on agenda items.

It was especially significant that the two sides sat down for business at this third full–dress meeting, awakened from the initial excitement over the opening of the barrier between the south and the north for the first time in two decades and a half. But, this session also saw the start of the stalemate of the talks with the clear exposure of the differences between the two sides.

The open session started with a keynote speech by Kim Tae–hui, the northern chief delegate, which was followed by ROKNRC chief delegate Lee Bom–sok's speech. After the two sides presented their respective positions as to the issue of solving the agenda item No. 2, Kim Tae–hui declared the adjournment of the meeting.

At the third full–dress meeting, Lee Bom–sok of the ROKNRC suggested that the following principles be applied to the substantive discussion of the agenda :

1. The project should be carried out on the basis of the Red Cross principles of humanitarianism and neutrality.

2. The project should be carried on in accordance with the wishes of separated families and relatives.

3. The project should not go beyond the frame of its original task of restoring severed blood relationships.

4. Any agreed individual project should be put into practice immediately without waiting for agreements on other matters.

Chief   Delegate Lee further laid down a set of guidelines for the implementation of the item No. 1 project of "ascertaining the fate and whereabouts, and informing thereof, of dispersed families in the south and the north," a project which he said was the most fundamental among all the projects. The guidelines were as follows :

ROKNRC Guidelines for Implementation of
Topic No. 1 of Full–Dress Talks

1. The two Red Cross Societies should take full control of the project.

2. The elements feared to impede the Red Cross spirit should be

eliminated.

3. The free will of the persons concerned should be respected absolutely.

4. Personal secrets of the persons concerned should be protected and should never be disclosed for other than humanitarian purposes.

5. The two sides should go into action immediately after an agreement was reached on this project.

6. Accuracy should be pursued to the maximum extent in collecting information on the fate and whereabouts of separated families, and that information obtained should be forwarded to the people concerned without delay.

The ROKNRC Chief Delegate also said that the task of finding out the fate and whereabouts of dispersed families and relatives could best be carried out by the following pattern of the international Red Cross tracing service, which had developed an effective technical system. Under this priniciple, he presented the following action program

ROKNRC Idea of Measures to Implement
Topic No. 1 of Full–Dress Talks

1. Project procedure

a. The two Red Cross Societies, upon receiving requests from dispersed families and relatives for searching for their families and relatives, will send letters of inquiry to the other side.

b. The two Red Cross Societies shall look into the matters given in the letters of inquiry promptly and send replies to the other side.

c. The two Red Cross Societies shall deliver the replies to the original inquirers without delay.

2. Forms to be used between the two Red Cross Societies.

The two Red Cross Societies shall use the same forms for inquiries and replies, which will have the following entries :

a. Items on Persons Being Sought

(1) Name

(2) Sex

(3) Date of birth or age

(4) Date of separation

(5) Occupation at the time of separation

(6) Address at the time of separation

(7) Other descriptions helpful in searching (including pictures)

(8) Names and addresses of persons who can help in search

b. Items on Inquirers

(1) Name

(2) Sex

(3) Date of birth or age

(4) Address

(5) Relations to the person being sought

–Letters of Reply on Fate and Whereabouts–

a. Items on Persons Being Sought

(1) Name

(2) Sex

(3) Date of birth or age

b. Confirmed Items

*Information of Living Persons

(1) Address

(2) Family situation

(3) Health condition

(4) Occupation

*Information on the Dead

(5) Date of death

(6) Place of death

(Front)

Letter of Inquiry of Present Conditions and Whereabouts of
Dispersed Families and Relatives in the South and the North.

Serial No.   Date Month Year

		Korean Writing	Sex		Date of Birth or Age	Date Month Year (Yrs.)
Person Being Sought	Name	Chinese Writing				
	Date of Separation		Date Month Year		Occupation at the Time of Separation	
	Address at the Time of Separation					
	Other Description Helpful for Search (Pictures May Be Attached on the Rear Page)					
	Names and Addresses of People Who Can Be Helpful in Search					
In-quirer	Name	Korean Writing	Sex		Date of Birth or Age	Date Month Year (Yrs.)
		Chinese Writing		Relation to the Above Person		
Address						

(Form 1-a) Use the rear page for more information.

89

(Rear)

(Attach Pictures Here)

(Additional Information)

90

(Front)

Reply on Present Conditions and Whereabouts of Dispersed
Fimilies and Relatives in the South and the North.

Serial No.   Date Month Year

Person Being Sought (Con-Firmed Facts)	Name	Korean Writing / Chinese Writing	Sex		Date of Birth or Age	Date Month Year (Yrs.)	
	Infor-mation on Living Person	Address					
		Family Situation					
		Occupation			Health Condition		
	Infor-mation on the Dead	Date of Death	Date Month Year		Cause of Death		
		Place of Death					
		Location of Tomb or Place of Keeping Memorial Tablet					
		Family Situation					
	Other Information (Attach Picture on the Rear Page)						
In-quirer	Name	Korean Writing	Sex		Age	Yrs.	
		Chinese Writing	Relation to the Above Person				
	Address						

(Form 1-b) Use the rear page for more information.

91

(Rear)

(Attach Pictures Here)

(Additional Information)

(7) Cause of death

(8) Location of tomb or place of keeping memorial tablet

(9) Family situation

(10) Other information (including pictures)

c. Items on Inguirers

(1) Name

(2) Sex

(3) Age

(4) Relation to the person being sought

(5) Address

3. Establishment of Project Office

The two Red Cross Societies will establish a "South–North Red Cross Project Office" at Panmunjom for exchange of documents of the inquiries on the present conditions and whereabouts of separated families and relatives.

Details on its establishment and operation will be decided through separated discussions.

4. Start of Project

The two Red Cross Societies will start exchanging documents for the family search service within one month after an agreement is reached on agenda item No. 1.

Together with this project implementation program, ROKNRC Chief Delegate Lee Bom–Sok presented the forms to be used for the family search service.

Meanwhile, NKRC Chief Delegate Kim Tae–hui, for his part, produced the following five principles for the discussion of the five agenda items :

1. The position of independence will be thoroughly maintained in the course of the talks.

2. The principles of democracy and freedom will be thoroughly observed in the course of discussion of questions raised.

3. The principle of promoting mutual understanding and trust and creating national harmony and grand unity through the conference project will be maintained.

4. The principle of Red Cross humanitarianism will be embodied thoroughly in the discussion of all problems.

5. In order to make the project come to fruition, the principle of carrying out the project as a nationwide undertaking will be realized thoroughly.

The NKRC chief delegate then made the following four–point proposal in connection with the "question of ascertaining the fate and whereabouts, and informing thereof, of dispersed families and relatives in the south and the north;"

1. In south Korea, all legal and social obstacles should be removed and favorable conditions and circumstances should be created so that the people concerned and their helpers can express opinions and engage in activities democratically and freely.

2. The two sides will dispatch adequate numbers of Red Cross publicity personnels to the areas of the other side.

3. The scope of family and relatives should be defined in accordance with the wishes of the persons seeking them, and the ways and means of finding out their present conditions and whereabouts , and the ways and means of providing such information should be decided on the basis of the seekers' democratic request and free will.

4. A "South–North Red Cross Joint Committee" should be formed and "Red Cross representatives' offices" should be established at places deemed necessary.

The ROKNRC proposal on agenda item No. 1 was concrete and practicable idea not only befitting the peculiar situation in Korea but conforming with the tradition and method of the international Red Cross project for search for missing persons. The NKRC proposal, on the other hand, in effect demanded the creation of favorable legal, social and political conditions for the subversive activities of northerners in the South, a proposition incorporating various issues that ran counter to the spirit of the July 4, 1972 South-North

94

Joint Communique that called the transcendence of the difference in ideas, ideologies and systems.

The wide gap between the positions of the two sides could not be narrowed. The only agreement reached at the third full–dress meeting was an increase in the number of newsmen covering the talks by 5 to 25 on each side.

(5) Fourth to Seventh Full-Dress Meetings

Impasse reigned through the fourth, sixth and seventh full-dress meetings of the south-north Red Cross talks.

The north Koreans insisted on the political prerequisites they set fourth at the third full-dress meeting in an apparent attempt to delay and hinder substantive discussions. And, finally the full-dress talks came to a halt after the seventh full-dress meeting, following the August 28, 1973 north Korean statement of the suspension of the inter-Korean talks.

The fourth full-dress meeting opened on November 22, 1972 in the conference room of the ROKNRC Conference Secretariat at the foot of Namsan Hill in Seoul. Discussions were centered on agenda item No. 1, but the NKRC kept the talks from making any substantive progress by adhering to its demand for the creation of "legal and social conditions." The two sides only agreed on the establishment of a joint project management body as follows :

Agreement at Fourth Full-Dress Meeting of South-North Red Cross Conference

1. A South-North Red Cross Joint Committee and a South-North Red Cross Project Office will be established at Panmunjom with the duties of putting into practice agreements reached at the South-North Red Cross Conference.

2. Functions, operational procedures and composition of the Joint Committee and the Panmunjom Project Office will be decided

through separate discussions.

3. The formation of other organizations necessary for the implementation of agreements reached at the South-North Red Cross Conference will be discussed in the future.

Although a note of agreement was exchanged on the establishment of the Joint Committee and the Panmunjom Project Office at the close of the fourth full-dress meeting, the two sides failed to agree on any details as to the the functions of the two projected bodies.

The two proposed organizations have not been brought into existence despite the ROKNRC's repeated urging that the north Koreans cooperate in the establishment of the two bodies. It was apparent that the NKRC agreed to the setting up of the two bodies just as a "gesture of sincerity" in the talks and in fact had not the slightest intention of materializing the agreement.

At the fifth full-dress meeting held in Pyongyang on March 31, 1973, the ROKNRC maintained that the search for separated families and relatives could be done satisfactorily by the exchanges of letters of inquiry and reply between the two Red Cross Societies. As to the question of "improving legal and social conditions" as demanded by the north, the ROKNRC delegation urged the north Koreans to withdraw the demand just as the ROKNRC did not make an issue out of the socialist and Communist legal and social conditions in the North. The ROKNRC explained that it did not raise this issue because 1) the question goes beyond the competence and authority of the Red Cross, 2) the question goes against the spirit of the July 4 South-North Joint Communiuque, and 3) the ROKNRC is convinced that the Red Cross project can be successful only when the two sides act on the basis of mutual trust. The ROKNRC pointed out that the question of "legal and social conditions" is an issue that falls on the function of the South-North Coordinating Committee.

On the other hand, the NKRC claimed that people should be allowed to go to the area of the other side to find their separated families and relatives by themselves, and for this, the Anti-Communist

Law and the National Security Law in south Korea should be repealed to guarantee north Koreans' free travel to the south. North
Korea also demanded the inclusion of Korean residents in Japan in
the scope of separated families and relatives.

The ROKNRC maintained that the question of Korean residents in
Japan should be discussed as part of agenda item No.5, "Other humanitarian problems to be settled," which, it said, could cover not only
the Koreans in Japan but all other Korean residents abroad.

Prior to the fifth full-dress meeting, there were partial reshuffles of
Red Cross delegates and their advisors. At the ROKNRC delegation,
delegates Park Son-kyu, Mrs. Chong Hee-kyong and Soh Yong-hun
were replaced by Kim Yu-gap, ROKNRC Management Committee
member, Lee Byung-ho, ROKNRC Management Committee member,
and Choi Mun-hyun, ROKNRC youth counsellor, respectively, while
advisors Kim Jun-yop, Yang Hung-mo, Park Jun-kyu, Ku Bom-mo
and Song Kon-ho were replaced by Park Bong-sik, Son Jae-sok and
Ko Yong-bok, professors of Seoul National University, Kim Chin-bok,
editorial writer of the daily Seoul Shinmun, Lee Chong-ha, professor
of Yonsei University. At the NKRC delegation, advisors Kim Kil-hyon
and Kim Byong-shik were replaced by Kim Choo-chul, deputy secretary general of the Democratic Front for the Reunification of the
Fatherland, and Park Chae-ro, vice chairman of Chochongryon in
Japan.

The sixth full-dress meeting was held in Seoul May 9–10 as scheduled. The NKRC delegation laid down details on its earlier demand
for the "improvement of legal and social conditions" in the South, as
well as on its suggestions for the dispatch of Red Cross expounders
and the inclusion of Korean residents in Japan in the family reunion
project. It also demanded that advisors be allowed to speak at the
meetings.

As to the dispatch of the expounders, the NKRC elaborated that 1)
each of the lowest administrative units, "dong" in cities and "ri" in
other areas, should be assigned one Red Cross expounders, 2) such
expounders would explain the situation of the separated families and
relatives, and 3) the expounders should be guaranteed freedom of

speech, publication, assembly movement and inviolability of their safety and belongings.

The ROKNRC delegation rejected this as totally irrelevant to agenda item No. 1 and told the northerners not to waste time raising such a question. The ROKNRC made it clear that all projects agreed at the South-North Red Cross Conference and activities required for the implementation of these projects would not be impeded by any existing legal or social arrangements and that the Republic of Korea government was positively supporting the Red Cross in this regard. The ROKNRC stressed that therefore, it was utterly unnecessary to talk about legal and social conditions in the other side at the Red Cross talks.

The ROKNRC also said that the activities of the so-called Red Cross expounders could be done by the joint south-north Red Cross bodies whose establishment was agreed upon at the fourth full-dress meeting. Moreover, dispatch of such large numbers of expounders to the area of the other side for propaganda activities was feared to create unnecessary disputes on both sides.

On the other hand, the ROKNRC rejected the proposal to allow advisors to speak at the Red Cross talks as it would only create confusion in conference proceedings

The seventh full-dress meeting opened on July 11, 1973 in Pyongyang. At this meeting, the ROKNRC proposed the exchange of groups of tomb visitors between the two sides on the occasion of Chusok, a traditional holiday in Korea, as a means of providing a breakthrough in the deadlocked talks and as a pilot project aimed at promoting mutual understanding and trust,and carrying out the humanitarian project effectively. The proposal was as follows :

Considering the lack of progress on agenda item No. 1 concerning the question of ascertaining the fate and whereabouts, and informing thereof, of dispersed families and relatives despite prolonged discussions, the ROKNRC makes the following proposal in an effort to promote mutual trust and understanding which are the basis for the progress of the talks and to carry out more effectively the current Red Cross project between the south and north Korean Red Cross Societies.

The two sides will organize groups of separated families and relatives in their respective areas who seek to visit their ancestors' tombs on the occasion of Chusok and arrange their visits to the area of the other side as this year's project.

The two sides will hold a working-level meeting soon with two delegates and three attendants from each side to discuss matters for the realization of this project.

However, the NKRC rejected this proposal, which they claimed could be discussed only after the "favorable legal and social conditions" were created in south Korea. Instead, the NKRC demanded that a "joint communique" be issued by the two Red Cross delegations on the following matters :

　　1. Abrogation of present anti-Communist laws in the south,

　　2. Ban on anti-Communist activities and dissolution of anti-Communist organizations in the south,

　　3. Guarantee of freedom of activities for all people participating in the Red Cross Project,

　　4. Positive measures to ease current military confrontation and the situation of tension, and

　　5. Authorities' legal and administrative measures to the above effect.

Due to this politically-motivated north Korean demand, the seventh full-dress meeting of the South-North Red Cross Conference, too, ended without any substantive results. The two sides only agreed to determine the date of the eight full-dress meeting through the direct telephone line or their liaison offices at Panmunjom.

On August 28, 1973, north Korea abruptly issued the "August 28 Statement" through Radio Pyongyang, asserting that it could not continue dialogue with the south unless south Korea : 1) withdrew the

June 23, 1973 Foreign Policy Declaration, 2) stopped punishing anti-state criminals and legalized their political activities, 3) released all anti-state prisoners, 4) replaced the Seoul-side co-chairman of the South-North Coordinating Committee, and 5) agreed to include representatives of political parties, social organizations and people's delegates from all strata in the South-North Coordinating Committee.

This "August 28 Statement" not only suspended the Coordinating Committee meetings but brought the whole south-north dialogue, including the Red Cross talks, to a standstill.

c. Suspension of Dialogue by Pyongyang

At 6 p.m. August 28, 1973, Radio Pyongyang suspended its regular programs to announce what it called an "important broadcast," a lengthy statement in the name of Kim Young-joo, Pyongyang-side co-chairman of the South-North Coordinating Committee. In the statement, north Korea levelled all abuses against Lee Hu-rak, the then director of the Central Intelligence Agency and Seoul-side co-chairman of the Coordinating Committee, linking Lee to the kidnapping of Kim Dae-jung that occurred in Tokyo earlier on August 8. The statement declared a unilateral suspension of the operation of the Coordinating Committee, asserting, "We cannot sit together and discuss with Lee Hu-rak and other south Korean CIA 'gangsters' important state affairs because they persecute a democratic personage calling for a peaceful unification."

But the north Koreans let it be known that the real reason for their boycott of the dialogue was not the Kim Dae-jung incident but President Park's June 23 Special Foreign Policy Statement Regarding Peace and Unification. North Korea branded the June 23 Foreign Policy Statement as an "open manifestation of a two-Korea policy." It further charged south Korea with "cheating the people with the excuse of a south-north dialogue and forging two Koreas by perpetuating national division," contending that "south Korea has thus turned upside down the South-North joint Communique."

Meanwhile, Lee Hu-rak, Seoul-side co-chairman, called a special press conference on the following day, August 29, challenging north Korea to withdraw the "preposterous" statement of the day before and to stop the "unwarranted scheme" to torpedo the inter-Korean dialogue. Lee attributed the north Korean boycott to the June 23 Special Foreign Policy Statement, which, he said, north Korea thought would "deprive them of the rationale to continue to pursue their aggressive intent of seeking a Communist takeover of south Korea by force." The Seoul-side co-chairman pointed to the unreasonableness of the north Korean statement point by point as follows:

The fact that Lee Hu-rak was himself the Director of the Republic of Korea Central Intelligence Agency had never been a secret from the very beginning of the dialogue. At their first encounter in Pyongyang in. May 1972, Lee introduced himself to Kim Il-sung as Director of the ROKCIA, a national security outfit whose primary mission was to crack down on Communist agents operating in the Republic of Korea. To this self-introduction, Kim Il-sung replied, according to Lee, "I do welcome you and trust you because you have dared to come to Pyongyang in the very capacity of one in charge of ferreting out the Communists in south Korea."

Throughout the three rounds of the Coordinating Committee meetings, the Republic of Korea kept on asking that the two sides inaugurate a Joint Secretariat, jointly construct a Joint Secretariat building in Panmunjom and finalize necessary regulations relative to the operations of the Coordinating Committee, and its Executive Council and Joint Secretariat at the earliest possible date. But it was the north Korean side which had persistently ignored these Republic of Korea suggestions.

The north Korean side had never lived up to the earlier bilateral agreement on suspension of mutually hostile radio programs, continuing to agitate violent anti-government struggles.

The Republic of Korea proposed the implementation of wide-ranging business exchanges and cooperations between the two sides of Korea. But, north Korea had turned this down.

North Korea made the supension of the south-north dialogue a fait accompli. In the "Aust 28 Statment" of Kim Young-joo, north Korea uttered the boycott only of the operation of the Coordinating Commitee. But, the South-North Red Cross Conference, too, could not go unaffected. Following the seventh full-dress meeting held in Pyongyang July 10-13, 1973, the Red Cross talks were supposed to have the eighth full-dress meeting in Seoul. By refusing to answer telephone calls from the South over the direct south-north line after the seventh full-dress meeting, however, the NKRC made the discussion of matters related to the convening of the eighth full-dress meeting impossible, thus in fact bringing about a halt to the Red Cross talks.

In the "August 28 Statement," north Korea contended, "There are still wide differences in opinion and many problems to be settled between the South and the North. Under the circumstances, we recognize the need to carry on talks in the future as well. We call upon the authorities, various political parties, social organizations and individuals in all walks of life in south Korea to exert common endeavors to this end." But, this seeming "willingness to carry on the talks" was a mere trick designed to shift the responsibility for the suspension of the inter-Korean talks to south Korea. This was more apparent in the fact that as a condition to resuming the dialogue, north Korea laid down a demand that can by no means be accepted by south Korea. Part of the north Koreans statemet follows :

If south Korean authorities are truly interested in peaceful unification, they should respect the principles embodied in the South-North Joint Communique, withdraw their two-Korea policy, stop persecuting those struggling for the unification of the fatherland, and set free those arrested and imprioned patriots. The South-North Coordinating Committee should naturally reflect the view of the entire nation. To this end, the representatives of various political parties, social organizations and all walks of life in south and north Korea, in addition to the authorities, should be allowed to participate. Only under these conditions can the dialogue between the South and the North progress on the basis of a great national unity and independent peaceful unification of the fatherland be promoted effective.

The phrases used here are the same as those appearing in the concept of the so-called "south Korean revolution," a rationalized version of the North Korean policy to achieve unification under communism. To grasp their meaning correctly, some explanation is needed.

1. The north Korean demand for "observance of the principles envisaged in the Joint Communique," "withdrawal of a two-Korea policy." "stoppage of persecution of those struggling for the unification of the fatherland," and "release of arrested and imprined patriots" in effect represents their call that south Korea adopt a policy for "coalition with the Communists in place of anti-Communism," "retract the June 23 Special Foreign Policy Statement" and "set free those Communists imprisoned for their espionage activities." In other words, the prerequisite north Korea has attached to any resumption of the dialogue is that the Republic of Korea give up the free democratic system in favor of the Communist system.

2. The North Korean contention that the representatives of various political parties, social organizations and all walks of life should be allowed to take part in the South-North Coordinating Committee stems from their attempt to degrade the Coordinating Committee into the "grand national congress" they were demanding.

d. SNCC Vice Chairmen's Meetings

On November 15, 1973, the Seoul-side of the South-North Coordinating Committee, while calling for an early fourth plenary meeting of the Coordinating Committee over the direct telephone line, proposed that if the reorganization of the Coordinating Committee was really needed, this question be discussed through contacts between the two sides' executive members. In consequence, the two sides agreed to hold meetings of the two sides' vice chairmen of the Coordinating Committee at Panmunjom to discuss matters necessary for the resumption of the operation of the Coordinating Committee, including the question of reorganizaing the committee. A total of 10 vice chairmen's meetings were held at the Freedom House in the southern sector Panmunjom, and Panmungak in the northeren sector, by turn.

Vice Chairmen's Meetings Held

Classification	Place	Time
1st	Panmungak	December 5, 1973
2nd	Freedom House	December 19, 1973
3rd	Panmungak	January 30, 1974
4th	Freedom House	February 27, 1974
5th	Panmungak	March 27, 1974
6th	Freedom House	April 24, 1974
7th	Panmungak	June 28, 1974
8th	Freedom House	September 21, 1974
9th	Panmungak	January 8, 1975
10th	Freedom House	March 14, 1975

On December 3, 1973, two days before that first vice chairmen's meeting, Lee Hu-rak resigned as director of the Central Intelligence Agency and also as Seoul-side co-chairman of the South-North Coordinating Committee. The Seoul-side appointed vice chairman Chang Key-yong as acting co-chairman.

Meanwhile, on November 16 before the opening of the vice chairmen's meetings, north Korea delivered to the Seoul-side messages which the Worker's Party, the Democratic Party and the Chondogyo Chongwu Party of north Korea were sending to the Democratic Republican Party, the New Democratic Party, the Democratic Unification Party·and the bogus "Unification and Revolutionary Party."

The North Korean message was to propose the convening of a "Grand National Congress" attended by the "representatives of various political parties, social organizations and people in all walks of life in south and north Korea." This proposition was taken to suggest, though indirectly, north Korea's lack of interest in the resumption of the South-North Coordinating Committee.

At the vice chairmen's meetings where the Seoul-side was represented by Chang Key-yong and the Pyongyang-side by Ryu Jang-shik the Seoul side expressed its willingness to consider affirmatively the north Korean call for the expansion of the organization of the Coordinating Committee if such an offer was reasonable, asking the Pyongyang-side to lay down a concrete plan for the proposed reorganization. Also noting that inter-Korean relations were deteriorating due to the intensifying slander and provocations aginst the south by north Korea beginning in ealry 1973, the Seoul-side against called for the early normalization of the operation of the Coordinating Committee pursuant to the expressed provisions of the South-North Joint Communique and the Agreed Minutes on Formation and Operation of South-North Coordinating Committee.

Through the first and second vice chairmen's meetings, north Korea only indulged in disputing the anti-Communist policy of south Korea and denouncing the June 23 Special Foreign Policy Statement without showing any sincerity toward the issue of resuming operation of the Coordinating Committee. At the second meeting, the Seoul-side said that in consideration of the north Korean offer for the reorganization of the Coordinating Committee, it was willing to agree to increase the number of members from five to about ten on each side, as well as to allow the participation of the representatives of political parties and social organizations in addition to those of government authorities.

At the third vice chairmen's meeting, the Pyongyang-side came out with what it dared to call a "reorganization plan," which horrified the other side of the table with its preposterousness. North Korea suggested that the Coordinating Committee be composed of "five or more representatives each from the authorities, five to twenty representatives each from some 60 to 70 political parties and social organizations from each of the two sides and, in addition, representatives of people of various classes and strata," pushing the total number of "Committee members" from one side up to at least 350 and more than 1,500 at the most. North Korea explained that "people of various classes and strata" meant "workers, farmers, soldiers, working intelligentsia and youthful students" of north Korea and "laborers, farmers, soldiers, intellectuals, youthful students, 'nationalist-minded capitalists' and 'petit bourgeois" of south Korea. The Pyongyang-side then insisted that in the case of south Korea, those "political parties, social organizations and individuals opposed to unification of the country" should be excluded from participation in the expanded Coordinating Committee. Here, "those opposed to unification" meant "those opposed to communism." According to the logic of north Korea, "Opposition to communism is tantamount to opposing national unity, and opposing national unity, in turn, is tantamount to opposing unification."

Considering the reality of the Korean peninsula, where the two sides maintain different ideas and systems, namely, free democracy and communism, where the concept of "political parties" and "social organizations" differs widely between the two sides, and where the ways and means of forming general ideas among the people differ substantially between the two sides, north Korea's "reorganization plan" was in effect an attempt to force south Korea to accept a Communist political order. Aware of the utter unreasonableness of its own "reorganization plan," north Korea withdrew it at the fourth vice chairmen's meeting. The Pyongyang-side instead laid down a new proposal that a "south-north political conference" be formed among the representatives of various political parties, social organizations and people of various classes and strata in south and north Korea for the exclusive discussion of all issues related to unification, while keeping the Coordinating Committee as it was. In addition, the Pyongyang-side argued that if south Korea wants to resume the dialogue, it should first 1) withdraw the June 23 Special Foreign Policy Statement, 2) give up its anti-Communist policy, repeal the Anti-Communist Law and National Security Law and legalize the activities of the Communists, 3) cause the American forces in Korea to be withdrawn, and 4) accept north Korea's unification formula.

Under such circumstances, the vice chairmen's meetings simply could not register any progress.

As the south Korean people's feelings toward north Korea turned from bad to worse in the wake of the attempt on the President's life at a ceremony marking National Liberation Day on August 15, 1974, and as the discovery of a north Korean invasion tunnel beneath the truce line north of Korangpo in November the same year drew world wide attention, the Pyongyang-side attempted to terminate the vice chairmen's meetings in favor of lower-level spokesmen's contacts through mutual agreement. When the Seoul-side rejected this idea, north Korea unilaterally replaced its vice chairman at the Coordinating Committee in January 1975, naming Cho Myung-il, a plain member of the north Korea delegation to the South-North Red Cross Conference, as Pyongyang-side vice chairman in place of Ryu Jang-shik, thus one-sidedly down-grading the status of the vice chairmen. Even after this replacement, the vice chairmen's meetings could not last long. Around the time Kim Il-sung toured Beijing, East European countries and some leftist neutral countries in Africa in the wake of the Indochina debacle in the spring of 1975, north Korea indefinitely postponed the 11th vice chairmen's meeting slated for May 30 through mutual agreement. Contacts under the South-North Coordinating Committee were thus brought to a complete halt.

e. Red Cross Delegates' and Working-Level Meetings

(1) Delegates' Meetings

Keeping pace with the suspension of the operation of the Coordinating Committee following the "August 28 statement" of Kim Young-joo, north Korea torpedoed the Red Cross talks, too, by refusing to discuss matters necessary for the convening of the eighth full-dress meeing of the South-North Red Cross Conference. In an effort to resume the suspended full-dress meetings, the ROKNRC, in a telephone message on November 15, 1973, proposed a "chief liaison officers' meeting" to discuss details for convening the eighth full-dress meeting before the end of the year.

The liaison officers met at Panmunjom on November 21 the same year, where the ROKNRC proposed holding the eight full-dress meeting in Seoul on December 19.The NKRC ignored this offer and instead suggested that the two sides each send a "delegate" to the following liaison officers' meeting. With ROKNRC acceptance, the two Red Cross Societies resumed their formal contact at Panmunjom four and a half months after the suspension of the full-dress talks. A total of seven rounds of delegates' meetings were held from November 28, 1973, to May 29, 1974 between Kim Dal-sul from the ROKNRC and Cho Myung-il (who was appointed as the Pyongyang-side vice chairman of the Coordinating Committee in January 1975) from the NKRC.

At these meetings, the ROKNRC delegate, emphasizing that all problems should be discussed and solved through negotiations, said the full-dress meetings should be resumed promptly and unconditionally. Twice he offered dates for the eighth meeting – December 19, 1973 and April 9, 1974 – to be held in Seoul, but the NKRC delegate gave no response.

The NKRC demanded as "prerequisites to the resumption of the full-dress talks" that 1) the ROKNRC delegation to the full-dress meetings be reshuffled, 2) repression of "democratic people and youths and students" in south Korea be stopped, and 3) the eighth full-dress meeting be held in Pyongyang because the "atmosphere in Seoul is not suitable for the talks." The NKRC also suggested that "meetings preliminary to full-dress talks" be held with the alternate chief delegates of the two sides as senior members until the eighth full-dress meeting opened. The ROKNRC counter-proposed, as a compromise offer aimed at expediting the resumption of the full-dress talks while taking the north Korean position into account, that "temporary talks of the South-North Red Cross Conference" be held at Panmunjom to discuss the issue of resuming the full-dress talks, as well as to debate and solve the agenda topics of the full-dress meetings. The ROKNRC idea was that if and when agreement is reached on these problems to a certain extent, the two sides enter into full-dress talks. At the end, the two sides arrived at an agreement of the convening of south-north Red Cross working-level meetings at the sixth delegates' meeting held on May 22, 1974.

An Agreement on Holding South-North Working-Level Meetings

The delegates of the two Red Cros Societies agreed in their Panmunjom meetings as follows:

1. The delegates' meetings will be ended and the two sides will hold working-level meetings at Panmunjom with the alternate chief delegate (or deputy chief of delegation) to the full-dress meetings as the head of each side.

2. At the working-level meetings, preliminary discussions will be made of the agenda items of the full-dress talks, and at the same time the issue of resuming the full-dress talks shall be discussed and solved.

3. The working-level meetings will continue until the time when the full-dress talks are resumend.

4. The schedule, composition of delegation and operation procedures of the working-level meetings will be decided in separate talks.

(2) Working-Level Meetings

As a result of contacts betwwen the delegates of the two Red Cross Societies for more than half a year, the working-level meetings of the South-North Red Cross Conference began on July 10, 1974, at the conference room of the Neutral Nations Supervisory Commission at Panmunjom. A total of 25 rounds of the working-level meetings were held over a period of about three years until December 9, 1977. Their task was to conduct "preliminary discussions of the agenda topics of the full-dress meetings." The alternate chief delegates to the full-dress talks led their respective delegations. The times of the working-level meetings and the list of the members of the two delegations were as follows:

Working-Level Meetings Held

Year	Classification
1974	1st(July 10), 2nd(July 24), 3rd(August 28), 4th(September 25), 5th(November 5), 6th(November 29)
1975	7th(January 24), 8th(February 28), 9th(March 26), 10th(May 8), 11th(July 21), 12th(August 22), 13th(October 23), 14th(November 28)
1976	15th(February 12), 16th(April 10), 17th(June 9), 18th(August 20), 19th(October 19), 20th(December 10)
1977	21st(February 11), 22nd(April 28), 23rd (July 15), 24th(October 14), 25th(December 9)

List of Delegates

ROKNRC

> Kim Yon-joo, alternate chief delegate
>
> Kim Dal-sul, delegate
>
> Chong Choo-nyon, delegate

NKRC

> Ju Chang-joon, deputy chief delegate
>
> Cho Myung-il, delegate (replaced by So Song-chol at the seventh meeting, who was again replaced by Chong Chae-il at the 17th meeting)
>
> Kim Ryon-joo, delegate (who did not appear at the 20th and later meetings for unknown reasons)

At the first working-level meeting held on July 10, 1974, the ROKNRC expressed the hope that at the working-level meetings, the two sides 1) would be faithful to the original Red Cross mission, 2) would embody the spirit of humanitarian service, and 3) would conclude the working-level talks early for the resumption of the full-dress meetings. Stressing that the supension of the full-dress talks was attri-

111

butable wholly to the raising of political issues and interference in internal affairs by the NKRC, the ROKNRC delegation proposed that 1) the eighth full-dress meeting be held in Seoul on Aughst 30, 1974, and 2) a "project to trace, and notify thereof, the whereabouts and fate of aged parents" be conducted as a pilot project for the solution of the agenda item No. 1, "question of ascertaining, and notifying thereof, the whereabouts and fate of the dispersed families and relatives in the south and the north."

According to the ROKNRC proposal, this "old parents" project could be done in a simple process of exchanging letters of inquiry and reply. The separated parents and children could meet at Panmunjom or visit each other as they wished.

The ROKNRC offered the project in an effort to make a breakthrough in the discussions over agenda item No. 2. Locating old parents and ascertaining their present conditions were undisputably the most urgent taks of all the humanitarian problems involving separated families.

The NKRC repeated its claim of an "unfavorable atmosphere" in Seoul which allegedlly was prevently the resumption of the talks. As to the proposal for the "old parents" project, the north Koreans also said the improvement of legal and social conditions in the south was a perequisite to any Red Cross project. They then reiterated the demand that the two sides issue a joint statement on the problems of "circumstances" in south Korea. The north Korea-drafted statement was to call upon south Korea to :

1. Repeal the Anti-Communist Law, the National Security Law and presidential emergency decrees.

2. Disband all anti-Communist orgaizations and all government anti-Communist agencies.

3. Stop pursuing anti-Communist policies and making military provocations against the North.

4. Guarantee the participation of political parties and social organizations in the Red Cross family reunion project, and

112

5. Have the authorities concerned take necessary legal and administrative measures to the above-mentioned effects.

The working-level meetings were held in succession. But north Korea turned a deaf ear to the ROKNRC call for the early resumption of the full-dress meetings in its persistence on the demand for "improvement of circumstances," a political demand that definitely goes beyond the scope of the Red Cross movement. The ROKNRC, as part of its efforts to provide a breakthrough in the impasse, set forth details for the prior solution of the aged parents' project as follows at the sixth working-level meeting:

First, the south and north Korean Red Cross Societies will first carry out the "project of tracing, and informing thereof, the whereabouts and fate of aged parents" as a pilot undertaking for the solution of the agenda topic No. 1 of the full-dress meetings, "question of ascertaining, and notifying thereof, the whereabouts and fate of the dispersed families and relatives in the south and the north."

Second, "old parents" in this proposal means men and women aged 60 or more who are separated from their children and relatives in the south and the north.

Third, the method of tracing and notifying will be the same as the method of exchanging letters of inquiry and reply which was proposed by the ROKNRC on October 24, 1972 at the third full-dress meeting.

Fourth, depending on the progress of the project for "tracing, and informing thereof, the whereabouts and fate of aged parents," the two Red Cross Societies will arrange reunions, visits and exchange of letters between the aged parents, and their children and relatives as they wish, in the following ways:

1) Reunions
The South and north Korean Red Cross Societies will arrange free reunions at Panmunjom at time convenient for old parents and their children and relatives whose whereabouts have been traced. For this

purpose, the two sides will establish a "meeting place" at Panmunjom and provide all necessary facilities.

2) Visits

For aged parents and their children and relatives whose whereabouts have been traced, the two Red Cross Societies will arrange free mutual visits to the area of the other side in accordance with their wishes.

In principle, they will be allowed to make visits on the occasions of New Year's Day and Chusok Day (15th day of the eighth month by the lunar calendar) for periods of up to 15 days, but they may be allowed to make the visits at other convenient times when required by individual circumstances. The two Red Cross Societies will provide all necessary facilities for the mutual visits.

3) Exchange of Letters

The south and north Korean Red Cross Societies will arrange exchange of letters between aged parents and their children and relatives, and will jointly operate a "south-north mail exchange office" at Panmunjom.

Fifth, the two Red Cross Societies will promptly put into operation the "joint project office at panmunjom" whose establishment was agreed on at the fourth full-dress meeting so that the above-mentioned "meeting place" and "south-north mail exchange office" will be established and operated in it.

At the seventh working-level meeting held on January 24, 1975, the ROKNRC urged the NKRC to return to the original Red Cross posture and agree, at an early date, to the holding of the eighth full-dress meeting in Seoul as well as to the "aged parents" project. The ROKNRC also said that following the June 23 Special Foreign Policy Statement, the exchange of letters had been realized with separated families in the Soviet Union and Mainland China, leaving north Korea the only place in the world with which exchange of letters was impossible. The ROKNRC, then, emphasized the need for the two sides of Korea to open their doors to each other so as to alleviate the sufferings of the dispersed families early.

Nonetheless, the NKRC persisted on its demand for "improvement of social conditions" in the south, showing no interest in the "aged parents" project. The NKRC asserted that the June 23 Special Foreign Policy Statement was a "policy of splittism," arguing that "so long as the South pursues such a policy, no humanitarian projects can be realized, nor can the full-dress meetings be resumed."

The ROKNRC further proposed the exchange of pictures between aged parents and their separated children at the eighth working-level meeting held on February 28, 1975, and 1) the exchange of "groups of tomb visitors" between dispersed families on New Year days and Chusok and 2) the operation of a "meeting place" and a "south-north mail exchange office" at the 13th working-level meeting on October 23, 1975. The substance of the ROKNRC proposal for exchange of groups of tomb vistitors was as follows:

The ROKNRC delegation presents the following proposal of a humanitarian project with the purpose of fulfilling the wishes of the 10 million divided family members and all the 50 million Korean people, as well as of seeking a breakthrough in the currently stalemated Red Cross talks :

1) The south and north Korean Red Cross Societies will exchange groups of tomb visitors from the separated families on each side as a pilot project to restore mutual trust between the two sides and expedite solution of the problem of separated families.

2) Such exchange of gropus of tomb visitors will be made on such traditional holidays as Chusok, New Year's Day, lunar New Year's Day and Hansik Day.

3) The two sides will make the first exchange of "groups of tomb visitors among separated families" on Chusok Day this year. The number of people to be exchanged, the period of their stay in the area of the other side and other procedural matters shall be decided through mutual consultation. (The ROKNRC proposed the first group be composed of about 500 people on each side and be

allowed to stay in the area of the other side for a week.)

However, no sign of change was seen in the north Korean attitude. Simply repeating the sophistry that "the sufferings of dispersed families and relatives would be removed by themselves when national unification is achieved," the north Koreans insisted that the Red Cross talks should discuss 1) the June 23 Special Foreign Policy Statement, 2) the anti-Communist policy of south Korea, and 3) the U.S.military presence in south Korea.

Finally on March 19, 1978, one day before the scheduled 26th working-level meeting, the NKRC unilaterally declared through Radio Pyongyang the indefinite postponement of the 26th meeting on the ground that "the routine joint Korea-U.S. military exercise, Team Spirit '78, caused an artificial difficulty to the Red Cross talks." North Korea thus suspended even the working-level Red Cross talks, the last thread of the inter-Korean dialogue.

f. Cutoff of Direct Inter-Korean Telephone Line

Another consequence of the suspension of the two-channel south-north dialogue – the South-North Coordinating Committee and South-North Red Cross Conference – was the cut-off of the direct south-north telephone line.

The direct south-north telephone line was installed for the first time on September 22, 1971 at the first Red Cross preliminary meeting on September 20 that year, in which they agreed to establish their permanent liaison offices at the Freedom House and Panmungak at Panmunjom, respectively, and to install two circuits of direct telephone line linking between the two laison offices.

At the later secret contacts between working-level officials on the proposed visit to Pyongyang by a ranking south Korean official after the need arose for political contacts parallel with the Red Cross talks, the Seoul side proposed to Pyongyang the installation of a direct Seoul-Pyongyang telephone line. Under a mutual agreement, the historical direct telephone line linking Seoul and Pyongyang was inaugurated on April 29, 1972 on an informal basis.

During his meeting with Kim Il-sung, Lee Hu-rak, the then director of the Central Intelligence Ageny, who visited Pyongyang soon thereafter, emphasized the need for "a permanent channel of dialogue between the South and the North" with a view to forestalling unexpected incidents between the two sides. With Kim Il-sung's nodding, the temporary direct line was formalized and this was announced along with the South-North Joint Communique on July 4, 1972.

Afterwards, the number of circuits of the direct telephone line had swelled to 23, which included two circuits between the central offices of the south and north Korean Red Cross, 18 circuits for the South-North Red Cross Conference, two circuits between the Liaison Offices at Panmunjom, and one circuit between the respective offices of the South-North Coordinating Committee.

The direct telephone line had been highly conducive to preparation of procedural matters in south-north meetings and to the materialization of the mutual secret visits by south and north Korean ranking officials (Lee Hu-rak from the South and Park Sung-chul from the north) and the issuance of the South-North Joint Communique. It also rendered a valuable service by facilitating prompt contacts between the South and the North when there occurred unexpected incidents such as shooting in the Demilitarized Zone and kidnapping of fishermen in the Yellow and Eastern seas. The hotline thus enabled them to keep such incidents from further aggravation.

As for the operation of the direct south-north telephone line, the Seoul-Pyongyang line of the Coordinating Committee used to be in operation between 9-12, a.m. and 4-8 p.m. every day, another Seoul-Pyongyang line between the head offices of the south and north Korean Red Cross 10-12 a.m. to 4-6 p.m. every day, and the one linking the Freedom House and Panmungak from 9. a.m. to 4 p.m. every day excepting holidays.

During the period of operation of the direct telephone line until its suspension, there were a total of 5,637 trial conversations over the line (1,108 by the Coordinating Committee, 1,850 by the Red Cross and 2,679 by the Panmunjom Liaison Offices) and 1,051 business conversations (238 by the Coordinating Committee, 45 by the Red Cross and 768 by the Liaison Offices). In addition, when meetings of the Coordinating Committee or the Red Cross talks were held in Seoul or Pyongyang, the direct line was in frequent use for press purposes. Even after north Korea unilaterally suspended the dialogue on August 28, 1973, the direct telephone continued to be operational for a considerable period.

On August 30, 1976, shortly after the axe-murder of two American officers at Panmunjom by north Korean guardsmen on August 18, the ROKNRC tried to send a telephone message to the north Korean side to discuss the issue of securing repatriation of a fishing boat, "Shinjin-ho No. 3," and its crewmen, which were hijacked by the north Koreans while the fishermen were in a peaceful fishing operation in the Eastern sea. The NKRC refused to accept the telephone message.

g. Contacts between Seoul Delegates from SNCC and Pyongyang Delegates from DFRF

(1) January 19 Proposal to North Korea

In his New Year press conference on January 19, 1979, President Park Chng Hee made a positive proposal to north Korea, suggesting that the authorities of south and north Korea have talks unconditionally at any time, at any place and at any level to discuss the issue of resuming the stalled inter-Korean dialogue. President Park said in part :

I urge that the authorities of south and north Korea meet at any time, at any place and at any level, and discuss directly, without any preconditions and openheartedly, all problems pending between the two sides – ways to prevent a fratricidal war on the Korean peninsula, to assure prosperity for all our 50 million people and to achieve peaceful unification ; that is, the issues in all areas which have been raised by the two sides thus far.

This proposal was aimed at providing a breakthrough in inter-Korean dialogue in circumstances where the South-North Coordinating Committee and the South-North Red Cross Conference, both channels of dialogue opened through due agreement between the two sides, had remained supended over a protracted period.

In the proposal the Republic of Korea expressed willingness to discuss all the issues pending between the two sides, including those raised by the North, if and when the suggested authorities' meeting took place. By also suggesting expressly that it would consider holding inter-Korean meetings on any level, the South let it be known that it is willing to consider if necessary holding even a summit meeting between the two sides.

However, the responsible authorities of north Korea had kept mum toward this epochal proposal by the Republic of Korea. The first north Korean reaction of any sort came on January 23, 1979 when a mere social organization called "Democratic Front for the Reunification of the Fatherland" (DFRF) issued a statement in response to the proposal, in which they said :

(We) propose the convocation of a whole-nation conference attended by the delegates of various political parties and social organizations in the south and the north.

This conference should be attended by the representatives of various political parties and social organizations of the north, the representatives of all the political parties and social organizations, including the Democratic Republican Party, and Patriotic personages in all walks of life in south Korea, and representatives of organizations of our brethren as well as individual personages abroad.

We propose that this conference be held in early September this year, and that for the successful preparation of the conference, a bilateral or multilateral preliminary meeting be held in Pyongyang in early June among working-level representatives of various political parties and social organizations at home and abroad.

In addition to proposing a "whole-nation conference" and a preliminary meeting instead of accepting the January 19 offer by the Republic of Korea, north Korea also suggested in the statement that 1) effective at 10 a.m. on February 1, 1979, the authorities of the two sides reaffirm the ideas and principles of the July 4 Joint Communique and officially declare their intention of observing them, 2) the two sides should stop issuing slanders and defamation against each other at the same time through all and every ways and means, including government-operated and private media, and 3) effective at 10 a.m. on March 1, 1979, the two sides should stop unconditionally all military actions that perpetuate enmity and threat the other side.

North Korea then had various offices and organizations issue statements in support of the offer of the "Democratic Front." Among them was the one made on January 25 by Park Sung-chul, a political commissar of the Central Committee of the Workers' (Conmunist) Party and vice president.

Here the government of the Republic of Korea, in a statement issued by the government spokesman (Minister of Culture and Information) on January 26, expressed the view that "the north Korean statement may well be an indication of Pyongyang's willingness to respect the matters already agreed on between the authorities of the two sides in the July 4 Joint Communique."

Pointing out that "just as all the inter-Korean agreements, including the July 4 Joint Communique, have been worked out through dialogue between the responsible authorities of the south and the north," the statement stressed that the future South-North dialogue can achieve desired objectives only when the dialogue is conducted by responsible authorities of the two sides.

The Republic of Korea government then proposed that a preliminary meeting be held as soon as possible, either in Seoul or Pyongyang, between the authorities concerned of the south and the north for the purpose of discussing all problems raised so far by the two sides, not necessarily waiting until June 1979, as suggested by the north Korean side. The statement called for a response directly from the responsible authorities of north Korea.

Reacting to this proposal of the Republic of Korea government, north Korea, in a statement released by the Secretariat of the Central Committee of the "Democratic Front" on January 27, said that a "working-level preliminary meeting" intended to discuss the convocation of a "whole-nation conference" should be held in early April instead of June, as originally suggested.

Thus north Korea, refusing to respond in the name of its responsible authorities to the south's call for a dialogue between responsible authorities, unveiled its attempt to manage an inter-Korean dialogue on a scenario of its own, namely, at times and at places it selects one-sidedly, on topics it dictates at its own option, and with participants it hand-picks by itself. To shed more light on their scheme to pursue propaganda gains over the inter-Korean dealings, North Korea mailed letters containing the January 23 statement of the "Democratic Front" to various personages and organizations of its choice.

The north Korea machination did not go unchallenged. In a statement released by the spokesman of the Ministry of Culture and Information on January 29, the Republic of Korea government pointed out that "the north Korean authorities have not made any responsible response to the Republic of Korea proposal, while a mere social organization continues to make an impracticable demand, indulging in political propaganda."

Urging that the directly responsible authorities of north Korea make a sincere response, the statment said, "The basic position of the Republic of Korea, as was already made clear, is that a preliminary meeting should be held between the responsible authorities of the two sides at a place agreed on between the two sides at any time before June this year without any preconditions so as to discuss all the problems raised between the two sides." The statement expressed the regret that the north Korean authorities did not make a sincere response although a considerable span of time had elapsed since the

121

proposal was offered by the Republic of Korea government.

While continuing to shun any responsible response , north Korea made a further propaganda move on January 31. In a statement released by their (North) Korean Central News Agency, North Korea one-sidedly declared that, pursuant to their January 23 statement made in the name of the Central Committee of the "Democratic Front," they would stop slandering of defaming south Korea effective 10 a.m. on February 1.

(2) Birth and Progress of Anomalous Contacts

With President Park's January 19 proposal as an added momentum, the Republic of Korea time and again urged the north Korean authorities to make a responsible response in efforts to resume the stalled dialogue. Nonetheless, north Korea ignored the call, demanding in the name of the "Democratic Front" the "fulfillment" of the spirit of the July 4 Joint Communique. The only thing to which North Korea showed an affirmative response was the South's call for advancing the time of preliminary contacts between the two sides.

Now that north Korea had raised the question of "fulfilling" the spirit of the July 4 Joint Communique, the Republic of Korea felt the need to terminate the unnecessary "war of statements" by early resuming the business of the South-North Coordinating Committee (SNCC), an organization established and operated for the purpose of embodying the basic spirit of the July 4 Joint Communique, and also by restoring the severed direct telephone line between the South and the North.

Min Kwan-shik, Seoul-side acting co-chairman of the SNCC, called upon north Korea in a statement of January 31, 1979 to commit itself to the fulfillment of the spirit of the Joint Communique not in words but in deeds by agreeing to resume the SNCC operation. The statement read in part :

It is my belief that the most effective and correct way to assure a rededication to

122

the spirit and principles, as well as a faithful implementation of the agreements, of the South-North Joint Communique is to have the operation of the South-North Coordinating Committee brought back to normalcy, for it is this Committee which is entrusted with the authority to preserve and implement the spirit, principles and agreements of the Joint Communique. Therefore, I urge the Pyongyang side that it agree to normalize the heretofore interrupted operation of the South-North Coordinating Committee at the earliest possible date.

Furthermore, for the evident reason that the bilateral issues and problems arising in relations between the, south and the north can in no way be resolved simply by serving unilateral notification or by making one-sided allegations, I also urge the Pyongyang side that it agree to have the Seoul-Pyongyang direct telephone line, presently out of operation, having been unilaterally disconnected by Pyongyang brought back to normal operation immediately in order to have communication between the south and the north conducted speedily and in a productive manner.

In the statement, the Republic of Korea expressly sought to have inter-Korean dialogue resumed in a productive and efficient manner by all means by calling for the normalcy of business of the SNCC, the existing machinery for dialogue, along with a meeting between the responsible authorities of the two sides regardless of time, place and level.

In an apparent reaction to this January 31 call by the SNCC Seoul side, north Korea, in a statement released by the Secretariat of the Central Committee of the "Democratic Front" on February 5, dared to deny the existence of the Coordinating Committee, contending, "We cannot fulfill the great national task in conformity with the wishes of the people merely with such a limited organization as the Coordinating Committee. It has already been rendered irrational and has lost its raison d'etre." North Korea instead demanded the formation of a Preparatory Committee for National Unification as a preliminary consultative body designed to prepare "machinery for nationwide dialogue and conference" such as the "whole nation conference" which they proposed. North Korea then suggested that liaison delegates of the two sides meet at Panmunjom at 12 noon on February 20 to discuss the formation of the Preparatory Committee for National Unification.

On February 12, north Korea announced in a press release from the Secretariat of the Central Committee of "Democratic Front," that they would send four liaison delegates representing the "Democratic Front" to the place and at the time they unilaterally dictated so as to discuss the "inauguration of the Preliminary Committee."

Faced with this one-sided move from north Korea, the government of the Repulic of Korea, in a press conference held by the government spokesman on February 12, reaffirmend that there was no change in its basic stand expressed in January 19 proposal that "the responsible authorities of the south and the north meet at any time, any place and on any level, without any preconditions, to discuss all the issues raised by the two sides." The spokesman stressed that it is essential to have the South-North Coordinating Committee function properly all the more because north Korea has raised an issue over the Coordinating Committee, an organization that oversees the implementation of the July 4 Joint Communique and other inter-Korean agreements.

The Seoul side of the South-North Coordinating Comittee, too, in a statement issued by its spokesman Lee Dong-bok on the same day, pointed out the unreasonableness of the north Korean assertions that "the Coordinating Committee has lost its reason for existance," "the Coordinating Committe is machinery of only a limited scope," and "a preparatory Committee for National Unification should be formed in place of the Coordinating Committee."

Stressing that "the Coordinating Committee, under an agreement between the two sides, in fact offers an all-embracing forum of dialogue with a view to dealing, in a far-reaching scope, with the full range of problems that may arise in the process of reaching independent and peaceful unification," the Seoul-side spokesman said that the easiest way for the two sides of Korea to bring the south-north dialogue to resumption is to normalize the SNCC operation by calling, without any preconditions, the SNCC's fourth plenary meeting into session in Pyongyang, in accordance with the agreement to hold the SNCC plenary meetings in Seoul and Pyongyang alternately, putting an end to the long interruption since the SNCC's third plenary meeting held in Seoul in June, 1973.

The Seoul side then proposed that the two sides' SNCC vice chairmen meet at the Freedom House in Panmunjom at 10 a.m. on February 17, 1979 to discuss procedural matters necessary for the fourth plenary meeting.

In reaction, north Korea, in a statement issued by the spokesman of the Secretariat of the "Democratic Front" Central Committee on February 13, argued that it would send the four delegates whom it had already chosen for discussion of the formation of the Preparatory Committee for National Unification to conference room of the Neutral Nations Supervisory Commission (NNSC) at Panmunjom at 10 a.m. on February 17.

After north Korea made this self-seeking assertion, the Seoul side of the SNCC, in its spokesman's statement on February 15, stated that it would not be inflexible about the suggested contact points, since the sites offered by the two sides are both within the Panmunjom area.

Noting that the South is engaged in an effort to reopen the South-North dialogue in accordance with the principles and agreements stipulated in the July 4 South-North Joint Communique, the Seoul-side statement said, "Therefore, it is naturally our primary concern to have the SNCC operation brought back to normalcy. We intend to make use of the Panmunjom contact of February 17 to have our aforementioned position conveyed to the Pyongyang side through those persons whom the Pyongyang side dispatches to the contact at Panmunjom." In the statement, the Seoul side made public a list of the four delegates of the SNCC Seoul side who would attend the Panmunjom contact.

Thus, with a proposal by the SNCC Seoul side for a meeting of vice chairmen on February 17, and with the north Korean decision to send the four liaison delegates of the "Democratic Front" to Panmunjom on the same date to discuss the issue of the Preparatory Committee for National Unification, anomalous contacts were bound to take place at Panmunjom between the two delegations with different natures, purposes and qualifications.

Three rounds of anomalous contacts were held at the NNSC conference room at Panmunjom on February 17, March 7 and March 14, between the SNCC Seoul side calling for an SNCC vice chairmen's meeting to discuss the issue of holding the long-delayed SNCC fourth meeting, and a delegation of north Korea's "Democratic Front" insisting on contacts between "liaison delegates" of the two sides to discuss the formation of the Preparatory Committee for National Unification aimed at preparing for a so-called "whole nation conference." The delegates of the two sides were :

SNCC Seoul Side
Min Kwan-shik, vice chairman of SNCC Seoul side
Hahm Byong-choon, a member of SNCC Seoul side
Chong Hong-jin, executive member of SNCC Seoul side
Lee Dong-bok, spokesman for SNCC Seoul side

"Liaison Delegates" of North Korea
Kwon Min-jun, vice chairman of Central Committee, Workers' Party (representative of Workers' Party)
Lee Chang-son, a minister of Administration Council (representative of Pyongyang government)
Kim Sok-jun, vice chairman of Central Committee, Korean Democratic Party (representative of Korean Democratic Party)
Paek Jun-hyok, deputy director of Secretariat, Central Committee, Democratic Front for the Reunification of the Fatherland

These contacts, anomalous as they were, drew keen concern from within and without the nation, inasmuch as they were the first talks ever to take place between the two sides of divided Korea since north Korea put off indefinitely the 11th SNCC vice chairmen's meeting originally slated for May 30, 1975, and subsequently the 26th working-level meeting of the South-North Red Cross Conference set to be held on March 20, 1978.

The contacts, however, turned out to be a "dialogue of the deaf," failing to register any achievements due to the conflicting stands of the two sides, with the Republic of Korea advocating substantial and effective talks either between the two sides' responsible authorities as suggested in the January 19 proposal or through resumption of the SNCC business, and with north Korea demanding "liaison delegates' meeting" aimed at discussing the establishment of the Preparatory Committee for National Unification.

At the first contact held on February 17, 1979, the SNCC Seoul side explained its basic stand with regard to resumption of the dialogue, and proposed to the SNCC Pyongyang side as follows for the normalization of the SNCC business :

First, that the fourth plenary SNCC session be held in Pyongyang on April 3, 1979 ;

Second, that the direct South-North telephone circuit of the SNCC be reopened at 9 a.m. on February 20, 1979 for speedy and smooth communication between the two sides ; and

Third, that the two sides' SNCC officials make a contact at Panmunjom at 10 a.m. on March 7, 1979 to discuss ways to normalize the SNCC operation.

At the same time, SNCC Seoul side stated that if it is necessary to expand the organization of the SNCC, it is willing to discuss this question. Reminding the Pyongyang side that at the second vice chiarmen's meeting held on December 19, 1973, the Seoul side proposed a plan to expand the SNCC organization by increasing the number of each side's members from five to ten or so and by enabling some members of political parties and social organizations to participate in it, the Seoul side said, "Our side made it clear that we are still willing to agree to discuss the expansion and reorganization of the SNCC at any time within the framework of rationality and efficiency."

The SNCC Seoul side also said that consolidation of peace and restoration of trust between the two sides must be based on mutual agreement, and that substantial and effective solution can no doubt be expected only when such an agreement is made between the responsible authorities of the two sides, with due power to guarantee the implementation of agreed matters under their responsibility in their respective areas.

Emphasizing that it is for this self-evident reason that the Republic of Korea has been calling for a direct dialogue between the responsible authorities of the two sides, the Seoul side urged the Pyongyang side to agree to have talks between the two sides' responsible authorities. Meanwhile, the Pyongyang side contended at the first-round contact that "this is no time merely to coordinate inter-Korean relations, as it was at the incipient stage of the dialogue. We must create a new organization such as the Preparatory Committee for National Unification and take necessary working-level measures." North Korean then suggested that the two sides immediately discuss at the first working-level contact the procedures for inauguration of the Preparatory Committee for National Unification which they proposed.

After the first contact was adjourned, Lee Dong-bok, SNCC Seoul-side spokesman, and Paek Jun-hyuk, deputy director of the Secretariat of the Central Committee of North Korea's "Democratic Front," had a closed-door meeting on the afternoon of the same day to discuss working-level issues related to the reopening of the severed direct south-north telephone line. However, the meeting broke up after north Korea refused the reopening of the telephone line installed between the two sides of the SNCC.

The second-round contact was held at the conference room of the Neutral Nations Supervisory Commission at Panmunjom on March 7, 1979, where the two sides explained their respective stands and discussed the issue of resuming the inter-Korean dialogue. Nevertheless, they failed to narrow their differences.

The SNCC Seoul side said Quiting the contact, "We cannot but express deep regret over the fact that the Pyongyang side of the SNCC failed to make any response to our side's three-point proposal made at the February 17 contact, and that as was the case at the February 17 contact, the Pyongyang side is represented at this contact, a forum supposedly between the two sides' SNCC officials, by a social organization which we do not recognize as the other side in a dialogue." The Seoul side let its firm position be known that the "Democratic Front" of north Korea cannot be accepted as the other side in an inter-Korean dialogue.

However, north Korea denied the existence of the SNCC itself, asserting "the SNCC already lost its function five years ago and no longer exists today," and instead insisted on the formation of the Preparatory Committee for National Unification.

The third contact between the SNCC Seoul-side delegates and north Korea's "liaison delegates" was held on March 14, 1979. North Korea was represented at the third contact, too, by the delegates of the "Democratic Front" in defiance of the South's call for attendance by either SNCC officials or responsible north Korean authorities.

At the March 14 contact, the SNCC Seoul side reminded north Korea that at the previous two contacts, the Seoul side 1) proposed that the fourth plenary meeting of the SNCC be held in Pyongyang on April 3 to normalize the SNCC operation, 2) clarified expressly that the SNCG is by no means so limited in function as only to coordinate the inter-Korea relations, and 3) suggested that the SNCC be expanded so as to allow the representatives of political parties and social organizations, in addition to those of authorities, to participate ; and that in the course of creating the proposed five subcommittees of the SNCC, yet broader participation should be promoted in the respective areas. The SNCC Seoul side then proposed that the anomalous contacts, held three times without any achievements, be done away with and instead contacts be held between working-level delegates who can be mutually trusted, in order to prepare for a normal inter-

Korean dialogue. The Seoul side specifically offered :

1. The contacts shall be attended by three working-level delegates from each side.

2. The site of the first contact shall be the NNSC conference room at Panmunjom.

3. The time of the first contact shall be 10 a.m. on March 28, 1979.

4. At these contacts, the two sides may discuss :

a. The question of normalizing the SNCC business.

b. The question of convening a meeting between the authorities of the South and the North.

c. Other issues raised between the two sides.

"We look forward to affirmative response from the Pyongyang side. From our side, three working-level delegates will come to the site given above on March 28," the Seoul side said.

Meanwhile, north Korea, at the third contact, put forth a seemingly fresh suggestion that the name of their delegation would be changed to "liaison delegates of political parties, social organizations and authorities," but only on a set of conditions.

The conditions were that the southern delegates withdraw their representation of the SNCC based on the fact that "the SNCC no longer exists," and that " it should be recognized that all the proposals made and steps taken by our side since January 23, 1979, remain effective, based on the recognition that (the change in the name of our delegation) cannot have any substantial effect on the contacts of liaison delegates already held." In other words, north Korea showed willingness to remove the title of "Democratic Front" on these incongruous conditions, while making no change whatsoever in their basic stand or demands.

The March 14 contact ended without agreeing on the time of a future contact, thus bringing an end to the anomalous contacts or "dialogue of the deaf." At the third and final contact, the SNCC Seoul side suggested that a working-level delegates' meeting be held on March 28, whereas north Korea stuck to the contention that another contact of the same nature be held on April 5. Thus, an additional effort of the Republic of Korea to have the South-North Coordinating Committee brought back to normalcy went up in smoke.

(3) Miscarriage of Working-Level Delegates' Talks

On March 26, 1979, the spokesman of the Republic of Korea government, recalling that the SNCC Seoul side proposed at the March 14 contact a meeting of working-level delegates who can be mutually trusted at the NNSC conference room at Panmunjom at 10 a.m. on March 28, in place of the anomalous contacts held in the past, made public in a statement the list of the working-level delegates of the authorities of the Republic of Korea as follows :

Chief delegate : Dong Hoon, vice minister of the National Unification Board

Delegate : Ro Chang-hee a minister-counselor at the Ministry of Foreign Affairs

Delegate : Rhee Kyung-sik, deputy spokesman of the Ministry of Culture and Information

The statement expressed the hope that "all the issues raised so far by the two sides would be discussed open-mindedly, in closed sessions if necessary, at the working-level delegates' contacts, so as to facilitate the early normalization of the inter-Korean dialogue."

Notrh Korea, in a statement issued by a "liaison delegation of political parties, social organizations and authorities" on March 27, merely reiterated their past stand, contending that their four liaison delegates who represented the Democratic Front in the past contacts would attend future contacts in the capacity of the "liaison delegation of political parties, social organizations and authorities." North Korea proposed in the statement that the "fouth liaision delegates' contact" be held at Panmunjom on April 2.

In the meantime, the working-level delegation of the authorities of the Republic of Korea entered the SNCC conference room at panmunjom at 10 a.m. on March 28 as announced and waited for a north Korean working-level delegation. But the north Korean delegation did not appear, leading to the miscarriage of the working-level delegates' talks.

Upon the miscarriage, Dong Hoon, the chief dlegate of the working-level delegation of the authorities of the Republic of Korea, issued a statement at Panmunjom urging north Korea to reconsider its stand and come forward to the forum of inter-Korean dialogue. The statement read in part:

...In an effort to resume meaningful dialogue, our side made an epochal proposal on January 19 calling for a meeting between the competent authorities of the South and the North at any time, at any place and at any level. We are here today based on that proposal.

This channel of direct dialogue between the authorities of the two sides is and will be open always.

At the same time, we wish to emphasize once again that the South-North Coordinating Committee which is the product of a bilateral agreement cannot be negated unilaterally. It is, therefore, obvious that by normalizing the functions of the Committee, the two sides can always utilize it as an appropriate channel for dialogue.

We call upon the north Korean side to respond positively to the aspiration of the 50 million Korean people and the demand of public opinion throughout the world, and come to the table of dialogue between the competent authorities without any further delay.

h. South-North Table-Tennis Talks

While contacts abnormal though were going on between the south an the north following the epochal January 19 proposal of the Republic of Korea, north Korea suddenly proposed on February 20, 1979 that the delegates of north-south table tennis associations meet at Panmunjom at 10 a.m. February 27 to discuss the issue of forming a single team for the 35th World Table Tennis Championships slated for April 23 through May 6, 1979 in Pyongyang. The proposal was made in a letter broadcast in a north Korea radio, which was signed by Kim Yu-soon, chairman of the north Korean Sports Guidance Committee, and Kim Duk-jun, president of the north Korean Table Tennis Association (NKTTA). The letter was addressed to Park Chong-kyu, chairman of the Republic of Korea Amateur Sports Association, and Chae Yong-chol, president of the Republic of Korea Table Tennis Association (ROKTTA).

Here, reminding the north Korean side of the fact that the Republic of Korea, has at every opportunity proposed to north Korea practicable exchanges and cooperation in the conviction that removal of mutual misunderstanding and distrust and improvement of south-north relations by means of expanded personal and material exchanges would be a shortcut to the restoration of national homogeneity, the Republic of Korea Amateur Sports Association and the ROKTTA decided to send four delegates to Panmunjom at 10 a.m. February 27 to discuss with north Korean delegates the question of forming a single south and north Korean table tennis team for the 35th World Table Tennis Championships to be held in Pyongyang. The two south Korean associations then made public a radio notification to north Korea on the afternoon of February 24 concerning south-north ping-pong talks, saying in would send a delegation to Panmunjom on February 27.

Delegation of the Republic of Korea Table Tennis Association

Delegate:Chae Yong-chol, president, Republic of Korea
       Table Tennis Association
Delegate:Lee Chong-ha, vice chairman, Republic of Korea

Amateur Sports Association
Delegate:Chon Yong-sok, managing director, Republic of
Korea Table Tennis Association
Delegate:Chong Choo-nyon, director, Republic of Korea Table
Tennis Association (spokesman)

Meanwhile, the NKTTA, in a statement by its spokesman, announced on February 24 that for the discussion of the issue of forming a single south-north ping-pong team, it would send a delegation consisting of four men — Kim Duk-jun, president of the NKTTA, chief delegate ; Park Mu-song, vice president of the NKTTA : Kim Dok -ki, chief secretary of the KNTTA ; and Kim Sun-il, member of the NKTTA. Thus, the first meeting of the South and the North Korean Table Tennis Associations was set to be held at Panmunjom at 10 a.m. on February 27, 1979 and, therefrom, another three rounds of meetings (March 5, March 9, March 12) were succeeded.

At the first meeting that lasted one hour and 46 minutes, the ROKTTA delegation expressed the hope that with the discussion of the question of forming a single south-north ping-pong team as a momentum, sports exchanges will be realized in all fields between the south and the north. Noting that the Reublic of Korea has on many occasions proposed sports exchanges between south and north Korea as well as the formation of single south-north team for international games, the ROKTTA delegation expressed its basic positions with regard to the question of forming a single table tennis team as follows :

First : The question concerning the formation of a single table tennis team of south and north Korea must abide by the spirits and provisions of the International Table Tennis Federation's charter.

Second : All questions inevitably related to the formation of a single table tennis team of south and north Korea have to be amicably resolved and agreed upon.

134

Chae Yong- chol, president of the ROKTTA, said that in view of the fact that the time for making the draw of the game schedule of the 35th World Table Tennis Championships had already been set for March 14 and 15, and that selection and training of players and various other problems incidental to the formation of a single team, the single team issue should be settled by March 12 at the latest.

Stressing that the participation of a Republic of Korea table tennis delegation in the 35th World Table Tennis Championships cannot be hampered due to any delay in the solution of the issue of forming a single team, Chae said that should no agreement be reached on the single team issue by March 12, the NKTTA should guarantee the particiaption of a south Korean team in the world ping-pong matches, and take all necessary steps to enable a south Korean team to enter Pyongyang by way of Panmunjom.

On the other hand, the north Korean side tried from the outset to display a seemingly positive posture by calling for an agreement on the basic principle of the formation of a single team, and, at the same time, suggested a series of procedural matters.

As for the formation of a joint team, north Korea was suggesting : "1) a joint team shall consist of 18 players who, on the basis of selecting the best qualified players, would include those in the list of the world's best players as announced by the International Table Tennis Association, with the rest to be filled from the two sides in an equal number each, 2) the selected players shall undergo joint training in Pyongyang prior to the matches, and all conveniences shall be provided to south Korean players during their stay in pyongyang, 3) the co-head system shall be employed, under which the head of a joint delegation shall be two, one from each side, and 4) the name of a single team shall be "Koryo," a name which neither side has ever used in the past."

At a glance, these suggestions may seem explainable. In effect however, they all were trivial matters void of any key and substantial questions and intended for use only in their propaganda.

At the second-round meeting between the south and north Korean

135

Table Tennis Association held at the NNSC conference room at Panmunjom at 10 a.m. March 5, 1979, Chae Yong-chol, president of the ROKTTA, said that it is highly significant for the two sides of Korea to have the ping-pong talks, and emphasized that the issue of a ping-pong team should be tackled as part of overall sports exchanges between the south and the north. He said this was all the more so considering the fact that had sports exchanges been materalized between the two sides, participation in international sports event under joint teams could be settled much more easily.

As the north Korean delegation made it plain at the meeting that it won't guarantee the de jure right of the ROKTTA to take part in the world championships as a due member of the International Table Tennis Federation, the delegation of the ROKTTA, questioning if the north Korea offer for a single team wasn't intended to block a south Korean team's participation, strongly demanded that the NKTTA first guarantee the de jure right of a south Korean delegation to participate in the Pyongyang Championships separately.

The north Korean delegation, however, shunned to answer this challenge, and instead merely repeated its insistence on a prior agreement on the principle of the formation of a single south-north table tennis team. North Korea, thus, itself added to the suspicion that Pyongyang is determined to keep a south Korean team from taking part in the world championships.

With these inconsistences, north Korea was repeating its one-sided demand for "unconditional agreement of the formation of a single team" while emphasizing the "significance" of its proposals for a "unified team." In this way, north Korea was attempting to cover up its intention of blocking a south Korean team's participation in the Pyongyang Championships as well as to gain the propaganda effect that "Pyongyang is truly interested in south-north collaboration and realization of national unification."

Chae Yong-chol, president of the ROKTTA, also stressed at the third meeting held at Panmunjom on March 9, 1979 that formation of a single table tennis team should be realized on the principle of overall sports exchanges between south and north Korea, urging that

136

north Korea, based on this spirits, should first guarantee the participation of a south Korean team in the Pyongyang Championships.

Nevertheless, north Korea's chief delegate Kim Duk-jun, shunning this guarantee, simply renewed a call that the two sides discuss various procedural matters related to the formation of a joint team, thereby making it evident again that north Korean remains resolved to prevent a south Korean delegation from taking part in the Pyongyang Championships.

At the fourth meeting on March 12, 1979, the ROKTTA delegation, reminding the north Koreans of its stand that the issue of a joint team should be solved by March 12 at the latest because the time for making the draw of the game schedule has already been set for March 14 and 15 and because the time needed for the selection and training of players and various other matters that would inevitably ensure, pointed out that north Korea's rejection of a prior guarantee for a south Korean Table Tennis team's participation has made it impossible to form a single team. The ROKTTA delegation noted that even the International Table Tennis Federation has called for such prior guarantee for the ROKTTA which has the every right to take part in any world table tennis matches as a rightful member of the International Table Tennis Federation.

At this point, north Korea, in an attempt to shift the responsibility for the breakup of the ping-pong talks to the ROKTTA, produced another version of its deceptive offer that was substantially the same as the original demand for "unconditional prior agreement on the principle of forming a joint team."

The new overture of north Korea was that the draft "agreement" it laid down at the second-round talks be rewritten to include the clause that the de jure right of the ROKTTA to take part in the 35th World Table Tennis Championships would be "recognized" but only on the condition that this de jure right would take effect only from the time the two sides sign and exchange the letter of agreement on the formation of a joint team.

Here, the ROKTTA delegation stressed that the meeting between the south and the north Korean Table Tennis Associations ought to be held in such a way as to strive for the realization of over-all sports exchanges between the two sides. It said it is erroneous for north Korea to attempt to one-sidedly restrict the function of the meeting only to the Pyongyang Championships. It then urged that the two sides first agree on a joint statement guaranteeing the de jure right of a Republic of Korea delegation to participate in the 35th World Table Tennis Championships. But, north Korea rejected it outright.

Thus, the controversy developing over north Korea's overture for the formation of a single south-north ping-pong team aimed at keeping a south Korean delegation from entering Pyongyang was brought to an end, only leaving behind the blur of pure sportsmanship having been trampled down upon and exploited for propaganda again.

i. Working-Level Contacts for Prime Minister's Meeting

(1) Initiation of Working-Level Contacts

On January 11, 1980, north Korea broadcast an announcement in the name of the(north) Korean Central News Agency that it would send two messengers to the conference room of the Netural Nations Supervisory Commission at Panmunjom at 2 p.m. on January 12 to deliver to the south letters containing an "important proposal related to the issue of national unification."

The SNCC Seould side sent two liaison officers to Panmunjom on January 12 to receive the North Korean letters.

The letters turned out to have been addressed to ten persons of their own choice in various circles of the South, which were signed by Kim Il, North Korea's vice president and concurrently secretary of the Workers' (Communist) Party and chairman of the Committee for Peaceful Reunification of the Fatherland. Another letter, signed by Lee Jong-ok, North Korea's' premier, was addressed to then prime Minister Shin Hyon-hwak.

Though wordings differed slightly depending on recipients, the letters carried almost identical contents, suggesting personal meetings. The contents of the letters were as follows in substance :

Now we should find a notional outlet by expelling alien forces and realizing unification through collaboration and unity between our same Korean people...

Sould the dialogue resume, we are willing to hold North-South authorities' meetings along with a broad political conference we have already proposed, and further to promote even a high-level authorities' meeting.

It is in this context that I propose to meet you in person and exchange opinions openheartedly.

The sooner our contact takes place, the better it will be. The venue may well be Panmunjom, Pyongyang or Seoul. A third country will also be acceptable···

Meanwhile, north Korean radio broadcasts reported on January 22 that similar letters also signed by Kim Il had been sent to ten Korean residents living in the United States, Japan, West Germany and elsewhere. The ten overseas recipients as bared by North Korea were all anti-Seoul dissidents with the single exception of the chairman of Mindan, a pro-Seoul Korean residents' association in Japan.

The Republic of Korea, studying the letters from north Korea, differentiated the nature of Lee Jong-ok's letter to Prime Minister Shin Hyon-hwak from that of the letters from Kim Il to a score of individuals at home and abroad, tending to accept Lee Jong-ok's message as an indication of north Korea's affirmative response to the call for a meeting between the authorities of the two sides suggested by the South, in view of the fact that the north Korean premier's letter, referring to south Korea by its official title, the "Republic of Korea," proposed a meeting between the two sides' prime ministers.

In his New Year press conference held on January 18, 1980, the then President Choi Kyu-hah disclosed the stand of the Republic of Korea government in regard to this issue, saying :

...North Korea has sent us a letter suggesting a meeting of the prime ministers

of south and north Korea.

Hopefully, we can interpret this as the first comparatively positive response from the North toward our ceaseless efforts to pursue dialogue between the responsible authorities of south and north Korea.

I wish to disclose that I have instructed the relevant offices to examine positively the possiblility of dialogue between the prime ministers of south and north Korea. Accordingly, our government's position on this matter will be communicated to north Korea in the near future.

On January 24, 1980, the Republic of Korea sent Prime Minister Shin's reply to the January 12 letter from Lee Jong-ok, north Korean premier, to north Korea through liaison officials of the South-North Coordinating Committee at Panmunjom. Prime Minister Shin's message read in part :

...We have urged all along that the two sides, transcending differences in ideologies and systems, must first build up mutual understanding and trust by opening the way for humanitarian reunion of the 10 million separated family members, as well as realizing a wide range of inter-Korean exchanges and cooperation in economic, social, cultural and sports fields. We have also proposed, over and over again, to hold a meeting between responsible authorities of south and north Korea.

In keeping with our consistent position, I hope that the prime ministers of south and north Korea will meet in person as soon as possible.

To arrange all the necessary procedures for a meeting of the prime ministers of the two sides, I propose to you that a preparatory meeting between working-level representatives of the two sides be held as follows :

Delegation : Three delegates including a vice-ministerial level senior representative and a few assistants from each side.

Venue of meeting : Freedom House at Panmunjom or a place to be agreed on by both sides.

Time : 10 : 00 a.m. Wednesday, February 6, 1980.

In response, North Korea, in a message sent to the South through Panmunjom on January 30, in effect agreed to the southern offer except that they counter-proposed that the meeting take place at the conference room of the Neutral Nations Supervisory Commission.

Thus the two sides agreed to hold the first working-level contact at the NNSC conference room at Panmunjom at 10 a.m. on February 6, 1980. Both sides made public the lists of their respective delegates as follows on February 5.

Republic of Korea Delegation
Chief delegate : Kim Young-choo, an ambassador of the Ministry of Foreign Affairs
Delegate : Chong Chong-shik, director of the Office of Policy Planning, National Unification Board
Delegate : Lee Dong-bok, director of the South-North Dialogue Office

North Korean Delegation
Chief delegate : Hyon Jun-guk, deputy director of Central Committee of the Workers' Party and concurrently councilor of the State Council
Delegate : Paek Chun-hyok, bureau director of the State Council
Delegate : Yim Chun-gil, bureau director of the State Council

(2) Progress of Working-Level Contacts

The Working-level contacts intended to discuss procedural matters were held a total of ten times before they were torpedoed by north Korea, with each side represented by three delegates plus two assistants.

141

Working-Level Contacts Held

Classifica-tion	Place	Time
1st	Conference Room, SNCC	February 6, 1980
2nd	Panmungak	February 19, 1980
3rd	Freedom House	March 4, 1980
4th	Panmungak	March 18, 1980
5th	Freedom House	April 1, 1980
6th	Panmungak	April 18, 1980
7th	Freedom House	May 6, 1980
8th	Panmungak	May 22, 1980
9th	Freedom House	June 24, 1980
10th	Panmungak	August 20, 1980

Question of Procedural Matters for Working-Level Contacts and Prime Ministers' Talks

At the first working-level contact, the Republic of Korea delegation, expressing the hope that "the contacts would become a first step toward resumption of the long-suspended inter-Korean dialogue, with a view to consolidating progress toward peaceful unification of the divided country," proposed procedural matters necessary for a meeting between the south and north Korean prime ministers as follows :

The Republic of Korea working-level delegation proposes the following procedural matters for the proposed meeting between the prime ministers of south and north of Korea, with a view to realizing the prime ministers' talks effectively at an early date.

(1) Time of the Meeting

The time of the meeting between the prime ministers shall be decided after the two sides arrive at an agreement on the rest of the procedural matters.

(2) Venue of the Meeting

The proposed meeting between the prime ministers shall be held a

142

third country preferably in Geneva, Switzerland.

(3) Agenda of the Meeting

The agenda of the meeting between the prime ministers shall be agreed on, in principle, at the current working-level contacts.

(4) Composition of Assistants

The prime ministers shall be accompanied each by two assistants of ministerial and/or vice ministerial rank and two assistants of the rank of assistant minister and/or bureau director, in addition to a few staff members for documentation, communication, liaison and public information.

(5) Arrangements inside the Conference Room

The two sides shall not use any special markings inside the conference room except the name plates of the prime ministers placed on the conference table.

(6) Documentation

Documentation of the meeting shall be made by each of the two sides in ways convenient to themselves. They may employ stenographers and tape-recorders.

(7) Agreements

The two sides shall prepare respectively written agreements in duplicate and shall exchange one of the duplicate copies duly signed.

(8) Sessions

The meeting shall be held behind closed doors. Depending on mutual agreement, the prime ministers may have an exclusive meeting.

(9) Press Briefings

The two sides shall conduct press briefings separately in ways convenient to themselves. Upon agreement, however, they may conduct a press briefing jointly.

At the first contact, however, north Korea unveiled its ulterior scheme to manipulate the prime ministers' meeting and make it a

143

mere part of the "south-north political conference" they had offered when, although having come to the conference table to prepare for the prime ministers' talks, they argued, "The proposed prime ministers' contact should be realized as part of multilateral contacts between politicians of the South and the North.

North Korea then made the following seven-point proposal in connection with the procedural matters of the prime ministers' meeting, including the offer that the venue of the meeting should be Pyongyang and Seoul by turn.

(1) The venue of the meeting of the prime ministers shall be Seoul and Pyongyang by turn ;

(2) Those who accompany the prime ministers shall be 60 persons, including 30 assistants specialists and technical personnel, and an additional 30 pressmen ;

(3) The personal security of the delegates and accompanying members shall be guaranteed through the exchange of memoranda at the time of each contact ;

(4) The contact shall be flexible in style. It may be opened to the public or held behind closed doors, depending on need at each session ;

(5) In the light of past conference experience, press briefings shall be made simultaneously upon the preparation of a documented agreement ;

(6) The duration of stay of a delegation in the other side's area shall be four to five days. The host side shall be responsible for the personnel of the other side ; and

(7) It would be reasonable and realistic to determine these procedural matters at this working-level contact so as to realize the prime ministers' contact at an early date.

At the second working-level contact held on February 19, 1980, the two sides, discussing matters brought up at the first contact, could reach agreement only on rather minor items such as the issues of whether to open the prime ministers' meeting, preparing documentation of agreement, press coverage, etc. however, the two sides showed a wide discrepancy over the vital questions of the venue of, and agenda topics for, the proposed meeting.

Meanwhile, the debate of the issue of assistants and attendants to accompany prime ministers was shelved unitl the venue of the prime ministers' meeting was determined, in as much as the number of assistants and attendants required was bound to change depending on the place of the proposed meeting.

The items agreed upon between the two sides at the second working-level contact with respect to the procedural matters for the prime ministers' meeting were as follows :

1) Whether to Open Meeting

The meeting shall be either opened to the public or held behind closed doors, depending on agreement at the time of each meeting.

2) Agreements

The two sides shall each prepare written agreements in duplicate and exchange one of the signed duplicate copies.

3) Documentation

Documentation of the meeting shall be made at each side's convenience, by means of stenography, tape-recording and/or video-taping.

4) Press Briefings

The two sides shall separately conduct press briefings in a way convenient to each side, unless a joint press briefing is agreed on.

5) Time of the Meeting

The time of the meeting shall be decided depending on progress of the working-level contacts.

6) Facilities and Markings

No markings shall be used in the conference room, except for the name plates of the prime ministers which shall be placed on the table.

Meanwhile, the Republic of Korea working-level delegation proposed in connection with the procedural matters for the working-level contacts that 1) the contacts be held behind closed doors in order to

145

ensure effective progress of the contacts, 2) starting from the second contact, the working-level contacts be held alternately at the Freedom House and Panmungak, and 3) the existing direct South-North telephone line be used for easier mutual liaison.

In response, north Korea suggested that the first contact be opened to reporters, which was agreed on by the southern side. Whether or not to open the second and later working-level contacts was to be determined at the beginning of each contact, as suggested by the north Korean delegation. The Republic of Korea delegation's ideas on the venues of working-level contacts and use of the direct South-North telephone line were adopted as north Korea did not object to them. During the time the working-level contacts were in progress, two direct telephone circuits were operated between the working-level delegations of the two sides.

—Question of Title of Prime Ministers' Dialogue—

With respect to the issue of the title of the prime ministers' meeting a question that reflects the nature of the meeting, the Republic of Korea working-level delegation, noting that the two sides referred to the proposed prime ministers' meeting by various different titles, suggested at the times of the fourth and sixth contacts that they adopt and use a single uniform title for the meeting. The Republic of Korea delegation reasoned that it is awkward for the South and the North to use different titles such as "seeing," "contact" or "dialogue," and that a single title was needed even in the sense of making clear the nature of the meeting between high authorities like prime ministers. The Republic of Korea delegation then suggested "Meeting between the Prime Ministers of the South and the North" as the official title of the proposed talks.

However, north Korea rejected the suggestion sticking to their insistence on "seeing" or "contact" on the grounds of the principle of expediency. This north Korean attitude pointed to their underlying intent not to make the proposed prime ministers' talks a serious business meeting.

146

–Question of Venue of Prime Ministers' Meeting–

At the second contact on March 14, the Republic of Korea delegation, discussing the issue of the venue of the prime ministers' meeting, said, "our side does not mean that it is dead opposed to some of the proposed sites being talked about, or is sticking to some others," explaining that because north Korea suggested in its January 11 letter that the proposed meeting may be held either at Panmunjom or in Pyongyang and Seoul, and even a third country would be acceptable. The Republic of Korea delegation had simply chosen a third country from among the several given alternatives, and therefore it was not the Republic of Korea delegation that first offered a third country as the venue. It then stated that in view of the past experience in inter-Korean dialogue, it would be good if a third country were chosen as the venue of the proposed meeting.

The Republic of Korea delegation added, "Our preference for Geneva does not necessarily mean that the venue should always be Geneva. We simply suggested Geneva in view of various favorable conditions of the city for international conferences." It then showed flexibility, suggesting "the question of which third country should be the site can be solved through mutual discussion."

North Korea, however, rejected the Republic of Korea delegation's choice of a third country. In a show of a somewhat ambiguous posture, the north Korean delegation insisted that it suggested a third country in its January 11 message only as possible alternative under "unavoidable circumstances."

The two sides continued to discuss the venue issue at the third and fourth contacts, ending in counter-proposals that the venue of the proposed meeting be Panmunjom. Based on these offers, the two sides agreed on the issue of venue as follows :

1) The venue of the prime ministers' dialogue shall be Panmunjom, with conferences to take place at the Freedom House and Panmungak alternately.

2) In the event either of the prime ministers wishes to change the venue, the two prime ministers shall consult about the matter.

In addition, the two sides agreed to discuss and settle the issue of which of the two — Freedom House or Panmungak — should be the venue of the first round of the prime ministers' talks when the time of the first meeting of the prime ministers' dialogue was determined.

The two sides also reached an agreement in principle on some of the procedural matters incidental to the solution of the venue of the meting, such as the number of assistants and attendants who would accompany the prime ministers to their meeting, the issue of extending support and convenience for press converage, and crossing of the Military Demarcation Line by participants. For the adjustment of some wordings and expressions of the agreement, the two sides decided to have one   working-level delegate from each side meet and discuss these at an appropriate time later.

—Question of Agenda of Prime Ministers' Meeting—

At the second contact held on February 19, 1980, the Republic of Korea delegation stated on the issue of agenda that "the agenda for the prime ministers' meeting should be arranged beforehand so that the prime ministers could discuss substantial matters when they meet."

However, north Korea opposed the advance fixing of agenda topics, contending that "there is no need to restrict the scope and contents of the discussion of the prime ministers by determining in advance the topics for their meeting."

At the third contact of March 4, north Korea made an aboutface and agreed in principle on the advance determining of agenda topics, facilitating some progress in the issue of agenda. At the fourth contact held on March 18, the two sides put forth their respective versions of agenda topics for the prime ministers' talks as follows :

South Korea

Item One:The question of fostering mutual trust between the south and the north.

1) The question of laying the foundation for the promotion of

mutual trust and understanding as well as restoration of national homogeneity between the south and the north of Korea through exchanges and cooperation between the two sides.

2) The question of implementing humanitarian measures aimed at easing the suffering and lessening the inconvenience of the people resulting from the division of the country.

. Item Two : The question of establishing peace on the Korean peninsula.

Item Three : The question of peaceful unification of the fatherland.

North Korea

Concerning the expediting of independent and peaceful unification of the fatherland through collaboration and unity in all areas of the South and the North.

Discussing the issue of the agenda topics of prime ministers' talks at fourth contact and again at the sixth and the seventh contacts, the Republic of Korea working-level delegation stressed that "unification cannot be achieved merely by unrealistic slogans or by one-sided propaganda rhetoric, but can be realized only when the two sides first take realistic and practical steps, and gradually expand the scope of such steps, as a means of laying the foundation for peaceful unification."

Pointing out that inasmuch as the prime ministers' talks are to be a meeting intended to discuss matters important for the nation, the agenda to be taken up must be concrete, reasonable and realistic, the Republic of Korea delegation said "our side's draft agenda does not restrict in any way the items subject to discussion at the prime ministers' talks, but has been prepared based on the realistic and reasonable order of priority for the processes and stages necessary for realization of the ultimate goal of peaceful unification," ROK delegation stressed.

At the same time, the Republic of Korea delegation showed flexibility over the issue of agenda topics by saying, "Our side does not insist

149

on item-by-item separate discussion alone, and the order of the agenda topics does not necessarily indicate any strict restriction on the order of discussion." It added that depending on mutual agreement at the time of the prime ministers' talks or at mutual conveniences, package discussion to a certain extent or overall discussion might be made of the agenda, while individual could also be held in principle in order of the topics given.

The south Korean delegation, however, argued that their draft agendum, being "comprehensive and single," is "better oriented toward unification" and "can better serve" to realizing the prime ministers' talks than north Korea's, denouncing as "divisive" the draft agenda offered by the southern side.

In reaction, the Republic of Korea delegation, in a speech made at the eighth working-level contact, stated that altough the two sides both insist they pursue independent and peaceful unification, it is apparent that they think of basically different approaches toward national unification. The southern delegation said that contrary to the concrete and reasonable draft agenda advanced by itself, the north Korean agendum is so vague that there is no way to know what it was intended for. It added that even if the northern agendum was adopted, therefore, it could not mean any agreement at all on the issue of agenda.

Pointing out, then, that north Korea attaches unilateral political meaning to the words "collaboration" and "unity" used in their draft agendum, the Republic of Korea delegation said in the same speech that the seditious meanings of the words and use of them in the draft agendum indicate that north Korea continues to pursue communization of all Korea by means of violent revolution in the South. The speech said in part :

Remarks by high authorities and official documents of your side assert, collaboration enables the broad masses of the south and the north to awaken themselves to national and class ideas, to rally firmly around the Leader, and to embark

150

resolutely on struggles for unification of the fatherland along the path dictated by the Leader.... Collaboration also enables all the problems pending between the South and the north to be settled on the basis of the socialistic capability of the northern half....'.

Similarly, the political meaning of the word 'unity' your side is using is to 'enable south Korean authorities to do away with their anti-Communist principles and to ally themselves with communism.'

Moreover, your side defines 'independent and peaceful unification' as unification achieved with the 'united strength of the socialistic forces of the northern half and the patriotic ad democratic forces of the south after the American aggressors are driven out, colonial rule is liquidated and a genuine people's regime is established in south Korea.'

Thus seen, it is more than apparent why your side insists on the use of the words 'collaboration' and 'unity' in the agenda for the prime ministers' talks. In other words, you side is not interested in the discussion of a formula independent and peaceful unification at the proposed meeting. Instead, all you are after is that, in the event these words at issue were adopted in the agenda, your side wohuld maintain that our sisw had accepted even the political meaning your side has arbitrarily imposed on these words.

It is apparent that your side's intention, as can be assessed in your draft agendum, is not to seek improvement of inter-Korean relations and genuine peaceful unification of the fatherland through dialogue, but to attempt to use even the proposed talks between the prime ministers – high authorities of the south and the north – as a means of fostering conditions for the so-called 'revolution in south Korea,' part of your traditional intent of pursuing unification within the framework of your own system.

At the ninth working-level contact of June 24, 1980, the Republic of Korea delegation proposed, for the sake of the early realization of the prime ministers' talks, comprehensive new agenda topics – in effect a compromise of the two sides' contentions – along with the time and the venue of the first round of the proposed prime ministers' meeting, as follows :

First, the question of agenda topics for the prime ministers' meeting.

The agenda items for the prime ministers' meeting shall be ;

Item No.1 – The question of fostering mutual trust and easing tensions between the south and the north of Korea through exchanges and cooperation between them.

–Item No.2 – The question of peaceful unification of the fatherland.

Second, the question of the time of the first round of the prime ministers' meeting ;

The first round of the prime ministers' meeting shall be held sometime during the coming month of August or September at the latest. In line with the spirit of the agreement on holding the prime ministers' talks in the two sectors of Panmunjom by turn, the second round shall be held one month after the first.

Third, the question of the venue of the first round of the prime ministers' meeting ;

The venue of the first round of the prime ministers' meeting shall be determined between Freedom House and Panmungak, according to your side's preference.

Notwithstanding this fresh suggestion, the North Korean delegation, raising issues out of some internal affairs in the South nor related in any way to the business of the working-level contacts, refused to discuss the question of agenda topics itself, asserting, "Since the Prime Minister of the South who signed the credentials exchanged at the first working-level contact has resigned, it is meaningless to continue discussion."

(3) *Stalemate and Suspension of Working-level Contacts*

Beginning barely one month after the first round working-level contact of February 6, 1980, North Korea worked to throw cold water upon the conference atmosphere. By staging armed provocations against the other side in the dialogue led objective observers to suspect whether the North was really interested in the contacts to prepare for the prime ministers' talks.

Their more outright move to suspend the working-level contacts began to appear at the eighth-round contact of May 22,1980 when the North Koreans refused to discuss substantial matters on the excuse that "there is no south Korean Prime Minister who signed the credentials of the southern working-level delegates."

At that time in the Republic of Korea, there was an Acting Prime Minister pending the confirmation of his appointment by the National Assembly, which was then in recess. For the north Koreans to dispute the capacity of the Acting Prime Minister represented their ignorance of accepted political practices and, at the same time, a crafty attempt to blame the Republic of Korea for the suspension of the working-level contacts, a breakoff which the north Koreans themselves contemplated, as they saw no chance to gain what they planned to reap through the prime ministers' talks.

Moreover, from the ninth contact, north Korea showed half-heartedness toward the working-level contacts. North Korea's chief delegate Hyun Jun-guk was himself absent from the contacts on account of "illness." and, contrary to the customary practice of holding the contacts roughly at two-week intervals, north Korea insisted on holding the ninth contact one month after the eighth, and the tenth two months later. Going a step farther, the north Korean delegation, showing up for the tenth contact of August 20, 1980 , argued at the outset that the 10th contact itself should be postponed until September 30, refusing to enter any business discussion. The tenth contact thus had to adjourn after agreeing only to have the next contact on September 26.

153

On September 24, 1980, barely two days before the scheduled 11th contact, north Korea in a radio broadcast unilaterally declared the suspension of the working-level contacts, and refused to receive telephone calls from the south over the direct south- north line. With this, the working-level contacts came to a camplete breakdown barely seven months after they were initiated on February 6, 1980. The channel of inter-Korean dialogue was blocked once again.

Despite the one-sided torpedoing by north Korea, the Republic of Korea delegation, in a statement on September 26, openly laid down a six-point proposal intended for the alleviation of tensions and substantial improvement of inter-Korean relations, as follows :

1) The agenda of the proposed prime ministers' meeting shall not be discussed any more at the working-level contacts, and instead be discussed and determined directly between the two prime ministers when they meet in the proposed conference.

2) The first round of the prime ministers' meeting shall be held sometime durng the second week (November 3–8) of November 1980, with the second round taking place within a month after the first.

3) The venue of the first-round prime ministers' meeting shall be chosen between the Freedom House or Panmungak at Panmunjom, as agreed on between the South and the North, or between Seoul or Pyongyang, as north Korea prefers, with the second-round taking place at a comparable place in the other side. Subsequent rounds shall take place in the two areas by turn.

4) Other minor procedural matters requiring mutual concurrence of the holding of the prime ministers' meeting shall be discussed and settled through separate contacts between one delegate each from the two sides, who shall be accompanied by some specialists. Agreements reached at such separate contacts shall be finalized subject to joint confirmation by the chief delegates of the two sides.

5) The 11th working-level contact shall be held on October 7, 1980 at Freedom House to discuss these new proposals of ours.

6) In due recognition of the need to ease the tensions and improve relations between the two sides of divided Korea, and to consolidate peace and stability on the Korean peninsula, the south and the north of Korea shall continue, without interruption, to operate the two Seoul-Pyongyang direct telephone lines hitherto operated between the delegations of the two sides for the working-level contacts.

However, north Korea dismissed this epochal six-point compromise proposal. They even cut off the direct South-North telephone line, with the telephone conversation held at 10:30 a.m. on September 25 as the last call made over the direct line. North Korea thus made it known expressly that from the beginning they were not interested in the easing of tensions and bringing about durable peace and stability on the Korean peninsula.

Soon thereafter, on October 10, 1980, north Korea staged yet another political farce by launching the sixth congress of the Workers' Party, the proposal for what is called a "Democratic Confederal Republic of Koryo" an oft-used time-worn propaganda gambit of Kim Il-sung's making.

Part Two

Unfolding of Diverse South-North Dialogue and Propusion of Pilot Projects

1. North Korea's Logic of Dialogue

From the beginning of the south-north dialogue of the 1970s, there was indwelling in the dialogue contradictions that inevitably doomed the talks. In order to ease in a peaceful manner the distrust and tension that had built up between the two sides of Korea over a quarter century after national division, the two sides ought to have sought agreements through dialogue and sincerely carry out what were agreed on.

However, the north's basic stance toward the dialogue was based on a predatory logic that might be summed up as "negotiations to keep mine and claim yours as mine." In other words, the north came to the conference table only to foster conditions conducive to achieving unification under communism.

No sooner had the South-North Coordinating Committee begun formally functioning and plenary sessions of the Red Cross Conference started than north Korea began deliberately obstructing the progress of such dialogue by ignoring those agenda agreed between both parties, by posting conditions absolutely unacceptable to the other side on the basis of some unessential and vague expressions in the criteria and rules, and by insisting the other side accept the demands as preconditions for further dialogue.

At the South-North Coordination Committee, for instance, the North was least interested in putting the Committee's working function in order or finding out mutually agreeable projects. Instead, by means of arbitrary and biased interpretation of the "three principles for unification" stipulated in the South-North Joint Communique, north Korea outrageously meddled in and criticized the domestic and foreign policies of the Republic of Korea.

North Korea demanded that the Republic of Korea repeal its Anti-Communist Law and National Security Law, release all prisoners convicted under these laws, legalize the activities of Communists in the Republic of Korea, and thereby abandon its anti-Communist policies in favor of pro-Communist policies – all these voluntarily and without north Korean reciprocity, on the ridiculous ground that these south Korean laws contravened the agreed principle for unification calling for national unity.

It also demanded that the Republic of Korea accept its five-point military proposal as another precondition of further dialogue. This proposal was aimed at the unconditional withdrawal from south Korea of U.S. troops, a vital part of the south-north military balance, and at preventing the modernization of the south Korean armed forces. North Korea declared that "the progress of the dialogue, the improvement of the south-north relations, or the settlement of the unification issue would all be impossible" unless and until the Republic of Korea accepted its "five-point military proposal."

North Korea, quibbling that the June 23 Declaration of the Republic of Korea was a "policy to split the nation and fix two Koreas," further demanded that the south retract it and instead accept the north Korean "peaceful unification formula" unconditionally.

North Korea did not stop there in being unreasonable. As it agreed on one hand to inaugurate the South-North Coordinating Committee as an organ to implement the "agreements and decisions on all matters related to unification," it was engaged on the other hand in undermining the legal functions of the Committee.

After the announcement of the Joint Communique, in which the south and north had agreed on the founding of the South-North Coordinating Committee, and before the formal activation of the Committee, Kim Il-sung told the Mainichi Shinbun of Japan in an exclusive interview on September 17, 1972 that:

We intend to organize and operate the South-North Coordinating Committee as soon as possible in order to promote the matters stipulated in the South-North Joint Communique and solve various problems involved in the pursuit of unification.

However, the unification issue cannot be completely solved through the limited contacts and negotiations at the South-North Red Cross Conference and South-

North Coordinating Committee. In order to solve the fundamental problems for national reunification, wider and more diversified contacts and negotiations must be arranged between the south and north for many years and to discuss a series of practical plans to materialize autonomous and peaceful unification.

Therefore, I call urgently for political negotiations through, say, a joint conference of various political parties and social organizations of the south and north, a conference between the authorities of the south and north, or a joint conference of representatives from our Supreme People's Assembly and their National Assembly.....

The South-North Coordinating Committee, inaugurated at the end of November 1972, had scarcely held two sessions when Kim Il-sung spoke as follows in a speech at a mass rally held in Pyongyang on April 16, 1973 welcoming Prince Norodom Sihanouk of Cambodia :

We propose that the South-North Coordinating Committee be expanded by adding representatives from various political parties and social organizations of the south and north, or that a political negotiation conference be convened with the participation of representatives from various political parties and social organizations along with personages from various fields and classes of the south and north separately from the South-North Coordinating Committee, which in this case will be left alone to attend its own projects... .

Here Kim Il-sung unmistakably suggests that north Korea, in agreeing on founding and operating the South-North Coordinating Committee, had no intention in the first place to operate the Committee in good faith in accordance with the agreed "rules" but merely to inaugurate and then change it into a so-called "South-North Political Conference" or "Grand National Congress," or to use it as a stepping stone leading to separately convening a "Political Conference."

Such dialogue logic from north Korea becomes more obvious at the South-North Red Cross Conference table. This conference is designed to solve the problem of dispersed families through the good offices of the Red Cross machinery since the distress of national division is most deeply felt by such family members as the political settlement of the division is being delayed indefinitely. This was to contribute to the settlement of the unification issue through the implementation of this program to reunite dispersed families.

The mission of the South-North Red Cross Conference, according to its agreed agenda, was to find practical procedures and methods for 1) the search for the whereabouts and fate of the dispersed family members and notification of kin, 2) mutual meetings and visits among the dispersed family members, 3) exchange of correspondence, 4) reunion, and 5) other humanitarian problems.

But, as in the case of the South-North Coordinating Committee, the north Korean intention was not to carry out these steps but to use this Conference as a stepping stone for some other purposes.

Under the twisted logic that "the humanitarian problem existing in the country can be automatically solved upon national unification" and that "therefore the humanitarian works cannot be handled separately from the unification issue but should be promoted only as a part of the unification issue," North Korea refused the discussion of the agreed agenda and insisted on what it called "the improvement of the legal conditions and social environments" as a precondition to discussion of the original agenda.

The north Korean demands for "the improvement of legal conditions and social environments" included :

1) That south Korea repeal all anti-Communist laws including the Anti-Communist Law and the National Security Law,

2) That all anti-Communist activities be prohibited in south Korea and all anti-Communist organizations and agencies be dissolved,

3) That all dispersed family members and their guides, and pertinent officials coming from north Korea be guaranteed the freedom of speech, publication, assembly and passage as well as the inviolable rights of their bodies and posessions,

4) That the U.S. force stationed in south Korea be withdrawn, and

5) That the search for the dispersed family members be conducted by such members and their counterparts by directly and freely travelling without interference by the Red Cross organs but with the help of cooperators and officials concerned.

These assertions of north Korea were, of course, outside the realm of the matters discussible at the Red Cross talks because of their political nature. Still, the more basic problem was the ulterior motive lurking behind such demands.

The contentions and attitude made by the north in the course of the dialogue, indicated that north Korea was trying to use dialogue as a means of realizing their scheme to communize the south and to embody the united front strategy taking advantage of unrest in the south. Their stereotyped tactics was that whenever their scheme turned out to have little chances, they unilaterally suspended an ongoing dialogue, attempting to shift the blame of such suspension to the south.

This ulterior motive of north Korea was more evident in the inter-Korean relations of the early 1980s. When the internal situation of south Korea grew unstable in the wake of the sudden death of President Park in October 1979, north Korea urged inter-Korean working-level contacts, supposedly to prepare for talks between the prime ministers of the two sides, in an attempt to manipulate the contacts for their intensified propaganda against the south, taking advantage of the social unrest.

As the Republic of Korea, however, regained stability while the South-North contacts were encountering rough sailing due to conflicting views on the key issues of the title and agenda topics of the prime ministers' meeting, north Korea shunned the debate on substantial issues, setting forth prerequisites over some internal affairs of south Korea before they finally broke off the working-level contacts altogether on September 24, 1980.

In short, what north Korea is really after is not a dialogue and cooperation between the south and the north but confrontation and split. Therefore, the very thing the north tries to obtain through a South-North dialogue is a license to carry out what they call a "revolution in south Korea."

On July 3, 1972, on the eve of the announcement of the historic South-North Joint Communique, Central Radio of north Korea broadcast a commentary titled "the Interrelation between the south Korean Revolution and the Fatherland Unification" in connection with the 'Comprehensive Business Report' presented by Kim Il-sung at the Fifth convention of the Workers'(Communist) Party. The political commentary said in part:

> The unification of the fatherland can be accomplished only upon the accomplishment of the south Korean revolution. The south Korean revolution becomes the precondition for fatherland unification. The south Korean revolution concerns south Korea alone, but the unification of the fatherland covers all areas of south and north Korea.
>
> The south Korean revolution poses the task of an anti-imperialist people's democratic revolution for the liberation of the south Korean people in terms of nation and class, while the fatherland unification involves the task of accomplishing the national liberation revolution on the pan-national basis under the banner of the Democratic People's Republic of (north) Korea.
>
> Though there are peaceful and non-peaceful methods for the unification, there is only a violent way to accomplish the south Korean revolution. There cannot be a peaceful method of carrying out the south Korean revolution. The south Korean revolution, aimed at crushing the American aggressors and their agents and at winning a people's regime, can never be carried out by peaceful means. The south Korean revolution can be won only by revolutionary violence.

The "independent peaceful unification" north Korean mentions calls for the realization initially of a "national liberation and people's democratic revolution" and then of 1) the withdrawal of U.S. forces from Korea, 2) step-down of the Republic of Korea government and 3) the establishment of a people's regime, so that a people's regime in

the south and the Kim Il-sung regime in the north can work together
to materialize a peaceful unification. It thus can be easily noted that
north Korea wants to use the dialogue only for the purpose of creating conditions and environments favorable to a south Korean revolution, which is a premise for the accomplishment of the north Korean
version of peaceful unification.

Apart from this ulterior motive of the north, the South-North dialogue in the 1970s was significant in that multiple forms of a dialogue
were made after a long period of disruption between the south and
the north. Still, the dialogue gave a great disappoinment to the whole
people who were anxious for a productive dialogue.

2. Efforts of the Republic of Korea to Promote Uni-
fication

a. Proposal for Top Leaders Meeting

Even after the South-North dialogue was unilaterally suspended by
north Korea, the Republic of Korea has untiringly sought resumption
of the dialogue.

As the north's attempt to try a Vietnam War-style "national liberation war" was thwarted and the south wisely surmounted the political
vacuum caused by the death of President Park, north Korea closed
the door of dialogue tight. And, even after the turn of the 1980s, the
north adhered to the policy of south Korean revolution and refused
to recognize the south Korean goverment.

It was against this backdrop that in a policy statement on January
12, 1981, President Chun Doo Hwan invited north Korea's Kim Il-
sung to "visit Seoul without any conditions attached and free of any
burden," saying that he himself was prepared to "visit north Korea at
any time" if he were invited on the same terms.

Part of President Chun's 1981 policy statement relating to the invitation was as follows :

It is not my intention today to argue over things past. To provide decisive momentum to creating mutual trust between the south and the north of Korea, epochal momentum to preventing a recurrence of tragic, fratricidal war, and historic momentum to paving the way to peaceful unification through unconditional resumption of the suspended dialogue, I hereby solemnly propose that the highest authorities of the south and the north exchange visits.

I invite President Kim Il-sung of north Korea to visit Seoul without any condition attached and free of any burden.

I will ensure that his personal safety is fully guaranteed during his stay in Seoul. I will extend all possible cooperation to him if he wishes to travel to any place of his choice in order to take a first-hand look at the actual situation in Seoul, other cities, or tural areas.

I also want to make it clear that I am prepared, at any time, to visit north Korea if he invites me on the same terms as I offer.

The purpose of the proposal for an exchange of visits between the highest authorities of south and north Korea was to provide 1) decisive momentum for creating mutual trust between the two sides, 2) firm momentum for preventing a recurrence of tragic, fratricidal war, and 3) historic momentum for paving the way to peaceful unification through unconditional resumption of the suspended dialogue.

The January 12 proposal was epochal in itself. For, mutual visits by the top leaders of the two sides, rather than having a conference with little chance for success and without the base of trust, would serve to remove the ground of mutual misunderstanding and provide a base for mutual trust through the mutual opening of their societies, thus becoming a decisive momentum to removing the danger of recurrence of war by miscalculation. Moreover, if and when north Korea accepted the offer for mutual visits, contacts and dialogue of various types would take place between the two sides in the course of translating the proposed visits into action, thereby providing a natural impetus to resuming the suspended inter-Korean dialogue.

Nonetheless, north Korea turned down the January 12 proposal. In a statement issued on January 19, 1981, one week after the proposal, by Pyongyang's vice president Kim Il in his capacity as chairman of the "Committee for the Peaceful Reunification of the Fatherland," north Korea denounced the proposal for mutual visits as a divisive scheme designed to perpetuate 'two Koreas' instead of being aimed at facilitating peaceful unification. North Korea then demanded as conditions to resuming the inter-Korean dialogue 1) dismissal of the incumbent government of south Korea and creation of a new regime sympathetic to communism, 2) freeing of Kim Dae-jung and other "political prisoners," 3) abrogation of laws on anticommunism, and dissolution of anti-Communist offices and organizations, 4) withdrawal of the June 23 special foreign policy statement, and 5) pullout of the U.S. forces in Korea. North Korea, in the same statement, levelled vulgar personal attacks on President Chun, making it clear that they would not enter into any talks with the incumbent government authorities of the Republic of Korea.

About five months later, on June 5, 1981, President Chun proposed a "direct meeting between the highest authorities of south and north Korea." The overture was announced in an opening address President Chun made in his capacity as the chairman of the Advisory Council on Peaceful Unification Policy at the inaugural meeting of that constitutional organization. The part of the speech on the proposal was as follow:

On this occasion, I renew my call to President Kim Il-sung of north Korea to accept my January 12 proposal that we visit each other free of any obligation and without any condition attached. It does not matter whether President Kim visits Seoul first or I visit Pyongyang first. The north Koreans can choose.

Furthermore, I would like to extend the scope of my invitation. Should some unavoidable circumstance prevent President Kim from accepting my proposal or from inviting me to visit north Korea, I suggest that we meet each other at some other place for frank face-to-face talks. I leave the choice of venue to the north Korean authorities. It could be either Panmunjom, or a third country, or any other place convenient to them.

The proposal, manifesting the south's strong will to bring about peaceful unification of the country, was a more advanced and concrete form of his earlier January 12 proposition in which the President offered an exchange of mutual visits between the highest authorities of the two zones of Korea.

Rather than a mere supplement to the January 12 overture, the June 5 proposal was epochal and significant in that the President boldly sought improved inter-Korean relations and a further advance toward unification by leaving the choice of the time and venue of a meeting to Kim Il-sung.

The proposal earned broad support at home and abroad as it was stressed that a divided nation's unification cannot be achieved by force of arms under any circumstances and that if a war occurs, it could only lead to self-destruction of the nation, where there would be neither victor nor loser.

Whereas an exchange of visit between the highest authorities of the two zones of Korea was suggested in the January 12 proposal, the June 5 offer suggested that he and Kim Il-sung meet at any time and any place to discuss frankly all questions raised by both sides, including the proposed exchange of visits and both south and north Korean unification formulae, adding that the time of the meeting would be the sooner the better.

Also in the June 5 proposal, he advocated that both south and north Korean authorities open their societies to the entire Korean people who have the right to make decisions concerning unification. Here, the Presidennt was expressing his strong desire to realize peaceful unification in the 1980s by forcing the north Koreans to abandon their dream of communizing the entire Korean peninsula, thereby fostering national trust between the two divided sides.

The June 5 proposal contained more practical and concrete contents than the January 12 offer, except for the suggestion of an exchange of visits between the highest authorities. The fact that the President kept the door to conference topics wide open by suggesting that the proposed meeting discuss all the issues raised so far between the two sides points to his resolve to tackle the unification issue affirmatively.

Another important aspect of the June 5 proposal was the President's step of giving flexibility to the north Koreans by suggesting that if their situation did not permit the prompt and complete opening of their society, exchanges could begin first in the athletic, culural, academic, postal and economic fields, with gradual progress made toward all-out exchanges and a complete opening.

He further let it be known that he is determined to carry on unification efforts more broadly when he expressed the hope that the north Korea would consult constructively with any person representing the Republic of Korea any place in the world, or could work through an authoritative international organization to deal with the matter.

North Korea showed a negative response to the June 5 proposal, too. In newspaper and radio commentaries on June 10, 1981, north Korea, denouncing the Republic of Korea vehemently, asserted that the "June 5 proposal is aimed at some impure purpose rather than being intended to discuss the question of unification." Again in a message sent on July 1, 1981 to the so-called Council for Acceleration of Peaceful Unification in north Korea, allegedly composed of former south Korean politicians, on the occasion of the Council's 25th anniversary, Kim Il-sung personally rejected the June 5 proposition, contending, "We cannot have dialogue or contact of any kind with the incumbent south Korean government."

The south's sincerity toward the proposed top leaders meeting was again amply displayed on January 18, 1983, when concrete topics for the summit meeting were suggested in a policy address made at the plenary meeting of the 115th extraordinary National Assembly session. The four topics sugested were :

(1) The question of taking effective measures to ease tensions and

prevent the recurrence of war between the south and the north.

(2) The question of discussing comprehensively the Formula for National Reconciliation and Democratic Unification and a unification idea advocated by the north.

(3) The question of preventing the waste of national energies through excessive competition between the south and the north at international arenas.

(4) The question of providing an impetus to fostering international conditions for the acceleration of peaceful unification.

b. Proposal for 20 Pilot Projects

The Republic of Korea, in a statement issued by the Minister of National Unification on February 1, 1982, proposed to north Korea that the two sides together implement 20 practicable pilot projects to realize the Formula for National Reconciliation and Democratic Unification.

Making clear the policy of the Republic of Korea to meet the wishes of all Koreans that democratic unification must be realized through national reconciliation, the statement said, "The government of the Republic of Korea asks the north Korean authorities to agree to translate promptly the pilot projects into action, in keeping with the spirit of the unification formula announced by President Chun Doo Hwan." The 20 pilot projects proposed were as follows :

(1) The connecting and opening of a highway between Seoul and Pyongyang as a means of guaranteeing free passage between the south and the north.

(2) The realization of postal exchanges and reunion of separated families, thereby easing their sufferings.

(3) The designating and opening of the area north of Mt. Sorak and south of Mt. Kumgang as a joint tourist zone.

(4) The joint management of homeland visits by overseas Korean residents and their free travel between the two sides by way of Panmunjom.

(5) The opeing of the harbors of Inchon and Chinnampo to facilitate free trade between the south and the north.

(6) The allowing of free listening to each other's regular radio programs through the removal of tricky propaganda and jamming facilities for the promotion of mutual understanding between the south and the north.

(7) The participation of north Korean delegations in the 1986 Asian Games and 1988 Olympiad, and their entry into the south by way of Panmunjom.

(8) The allowing of all foreigners wishing to visit the south and the north free access to the two areas by way of Panmunjom.

(9) The creation of joint fishery zones for the convenience of fishermen of both the south and the north.

(10) The conducting of mutual goodwill visits from various circles, such as politicians, businessmen, youths and students, workers, writers and artists, and sportsmen, to improve relations and foster trust between the south and the north.

(11) The guaranteeing of free press coverage by the journalists of the two sides in each other's area to facilitate the correct reporting of the realities of the societies of the south and the north.

(12) The undertaking of joint research on national history for the purpose of preserving and developing the national culture.

(13) The exchange of goodwill matches in various fields of sports and participation in international games under single delegation between the south and the north.

(14) The trading of products of daily necessity for the convenience of residents of both sides.

(15) The joint development and utilization of natural resources between the south and the north to enhance the national economy.

(16) The exchange of technicians and exhibitions of manufactured products to contribute to the industrial development of the south and the north.

(17) The creation of sports facilities inside the Demilitarized Zone for goodwill matches between the south and the north.

(18) The conducting of a joint academic survey to study the ecological system of the fauna and flora inside the Demilitarized Zone.

(19) The complete removal of military facilities from within the Demilitarized Zone in order to alleviate military tensions between the south and the north.

(20) The discussion of measures to control arms between the south and the north, and the installing and operation of a direct telephone line between the officials responsible for the military affairs of the two sides.

North Korea rejected the proposal for 20 inter-Korean projects. In a statement issued by the Committee for Peaceful Reunification of the Fatherland, the north asserted, "The so-called 20 pilot projects are nothing new and only an extremely small part of the measures which our side has historically proposed for inter-Korean collaboration and exchanges."

To be true, the north, too, had suggested inter-Korean exchanges, connecting of communications facilities, etc. for the restoration of mutual trust and laying a foundation for unification, as they asserted. This eloquently indicates that there is no reason, therefore, why the north should reject the offer. Their rejection represented only logical contradiction of their own.

c. Proposal for High-Level Delegates' Meeting

As the new unification formula and the 20 pilot projects, both proposed by the Republic of Korea, drew growing support both at home and abroad, and the north Koren rejection of them came under worldwide censure, north Korea demanded a "joint meeting between south and north Korean politicians" in a statement signed by the Committee for the Peaceful Reunification of the Fatherland on February 10, 1982.

In the statement, north Korea hand-picked the 50 "participants" who would "represent" south Korea at the "joint meeting", in disregard of the existing political parties and social organizations in the south, let alone the Republic of Korea government authorities. North Korea argued that these 50 "representatives of the south" would meet 50 north Korean representatives in a "joint meeting of south and north Korean politicians" in the form of multilateral and round-table talks.

This absurd and unrealistic demand notwithstanding, the Republic of Korea has made untiring efforts to bring the intransigent north Koreans to the forum of dialogue. In a statement issued by Minister of National Unification Sohn Jae-shik on February 25, 1982, the Republic of Korea, urging north Korea to rectify its attitude, proposed a meeting of high-level delegates between south and north Korea in the hope of advancing through dialogue the peaceful unification desired by all Koreans. The contents of the proposal for an inter-Korean high-level delegates meeting were as follows:

1) South and north Korea should hold a high-level delegates' meeting in Seoul, Pyongyang or Panmunjom within the month of March 1982;

2) The high-level delegates' meeting between the south and the north should discuss:

–The question of holding a meeting between the top leaders of south and north Korea to organize a Consultative Conference for National Reunification for the drafting of a constitution for a unified Korea, and also to promote the normalization of relations between the south and the north.

–Questions concerning the meeting proposed by north Korea on February 10, 1982, and

–Various issues that must be urgently settled to promote exchanges, cooperation, the opening of the two societies to each other and relaxation of tensions between the south and the north.

3) Each delegation to the meeting between the south and the north should be composed of nine delegates headed by a cabinet-rank official.

List of Republic of Korea Delegation
Chief Delegate: Roh Tae-woo, Second Minister for State Affairs;
Deputy Chief Delegate: Kim Sang-koo, Deputy Secretary General

of the Advisory Council on Peaceful Unification Policy

Delegates : Lee Young-il, National Assemblyman (Democratic Justice Party)

Kim Moon-suk, National Assemblyman (Democratic Korea Party)

Kang Ki-pil, National Assemblyman (Korea National Party)

Baik Chan-kee, National Assemblyman (Democratic Socialist Party)

Lee Hong-koo, Consultant to the Advisory Council on Peaceful Unification Policy

Kim Tae-suh, Consultant to the Advisory Council on State Affairs

Song Han-ho, Director of the Office of South-North Dialogue, National Unification Board.

In the proposal for a high-level delegates' meeting, the Republic of Korea showed broad-mindedness intended to settle, through sincere dialogue, any problems pending between the South and the North, even including the issue of convening a "joint meeting between south and north Korea" offered by the North. Moreover, nationwide views were fully reflected in the composition of the Republic of Korea delegation to the proposed meeting. Its members included representatives of government authorities, political parties, the Advisory Council on Peaceful Unification Policy and the Advisory Council on State Affairs.

By naming the delegation of leading personages from relevant areas, the competency of the delegation was fully ensured. The delegation was duly empowered to solve the issue of resuming the inter-Korean dialogue and other questions pending between the two sides. Even undue contentions raised by north Korea were not outrightly rejected. Instead, they were given an opportunity to explain their stand at the table of dialogue.

3. Formula for National Reconciliation and Democratic Unification

a. Background

As was seen in the foregoing, various types of dialogue were tried between the two zone of Korea in the 1970s, and a set of principles for peaceful unification was declared by the Republic of Korea government. However, due to north Korea's sincerity and persistent policy to communize all Korea by force of arms, no single productive agreement has ever been worked out between the south and the north.

Upon the inauguration of the new age, the Republic of Korea government, in an approach toward creating an independent national country in the 1980s, reflected on itself cooly over the past dialogue and resolved to depart resolutely from the past method in favor of a fresh start. It was as part of this bold decision that the south proposed a South-North top leaders meeting. Due to the north's rejection, however, there was little chance for the early realization of a top leaders meeting.

It was against this backdrop that President Chun Doo Hwan pronounced in his policy address on January 22, 1982, the Formula for National Reconciliation and Democratic Unification at the home and abroad. The formula was prepared originally as a comprehensive unification idea for presentation at a metting between the top officials of south and north Korea should it be held. The announcement of the formula was intended in part to enable north Korea to understand correctly the real intention of the south, removing any suspicion if might have harbored, prompting itself to agree to a South-North dialogue including a top leaders meeting at an early date.

The part of President Chun's policy statement, devoted to the proposal to the north was as follows :

Recent history teaches us that Korea will never be united as long as the south and the north each insists on a unification formula intended to advance only its own ideology, ideals and institutions. If we are to be successful, unification must be sought from the realization that the Korean people have been a single ethnic family from time immemorial, sharing a common descent, history, culture and tradition.

Unification must not be pursued exclusively or arbitrarily by any specific class or group, nor should it be sought by force of arms or other violent means. I am firmly convinced that unification must be accomplished on the principle of national self-determination and through democratic and peaceful procedures that reflect the free will of the entire people.

It was with an open mind and a desire to seek such a democratic and peaceful path to unification that last year I proposed on January 12 and again on June 5 an exchange of visits and a face-to-face meeting between the top leaders of south and north Korea. I want to make it clear that every possible effort has been—and will continue to be made by the Republic of Korea Government to realize these proposals.

At the same time, I would like to make use of this occasion to disclose a new peaceful unification formula that was originally prepared in anticipation of a South-North summit meeting. I do so with a view to providing the north Korean authorities and the rest of the world with an opportunity to comprehend our genuine intent. It is my conviction that the most reasonable way to peaceful unification is to adopt a constitution of a unified Korea testifying to the commitment of the entire people to unification—a commitment attained through the promotion of national reconciliation—and to then establish a unified state on the terms and conditions laid down in the constitution.

I suggest that, to have the said constitution adopted, the south and the north organize a Consultative Conference for National Reunification(CCNR) with participants from the two sides representing the views of the residents in their respective areas and authorize this body to draft a constitution presenting the terms and conditions of a unified Democratic Republic of Korea committed to the ideals of nationalism, democracy, liberty and individual well-being. I would further suggest that, when such a draft constitution is drawn up, the two side make it into law through free, democratic referendums held throughout the whole peninsula. The unification of the country can then be accomplished by organizing a unified legislature and establishing a unified government through a general election held under the

176

constitution of the unified Korea.

It is my understanding that such issues as the political ideology, the name of the country, the basic domestic and foreign policy directions, the form of government and the methods and dates of the general elections for a unified legislature will have to be discussed and agreed on in the CCNR in the course of drafting the constitution. It is our intention to present our own draft of a constitution for a unified country to the CCNR. If north Korea genuinely desires an independent and peaceful unification, it will also have to present a draft constitution for a unified country before the CCNR, so that the two versions can be studied and forged into a single draft.

It is essential to promote trust between the south and the north and steadfastly eliminate from national life all impediments to unification to facilitate the historic drafting of a unified constitution. Accordingly, the unnatural relations between the south and the north which have resulted in self-inflicted injuries must be brought to an end and replaced by normal contacts that promote the national well-being.

To achieve this end, I hope that the south and the north will first normalize relations and, within the framework of these normalized relations, take concrete steps to bring about national reconciliation. I therefore propose, as a practical arrangement leading to unification, the conclusion of a Provisional Agreement on Basic Relations between south and north Korea featuring the following provisions :

First, relations between south and north Korea shall be based on the principle of equality and reciprocity pending unification.

Second, the south and the north shall abandon all forms of military force and violence, as well as the threat there of, as a means of settling issues between them and seek peaceful solutions to all problems through dialogue and negotiation.

Third, south and north Korea shall recognize each other's existing political order and social institutions and shall not interfere in each other's internal affairs in any way.

Fourth, the south and the north shall maintain the existing regime of armistice in force while working out measures to end the arms race and military confrontation in order to ease tensions and prevent war on the Korean peninsula.

Fifth, in order to eliminate national suffering and the inconvenience resulting from the partition of the land and to promote an atmosphere of national trust and reconciliation, the south and the north shall progressively open their societies to each other through various forms of exchange and cooperation. To substantially advance the interests of the people, the south and the north shall facilitate free travel between the two halves of the peninsula, including the reunion of separated families and shall promote exchanges and cooperation in the fields of trade, transportation, postal service, communications, sports, academic pursuits, education, culture, news gathering and reporting, health, technology, environmental protection, and so forth.

Sixth, until unification is achieved, both parties shall respect each other's bilateral and multilateral treaties and agreements concluded with third countries, irrespective of differences in ideologies, ideals and institutions, and will consult each other on issues affecting the interests of the Korean people as a whole.

Seventh, the south and the north shall each appoint a plenipotentiary envoy with the rank of cabinet minister to head a resident liaison mission to be established in Seoul and Pyongyang. The specific functions of the liaison missions shall be determined by mutual consultation and agreement with both parties providing the liaison mission from the other party with all necessary facilities and cooperation to ensure its smooth functioning.

It is my earnest hope that north Korea will expeditiously accept the proposal for a meeting between the top leaders of the south and the north in order to conduct frank and openminded discussions on all issues noted above.

I propose to north Korea that high-level delegations from the south and the north, headed by cabinet-rank chief delegates, meet together at the earliest possible date in a preparator conference to work out the necessary procedures for a south-North summit meeting. I want to make it clear that if north Korea is agreeable to the proposal for a preparatory conference, the Government of the Republic of Korea has already made the necessary preparations to send a delegation.

b. Major Contents

The unification formula of the Republic of Korea puts forward a set of concrete procedures leading to peaceful unification, ranging from the preparation of a unified constitution to the inauguration of a Unified Democratic Republic by means of general elections.

Suggestion for Formation of Consultative Conference for National Reunification.

The unification formula clearly states that under the basic principle that "unification must be accomplished on the principle of national self-determination and through democratic and peaceful procedures that reflect the free will of the entire people," the most reasonable way to peaceful unification is to adopt a constitution for a unified Korea and then to establish a unified state on the terms and conditions laid down in the constitution.

In other words, the formula suggests that 1) a Consultative Conference for National Reunification be formed with representatives of the residents of the two sides,   2) the Consultative Conference draft a unified constitution for the establishment of a nuifed democratic republic of Korea committed to the ideals of nationalism, democracy, liberty and individual well-being, 3) the unified constitution thus drafted be confirmed and promulgated through free national referendums held in a democratic manner throughout the whole peninsula, and 4) the unification of the country be then accomplished by organizing a unified legislature and establishing a unified government through a general election held under the unified constitution.

The proposal stressed that such issues as political ideology, the name of the country, basic domestic and foreign policy directions, the form of government and methods and dates of the general elections for a unified legislature should be discussed and agreed on at the Consultative Conference for National Reunification in the course of drafting the constitution.

Suggestion for Conclusion of a Provisional Agreement on Basic Relations between South and North Korea.

The most realistic and reasonable method is to accomplish unification on the terms provided by a unified constitution prepared by a Consultative Conference for National Reunification and endorsed by

179

a national referendum.

However, since the reality is that such a historic task can hardly be completed smoothly over a short period of time because of the difference in ideologies, systems, and sense of values, as well as the deep-rooted confrontation situation, the Formula for National Reconsiliation and Democratic Unification put forth a set of supplementary measures to turn the inter-Korean relationship into a peaceful and normal one, pending the realization of a unified state under the provisions of a unified constitution. Such measures are duly envisaged in a Provisional Agreement on Basic Relations between South and North Korea, which the new unification formula proposed. Highlights of the proposed Provisional Agreement, aimed at supplementing the whole process of unification to be achieved under procedures provided by a unified constitution, are as follows :

1) Respect for the principles of reciprocity and equality in mutual relations pending the time of unification.

2) Renouncing of the use of force of arms or other violence in favor of solving of disputes peacefully through dialogue.

3) Recognizing of each other's political order and social system, and non-interference in each other's internal affairs.

4) Maintaining the existing armistice system, and discussion of measures to end the arms race and dissolve the state of military confrontation.

5) Promotion of opening of the societies of the two sides through multi-faceted exchanges and cooperation (in reunion of dispersed families, trade, transportation, postal service, communications, sports, academic pursuits, education, culture, press, health, technology, environmental protection, etc.)

6) Respecting each other's bilateral and multilateral agreements concluded with third countries, and consultation on matters affecting the interests of the Korean nation pending the time of unification.

7) Establishment of respective permanent liaison missions in Seoul and Pyǫngyang.

c. Major Features

The major features of the Formula for National Reconciliation and Democratic Unification are as follows :

Presentation of Master Plan for Peaceful Unification

*(1) Principles for Unification:*The formula expressly lays down the principle of peaceful unification, not unification by means of arms or violence, of democratic unification, not unification under communism, and of national unification, not unification by classes.

In other words, the formula stresses that :

1) Neither side should insist on a unification formula of its own in adherence to its own ideology, ideas and system.

2) Unification must not be pursued exclusively or arbitrarily by any specific class or group.

3) Unification must not be sought by force of arms or other violent means.

4) Unification must be accomplished on the principle of national self-determination and through democratic and peaceful procedures that reflect the free will of the entire people.

*(2) Course Leading to Unification:*The Formula for National Reconciliation and Democratic Unification clearly sets forth a course of unification starting from the reality of national division and ending in the completion of unification. In other words, the formula provides that the two sides first form a Consultative Conference for National Reunification with representatives of the residents of the two sides to draft a unified constitution, which can be finalized through national referendum held in a free and democratic manner throughout the whole peninsula. A unified democratic republic pursuing the ideals of nationalism, democracy, liberty and welfare can then be accomplished by organizing a unified legislature and establishing a unified government through democratic general elections held under the provisions of such a unified constitution.

*(3) Pursuit of National Reconciliation to Foster Conditions for Unification:*Another feature of the new unification formula is that it ex-

181

pressly provides the form and policy of a unified nation which will not tolerate any discrimination by classes or groups. By stressing that "unification can be realized only when we promote it from the realization that the Korean people have been a single ethnic family from time immemorial, sharing a common descent, history, culture and tradition." the formula makes clear that the kind of unification the Republic of Korea pursues in democratic unification, featuring national reconciliation, rather than unification realized under communism based on class revolution.

To accomplish such a unification, the new formula suggests that the south and north of Korea jointly undertake a set of measures to ensure national reconciliation, transcending differences in ideologies through the conclusion of a Provisional Agreement on Basic Relations between south and north Korea.

Overcomming Sense the Sense of Confrontation

While laying down realistic procedures to overcome national division and pursue unification with the nation's own independent efforts, the unification formula shows the south's sincerity and magnanimity to broaden the horizon of mutual agreement to the utmost possible extent through dialogue by taking north Korea's ideas into consideration and even affirmatively encompassing part of them.

In other words, the formula proposes nationwide machinery for dialogue like the Consultative Council for National Reunification, designed to draft a unified constitution, thereby including in the subjects of discussion even such north Korean ideas of a propaganda nature as a "grand national conference," "nation wide conference" and "meeting to expedite national unification." Also by suggesting that proposals advanced by the two sides be discussed in the course of drafting a unified constitution, the new formula made it express that the Republic of Korea is willing to discuss the north Korean idea of a "confederation system" at any time.

In addition, the unification formula suggests that such issues as political ideology, the name of the unified country, basic domestic and foreign policy directions, the form of government and methods and procedures for general elections for a unified legislature be discussed and agreed on through a unified constitution to be prepared by the Consultative Conference, making it express that even north Korean ideas related thereto can be discussed.

Continuity of Unification Policy

The Formula for National Reconciliation and Democratic Unification retains and makes more concrete the basic spirit underlying the Republic of Korea's unification policy that "unification must be achieved through alleviation of tension and restoration of national trust." In other words, the new formula concretely incorporates the provisions of Items 1 and 2(consolidation of peace and restoration of mutual trust) of the existing Principles for Peaceful Unification into the seven items of a suggested Provisional Agreement on Basic Relations between South and North Korea. Similarly, the provisions of Item 3(Unification through General Elections) of the Principles is reflected in the suggested series of unification procedures.

Besides, a Provisional Agreement on Basic Relations envisaged in the unification formula encompasses the contents of the Inter-Korean Nonaggression Agreement proposed on January 18, 1974, and part of the Special Foreign Policy Statement Regarding Peace and Unification of June 23, 1973.

Chart of the Unification Formula

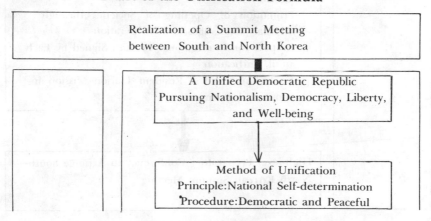

183

Formation of the Consultative Conference for National Reunification with Representatives of the People from the south and the north

↓

Drafting of a Constitution for a Unified Korea Providing: the Name of the Unified Country, the Form of Government, Basic Policies, General Elections.

↓

National Referendums to Make the Draft Constitution into Law.

↓

Democratic General Elections under the Constitution to Form a Unified Legislature and a Unified Government.

Proposal to North Korea

National Reconciliation to Be Achieved by Concluding A Provisional Agreement on Basic Relations between South and North Korea

1) Maintaining Relations on the Principle of Reciprocity and Equality
2) Peaceful Solution of Issues through Dialogue
3) Recognition of Each Other's Socio-Political System and Norinterference in Internal Affairs.
4) Adherence to the Armistice Agreement, an End to the Arms Race and Termination of the Military Confrontation
5) Promotion of Opening of Societies through Mutual Exchanges and Cooperation
6) Respect for International Treaties Signed by Each until Unification
7) Establishment of a Resident Liaison Mission in Seoul and Pyongyang

High-level Preparatory Conference to Arrange South-North Korean Summit Meeting

4. Dialogues in Several Areas

a. Overview

Beginning late 1984, dialogues were held briskly between south and north Korea in several areas, which included the South-North Red Cross Conference, an economic meeting, preliminary contacts for parliamentary talks, and a sports conference held under the aegis of the International Olympic Committee.

If the inter-Korean talks held in the 1970s, such as the preliminary Red Cross talks begun in September 1971 and the South-North Coordinating Committee meetings held in the wake of the historic July 4, 1972, South-North Joint Communique, could be taken as the Phase 1 of the South-North dialogue, then the various talks and contacts made in the 1980s can be called the Phase 2 of the dialogue.

Even after the initial dialogues were suspended due to north Korea's Kim Young-joo statement of August 28, 1973, there were contacts between the two sides on many occasions. In particular, after the birth of the Fifth Republic, an intermittent dialogue, such as a meeting to discuss the issue of fielding a single Korean delegation to the Los Angeles Olympics and of sports exchanges, was held between the south and the north. But all these talks and contacts ended as one-shot affairs without registering any tangible achievements.

The Phase 2 dialogue was diverse and brisk in terms of content. In qualitative aspects, too, the dialogue served to move a step forward the inter-Korean relationship as it reaped concrete and realistic achievements such as the exchange of dispersed family hometown visitors and art troupes amidst unprecedentedly high expectations and concern about the dialogue at home and abroad.

The Phase 2 dialogue was the result of the nations's burning desire for peaceful unification and of the positive and multi-pronged efforts the Republic of Korea government had made consistently to promote dialogue based on such a national craving.

North Korea, too, agreed to the dialogue in a bid to improve their overseas image which had fallen as a result of their involvement in the terrorist bombing in Rangoon, Burma, to foster an atmosphere ripe for their idea of a tripartite meeting aimed at engineering the pullout of U.S. forces from Korea, and to facilitate their approach to the West to surmount their continuing economic stagnation.

On January 12, 1981, south Korean President Chun Doo Hwan proposed mutual visits by the top leaders of south and north Korea as a means of providing an epochal momentum to facilitating peaceful unification through confidence building, the prevention of fratricidal conflict and the resumption of suspended dialogue between the south and the north. Again on June 5 the same year, President Chun suggested a meeting between the top leaders of the two sides, calling for the opening of the societies of south and north Korea to each other. The President said that even if the north were not in a position to open up its society completely, contacts could initially begin with sports, cultural, postal and economic exchanges, leading steadily up to complete exchanges and openings.

Moreover, in his New Year policy speech on January 22, 1982, President Chun announced before the world a Formula for National Reconciliation and Democratic Unification, in which the President stressed that the most reasonable way of achieving peaceful unification is to realize national reconciliation between the south and the north, to adopt a unified constitution by pooling the nation's will to unification, and then to accomplish a unified state under the terms of such a constitution.

President Chun further proposed to the north Korean authorities that as a practical method of ensuring the smooth preparation of a unified constitution and facilitating national reconciliation pending the time of unification, the two sides conclude a Provisional Agreement on the Basic Relations between South and North Korea consisting of seven items including clauses stipulating exchanges and cooperation between the two sides.

Based on the spirit of the Formula for National Reconciliation and Democratic Unification, the government of the Republic of Korea on February 1, 1982, proposed 20 inter-Korean pilot projects which could be implemented forthwith and which were all related to the mutual opening of society, exchanges and cooperation, and the alleviation of tensions. Also, the south called on the north time and again to agree substantially to resolve problems pending between the two sides through dialogue.

In his summer press conference on August 20, 1984, President Chun proposed mutual trade and economic cooperation between the south and the north so that the two sides could restore the national bond and realize co-prosperity, suggesting that "if the north agrees, we are willing to provide the north free of charge with the kind of technology and materials that can significantly contribute to the enhancement of the lives of the north Korean compatriots."

North Korea, which was invariably negative toward the south's series of proposals, offered relief materials to the south on September 8, 1984, in connection with a flood in some areas of the south.

At that time, south Korea was fully able to rehabilitate the flood damages through its own efforts and resources. This was why the south even declined an offer of assistance from the International League of Red Cross Societies. However, in the hope of setting a precedent for mutual assistance and providing a breakthrough in the improvement of inter-Korean relations, the south decided to accept the north's offer. North Korean flood relief materials were thus delivered and received between the south and north Korean Red Cross offices from September 29 through October 4, 1984.

With a view to using the occasion of the delivery and receipt of the relief materials to realize broader exchanges and cooperation between the two sides, the Republic of Korea National Red Cross, in a message signed by its president, Yoo Chang-soon, proposed on October 4, 1984, immediately after the delivery and receipt of the flood relief materials, the resumption of the suspended Red Cross talks. Also, Deputy Prime Minister and Economic Planning Minister Shin Byung-hyon proposed on October 12, 1984, a south-north economic meeting.

The north finally accepted the south's offers, and the south-north economic meeting was opened on November 15, 1984, for the first time. On

November 20, 1984, a preliminary contact was held at Panmunjom to prepare for the resumption of the full-dress talks of the South-North Red Cross Conference which had been suspended for about 10 years. On May 29 the following year, 1985, the eighth full-dress meeting of the South-North Red Cross talks was held in Seoul.

Meanwhile, the Supreme People's Assembly of north Korea proposed on April 9, 1985 when the second economic meeting and the eighth Red Cross meeeting were forthcoming, that a south-north parliamentary meeting be held to discuss the issue of jointly declaring nonaggression.

The National Assembly of the Republic of Korea stressed that it was proper for the government authorities of the two sides to discuss the nonaggression issue since they have the competence and responsibility to execute such a declaration. Nevertheless, the south proposed preparatory contacts to discuss various issues related to opening an inter-Korea parliamentary meeting. As a result, the first parliamentary contact was held at Panmunjom on July 23, 1985.

Beginning November 1984, in a period of little more than a year, south and north Korea thus had a total of 16 exchanges and contacts, which included five economic meetings, three Red Cross meetings and two preliminary contacts for a south-north parliamentary conference.

At the Red Cross talks, in particular, significant progress was registered in the discussions of the five agenda topics on dispersed families. Moreover, though the size was limited, an exchange of dispersed family hometown visitors and art troupes was realized to mark the first case of private citizens traveling back and forth between the two sides since national division. During the four-day hometown visits beginning September 20, 1985. 65 of the 100 visitors met 92 of their relatives in Seoul and Pyongyang despite the long disruption of more than 40 years. At the economic meetings, the two sides reached an accord in principle on the creation of a joint economic cooperation organization co-headed by a deputy prime minister-level official of each side and neared an agreement on commodity exchanges and various other economic cooperation. At the parliamentary contacts, also, the two sides shared opinions on many issues other than a few including the topics of the proposed parliamentary meeting, agreeing in principle to hold a parliamentary meeting.

Despite this progress in inter-Korean contacts, however, north Korea unilaterally suspended the dialogue using the annual Team Spirit military exercise in the south on January 20, 1986 as an excuse. The north had subsequently rejected the repeated calls of the south for the resumption of the suspended dialogue, thus terminating the Phase 2 South-North dialogue about a year after its initiation.

As the north itself stood in the way to the dialogue as they did in the dialogue during the 1970s by setting forth undue preconditions, the efforts to resolve national issues through direct dialogue between the two sides had gone nowhere. However, though the period was rather short, the Phase 2 dialogue had laid down a significant foundation by, for instance, setting a precedence for mutual assistance in inter-Korean exchanges and cooperation. It would thus be recorded as a significant period that had marked a new milestone in the history of national unification.

b. South-North Sports Talks

On March 30, 1984, north Korea, which had persistently rejected the proposal made by the Republic of Korea Amateur Sports Association(K-ASA) on June 19, 1981, for the fielding of a single inter-Korean delegation to the Olympics and other international sports events, proposed a south-north sports meeting to discuss the issue of sending a single south-north delegation to the 23rd Olympic Games slated for July the same year in Los Angeles and subsequent Asian and world championships matches. The offer, made in a letter from Kim Yu-sun, chairman of the North Koran Sports Guidance Committee and the North Korean Olympic Committee, to KASA President Chung Ju-young, came at a time when tensions were building up on the Korean peninsula more menacingly than at any other time in the past due to a series of grave provocations committed by north Korea such as the terrorist bombing in Rangoon, Burma, and the abduction of Film Director Shin Sang-ok and Actress Choi Eun-hee.

At first, the KASA was sceptical about the north Korean offer because it was almost impossible technically to discuss and form a single Korean delegation at a time when barely two months were left before the deadline for final entry for the Los Angeles Olympics and because the north had not admitted to or apologized for the terrorist bombing they perpetrated in Burma. However, in an effort to use the occasion to expand inter-Korean personnel and material exchanges and cooperation, the south accepted the north's proposal and sent the following message to the north on April 2, 1984 :

I received your letter of March 30, and first of all, I am compelled to point out the lack of any mention about the terrorist atrocity in Burma last October 9. In that attempt on the life of our Head of State, most of the members of our diplomatic delegation were murdered en masse.

It was not only a crime against compatriots who share the same blood and all other peace-loving peoples of the world, but also constituted a flagrant violation of the Olympic spirit which pursues peace and the unity of all mankind.

Even between athletes and athletic officials an apology for such heinous criminal conduct, in which compatriots were slain en masse, would be appropriate. We have demanded on several occasions in the past and will demand that the north Korean authorities take appropriate measures to atone for the Burma atrocity.

Nevertheless, we have decided to review affirmatively your proposal for talks between south and north Korean sports officials in the pure spirit of sportsmanship, separate from any other pending issue.

On many occasions, we have already urged that single delegations be formed to take part in the 23rd Olympics in Los Angeles this coming July and in various future world championships.

On June 19, 1981, Cho Sang-ho, then president of the Korean Olympic Committee, proposed that single inter-Korean teams be formed for the 1984 Los Angeles Olympics and the 1982 New Delhi Asian Games, and suggested to your side that an inter-Korean sports delegates meeting be held as soon as possible.

When we made the offer for joint participation as a single inter-Korean team three years before Los Angeles Olympics, we expected north Korea to respond affir-

matively without hesitation. Again in the proposal for 20 inter-Korean pilot projects which the government of the Republic of Korea put forth to north Korea on February 1, 1982, we called for an exchange of goodwill games in the south and the north, the formation of single teams for various international matches, and goodwill exchanges between people in the athletic world.

All these proposals were advanced from the perspective of national reconciliation, and, therefore, there was no reason whatsoever why you shouldn't have accepted them. But you did not.

It is fortunate, however, that you have, albeit belatedly, responded affirmatively to our offer to form single teams for the 1984 Olympics and various other international games.

We expect that south and north Korea will be able to form single delegations to take part jointly not only in the Los Angeles Olympics but also in the 1986 Asian Games and the 1988 Olympics to be held in Seoul.

The south and the north came in third and fourth, respectively, in the New Delhi Asian Games in 1982. Though we failed to win the glory of winning first place, we proved our people's ability to all the world. Had we formed a single delegation for the New Delhi Games, we might have even won first place.

Considering that West and East Germany held some 200 meetings over a period of more than five years from June 1951 to November 1956 before they could form a single team for the Olympics in the 1950s, it can't be said there is enough time to prepare for the 1986 Asian Games and the 1988 Olympics in Seoul not to mention the Los Angeles Olympics in 1984.

Therefore, we had better hold various goodwill games in Seoul and Pyongyang in turns even beginning right from this April so that we can strongly demonstrate both at home and abroad our mutual determination to form single teams and hasten without the slightest delay the selection of players to participate on single inter-Korean teams in the Los Angeles Olympics and other international games.

In order to facilitate the smooth progress of the talks to arrange for such single teams and sports exchange programs, a direct telephone line should be opened between south and north Korea.

To discuss these questions, we propose the following :

Time of first meeting : 10 a.m., April 9, 1984

Site : Conference Room, Neutral Nations Supervisory Commission, Panmunjom

Delegations : Four delegates each, with the senior delegates being the deputy heads of the sports associations and Olympic committees.

Agenda :

1. The question of forming single inter-Korean teams for the 1984 Los Angeles Olympics, 1986 Asian Games, 1986 Asian Games, 1988 Olympics and other international games to be held in the days ahead.

2. The question of holding inter-Korean athletic exchanges.

I Look forward to your affirmative response.

(1) First Meeting

Because north Korea agreed to the south's proposal, the first south-north sports meeting was held at 10 a.m. April 9, 1984, at the conference room of the Neutral Nations Supervisory Commission. The two delegations were as follows :

Delegation of the South

Chief Delegate : Kim Chong-kyu, vice presidnet of the Korean Amateur Sports Association and the Korean Olympic Committee.

Delegate : Kim Chong-ha, chairman of the Korean Handball Association and concurrently permanent member of the Korean Olympic Committee.

Delegate : Lee Chong-ha, a member of the Korea University Sports Committee

Delegate : Im Tae-sun, a director of the Korean Soccer Association and concurrently a member of the Korean Olympic Committee

Delegate : Nam Chong-mun, a director of the Korean Table Tennis Association and concurrently director of the Korean Amateur Sports Association.

192

Delegation of the North

Chief Delegate : Kim Duk-jun, vice chairman of the North Korean Olympic Committee

Deputy Chief Delegate : Pak Mu-song, deputy chief secretary of the North Korean Olympic Committee

Delegate : Kim Se-jin, a member of the North Korean Olympic Committee and concurrently vice chairman of the North Korean Sports Technique Guidance Committee

Delegate : Suh Myong-ho, a member of the North Korean Olympic Committee.

Delegate : Sok Tae-ho, a member of the North Korean Olympic Committee.

Because the north's chief delegate Kim Duk-jun could not attend for reasons unknown, four delegates form each side attended the first meeting.

At the meeting, the south's delegation stressed that the sports persons of the two sides of Korea cannot engage in any exchanges and cooperation freely under the circumstances in which north Korea committed acts of grave provocation such as the Burma terrorist bombing and the kidnapping of Choi Eun-hee and Shin Sang-ok. The Seoul delegation then demanded that the north duly admit to and apologize for the incidents and take appropriate measures to atone for them.

The south's delegates went on to say that how the north reacts to these demand would serve as a yardstick to measure their sincerity toward the sports talks, and also would directly affect the question of the personal safety of the south's athletes and sports officials in the event they jointly participate in international matches in the north in an exchange of games to form single teams for international competitions.

Reminding the north's delegation of the fact that Seoul had repeatedly called for inter-Korean sports exchanges and the formation of single teams to take part in international matches, the south's delegation suggested that various inter-Korean sports matches be held on both sides right from April to manifest at home and abroad the Koreans' resolve to form single

193

delegations. It noted that the remaining time was not sufficient for the two sides to discuss and form single teams for the 1986 Asian Games and the 1988 Olympics much less the 1984 Los Angeles Olympics.

From this basic standpoint, the south suggested, as the agenda topics of the sports meeting, 1) the question of forming single inter-Korean teams for the 1984 Los Angeles Olympics, the 1986 Asian Games, the 1988 Olympics and other international games to be held in the days ahead, and 2) the question of holding inter-Korean sports exchanges.

The south's delegation then advanced the following seven-point proposal in connection with the first topic of the agenda, that was, the question of forming sigle teams for international games.

1. Selection of Athletes

a. The best-qualified athletes shall be selected through selection matches held according to the sporting event.

b. Selection matches shall be held in places in south and north Korea such as Seoul and Pyongyang.

c. Details shall be determined by committees to be set up according to the sporting event.

2. Formation of Delegations

Delegations shall be formed through mutual discussion based on the IOC Charter, and other documents.

3. Training of Athletes

a. The existing facilities in the south and the north shall be used to the utmost extent possible in training the selected athletes. If necessary, joint stadiums shall be prepared in the Demilitarized Zone.

b. Other matters necessary for training shall be resolved as agreed on between the sports organizations of the two sides.

4. Expenses for Delegations

The expenses for the delegations shall be in principle borne jointly.

5. Flag of Delegations

The word "KOREA" in Roman letters below the Olympic symbol of five rings.

6. Anthem for Delegations

194

"Arirang" shall be the anthem of the delegations.

7. Title of Delegations

The title of the delegations shall be "Korea" in English and "Taehan" in Korean.

Meanwhile, the north's delegation asserted that the Burma incident and the abduction of Choi Eun-hee and Shin Sang-ok were fabricated by the south and had nothing to do with the sports talks. When the meeting entered the discussion of operational and procedural matters, the north's delegation agreed to discuss various issues such as the selection of a conference site and the operation of a direct inter-Korean telephone line. They even suggested as agenda topics 1) the issue of the participation by the north and the south in the 23rd Olympic Games and subsequent international games as single teams, and 2) the issue of carrying out collaboration and exchanges between the north and the south in the area of sports.

At this point, however, the north made an abrupt aboutface and insisted repeatedly that unless the south's delegation retracted its remarks about the Burma incident and the kindnapping of Choi Eun-hee and Shin Sang-ok, they won't carry on the talks any further. They then walked out of the conference room unilaterally, rejecting the south's suggestion that the two sides should at least decide on the time of the next meeting.

After the meeting broke up, the Seoul side regretted the insincere attitude the north showed at the sports meeting that culminated in their one-sided walkout from the meeting. This regret was expressed in a press conference held by chief delegate Kim Chong-kyu and in a statement issued by Chung Ju-young, president of the Korean Amateur Sports Association. The south stressed that the sports meeting should be resumed at an early date to discuss concretely the "question of forming single inter-Korean delegations for the 1984 Los Angeles Olympics, the 1986 Asian Games, the 1988 Seoul Olympics and other future international games as well as the question of sports exchanges between south and north Korea." It then proposed that a second meeting be held at the conference room of the Neutral Nations Supervisory Commission within that week, saying

195

that details of the proposal would be furnished in a message later.

(2) Seond Meetting

As a result of two calls made by the south on April 12 and April 17 for the resumption of the sports talks, the second inter-Korean sports meeting was held for four hours and thirty-seven minutes on April 30, 1984, with the participation of five delegates from cach side.

From the very beginning, the north's delegation tried to shift the blame for the breakup of the first meeting to the south, asserting that the Burma incident was the south's fabrication. The meeting thus failed even achieve any tangible business.

The delegation from the south expressed regret at the one-sided walkout by the north's delegation at the first meeting, urging the north to try to carry out the meeting sincerely in an air of mutual trust and harmony based on sportsmanship and brotherly love.

The south's delegation stressed that the incidents like the terrorist bombing in Burma and the abduction of Choi Eun-hee and Shin Sang-ok basically undermined the atmosphere of inter-Korean trust and harmony and ran squarely counter to the south-north dialogue. It then again urged the north to take acceptable measures, pointing out that the way north Korea handles the Burma incident would be linked to the basic issue of whether the north is truly interested in dialogue.

As for the question of the agenda, the south's delegation called for the adoption of the two-point agenda it advanced at the first meeting, saying that its version, in fact, incorporated even the north Korean idea on the agenda issue and its wording was clearer than the north's. It then suggested that inasmuch as the Los Angeles Olympics were already at hand, "matches to select athletes for a single team be held promptly in Seoul and Pyongyang in turns" and that committees by sporting event be formed to discuss details related to the selection of athletes.

Meanwhile, the north's delegation, by redressing the idea they advanced at the first meeting, produced an eight-point suggestion for the formation of single team and another five-point idea on the forming of a single team to take part in the Log Angeles Olympics. They then called for prior debate of their ideas, trying to give the impression that they were positive toward the talks. The new north Korean ideas were as follows :

–Idea for Formation of Single Team –
1. Principle and Method of Selection of Athletes
a. Selection of best qualified athletes.

b. The sites of selection matches shall be in the areas of the south and the north and if necessary, in the Demilitarized Zone.

c. Athletes and guidance members shall be selected from among those of the south and the north by sporting event.

2. Training of Athletes
The facilities of the south and the north shall be used in turns. If necessary, training may be held at third places.

3. Finance and Guarantee of Conditions
Expenses shall be borne by the side which offers the sites. In the event training is held at a third place, expenses shall be borne jointly.

4. Members of Delegations
The number of delegation members shall be determined through mutual agreement and based on the IOC Charter and the regulations of the various sports federations.

5. Title of Single Delegation
"Koryo" and also "Koryo" in English.

6. Flag of Single Delegation
The Korean map in brown color on a white back ground with the inscription "KORYO" in English below the map.

7. Anthem of Single Delegation
"Arirang"

8. Establishment of Joint Secretariat for Single Team (Panmunjom)
Disposition of working matters such as the formation and preparation of single team.

–Idea for Formation of Single
Team for Los Angeles Olympics–

1. The sporting events to be participated in shall be determined through discussions between the south and the north.

2. The selection of athletes shall be completed by May 20.

3. Selection of Athletes

a. Selection shall be made in principle through selection matches.

b. In the sporting events where the teams are qualified to take part in the Olympics through preliminary games, the qualified teams shall absorb outstanding athletes from the other side.

c. In other events, the two sides shall recommend and select participating athletes based on their latest records made abroad or at home.

4. Joint training shall be conducted from June 1 until prior to departure.

5. Other matters shall be resolved based on the ideas for the formation of single team and through discussions between delegates of the respective sporting events.

As the north's delegates disputed the internal affairs and system of the south, the conference atmosphere was unprecedentedly tension-packed. The second meeting thus ended without any discussion of the agenda issue. The two sides decided to determine whether to hold the third meeting through several messages.

(3) Third Meeting

The third meeting, attended by five delegates from each side, was held at the conference room of the Neutral Nations Supervisory Commission on May 25, 1984.

At the meeting, the north's delegation, setting forth new prerequisites, demanded the south's advance acceptance of their prerequisites while rejecting the repeated calls of the south for the discussion of agenda topics. The third meeting thus came to an end without even entering debate on essential issues.

It was especially noteworthy how the north would behave at the third meeting as the meeting came one day after north Korea joined the Prague declaration by the sports officials of 11 Communist-bloc countries boycotting the Los Angeles Olympics.

Pointing out that no progress had been registered at the talks despite the fact that the Los Angeles Olympics was merely two months away and that one and a half months had elapsed since the meeting began, the Seoul delegation urged that the two sides discuss the two-point agenda produced at the first and second meetings, producing details about the ideas.

In particular, regarding the second item, "the question of carrying out south-north sports exchanges," the south's delegation laid down a seven-point method of implementation, expressing the hope that a debate would be made smoothly at the third meeting. The seven-point method was that 1) sports matches shall be held between the south and the north, 2) mutual participation in each other's domestic sporting events shall be guaranteed, 3) athletes and sports officials shall be allowed to travel back and forth between the south and the north, 4) skills and materials related to sports shall be exchanged between the south and the north. 5) journalists shall be allowed to visit each other's areas to cover sports events, other sports activities and facilities, 6) conveniences shall be mutually provided for the training of athletes in each other's areas, and 7) lectures on sports shall be held jointly between the south and the north, and joint sports facilities shall be created inside the Demilitarized Zone, the cost of which will be covered jointly by the two sides.

However, the north, in trying to shift the blame for the breakoff of the talks to the south, insisted that the previous two meetings broke up because the southern side made "political provocations" having nothing to do with the essential issue of the sports meetings. The north's delegation then set forth two prerequisites for normalizing the talks: 1) the south must admit to and apologize for obstructing the formation of a single team for the Los Angeles Olympics by making political remarks at the sports meetings, and 2) the south must guarantee that it would not raise any political issue or make political provocations at the meetings. The north thus refused to discuss agenda topics despite the south's repeated urging, and one-sidedly suspended the third meeting. They refused even to set the time of the fourth meeting, asserting that the issue of the next meetng could be discussed through letters.

Meanwhile, in a message delivered to the north on May 29, 1984, Chung Ju-young, president of the Korean Amateur Sports Association, suggested that the fourth sports meeting be held at Panmunjom on June 1. In the message, Chung again asked the north to reflect on their attitude, pointing out that the posture they showed at the third meeting made onlookers doubt if the north was truly interested in the formation of a single inter-Korean delegation to participate in the Los Angeles Olympics.

North Korea did not respond until they belatedly sent a letter to the south on the afternoon of June 1, informing the south that they would not attend the fourth meeting unless the preconditions they produced at the third meeting were met.

The north's maneuvering showed that from the beginning their policy was to join with their fellow socialist countries in boycotting the Los Angeles Olympics.Nonetheless,they proposed a single team only to find an excuse to shift the blame for the formation of a single inter-Korean team on the south and also to block the south's demand for an apology over the Burma incident on the grounds that such a demand only stood in the way of sports talks, thereby attempting to shun international censure over the issue.

Despite the entire nation's desire and the sincere efforts of the south to make the talks a success, it was made impossible for south and north Korea to field a single team to the Los Angeles Olympics.

Chung Ju-young held a press conference on June 2, the deadline for the final entry for the Los Angeles Olympics, to explain that it had become unavoidable for the south and the north to participate in the Olympics separately. Chung said that despite the failure to form a single team for the Los Angeles Games, "there would be no change in the policy of his

Olympic Committee to continue to promote sports talks to discuss and form single teams for various international games as well as to resolve the question of inter-Korean sports exchanges." He then called on the north once again to agree to resume the sports talks at an early date.

On the other hand, the North Korean Olympic Committee on June 2 formally announced their boycott of the Los Angeles Olympics. The north attempted to justify their boycott with the unreasonable argument that "no safety of athletes can be guaranteed in a place where anti-Communist and anti-socialist schemes are openly conspired" and that "separate participation in the Olympics would run counter to national wishes."

North Korea also asserted that the Olympics "should be held in a place where the athletes of all countries can take part in games safely and freely without any political pressure or any mental or physical constraint," adding that "as we believe this is the most exigent issue facing the future Olympic movement, we shall spare no efforts in the resolution of the question in cooperation with all National Olympic Committees." These remarks show well that they were not seriously concerned with the formation of a single team from the beginning of the sports meeting.

c. Delivery and Receipt of Relief Goods and Working-Level Contacts

(1) Initiation of Working-Level Red Cross Contacts

In his summer press conference on August 20, 1984, President Chun Doo Hwan stressed that "such abnormal inter-Korean relations as exist today should be done away with at an early date and instead an age of inter-Korean exchanges and cooperation should be opened to facilitate national reconciliation and peaceful unification." Expressing willingness to enter into "inter-Korean trade and economic cooperation," the Prsident said that if north Korea agrees "we are willing to provide the north with various technologies and commodities free of charge which would substantially contribute to improving the lives of our brethren there."

President Chun pointed out that "the south produces high-quality daily necessities, medicines, automobiles and various machines in large amounts for both domestic consumption and export to the world market, while north Korea is exporting such resources as coal and iron ore, which the south lacks." Stressing that he sees no reason why south and north Korea cannot trade and cooperate with their brethren when they are doing so with third countries, the President urged the north to join in the efforts of the Republic of Korea to promote national reconciliation and unification.

President Chun's proposal was intended to forestall the waste of national energies stemming from the abnormal conditions of inter-Korean relations and also to lay a solid foundation for unification by enriching mutual trust through exchanges and cooperation. At the same time, the overture embodied the south's determination to help resolve the chronic economic stagnation north Korea suffers and the resultant plight of the north Korean people, and thereby pursue the co-prosperity of the 60 million Korean people.

As of yet, no signs of improvement in the inter-Korean relationship were seen because the north, in a commentary appearing in the *Rodong Shinmun* on August 25, 1984, rejected the proposal. It was around this time the North Korean Red Cross (NKRC) suddenly on September 8, 1984, said in a radio broadcast that the NKRC decided to provide flood victims in south Korea with 225,950 bushels of rice, 500,000 meters of fabric, 100,000 tons of cement and various medicines. It then asked the Republic of Korea National Red Cross (ROKNRC) for positive cooperation in the "speedy delivery" of the materials to flood victims.

In response, the ROKNRC said that although some human and material losses were suffered in the heavy rains in August, relief and rehabilitation work had been completed in a short span of time thanks to the concerted efforts and warm-heartedness of the people. Accordingly, the ROKNRC said, it had already declined an offer for assistance by the International League of Red Cross Societies. Nevertheless, the ROKNRC decided to accept the north Korean offer in the hope that such an occaion could be used profitably in providing a breakthrough in the efforts to improve inter-Korean relations. The ROKNRC president issued the following statement on September 14, expressing the hope that contacts between working-level officials of the two Red Cross Societies could be held at an early date to discuss procedures for the receipt of the proposed materials.

In a press conference on last August 20, President Chun Doo Hwan emphasized the need for inter-Korean economic exchanges and cooperation and announced a willingness to provide north Korea free of charge with the kind of expertise and materials which would be helpful in improving the lives of the north Korean people.

Our proposal for the provision of daily necessities to the north Korean people stemmed from pure brotherly love and a humanitarian spirit. It was hoped that they would help meet the north Korean people's need for such daily necessities as household items and medicines.

While north Korea expressed a negative attitude toward our humanitarian proposal, the North Korean Red Cross announced in a radio broadcast last September 8 that it would provide 225,950 bushels of rice, 500,000 meters of fabric, 100,000 tons of cement and various medicines to the victims of our recent flood.

Some people were left homeless or suffered property damage in the flood in Seoul and some provincial areas. But we have been able to rehabilitate them completely in a short span of time thanks to the concerted efforts of the people. We have thus completed the work of repairing the flood damage. Yet we appreciate the concern of the North Korean Red Cross for our suffering caused by the flood.

In line with the spirit of the humanitarian proposal made by President Chun last August 20, the Republic of Korea National Red Cross hereby accepts the offer of the North Korean Red Cross. We hope that the materials specified by north Korea will be delivered to us within this month. It would be good if the North Korean Red Cross were to carry the goods to either Inchon or Pusan Harbor by ship.

When the International League of Red Cross Societies offered assistance last September 3 for our flood victims, we politely declined it because we could fully rehabilitate them with our own efforts. Nevertheless, we accept the north Korean offer in the sincere hope of paving the way for genuine mutual assistance between fellow Koreans beginning with humanitarian areas, and for improving inter-Korean relations.

Should any calamities occur in north Korea in the future, we will not spare our efforts to provide materials from a humanitarian standpoint. We hope that this new contact and exchange to be realized between the Red Cross Societies of south and north Korea will serve as an occasion to foster an atmosphere of reconciliation and mutual assistance between south and north Korea, and that such humanitarian exchanges will be expanded.

We hope that working-level officials' contacts will be held at an early date between the two Red Cross societies to discuss procedures to receive the goods offered by the North Korean Red Cross.

The NKRC said in a radio broadcast on September 14 that they agreed to working-level contacts and would send five delegates headed by Han Ung-sik, vice chairman of the Central Committee of the North Korean Red Cross, to the conference room of the Neutral Nations Supervisory Commission at Panmunjom at 10 a.m. September 18, 1984.

The ROKNRC, in a radio message on September 15, announced the list of its five delegates headed by Lee Yong-duk, the vice ROKNRC president. The NKRC, too, notified the south of the list of its delegates on September 17. working-level contacts were thus set to open between the south and north Korean Red Cross societies. The list of the two delegations was as follows:

ROKNRC Delegation

Chief delegate : Lee Yong-duk, ROKNRC vice president
Delegate : Cho Chol-hwa, ROKNRC secretary general
Delegate : Song Yong-dae, a member of the ROKNRC's Disaster Relief Committee
Delegate : Choi Eun-bom, director of the ROKNRC Relief Ser-

vice Department

Delegate : Lee Jun-hi, advisory member for ROKNRC Social Services

NKRC Delegation

Chief delegate : Han Ung-sik, vice chairman of the NKRC Central Committee

Delegate : Choi Won-sok, a permanent member of the NKRC Central Committee

Delegate : Choi Ki-bong, director of the NKRC Central Committee

Delegate : Paek Yong-ho, deputy chief secretary of the NKRC Central Committee

Delegate : Lee Nam-in, vice chairman of the NKRC Nampo Committee

(2) Working-Level Contacts and Delivery and Receipt of Relief Materials

An inter-Korean Red Cross working-level contact was held at the conference room of the Neutral Nations Supervisory Commission at 10 a.m. September 18, 1984, which lasted no shorter than six hours and 35 minutes.

At the contact, ROKNRC chief delegate Lee Yong-dok said it was good for the NKRC to show concern about the south's flood damages and to offer materials for flood victims, and suggested the following procedures for the delivery and receipt of the materials.

First, the materials should be delivered and received between the Red Cross Societies of south and north Korea.

Second, the delivery and receipt of the materials should be completed by the end of September.

Third, the mateials should be transported by ship.

Fourth, taking the distance into consideration the point of the delivery and receipt of the materials should be Inchon Harbor.

205

Fifth, all the materials should delivered and received on a packaged basis.

Sixth, to facilitate business related to the delivery and receipt of the materials, a direct inter-Korean telephone line should be operated.

ROKNRC chief delegate Lee explained that under the regulations of the International League of Red Cross Societies and general practices, relief goods are usually delivered to the place designated by the recipient side. So it would be most convenient to use Inchon Harbor for the speedy and effective transport of the materials since it is the shortest distance from the port of Nampo, north Korea. The NKRC, on the other hand, insisted that the materials be transported by both land and sea and suggested Seoul and the harbors of Sokcho, Inchon and Pusan as points of delivery.

As for the method of delivery, the NKRC maintained that the materials should be delivered and received in ceremonies attended by north Korean officials and pressmen, who, they argued, should be allowed to visit the scenes of flooding to "console" the flood victims.

Initially the ROKNRC suggested that the materials be transported to the south by sea only, but later agreed in principle to land transport as well, as the north asserted that the materials had already been assembled at Kaesong for overland transport. Regarding sea transport, the ROKNRC counter-proposed that Pukpyong Harbor be used instead of Sokcho as suggested by the north, saying that Pukpyong has better harbor facilities than Sokcho. The NKRC accepted the proposal and an agreement was thus reached on the use of Inchon on the west coast and Pukpyong on the east coast.

Regarding overland transport, however, the two sides could not come to terms. The ROKNRC suggested that the goods should be transported overland to an area south of Panmunjom, whereas the north insisted the materials should be transported all the way to Seoul.

Despite repeated calls by the ROKNRC for a delivery point south of Panmunjom, the NKRC delegates unilaterally walked out of the conference room, saying that the next contact should be on September 21. Thus the inter-Korean Red Cross contacts, held for the first time in seven years after the 25th Red Cross working-level meeting of December 1977, ended without any substantial achievement as the north contravened the spirit of humanitarianism.

After the working-level contacts, both Lee Yong-duk, ROKNRC chief delegate, and Yoo Chang-soon, ROKNRC president, each issued a statement expressing regret over the failure to reach any agreement on the delivery and receipt of materials due to insincerity on the part of the north.

ROKNRC President Yoo, in particular, said that "if north Korea is truly interested in offering materials, it should, witout sticking to preconditions, transport materials to Inchon, Pukoyong and Panmunjom by ship or truck by the end or September." He let it be known that "if only the north informs the south about a concrete plan to deliver all the materials by the end of September, the south would take steps necessary for the receipt of the materials in the most speedy and simple manner."

The text of ROKNRC President Yoo's statement was as follows :

As was already reported, the inter-Korean working-level contacts held at Panmunjom today broke off as the north Korean delegation walked out of the conference room unilateraly despite our delegation's call for continuous discussion to resolve all questions today.

Today's inter-Korean Red Cross working-level contacts were designed to discuss procedures for the delivery of the materials the North Korean Red Cross offered to our flood victims, to the Republic of Korea National Red Cross. Nevertheless, the north Korean side held fast to the incomprehensible assertions from the outset that in disregard of the principles and practices of international Red Cross activities, they would carry the materials aboard their trucks directly to flood victims all across the country and console them.

In accordance with Red Cross practices in which recipient countries designate the points of the delivery of materials, we gave the harbor of Inchon as the site of the delivery of materials to enable us to receive their materials in the most speedy and convenient way. And we made concessions and showed sincerity by additionally designating Pukpyong and Panmunjom as the sites of delivery as the north wished.

The north Korean side, however, turned a deaf ear to our effort to select Inchon, Pukpyong and Panmunjom as the sites of the delivery, and discuss other procedural matters. They instead insisted to the end on carrying the materials to Seoul, thus revealing that their offer for materials was not motivated by genuine humanitarianism and brotherly love.

We believe that unless there is a basic change in their attitude, any continuation of the inter-Korean Red Cross contacts would be totally meaningless.

We regret that due to north Koreas insincerity, no agreement was reached on such a simple matter as could be fully resolved with today's single-day contacts.

If the north is truly interested in offering materials, they can simply transport them to Inchon, Pukpyong and Panmunjom by ship and automobile by the end of month without insisting on other conditions.

If north Korea informs us in advance of a concrete plan to deliver materials completely by the end of September, we shall take necessary measures to receive the materials in the most speedy and simple manner.

Meanwhile, because the voice of wariness was raised against the "ulterior motives behind the north's offer veiled with humanitarianism" and public opinion at home and abroad had turned unfavorable to the north because of the unreasonable insistence they showed during the contacts and their unilateral walkout, the north made an abrupt aboutface on September 19, saying, in a statement issued by their chief delegate to the working-level contacts, that they would transport the materials to Inchon, Bukpyong and Panmunjom as designated by the ROKNRC.

The ROKNRC accepted the delivery schedule the north offered in its changed attitude, thus paving the way for the delivery and receipt of materials for flood victims between the two Red Cross Societies. Following concrete discussions, through the exchange of telephone messages at eight separate times, of matters related to the delivery and receipt of materials, such as the method of delivery and conveniences for north Korean personel and their personal safety, the two Red Cross Societies completed the delivery and receipt of the materials for flood victims in four days from September 29 through October 4.

Another achievement incidental to the Red Cross project was the reopening of a direct inter-Korean telephone line effective September 29, 1984, eight years and one month after the suspension of the hotline. The north belatedly agreed to the repeated calls for the operation of a hotline made by the south during the working-level contacts. The operational guidelines of the direct south-north telephone line which the two sides tentatively agreed on during the working-level contacts of September 18 and finally confirmed in their telephone messages of October 8 and October 11, were as follows:

– Operational Guidelines for the Direct South-North Telephone Line –

1. A direct telephone line between south and north Korean Red Cross Societies shall be operated continuously in the future.

2. The direct south-north Red Cross telephone line shall in principle be operated between 9 to 12 a.m. in the morning and between 2 to 5 p.m. in the afternoon every day except for Sundays and the public holidays of either of the two sides. However, if both sides consider it necessary, the direct telephone line shall be operated at pre-determined times and dates without being bound by the times and dates given above.

3. Either of the two sides shall notify the other side of its public holiday 24 hours in advance.

4. Test calls between communications working-level officials of the two sides shall be made between 8 to 9 a.m. every day. On odd days, the south shall make test calls and on even days the north. If anything unusual happens on the circuit of the direct telephone line, a check shall be asked at any time.

5. The secrecy of the contents of telephone coversation of the direct

south-north Red Cross telephone line shall be guaranteed through mutual agreement.

d. South-North Red Cross Conference

(1) Red Cross Preliminary Contacts and Full-Dress Talks

With a view to expanding exchanges and cooperation between the south and north Korean Red Cross Societies with the delivery and receipt of relief materials as the momentum, the Republic of Korea National Red Cross proposed the resumption of the suspended south-north Red Cross talks. The offer was made in a message delivered to Son Song-pil, chairman of the Central Committee, North Korean Red Cross, through Han Ung-sik, chief NKRC delegate to the Red Cross working-level contacts and one of the senior NKRC officials who came to the south to deliver the materials for flood victims to the ROKNRC, on October 4, 1984, when the delivery and receipt of the relief materials were ended.

The full text of the message, which ROKNRC President Yoo Chang-soon made public in a press conference on October 6, was as follows:

It pleases me greatly that the Red Cross Societies of south and north Korea have successfully completed the delivery and receipt of materials for our flood victims. I appreciate the efforts your side made to send the materials by mobilizing a considerable number of personnel and transportation means. Let me inform you know that the materials we received are being distruibuted equally to flood victims.

The giving and receiving of the materials between the Red Cross Societies of south and north Korea was a historic event transcending the barriers of division in the aspects of brotherly love and humanitarianism.

In this sense, I believe the humanitarian project we have accomplished recently will serve as a good precedent for broadening the avenue for new contacts and exchanges between south and north Korea which have dissociated themselves from each other.

All the compatriots of the south and the north hope that the recent flow of materials for flood victims will not end as merely a giving and taking of materials but will grow into a broader humanitarian project to help reunite the families and relatives dispersed in the south and the north.

To look back, no less than 13 years have passed since we began the south-north Red Cross conference to realize the reunion of 10 million separated family members. It is heartbreaking that we have thus far made little progress toward resuming the suspended talks, let alone mitigating even a bit the pains of the separated relatives.

It is indeed unfortunate and deplorable that in spite of today's international trend of mutual visits and exchanges made beyond the boundaries of ideologies and systems, the reality of south and north Korea remains to be such that people have no way to learn the fates of their families and relatives and to exchange letters with them despite their being relatively so near on the same land.

Therefore, to facilitate the exchange of information and open the way for reunion between separated families on the two sides is an ardent wish of all the Korean people and also a solemn mission our Red Cross workers should accomplish. It is a most urgent task we cannot afford to put off.

From this point of view, I am convinced that the recently rare inter-Korean Red Cross contact should, without fail, lead to talks aimed at realizing the reunion of dispersed families.

Beliveing that your side agrees in principle to our position that the South-North Red Cross Conference should be resumed as soon as possible, I hope that a meeting will be held by the end of this month, if possible. I look forward to an affirmative response from your side.

Chairman Son Song-pil of the NKRC Central Committee, in a telephone message on October 29, accepted the ROKNRC proposal for the resumption of the Red Cross talks, suggesting that preliminary contacts be held at the conference room of the Neutral Nations Supervisory Commission at Panmunjom at 10 a.m. November 20 to discuss matters related to the resumption of the suspended talks. Son also said his Red Cross would send three delegates to Panmunjom on that day.

In a telephone message on November 14, the ROKNRC notified the NKRC of the list of its three delegates – Chief delegate Cho Chol-hwa, ROKNRC secretary general, and delegates Song Yong-dae, a ROKNRC Disaster Relief Committee member, and Choi Eun-bom, ROKNRC Relief Service Department director. Two days later on November 16, the NKRC notified the ROKNRC that their delegates included So Song-chol, chief delegate and permanent member of the NKRC Central Committee, Park Yong-su, a delegate and NKRC Central Committee deputy director, and Park Dong-chun, a delegate and NKRC Central Committee division chief. Preliminary contacts were thus set to be held between the south and north Korean Red Cross societies.

At the preliminary contacts held at the conference room of the Neutral Nations Supervisory Commission at Panmunjom from 10 a.m. November 20, 1984, the two sides could reach an agreement easily since discussions were made in the form chiefly of reaffirming various operational procedures such as the topics, venue and the composition of delegations, based on what were already agreed on between the two sides through their preliminary contacts of 1971 and 1972.

ROKNRC Chief Delegate Cho Chol-hwa suggested that the two sides reaffirm the various items which both sides had already agreed to with respect to the operation of the full-dress south-north Red Cross meetings, and discuss any additional matters, if any, that needed to be agreed on. He then offered the following items for discussion.

1. The Venue of the Eighth Full-Dress Meeting

The venue of the eighth full-dress south-north Red Cross meeting should be Seoul in accordance with the arrangement made at the third south-north Red Cross preliminary meeting of October 6, 1971, that full-dress meetings would be held in Seoul and Pyongyang in turns.

2. The Topics of Full-Dress Meetings.

The topics of full-dress south-north Red Cross meetings should be, as agreed on at the 20th south-north Red Cross preliminary meeting of June 16, 1972, as follows :

1) The question of ascertaining, and notifying thereof, the whereabouts and fate of the dispersed families and relatives in the south and the north ;
2) The question of facilitating free mutual visits and free meeting among the dispersed families and relatives in the south and the north ;
3) The question of facilitating free postal exchanges among the dispersed families and relatives in the south and the north ;
4) The question of facilitating the reunions of the dispersed families according to their free individual wishes ; and
5) Other humanitarian problems to be settled.

3. The Delegations to Full-Dress Meetings
As agreed on between the two sides, delegations to the full-dress meetings shall be headed by Red Cross vice president-level officials and should each comprise seven delegates, seven consultants, 20 attendants and 25 press members.

4. The Operating of a Permanent Conference Liaison Office
The function of the permanent conference liaison office established under an agreement reached at the second south-north Red Cross preliminary meeting of September 29, 1971, shall be normalized, and the direct telephone line between the Freedom House and Panmungak reopened for operation.

5. Other Operational Procedures for Full-Dress Meetings
Matters related to personal safety, procedures for visits, period of stay and the schedule of talks, emblems, equipment and belongings, transportation, communications, activities outside the conference site, facilities at the conference site, recording of talks, whether to open the talks to the public, press coverage, conference proceedings, the drafting and announcing of agreements, and provision of conveniences, shall be in accordance with the agreement reached at the 25th south-north Red Cross preliminary meeting of August 11, 1972.

6. The Time of the Eighth Full-Dress Meeing

The time of the eighth full-dress south-north Red Cross meeting should be by the end of the month from the date of the conclusion of these preliminary contacts.

The NKRC delegation agreed basically to this ROKNRC proposal. But it demanded a readjustment of some of the items, contending that the Red Cross meeting had been suspended over a protracted period of time and the objective situation had changed much during the period.

As to the formation of the delegations, the NKRC suggested that the number of press members on each side be increased from 25 to 50 and the number of attendants be reduced from 20 to 15. The north reasoned that an increase in the number of press members was unavoidable because more publishing and press media had come into being during the period and because press and publishing equipment had become diversified. The ROKNRC, in response, suggested that the number of attendants remain at 20 as before but agreed to increase the number of press members to 50 as suggested by the NKRC. The two sides thus agreed to set the numbers of press members and attendants at 50 and 20, respectively.

In addition, the NKRC delegation, pointing out that the full-dress meeting would be resumed after a suspension of 11 years, tenaciously insisted on an exchange of art troupes so that the eighth and ninth full-dress meetings scheduled for Seoul and Pyongyang, respectively, could be held in a festive atmosphere.

The ROKNRC delegation rejected the NKRC idea, stressing that such festive programs are not compatible with the original aim of the Red Cross talks and the wish of the 10 million dispersed family members for the early conclusion of the Red Cross talks. It then suggested that the hosting side take charge of art performances as in the past.

The matters agreed on between the two sides at the preliminary contact were as follows :

1. The Venue of the Full-Dress Meetings

The eighth full-dress meeting shall be held in Seoul and the ninth full-dress meeting in Pyongyang.

2. The Topics of the Full-Dress Meetings

The topics shall be the five items agreed on at the 20th south-north Red Cross preliminary meeting of June 16, 1972:

1) The question of ascertaining, and notifying thereof, the whereabouts and fate of the dispersed families and relatives in the south and the north;

2) The question of facilitating free mutual visits and free meetings among the dispersed families and relatives in the south and the north;

3) The question of facilitating free postal exchanges among the dispersed families and relatives in the south and the north;

4) The question of facilitating reunions of the dispersed families according to their free individual wishes; and

5) Other humanitarian problems to be settled.

3. The Forming of Delegations to Full-Dress Meetings.

Each delegation shall be composed of seven delegates, seven consultants, 20 attendants and 50 press members.

4. The Operating of a Permanent Conference Liaison Office.

The function of the permanent conference liaison office at Panmunjom and the direct telephone line shall be restored immediately.

5. The Question of Whether to Open Full-Dress Meetings to the Public.

The eighth and ninth full-dress meetings shall be opened to the public. Afterwards, full-dress meetings shall be held in principle behind closed doors. However, they may be opened to the public if both sides agree.

6. Other Operational Procedures of the Full-Dress Meeting

Matters related to personal safety, procedures for visits, emblems, equipment and belongings, transportation, communications, activities outside the conference site, facilities at the conference site, and the provision of facilities, shall be in accordance with the agreement reached at the 25th south-north Red Cross preliminary meeting of August 11, 1972, and the additional agreement reached at the third full-dress meeting of October 25, 1972.

As to the time of the eighth full-dress meeting, the NKRC at first said it was leaving the time to be decided by the hosting side of the ROKNRC.

When the ROKNRC gave December 18–21, 1984, as the time, the NKRC, in an abrupt aboutface insisted that it be held on January 23, 1985, contending that no full-dress Red Cross meeting was held in December or January in the past. No time was thus agreed on, with the two sides agreeing to determine the time through mutual discussion over the direct telephone line.

The ROKNRC delegation, in a telephone message on November 22, proposed that the eighth full-dress meeting be held at 10 a.m. January 23, 1985, in Seoul in consideration of the north's opinion, saying that the period of the north's delegation's stay in Seoul should be three nights and four days from January 22 through January 25. On December 14 the same year, the NKRC agreed to the time.

On January 9, 1985, one day before both sides' liaison officials were supposed to meet to discuss working-level matters related to the north's delegation's stay in Seoul, however, the NKRC notified the ROKNRC in a telephone message that it was postponing the scheduled full-dress Red Cross meeting on the grounds of the Team Spirit training exercise set to begin on February 1 in the south. The north tried to shift the blame for the postponement of the Red Cross meeting on the south.

The Team Spirit exercise, on the excuse of which the north put off the Red Cross meeting, was a joint ROK-U.S. military training exercise held openly every year since 1976 solely for defensive purposes to help preserve peace on the Korean peninsula. The exercise has been so open that the south had on many occasions notified the north of the training in advance and invited it to send observers to the annual field maneuver.

In the past, moreover, various inter-Korean meetings had taken place regardless of Team Spirit exercises. During the Team Spirit '84 exercise, for instance, north Korea affirmatively responded to the south's proposal for sports talks and actually attended them in early April 1984. Thus, the postponement of the Red Cross talks by the north on the excuse of the Team Spirit exercise could not be justified under any circumstances.

Under the circumstance where the north unilaterally put off the scheduled eighth full-dress Red Corss talks on the excuse of the Team Spirit military training exercise in the south and rejected the repeated calls of the ROKNRC for the resumption of the talks, ROKNRC President Yoo Chang-soon sent a telephone message to Son Song-pil, NKRC Central Committee chairman, on March 25, 1985, again urging him to agree to the early holding of the eighth full-dress Red Cross talks which could not be held due to the north's unilateral boycott. In the message, Yoo suggested that the eighth full-dress meeting be held in Seoul at 10 a.m. May 15, with the north's delegation staying in Seoul from May 14 through 17.

The full text of ROKNRC President Yoo's message to the NKRC was as follows :

I regret that the eight full-dress meeting of the south-north Red Cross Conference, which we agreed to open on January 23 this year, has not been held for two months because of your unilateral postponement. All the compatriots were greatly disappointed by the postponement of the talks which were to be reopened after a 12-year suspension.

It is one of the most important tasks for those of us engaged in Red Cross activities to find the whereabouts of the families and relatives separated in the south and the north and to arrange for their reunion. Thus, the South-North Red Cross Conference cannot be delayed for any reason or excuse.

For this reason, I propose to hold the eighth full-dress meeting of the south-north Red Cross Conference at 10 a.m. May 15, 1985, in Seoul, with your delegation's stay in Seoul beginning on May 14 and lasting for four days until May 17.

As the host of the eighth full-dress south-north Red Cross meeting, I hope to hear from you concerning the meeting at least one month before its opening so that we can prepare for your delegation's stay in Seoul and make other necessary arrangements for the conference.

On April 4, 1985, north Korea, in a telephone message signed by Son Song-pil, NKRC Central Committee chairman, agreed to hold the eighth full-dress meeting as proposed by the south, but counter-proposed that it be opened on May 28. On the same day, the ROKNRC accepted the north's counterproposal, thus setting the stage for the eighth full-dress meeting of the south-north Red Cross Conference in Seoul May 27–30.

Before the opening of the eighth meeting, the two sides held liaison officers contacts three times – May 20, May 23 and May 25 – to discuss procedural matters related to the Seoul meeting and to exchange lists of delegation members. The lists of the two delegations were as follows :

ROKNRC Delegation

Delegates

Chief delegate : Lee Yung-dug, ROKNRC vice president

Delegate : Cho Chul-hwa, ROKNRC secretary general

Delegate : Song Yong-dae, member of the ROKNRC Disaster Relief Consultative Committee

Delegate : Lee Byung-ho, member of the ROKNRC Public Relations Advisory Committee

Delegate : Chung Yong-sok, member of the ROKNRC Youth Advisory Committee

Delegate : Lee Jun-hee, member of the ROKNRC Social Services Advisory Committee

Delegate : Lee Byung-woong, director of the ROKNRC General Affairs Department

Consultants

Cho Duk-song, editorial writer of the Chosun Ilbo

Kim Dong-hwan, lawyer and director of the Committee for the Promotion of Reunion between 10 Million Dispersed Family Members

Lee Kyung-Suk, professor of Sukmyung Women's University

Chung Si-song, member of the ROKNRC Dialogue Operations Committee

Ahn Byung jun, professor of Yonsei University

Rhee Sang-woo, professor of Sogang University

Han Sung-joo, professor of Korea University

218

NKRC Delegation

Delegation

Chief delegate : Li Jong-ryul, vice chairman of the NKRC Central Committee

Deputy chief delegate : So Song-chol, executive member of the NKRC Central Committee

Delegate : Han Yon-su, executive member of the NKRC Central Committee

Delegate : Pak Yong-su, director of the NKRC Central Committee's Compatriots Programs Department

Delegate : Kim Wan-su, director of the NKRC Central Committee's Culture and Propaganda Department

Delegate : Pak Dong-chun, deputy director of the NKRC Central Committee's International Department

Delegate : Kim Chang-hyun, deputy director of the NKRC Central Committ's Organization and Planning Department

Consultants

Kang Sok-sung, member and department director of the Workers' Party Central Committee

Kim Sok-jun, vice chairman of the Social Democratic Party Central Committee

Choe Hui-jun, vice chairman of the Chondogyo-Chong-wu Party Central Committee

Im Chun-gil, vice chairman of the committee for the Peaceful Reunification of the Fatherland

Kim Yong-nam, vice chairman of the General League of Professions

Kim Chang-ryong, vice chairman of the Central Committee, Socialist Working Youth League

Pak Jae-ro, vice chairman of the Chongryon Central Committee

219

In a statement issued in the name of Home Affairs Minister Chong Sok-mo on May 18, the government of the Republic of Korea announced that it would guarantee the personal safety of the members of the north Korean delegation, attendants and press members during their stay in, and trips to and from the south. Following these preparatory measures, the NKRC delegation, attendants and press members totaling 84 arrived in Seoul by way of Panmunjom at noon on May 27, 1985, to resume the full-dress Red Cross meeting after 12 years of suspension.

(2) Eighth Full-Dress Meeting

The eighth full-dress meeting of the South-North Red Cross Conference was held May 28–29, 1985, at the conference room of the Sheraton Hotel in Seoul. At the first-day session, begun with an opening declaration by ROKNRC Chief Delegate Lee Yung-dug, the cheif delegates of each side delivered a keynote speech. The speeches were preceded by greetings by ROKNRC's Lee and NKRC Chief Delegate Li Jong-ryul and congratulatory speeches by NKRC Consultant Kang Sok-sung and ROKNRC Consultant Cho Duk-song.

In his keynote speech. ROKNRC Chief Delegate Lee stressed that the objective of the south-north Red Cross talks is "to reunite the families and relatives dispersed in the south and the north at an early date and foster, in such a way, an atmosphere for national reconciliation and contribute ultimately to the peaceful unification of the homeland." Pointing out that "the important task we are now entrusted with is to discuss concretely and resolve the agenda topics one by one and implement agreed-on projects promptly," the ROKNRC chief delegate explained as follows the ROKNRC position with respect to the discussion of the five agenda topics which the two sides reaffirmed through their preliminary contacts :

– ROKNRC Proposal Regarding Discussion of Five Agenda Topics –

The first item on the agenda is the question of ascertaining, and notifying thereof, the whereabouts and fate of the dispersed families and relatives in the south and the north.

To resolve this, we believe it would be best to exchange letters of inquiry and replies between the two Red Cross Societies in accordance with the practices of the International Red Cross tracing service.

The second is the question of facilitating free mutual visits and free meetings among the dispersed families and relatives in the south and the north. this question could be resolved by fixing, in principle, the duration, frequency and places of such visits and meetings in utmost deference to the free wishes of the persons involved.

As for visits, it would be good to exchange large groups of visitors accompanied by adequate numbers of press members, whose freedom to report would be guaranteed, since huge numbers of would-be visitors are expected to turn out at the same time in the initial stage.

For meetings, measures should be taken to establish a meeting center at Panmunjom or to allow the people involved to meet at places they consider convenient.

The third topic is the question of facilitating free mail exchange between the dispersed families and relatives in the south and the north. Correspondence should be made in letters, postcards, or whatever form is most convenient to the people involved. The use of such communication means as telephones and telegraphs should also be made possible.

The freedom of communication should be thoroughly guaranteed, and delivery service should be made smoothly. When the Joint South-North Red Cross Panmunjom Project Office, the establishment of which was agreed on at the fourth full-dress meeting, is set up, it would be good to have the office execute a postal exchange service between the south and the north.

The fourth topic is the question of facilitating the reunions of dispersed families according to their free individual wishes. We should see to it that even before unification, the families dispersed in the south and the north are able to reunite and settle down together at places of their own choosing.

The fifth topic may include, through mutual discussion, humanitarian programs related to the issue of dispersed families, which are not contained in topics one through four. For example, the repatriation of relics and the remains of dead relatives, the relocation of tombs, etc., could be included.

ROKNRC Chief Delegate Lee then expressed the hope that the two sides would, at an early date, discuss and determine ways to implement the five topics and would be able to inaugurate the "South-North Red Cross Joint Committee" and the "South-North Red Cross Panmunjom Joint Project Office," which were agreed on at the fourth full-dress meeting as project implementation organizations, so that the project to search for dispersed families could be launched by August 15, 1985, at the latest.

Lee also suggested that even before a method of implementing the five topics is agreed on, a "dispersed families hometown visting groups" be exchanged on August 15 as a pilot project to expedite the dispersed family search program.

On the other hand, the NKRC chief delegate suggested that the five agenda topics be discussed on a package basis, insisting that "a fresh method should be employed in place of the old-fashioned means of the past" in order to ease the pains of the dispersed families and relatives at an early date. Arguing that if only the issue of free visits, which is no more than one of the multiple methods of resolving the dispersed family question, were settled, other humanitarian issues would be resolved by themselves, and the NKRC asserted that the issue of free visits be discussed before any other question. The north's delegation then set forth details about the procedures related thereto as follows :

– NKRC Proposal Regarding Free Visits –

1. Procedures for Free Visits

1) Visitors shall produce the letters of credence issued by the Red Cross organizations of each side.

2) Visitors shall notify the persons and places to be visited one month before their departure.

3) The destination of the visitors shall be the places where their families or relatives lived at the time of separation. The destination may be changed if need arises.

4) The period of stay in the other side shall be one month, but may be extended if the need arises.

5) The points of entry through the Military Demarcation Line

shall be Panmunjom and Chorwon. Such points may be increased through mutual agreement.

2. Visitor Eligibility

1) Families shall mean the members of a family at the time of separation, and their children.

2) Relatives shall include up to third cousins on the father's side and first cousins on the mother's side or the wife's.

3) Other relatives specifically requested may be included.

3. Conveniences and Guarantees of Safety

1) Panmunjom and Chorwon Joint Project Offices and a South-North Red Cross Joint Committee shall be established.

2) Conveniences such as lodging and boarding, transportation and communications shall be guaranteed by the Red Cross organization of the other side.

3) Should there be a need for emergency relief or medical care, the Red Cross organization of the other side shall offer it free of charge.

4) Measures for personal safety shall be taken by the authorities of each side at the recommendation of the Red Cross organizations.

5) Detailed discussions shall be made separately.

The NKRC delegation also proposed that in August 1985, which marks the 40th anniversary of national liberation, an art troupe of about 100 members personally led by the Red Cross president of each side be exchanged between the two side to stage congratulatory performances comprising mostly traditional songs and dances to foster a festive mood for the Red Cross talks.

At the second-day session, the ROKNRC delegation said that since the question of free visits raised by north Korea had already been agreed on and adopted as Agenda Topic No. 2, there was no need to discuss it again. As to the north Korean contention that "free visits are pivotal to resolving the issue of dispersed families," the ROKNRC chief delegate said the argument reminded him of the contention made by the NKRC at the third full-dress meeting that "the improvement of statutory conditions and the social environment is prerequisite" to the discussion of the agenda

223

topics. He then said that if their idea of free visits was not motivated to produce such political prerequisites as in the past or to dispute the south's internal issues, the question could be agreed on at any time.

Meanwhile, the NKRC delegation repeatedly called for an agreement on free visits only, contending that "free visits are commonly related to the five agenda topics and are most preferential and pivotal to alleviating the pains of separated families and relatives."

North Korea insisted that there still was no change in their position that it was reasonable for them to make an issue out of the south's internal affairs in the early 1970s. Under the circumstances, no progress was registered in the discussion of the project envisaged in the five agenda topics.

Here, in a bid to facilitate the substantial progress of the talks, the ROKNRC, accommodating the north's idea of the exchange of art troupes, proposed the exchange of both "dispersed family hometown visitors and art troupes," which the north accepted. In subsequent working-level delegates'contacts, the two sides agreed to exchange groups of dispersed families for hometown visits and art troupes on August 15, 1985, and to hold working-level delegates' contacts at Panmunjom on July 15 to discuss concrete procedural matters.

Although there was no tangible progress in substantial issues, the eighth full-dress Red Cross meeting was highly significant in that the talks were resumed after a 12-year suspension following the seventh full-dress meeting held in Pyongyang in July 1973.

(3) Ninth Full-Dress Meeting

The ninth full-dress meeting of the south-north Red Cross Conference was opened at the People's Cultural Palace in Pyongyang.

The first-day session was begun with an opening statement and greetings by Li Jong-ryul, chief delegate of the NKRC. Greetings by ROKNRC Chief Delegate Lee Yung-dug and congratulatory remarks by Cho Duk-song, a ROKNRC consultant, and Kang Sok-sung, an NKRC consultant, followed in that order. Before the two sides' chief delegates made keynote speeches, both sides confirmed an agreement reached on August 22, 1985, following three working-level contacts on the exchange of hometown visitors and art troupes. In the confirmation, the written agreement on the exchanges was read by the spokesmen of the two sides, which was then ascertained by the chief delegates.

At the meeting, ROKNRC Chief Delegate Lee Yung-dug produced three draft agreements, expressing the hope that the inter-Korean Red Cross talks that had dragged on for 15 years would be concluded at an early date and the family reunion project would be translated into action by the end of 1985, which happened to be the 40th anniversary of national liberation. He expressed the hope that all projects would be discussed and resolved on a package basis in light of the fact that at the eighth full-dress meeting, the two sides agreed to discuss the five agenda topics on a package basis and also arrived at an agreeement in principle on free visits. The draft agreements produced were an Agreement Regarding the Implementation of Projects Envisaged in the Five Topics, an Agreement on Procedures for Free Travel between Dispersed Families and Relatives in the South and the North, and an Agreement on the Formation and Operation of a South-North Red Cross Joint Committee and a South-North Red Cross Joint Panmunjom Project Office.

In addition, the south proposed the establishment of permanent Red Cross missions in Seoul and Pyongyang with a view to carrying out smoothly Red Cross projects, promoting close cooperation between the two Red Cross Societies and carrying out cooperation and liaison for each side's personnel staying in the other side's area.

The texts of the three draft agreements put forth by the south at the first session were as follows :

– Agreement Regarding the Implementation of Projects Envisaged in the Five Topics (Draft) –

The Republic of Korea National Red Cross and the Democratic People's Republic of Korea Red Cross agreed as follows at the ninth full-dress south-north Red Cross meeting in a humanitarian spirit and with a desire to pave the way for early reunions between the families and relatives dispersed in the south and the north :

First, the two sides shall implement the projects envisaged in the five topics in the following methods and procedures under the auspices and cooperation of the Red Cross Societies.

1. The project to ascertain, and notify thereof, the whereabouts and fate of the dispersed families and relatives in the south and north shall be implemented either through an exchange of letters of inquiry and letters of reply or through free travel by the people involved according to the free will of the dispersed families involved. The methods and procedures including the format for letters of inquiry for dispersed families and letters of reply shall be as suggested by the Republic of Korea National Red Cross at the third full-dress meeting.

2. The project to facilitate mutual visits and meetings among the dispersed families and relatives in the south and the north shall be implemented through free travel back and forth. As for meetings, the families and relatives shall be allowed to have meetings according to their wishes at a meeting center to be created at Panmunjom or elsewhere. The South-North Red Cross Joint Panmunjom Project Office shall be responsible for the establishment and operation of a Panmunjom meeting center.

3. Correspondence between the families and relatives dispersed in the south and the north shall be made in sealed letters or postcards at their convenience. They shall be allowed to make use of such communications means as telephones and telegraphs. The exchange of correspondence shall be entrusted to the South-North Red Cross Joint Panmunjom Project Office.

4. Means shall be explored to facilitate the permanent reunion of dispersed families in the south and the north at places of their own choosing. Working-level matters regarding such reunion shall be discussed and determined by the South-North Red Cross Joint Committee.

5. Other humanitarian projects to be settled shall be introduced to and steeled by the South-North Red Cross Joint Committee.

Second, procedures for free travel back and forth by dispersed families and relatives, which are necessary for the implementation of these projects, shall be determined separately.

Third, to guarantee the implementation of matters agreed on at the South-North Red Cross Conference, the two sides shall inaugurate early the "South-North Red Cross Joint Committee" and the "South-North Red Cross Joint Panmunjom Project Office," the creation of which was agreed on at the fourth full-dress Red Cross meeting. An agreement concerning the formation and operation of the "South-North Red Cross Joint Committee" and the "South-North Joint Panmunjom Project Office" shall be prepared separately.

Fourth, Red Cross missions shall be established and operated in Seoul and Pyongyang, with a view to smoothly implementing Red Cross projects for dispersed families and relatives in the south and the north, Promoting close cooperation between the Red Cross organizations of the two sides, and carrying out such business as cooperation and liaison for people staying in the other's area.

Fifth, this agreement shall go into force from the time the two sides affix their signatures and exchange signed copies, and shall continue to remain in force unless it is repealed through mutual agreement.

– Agreement on the Formation and Operation of a South-North Red Cross Joint Committee and a South-North Red Cross Joint Panmunjom Project Office (Draft) –

1. Purport

For the purpose of effectively carrying out various projects agreed on at the South-North Red Cross Conference, the two sides shall establish and operate a South-North Red Cross Joint Committee (hereinafter referred to as "Joint Committee") and a South-North Red Cross Joint Panmunjom Project Office (hereinafter referred to as "Joint Project Office").

2. Joint Committee

a. Function

(1) To guarantee the faithful implementation of matters agreed on between the two sides at the South-North Red Cross Conference, and to adjust and resolve all problems that occur in the course of implementing agreed matters.

(2) To discuss all humanitarian problems that arise in connection with the project for reunions between dispersed families and relatives in the south and the north and to make decisions about them.

b. Formation

The Joint Committee shall be composed of five members from each side, and the co-chairmen shall be of vice Red Cross president (vice chairman) level.

c. Operation

(1) Meetings of the Joint Committee shall in principle be held at Panmunjom. However, they may be held in Seoul or Pyongyang through mutual agreement.

(2) The Joint Committee shall have a regular meeting every three months and may have extraordinary meetings at the request of either side.

(3) Meetings of the Joint Committee shall be held behind closed doors. However, they may be opened to the public through mutual agreement.

(4) Matters of agreement reached at the Joint Committee shall be referred to the Joint Project Office for implementation.

3. Joint Project Office

a. Function

(1) To perform the business of exchanging letters of inquiry regard-

ing the whereabouts and fate of the dispersed families and relatives in the south and the north and the letters of reply.

(2) To perform the business of exchanging letters between the dispersed families and relatives in the south and the north.

(3) To perform the business of maintaining the meeting site at Panmunjom for dispersed families and relatives in the south and the north who wish to meet there.

(4) To perform various business related to the passage through Panmunjom of the dispersed families and relatives in the south and the north.

(5) To perform general clerical work related to the operation of the Joint Committee, and to carry out humanitarian projects referred to it by the Joint Committee.

b. Formation

The Joint Project Office shall be formed with a head of department-chief level from the central Red Cross organizations of each side and necessary clerical workers from each side. The organization and the number of clerical workers shall be determined separately through discussion.

c. Operation

(1) The two sides shall jointly construct and use the office building of the Joint Project Office at Panmunjom. However, pending the completion of the office building of the Joint Project Office, the Republic of Korea National Red Cross and the Democratic People's Republic of Korea Red Cross shall establish and operate the Joint Project Office at the "Peace House" and "Panmungak," respectively.

(2) The head of each Joint Project Office shall regularly hold a closed-door meeting once a week. A meeting may be held at any time at the request of either side.

(3) The two sides shall establish and begin to operate the Joint Project Office within one month after affixing their signatures on and ex-

changing this agreement.

(4) Details about the construction of the office building of the Joint Project Office and about the operation of the Joint Project Office shall be discussed and determined by the Joint Committee.

4. This agreement shall go into force from the time the two sides affix their signatures to it and exchange signed copies of it, and shall continue to remain in force unless it is repealed through mutual agreement.

–Agreement of Procedures for Free Travel between Dispersed Families and Relatives in the South and the North (Draft)–

1. The families to travel between the south and the north shall include those who were family members at the time of separation and their children born thereafter, and relatives shall include up to third cousins in collateral relations and first cousins on the wife's and mother's side.

2. The purpose of travel between the south and the north by families and relatives shall be to ascertain the whereabouts and fate of family members and relatives, and to have visits or reunions with them. If and when they wish to travel freely for other purposes, it shall be discussed and decided on by the South-North Red Cross Joint Committee.

3. The families and relatives traveling back and forth shall carry travel certificates issued by the Red Cross of the traveler's side. The certificates shall indicate the purpose of travel, destination, period of stay and other necessary information.

4. Each Red Cross shall notify the other of the families and relatives set to travel between the south and the north and their destinations one month before they are to depart.

5. The destination of those traveling back and forth between the south and the north shall be their hometowns, the place where they resided at the time of separation or the place where their family members or relatives now reside. If necessary, such destination may be changed with

230

cooperation from the other side's Red Cross.

6. The period of stay in the other side's area for the families and relatives traveling between the south and the north shall be less than one month. If necessary, the period may be extended with the cooperation from the other side's Red Cross.

7. The point of passage through the Military Demarcation Line by the families and relatives traveling between the south and the north shall be Panmunjom. Additional points of passage may be established through mutual agreement.

8. The Red Cross of the other side shall guarantee and be responsible for the provision of various conveniences such as lodging, boarding, transportation and communications for the families and relatives traveling back and forth between the south and the north.

9. In the event there is a need for emergency relief or medical care for the families and relatives traveling between the south and the north, it shall be offered free of charge by the Red Cross of the other side.

10. As for the issue of the security of the families and relatives traveling between the south and the north, the government authorities of both sides, through the good offices of both Red Cross Societies, shall guarantee and be responsible for the safe return of all members.

11. This agreement shall go into force from the time the two sides affix their signatures on it and exchange signed copies, and shall continue to remain in force unless it is repealed through mutual agreement.

These three draft agreements offered by the south covered all the implementation methods of resolving the five topics on a package basis, and incorporated even the ideas and demands north Korea voiced at the 8th full-dress meeting.

However, the NKRC delegation was opposed to the package discussion and resolution of the five agenda projects. Insisting that at the eighth meeting the two sides "reached an agreement on the package discussion of the five topics and on the question of allowing free visits as a comprehensive means of realizing the free visits," the north's delegation only produced a draft agreement regarding free travel. It demanded that the draft agreement be adopted first before the project implementation method and procedures are discussed.

In other words, the north Koreans, contrary to the principle of package discussion and solution agreed on between the two sides at the 8th meeting, were now demanding a phased resolution of the dispersed family issue. Their idea was to adopt an agreement on "free travel" at the first stage, discuss and resolve other means than "free travel" at the second stage, and then discuss procedural matters related to the concrete implementation of the topics.

Moreover, by setting the deadline for the discussion of procedures for the dispersed family question at September 1986, north Korea revealed the intent of delaying the substantial discussion of the dispersed family issue.

–North Korean Version of Agreement Regarding Free Travel (Draft)–

1. The agenda topics of the South-North Red Cross Conference shall be disussed on a package basis.

2. In the realization of agenda projects, a pivotal and comprehensive method shall be free travel. The projects shall be promoted through free travel in a way that conforms to the wish of the dispersed families and relatives.

(1) Dispersed families and relatives shall be allowed to travel to the area of the other side freely according to their own will and personally ascertain the whereabouts and fate of their families and relatives.

(2) Dispersed families and relatives shall be allowed to travel to the area of the other side freely according to their own will to visit their relatives, and freely meet their families and relatives at any place.

(3) Dispersed families shall be allowed to travel to the area of the other side freely to discuss and realize the issue of permanent reunion.

(4) Dispersed families and relatives shall be allowed to travel to the area of the other side freely to pay tribute to their ancestral tombs, dis-

pose of articles left by the deceased to relocate the remains.

3. Other methods raised in addition to free travel shall also be the methods of easing the pains of dispersed families and relatives.

4. Other methods related to the realization of each item of the agenda topics shall be discussed and determined after the adoption of an agreement on free travel.

5. Procedural matters shall be discussed together after the method of free travel and other methods raised were agreed on.

6. The method of easing pains of dispersed families and relatives and procedural issues related thereto shall be dealt with in September 1986.

The second-day sesion held on August 28 was to discuss chiefly what both sides had suggested during the first-day session. But the meeting ended without any serious debate because the north Korean side, making an issue of the incidence that occurred at the Moranbong Stadium on August 27, shunned any discussion of business.

Under the original itinerary, the members of the ROKNRC delegation were to observe "youth gymnastics" at the Students-Children Palace in Pyongyang on the afternoon of August 27 after the first-day session was over. But the ROKNRC delegates were instead taken to the Moranbong Stadium where they were shown highly propagandistic, mock battle-like gymnastics. Unable to stand the provocative show, the ROKNRC delegates walked out of the stadium halfway through it.

To everyone's eyes, it was clear what the north had sought when they staged the propaganda gymnastics by mobilizing 50,000 youths and 100,000 spectators. Since the north refused to explain the contents of the gymnastics beforehand by changing the site and time of the ROKNRC delegation's observation schedule, it was an apparent attempt of the north to exploit the Red Cross talks for political gains. The show was in express violation of the mutual agreement not to display any political events to the other side.

Nonetheless, the north created a tense atmosphere from the very start of the meeting by accusing the ROKNRC delegation of walking out and demanding that the ROKNRC make an apology. The north made the argument openly in breach of the agreement made at the first-day session that the second-day meeting would be held behind closed doors. Despite the repeated calls of the ROKNRC delegation for the debate of essential issues, the north refused. The meeting thus broke up without any progress.

(4) Tenth Full-Dress Meeting

The tenth full-dress meeting of the South-North Red Cross Conference was opened at 10 a.m. December 3, 1985, at the Sheraton Hotel in Seoul.

The meeting was begun in an atmosphere full of expectations as it came soon after dispersed family members, though their number was limited, had an emotional meeting of their long-missing families and relatives in their personal visits to their hometowns for the first time in the 40 years of national division.

At the first-day session, ROKNRC Chief Delegate Lee Yung-dug, in his keynote speech, produced the more concrete versions of the three draft agreements he first set forth at the ninth full-dress meeting, the three being an Agreement Regarding the Implementation of Projects Envisaged in the Five Topics, an Agreement on Procedures for Free Travel between Dispersed Families and Relatives in the South and the North, and an Agreement on the Formation and Operation of a South-North Red Cross Joint Committee and a South-North Red Cross Joint Panmunjom Project Office. Lee suggested that the draft versions be discussed on a package basis so as to adopt an integrated agreement. He said the two sides could thus wind up the Red Cross talks at an early date and go into the stage of project implementation.

Chief Delegate Lee said that while the draft versions the two sides produced at the ninth meeting had some points in common, such as those that dispersed family projects be undertaken in utmost deference to the free opinions of the families involved and that the five agenda topics be discussed as soon as possible and the results be adopted in an agreement, there were considerable differences as to the method of the debate of the

234

agenda topics as well as on the contents of a proposed agreement. Lee discussed the ROKNRC delegation's position regarding such differences is follows :

First, we believe that inasmuch as our two sides have already agreed to discuss and resolve the five topics on a package basis without regard to their order, methods for an item-by-item implementation of the five topics should naturally be considered for their comprehensive discussion and solution.

However, your side in effect shuns a package solution of the five topics. While demanding a package discussion of the five topics, your side insists that the issue of free travel should be tackled first and that the methods and procedural matters on issues other than free travel should be discussed and determined after an agreement was adopted on the question on free travel.

I believe that we should respect the package discussion of the five agenda topics since it is a matter agreed on between the two sides at the eighth full-dress meeting and since it is a method necessary even for effective progress in the discussion of agenda topics.

Second, regarding the contents of the agreements, our side produced comprehensive ideas containing concrete content regarding the implementation of projects envisaged in the five agenda topics, procedures for free travel and the formation and operation of organizations necessary for the implementation of projects. Your versions, however, lacked any comprehensive content.

Moreover, your side failed to produce any concrete ideas regarding items other than free travel and procedural matters related to the actual realization of topics, saying only that they would be discussed.

I believe that the shortcut to resolving the question of dispersed families is for our two sides to discuss and solve comprehensive and concrete contents of all related problems in order to wind up the south-north Red Cross talks that have lasted for no fewer than 14 years and to translate agreed-on projects into action at an early date. Even though the two sides show differences, we would be able to conclude the full-dress talks successfully at an early date if only we display the spirit of mutual understanding and reciprocity since we both mean to resolve the question of the separated families.

In this respect, I expect that your side would produce a comprehensive idea commensurate with our side's version and that the two sides' versions would be discussed at today's meeting. I believe that, otherwise, we could reach an agreement easily if we make discussions chiefly on our side's version since our side's draft version fully reflects even the content your side suggested.

The ROKNRC delegation then proposed that to expand and develop the good results of the hometown visiting program even before full-fledged visits and reunions are realized, hometown visiting groups of dispersed families be exchanged again on the occasion of the lunar New Year's Day of 1986, one of Korea's traditional holidays. Also, proposing that those who met their missing families in Seoul and Pyongyang and had to be separated again in September 1985 be allowed to exchange correspondence freely according to their free will, the south's delegation said that if the north agreed, a working-level meeting could be held separately to discuss concrete matters related thereto.

The texts of the three draft agreements presented to the meeting were as follows :

–Agreement Regarding the Implementation of Projects Envisaged in the Five Topics of Full-Dress South-North Red Cross Meeting (Draft)–

The Republic of Korea National Red Cross and the Democratic People's Republic of Korea Red Cross hereby agree as follows in order to pave the way under a humanitarian spirit for early reunions between the families and relatives dispersed in the south and the north :

First, the two sides shall implement the projects envisaged in the five topics via the following methods and procedures under the auspices and cooperation of the two Red Cross Societies.

1. The project to ascertain, and notify thereof, the whereabouts and fate of the dispersed families and relatives in the south and the north shall be

implemented either through an exchange of letters of inquiry and letters of reply or through free travel made with the cooperation of the two Red Cross Societies according to the free will of the dispersed families involved. Methods and procedures including the format for letters of inquiry for dispersed families and letter of reply shall be as suggested by the Republic of Korea National Red Cross at the third full-dress meeting.

2. The project to facilitate mutual visits and meetings among the dispersed families and relatives in the south and the north shall be implemented through free travel back and forth.

As for meetings, the families and relatives shall be allowed to have meetings according to their wishes at a meeting center to be created at Panmunjom or elsewhere. The South-North Red Cross Joint Panmunjom Project Office shall be responsible for the establishment and operation of a Panmunjom meeting center.

3. Correspondence between the families and relatives dispersed in the south and the north shall be made in sealed letters or postcards at their convenience. They shall be allowed to make use of communications methods such as telephones and telegraphs. The exchange of correspondence shall be entrusted to the South-North Red Cross Joint Panmunjom Project Office.

4. Reunions between dispersed families in the south and the north shall be realized by arranging the way for them to live at places of their own free choosing. Working-level matters regarding reunions shall be discussed and determined by the South-North Red Cross Joint Committee.

5. Other humanitarian projects to be settled shall be introduced to and settled by the South-North Red Cross Joint Committee.

Second, procedures for free travel back and forth by dispersed families and relatives, which are necessary for the implementation of these projects, shall be determined separately.

Third, to guarantee the implementation of matters agreed on by the South-North Red Cross Conference, the two sides shall inaugurate early the South-North Red Cross Joint Committee and the South-North Red Cross Joint Panmunjom Project Office, the creation of which was agreed on at the fourth full-dress Red Cross meeting. Agreements on the Formation and Operation of the South-North Red Cross Joint Committee and the South-North Joint Panmunjom Project Office shall be determined separately.

Fourth, Red Cross missions shall be established and operated in Seoul and Pyongyang, with a view to smoothly implementing Red Cross projects for dispersed families and relatives in the south and the north, promoting close cooperation between the Red Cross organizations of the two sides, and carrying out such business as cooperation and liaison for personnel staying in the other's area.

Fifth, this agreement shall go into force from the time the two sides affix their signatures and exchange signed copies, and shall continue to remain in force unless it is repealed through mutual agreement.

—Agreement on Procedures for Free Travel between Dispersed Families and Relatives in the South and the North (Draft)—

An agreement is hereby reached as follows on the procedures for free travel between the families and relatives dispersed in the south and the north, pursuant to the Agreement Regarding the Implementation of Projects Envisaged in the Five Topics.

1. The families to travel between the south and the north shall include those who were family members at the time of separation and their descendants born thereafter, and relatives shall include up to third cousins in collateral relations and first cousins on the wife's and mother's side.

2. The purpose of travel between the south and the north by families and relatives shall be to ascertain the whereabouts and fate of family members and relatives, and to have visits or reunions with them. If and when they wish to travel freely for other purposes, it shall be discussed and decided on by the South-North Red Cross Joint Committee.

3. The families and relatives who travel back and forth shall carry travel certificates issued by the Red Cross of his side. The certificates shall

indicate the purpose of travel, destination, period of stay and other necessary information.

4. Regarding the families and relatives traveling back and forth between the south and the north, the relevant Red Cross shall notify the other Red Cross of the list of such travelers, purpose of travels, destinations, duration of their stay in the other side's area and other necessary matters one month before their departure.

5. .The destination of those traveling back and forth between the south and the north shall be their hometowns, the place where they resided at the time of separation or the place where their family members or relatives now reside. If necessary, such destination may be changed with cooperation from the other side's Red Cross.

6. The period of stay in the other side's area for the families and relatives traveling between the south and the north shall be less than one month.

7. The point of passage through the Military Demarcation Line by the families and relatives traveling between the south and the north shall be Panmunjom. Additional points of passage may be established through mutual agreement.

8. The provision of various conveniences such as lodging, boarding, transportation and communications for the families and relatives traveling back and forth between the south and the north shall be the responsibility of the other side's Red Cross.

9. In the event there is a need for emergency relief or medical care for the families and relatives traveling between the south and the north, it shall be offered free of charge by the other side's Red Cross.

10. As for the issue of the security of the families and relatives traveling between the south and the north, the government authorities of both sides, through the good offices of both Red Cross societies, shall guarantee and be responsible for the safe return of all members

11. This agreement shall go into force from the time the two sides affix their signatures on it and exchange signed copies, and shall continue to remain in force unless it is repealed through mutual agreement.

−Agreement on the Formation and Operation of a South-North Red Cross Joint Committee and a South-North Red Cross Joint Panmunjom Project Office (Draft)−

An agreement is hereby reached as follows on the formation and operation of a South-North Red Cross Joint Committee and a South-North Red Cross Joint Panmunjom Project Office, pursuant to the Agreement Regarding the Implementation of Projects Envisaged in the Five Topics.

1. Purport

For the purpose of effectively carrying out various projects agreed on at the South-North Red Cross Conference, a South-North Red Cross Joint Committee (hereafter referred to as Joint Committee) and a South-North Red Cross Joint Panmunjom Project Office (hereafter referred to as Joint Project Office) shall be established and operated.

2. Joint Committee

a. Function

(1) To guarantee the faithful implementation of matters agreed on between the two sides at the South-North Red Cross Conference, and to adjust and resolve all problems that occur in the course of implementing agreed matters.

(2) To discuss all humanitarian problems that arise in connection with the project for reunions between dispersed families and relatives in the south and the north, and make decisions about them.

b. Formation

The Joint Committee shall be composed of five members from each side, and the co-chairmen shall be of vice Red Cross president (vice chairman) level.

c. Operation

(1) Meetings of the Joint Committee shall in principle be held at Panmunjom. However, they may be held in Seoul or Pyongyang through mutual agreement.

(2) The Joint Committee shall have a regular meeting every three

240

months and may have extraordinary meetings upon the request of either side.

(3) Meetings of the Joint Committee shall be held behind closed doors. However, they may be opened to the public through mutual agreement.

(4) Matters of agreement reached at the Joint Committee shall be referred to the Joint Project Office for implementation.

3. Joint Project Office

a. Function

(1) To perform the business of exchanging the letters of inquiry and replys regarding the whereabouts and fate of the dispersed families and relatives in the south and the north.

(2) To perform the business of exchanging letters between the dispersed families and relatives in the south and the north.

(3) To perform the business of maintaining the meeting site at Panmunjom for dispersed families and relatives in the south and the north.

(4) To perform various business related to the passage through Panmunjom of the dispersed families and relatives in the south and the north.

(5) To perform general clerical work related to the operation of the Joint Committee, and carry out humanitarian projects referred to it by the Joint Committee.

b. Formation

The Joint Project Office shall be formed with a head of department-chief level from the central Red Cross organizations of each side and necessary clerical workers from each side. The organization and the number of clerical workers shall be determined separately through discussion.

c. Operation

(1) The two sides shall jointly construct and use the office building of the Joint Project Office at Panmunjom. However, pending the completion of the office building of the Joint Project Office, the Republic of Korea National Red Cross and the Democratic People's Republic of Korea Red Cross shall establish and operate the Joint Project Office at the Peace House and Panmungak, respectively.

(2) The two heads (one from each side) of the Joint Project Office shall regularly hold a closed-door meeting once a week. A meeting may be held at any time at the request of either side.

(3) The two sides shall establish and begin to operate the Joint Project Office within one month after affixing their signatures on and exchanging this agreement.

(4) Details about the construction of the office building of the Joint Project Office and about the operation of the Joint Project Office shall be discussed and determined by the Joint Committee.

4. This agreement shall go into force from the time the two sides affix their signatures to it and exchange signed copies of it, and shall continue to remain in force unless it is repealed through mutual agreement.

However, the NKRC delegation, though it was calling for the package discussion of the five agenda topics, produced their idea of free travel in the form of a draft agreement, which they first advanced at the ninth full-dress meeting and was later supplemented, demanding that their draft agreement be adopted before everything else. The north's delegation also set forth a Proposal on Methods Other than Free Travel for those among dispersed families and relatives who cannot make free trips due to age, physical limitations and other reasons.

The gist of the NKRC offer was as follows:

–Gist of Agreement on Free Travel–

1. Principles of Free Travel

(1) Maximum respect for the personality of the dispersed families and relatives involved.

(2) Prohibition of any intervention or control that impedes in the humanitarian activities of the travelers.

(3) Prohibition of any physical constraints of the travelers.

2. Scope of Free Travel

(1) Families at the time of separation and their descendents.

(2) Third cousins on collateral relations and the first cousins on the wife's and mother's sides.

(3) Other relatives requested.

3. Procedures for Free Travel

(1) Would-be travelers shall file applications with their side's Red Cross authorities.

(2) Travelers shall notify the authorities concerned of the persons and places to be visited one month before their departure.

(3) The destination of the travelers shall be the places of residence of their families and relatives at the time of separation, the work places of their families and relatives, and other places of meeting.

(4) The duration of the travelers' stay shall be approximately one month.

4. Means of Travel and Points of Passage

(1) Transportation means for the travelers shall be either automobiles, trains, ships or airplanes depending on the desire of travelers.

(2) The points of passage for travelers shall be Panmunjom and Chorwon for land; Wonsan, Pusan, Nampo and Inchon ports for sea; and the Sun-an and Kimpo airports for air.

5. Guarantee of Conveniences for the Travelers

(1) Conveniences such as lodging, boarding, transportation, communications, etc., shall be provided by the other side's Red Cross organization.

(2) In case of the need of emergency relief and medical assistance, required services shall be provided by the other side's Red Cross organization free of charge.

(3) Details shall be discussed separately.

6. Guarantee of Personal Safety for the Travelers

(1) Steps to guarantee the personal safety of the travelers shall be taken by the authorities of the two sides through the good offices of Red Cross organizations.

(2) Detailed matters regarding the guarantee of personal safety

shall be discussed separately.

–Gist of Idea of Methods Other Than Free Travel–

1. Method of Ascertaining, and Informing Thereof, the Whereabouts and Fates of Those Families and Relatives Who Cannot Make Free Travel.

(1) Families and relatives dispersed in the south and the north shall request their sides' Red Cross organizations for such ascertainment.

(2) Families and relatives dispersed in the south and the north shall ascertain the whereabouts and fates by sending their trusted representatives to the other side's areas.

(3) Families and relatives dispersed in the south and the north shall ascertain the whereabouts and fates through contacts with the other sides' organizations or individual persons.

2. Method of Realizing Meeting Between Those Families and Relatives Who Cannot Make Free Travel.

(1) Meetings shall be made at Panmunjom, Chorwon and other places the persons involved want.

(2) Joint project centers shall be set up at Panmunjom, Chorwon and other places for the conveniences of such meetings.

3. Method of Realizing Exchange of Correspondence Between Those Families and Relatives Who Cannot Make Free Travel

(1) Exchange of such postal matters as letters and postcards.

(2) Use of communications methods such as the telephone and telegraph.

(3) Procedures for the exchange of postal matters and the use of the telephone and telegraph shall be discussed separately.

4. Method of Realizing Reunions of Those Families and Relatives Who Cannot Make Free Travel

(1) Realization of reunions through the exchange of letters between the persons involved.

(2) Realization of reunions in an arrangement made through their

relatives or trusted representatives.

(3) Realization of reunions through contacts with the Red Cross organizations of the two sides.

5. Method of Resolving Other Humanitarian Projects

(1) A person may dispose of the articles left by the dead and transfer the remains of the dead through a trusted representative.

(2) A person may dispose of the articles left by the dead and transfer the remains of the dead through contacts with the Red Cross organizations of the two sides.

(3) The method of ascertaining, and informing thereof, the fate of friends, and of realizing free visits and the exchange of letters between them, shall be the same as the case with dispersed families and relatives.

(4) Other problems to be raised through mutual agreement may be further discussed.

At the second-day meeting, the two sides exchanged supplementary speeches and engaged in substantial discussion, but without any progress.

In his speech, ROKNRC Chief Delegate Lee stressed again that in order to respect the principles of "package discussion of agenda topics" and the "free travel" agreed on at the eighth full-dress meeting and to resolve the issue of the five agenda topics at an early date, the north Korean side, too, should produce a comprehensive draft agreement. Pointing out that the NKRC idea of dividing dispersed families into those subject to free travel and those to non-free travel, contravened the principle of respecting the free will of the dispersed people involved, the ROKNRC chief delegate refuted in part the north Korean offer as follows :

First, your new proposal is prone to give rise to confusion and misunderstanding because it separately regulates the methods of the projects envisaged in the five agenda topics respectively for free travelers your side mentioned and for those who cannot make free visits.

For example, your side's draft agreement on free travel says that as a method of resolving the project of Topic No. 3, information could be conveyed orally or by letter to one's families and relatives in the other side's area by way of free travelers. On the other hand, your side says in your proposals on other methods that postal matters such as letters and postcards and such communications means as the telephone and telegraph can be available only to those families and relatives who cannot make free travel.

This is apt to cause the misunderstanding that only those who cannot make free travel would be allowed to use postal matters and communications methods while free travelers would be denied them.

A literal look at your side's offer shows much room for misunderstanding and confusion, as it gives the impression that the exchange of correspondence would be allowed not for free travelers but only for those who cannot make free travel.

Such misunderstanding and confusion derive purely from your side's unnecessary classification of those converable in the family search program into free travelers and those who cannot make free travel.

We'd better forestall and eliminate the basis of such misunderstanding. I therefore believe that dispersed families should not be categorized into free travelers and non-free travelers. What should be distinguished instead should be project methods such as free travel or the exchange of letters. I think that all dispersed families should be allowed to choose these project methods according to their free will.

It was under this principle and spirit that my ROKNRC delegation produced a proposal centered on a basic agreement on the implementation of the projects envisaged in the five agenda topics.

At the same time, your side's draft agreement on free travel and the proposal on other methods enumerate the methods of setting projects envisaged in the five topics in duplicate. In other words, there are methods of resolving agenda projects with regard to free travel, while there are separate methods for the same agenda projects in a proposal for other methods. This amounts to putting the cart before the horse.

As your side, too, well knows, the basic mission our south-north Red Cross talks should accomplish is to resolve the projects envisaged in the five agenda topics. The rightful order, therefore, should be that the resolution of agenda topics remains the core of an agreement, while its methods or procedures must be secondary.

In the resolution of the project of Topic No. 1, for instance, your side suggests *that free travelers will have no way to ascertain the fate and whereabouts of their missing families unless they directly travel to the other side's area, and that the method of finding out the fate and whereabouts through Red Cross organizations is available only to non-free travelers.*

Also, regarding the question of reunions, Topic No. 2, your suggestions are that non-free travelers are to be met at specific places like Panmunjom and Chorwon, whereas free travelers "can meet at any place they like." Your side thus eliminates non-free travelers. Your idea of family meeting thus carries the contradiction of its being hardly distinguishable in reality from the issue of visits.

Regarding the question of the exchange of correspondence, Topic No. 3, your side tries to set a distinction between free travelers and non-free travelers, as pointed out earlier, in disregard of the free will of the people involved. Further, regarding the question of reunions, Topic No. 4, your side unduly attempts to keep free travelers from contacting Red Cross organizations or exchanging letters, thus denying them any opportunity of reunion unless they "personally travel to the other side's area."

Also, regarding the question of other humanitarian issues, Topic No.5, covering the disposition of the remains of the dead or the articles left by the dead, your proposal, in a display of contradictions, blocks dispersed families from resolving the issue through Red Cross organizations unless they personally travel to the other side's areas.

I presume that this is the result of your side's negligence of the importance of the other methods in your over-emphasis of free travel, as well as from your attitude of putting the cart before the horse, in which your side regards the solution of the five agenda topics as only secondary.

The basic mission of the full-dress south-north Red Cross talks is in every respect to resolve the projects envisaged in the five topics. If this basic duty were understood clearly, there would be no denying that the issue of free travel or other methods should naturally be put secondary to the solution of the projects of the five topics.

Moreover, in your proposal regarding other methods, your side out of nowhere raised a new object of the projects, that is, "friends," which has nothing to do at all with any of the other objectives.

The issue of "friends" is not related in any way to the families and relatives dispersed in the south and the north. As your side remembers, this was the issue which your side raised in the course of preliminary meetings in the early 1970s and which the two sides already agreed to eliminate from the list of topics.

I do not understand what has prompted your side to raise the issue of "friends" again, an issue which does not befit even the contents of your proposal and which the two sides have already agreed to exclude from the scope of discussion.

However, the NKRC delegation only indulged in stressing the "just-ness" and "reasonability" of the proposals on free travel and other methods they produced at the first-day meeting, thus standing in the way of the progress of the talks. They further turned down the ROKNRC proposal for the second exchange of hometown visitors on the lunar New Year's Day of 1986 and for the exchange of correspondence between those who met during the exchange of hometown visitors in September 1985.

The two sides agreed to hold the 11th full-dress Red Corss meeting in Pyongyang on February 26, 1986, But it has not taken place as of the end of 1988 because north Korea suspended the south-north diaogue in early 1986 with the excuse of the Team Spirit military training exercise.

e. Exchange of Dispersed Family Hometown Visitors and Art Troupes

(1) Delegates' Contacts

To discuss the exchange of dispersed family hometown visitors and art troupes, which was agreed on at the eighth full-dress Red Cross talks, the two Red Cross delegations held two rounds of working-level contacts on May 29–30, 1985, immediately after the eighth meeting.

At the closed-door contacts attended by two delegates from each side, the two sides agreed to exchange groups of dispersed family hometown visitors and art troupes around August 15, 1985. To discuss concrete pro-cedural matters, they decided to hold working-level contacts at Panmun-jom on July 15.

– Agreement of Working-Level Contacts –

1. The two sides agreed to promote the exchange of hometown visiting groups and art troupes around the time of the 49th anniversary of national liberation on August 15, 1985. To discuss concrete matters such as procedures, the size of visiting groups and the period of stay, working-level delegates' contacts will be held at the conference room of the Neutral Nations Supervisory Commission at 10 a.m. July 15.

2. Working-level contacts shall be attended by three delegates and three attendants from each side.

3. The time of the 10th full-dress meeting of the South-North Red Cross Conference will also be discussed at the working-level contacts.

4. The working-level contacts shall be held behind closed doors.

(a) First Working-Level Delegates Contacts

The first working-level delegates contacts between the south and north Korean Red Cross Societies was held behind closed doors at the conference room of the Neutral Nations Supervisory Commission at 10 a.m. July 15, 1985, to discuss concrete methods and procedures for conducting the exchange of hometown visitors and art troupes.

The contacts were attended by three delegates from each side : Song Yong-dae, Lee Jun-hi and Lee Byong-wung from the south and Pak Yong-su, Kim Wan-su and Pak Dong-chun from the north.

The ROKNRC side, expressing the hope that the exchange of hometown visitors and art troupes, would be realized at an early date, set forth concrete matters for their implementation as follows :

– Matters Related to Basic Issues –

1. Name of Visiting Groups

The name of the visiting groups shall be "South-North Hometown Visitors and Art Troupes."

2. Composition and Size of Visiting Groups

(1) Each group, headed by the highest official of each central Red Cross organization (the president of the Republic of Korea National

Red Cross or the chairman of the Central Committee of the Democratic People's Republic of Korea Red Cross), shall be composed of hometown visitors, an art troupe, press members, guides and support personnel.

(2) The size of a hometown visiting group shall be 300, and an art troupe 100 including production staff and performers such as chorus members, dancers, musicians, etc.

(3) The number of press members shall be around 100.

(4) Guides and support personnel shall be 50 to 60 including the head of the group.

3. Method of Exchange

Visting groups shall be exchanged simultaneously.

4. Period of Visiting

The visiting period shall be September 20–26, 1985 (six nights and seven days).

5. Places and Method of Visits

The members of the hometown visiting groups shall be teamed by special cities, direct-controlled cities and provinces depending on the places to be visited, and shall be grouped into teams of appropriate numbers in special cities, direct-controlled cities and provinces for direct visits to their hometowns. They shall be accompanied by visiting press members.

6. Scope of Meeting

The meetings shall be with the direct ascendents and descendents of a family at the time of separation and any children they many have, up to third cousins on the father's side and first cousins on the mother's and wife's side. Depending on the visitor's wishes, other relatives whose fate and whereabouts have been confirmed may be included.

7. Place and Frequency of Performances of Art Troupes

(1) Places of mutual conveneince shall be provided for performances.

(2) The performances shall be once a day and shall total two to

three in number.

8. The Nature of Performances

(1) Performances shall be of an artistic nature with emphasis on national traditions, and without any ideological and political elements.

(2) Stage sets, props and music of nature praising specific persons, political propaganda or demagogy shall not be used.

(3) There shall be no moderator's exposition at the time of the performances.

9. Exchange of Scripts and Advance Check of Performance Sites

(1) Scripts shall be exchanged eight days before the visits.

(2) To check in advance the preparations for the performances, compositions, sets and sound and lighting effects, technical personnel including producers, stage directors and setting, lighting and sound technicians shall inspect the performance sites.

10. Duration of Performances

The performances shall be about 120 minutes in accordance with international practices.

− Matters Related to Administrative and Procedural Issues −

1. Guarantee of Personal Safety

A memorandum guaranteeing personal safety shall be delivered to the other side eight days before the visits, and a statement by the relevant authorities guaranteeing the personal safety shall be made public seven days before the visits.

2. Transportation and Communications

(1) The transportation of the members of the visiting groups, equipment and other necessary items between Seoul and Pyongyang shall be made with the vehicles (including equipment and personnel) of the visiting side.

(2) Vehicles for the head of the Red Cross and his attendants, business liaison by support personnel and for hometown visits by hometown

251

visitors shall be provided by the hosting side.

(3) During the visits, pouches shall be operated between Seoul and Pyongyang twice a day.

(4) For liaison and press purposes during the visits, the 20 existing direct south-north telephone circuits shall be used and, if ncessary, additional circuits shall be installed through mutual agreement.

(5) During the stay and transit of the members of hometown visiting groups in local areas, the hosting side shall guarantee the formation of communications networks so that the personnel of the visiting side could make communications contacts with their liaison center.

3. Press Coverage

The hosting side shall guarantee press coverage by the press members of the visiting side at the scenes of family reunions, and shall provide various conveniences for press   coverage.

4. Place of Passage and Passage Procedures

(1) The place of passage shall be Panmunjom.

(2) As for passage procedures, personnel shall be checked by the hosting side in their respective vehicles. Articles other than equipment and belongings shall be checked separately.

5. Time of Notification of Visitors' List

(1) The lists of hometown visitors shall be notified to the other side 15 to 20 days before the visits.

(2) The lists of the members of art troupes, press members and support personnel shall be notified to the other side eight days before the visits (at the time of the delivery of a memorandum guaranteeing personal safety).

6. Format of Lists of Hometown Visitors

(1) In the lists of hometown visitors, the section for hometown visitors shall be itemized with columns for the name, sex, age, hometown address, relationship with the persons to be visited, and a picture of each visitor.

(2) In the lists of hometown visitors, the section for the persons to be visited shall be itemized with columns for the name, sex, age, hometown address, the time of separation, and other information that could be of

help in locating a person or persons.

7. Format of Lists of Art Troupe Members, Press Members and Support Personnel

The lists of the visiting group members other than hometown visitors shall be itemized with columns for the name, sex, age, area of participation and a picture.

8. Insignia for Visitors

(1) Members of hometown visiting groups, art troupes and support personnel shall wear a Red Cross insignia marked with the side to which the wearer belongs.

(2) press members shall wear armbands in addition to the insignia of the visiting groups. Other matters shall be in accordance with the practices of the South-North Red Cross Conference.

9. Belongings

(1) Individual persons may carry daily necessities like clothes and cosmetics, cameras, video cameras, tape recorders, radios, simple medicines and stationery goods ncessary for reporting.

(2) Necessary supplies shall be stage costumes, chemicals, kits, musical instruments, special illumination tools, items necessary for performance such as stage settings, items for press coverage, items for recording, and other necessary administrative supplies.

10. Activities of Visitors and Matters to Be Respected in Carrying Belongings

(1) Visitors cannot propagandize on and praise or slander any specific thought, system and persons, and shall be prevented from carrying materials related thereto and hazardous items.

(2) No check, search or seizure can be made of the items carried by visting group members.

(3) In the event there occurs behavior or exists an item or items that contravenes the provisions of Paragraph (1) above, it shall be notified to the top official of the visiting group for action against it.

(4) Each visitor shall carry an identification card issued by the president (chairman) of the Red Cross of his or her side.

11. Itineraries

(1) Itineraries shall be delivered to the other side eight days before the visits, which shall then be determined through discussion.

(2) Visits by the top official of a visiting group to Red Cross offices, scenes of events or festivals and tourist sites of the other side shall be determined at the time of the discussion of the itineraries.

(3) Sight-seeing trips and visits to festivals or other events by art troupe members, too, shall be determined at the time of the discussion of the itineraries, which shall be conducted after the first performance.

12. Lodging

(1) The members of a visiting group shall be lodged and boarded at the same lodging facilities.

(2) Provision of an office inside the lodging facilities shall be guaranteed for the liaison and support business of a visiting group.

(3) Provision of a press room including photo processing and printing facilities inside the lodging facilities shall be guaranteed for preparing and transmitting of press items by press members.

13. Others

(1) During visits to the area of the other side, visitors shall follow the guideance and rules of the other side.

(2) The hosting side shall make provisions so that the visiting troupe can rehearse at the performance site prior to the formal presentations.

(3) Auxiliary workers for setting up the stages, ordinary lighting equipment and other needs related to the performances shall be provided by the hosting side.

(4) Performance programs shall be prepared, carried and distributed by the side presenting performance.

Meanwhile, the NKRC delegation, contrary to the agreement reached at the eighth full-dress meeting and the wishes of the dispersed families for direct visits to their hometowns, insisted that the places to be visited be restricted to Seoul and Pyongyang. Also, contrasting to their offer at the eighth meeting that the members of an art troupe should be 100, they now asserted that an art troupe should be composed of 300 persons.

254

In particular, whereas the ROKNRC delegation suggested that political elements that could irritate the other side and praise of specific individuals should be eliminated from the performances, the NKRC delegation asserted that the contents of the performances should not be controlled while demanding that the performances be televised live, and posters and other things used to advertise the performances.

But, the two sides, recognizing the need to make an advance check of performance sites, agreed in principle to implement the proposed exchange during the month of September instead of August as they had agreed earlier.

With respect to the issues of the places to be visited and the size of the visiting groups, the areas where the two sides showed a wide discrepancy, the two delegations decided to discuss them further during the second contacts. They agreed to have the NKRC further study the question of the places to be visited and the ROKNRC the issue of the size of the visiting groups.

The substance of the proposals advanced by the NKRC during the first contacts was as follows :

– Substance of NKRC Proposals –

1. Issues of Name and Composition of Visiting Groups, Period of Stay, and Time and Method of Exchange

(1) Name of Visiting Groups : Red Cross Art Troupes and Hometown Visiting Groups.

(2) Composition of Visiting Group : 700 persons in all – 300 for a hometown visiting group, 300 art troupe members, 50 press members and 50 working-level officials.

(3) Period of Stary in Other Side's Area : Three nights and four days.

(4) Time of Exchange of Visting Groups : Concurrence on ROKNRC suggestion for September.

2. Issue of Exchange of Art Troupes

(1) Contents and Duration of Performances : Contents shall be determined at each side's convenience, and the duration of performances less

255

than two hours.

(2) Frequency of Performances : Three to four times.

(3) Informing about Contents of Performances : Televising live, and use of performance posters.

3. Issue of Hometown Visiting Group

(1) Scope of Visitors : Those whose hometowns are in the area of the other side, the south or the north

(2) Meeting with families and relatives in Seoul and Pyongyang.

4. Issue of Conveniences and Safety Guarantee

(1) During the period of stay in the area of the other side, lodging, boarding and all other conveniences shall be guaranteed by the hosting side free of charge.

(2) Relevant authorities of each side shall issue statements guaranteeing personal safety, the original copies of which shall be exchanged three days before the visits.

(3) Detailed itineraries during the stay of a visiting group in the area of the other side shall depend on the guidance by the hosting side based on an advance mutual agreement.

(b) Second Working-Level Delegates Contacts

At the second working-level delegates contacts held on July 19, the NKRC delegation asserted from the outset that the proposals they made at the first contact were all realistic and reasonable, whereas the ideas of the ROKNRC lacked justification. They insisted that the places to be visited should be restricted to Seoul and Pyongyang.

On the other hand, the ROKNRC delegation showed a flexible posture. Recalling that the NKRC side was to review the question of the places to be visited and the ROKNRC delegation the issue of the size of the visiting groups, the ROKNRC delegation suggested that if hometown visitors could directly visit their hometowns, the size of both hometown visiting groups and art troupes could be fixed without much difficulty.

Nevertheless, the NKRC kept arguing unfoundedly that the two sides had in effect agreed at the eighth full-dress meeting to restrict the places to be visited to Seoul and Pyongyang. They asserted that the ROKNRC insistence on dircet hometown visits only stood in the way of the progress of the working-level contancts.

The ROKNRC delegation made it clear that at no time did the two sides agree during the eighth full-dress meeting to limit the places to be visited to Seoul and Pyongyang. It pointed out that the words "hometown visiting" implied direct hometown visits. The ROKNRC delegation then suggested that the issue of visiting places and other matters be discussed and resolved one by one.

Seeking a breakthrough, the ROKNRC delegation proposed that one delegate each meet separately 30 minutes after the end of the working-level contacts, but this was rejected by the north. The NKRC even refused to agree on the time of the next contacts, contending that the stands of the two sides differed basically, a further meeting could not result in any affirmative results. The NKRC demanded that the ROKNRC notify them over the direct telephone only when the south could agree to their idea.

(c) Third Working-level Delegates Contacts

Under an agreement reached at unofficial contacts between the working-level officials of the two Red Cross Societies at Panmunjom twice on August 17 and August 19, the third working-level delegates contacts were opened at 10 a.m. August 22, 1985, at the conference room of the Neutral Nations Supervisory Commission behind closed doors.

Since the two sides concentrated at the third contact on adjusting the wording of their respective versions of an agreement based on what were discussed at the unofficial contacts, they could reach, without much difficulties, a complete agreement on detailed procedural matters related to the exchange of dispersed family hometown visitors and art troupes.

They agreed to undertake the project by simultaneously exchanging the groups for four days, September 20–23, 1985, and to fix the number of each visiting group at 151–a group leader which should be the head of the central organization of each Red Cross, 50 hometown visitors, 50 art troupe members, 30 press members and 20 support personnel. The two sides also decided to make Seoul and Pyongyang the only places to be visited.

The text of the agreement reached was as follows :

– Agreement Regarding the Exchange of Groups of South-North Dispersed Family Hometown Visitors and Art Troupes –

At the third working-level delegates contacts of the eighth full-dress Red Cross meeting held on August 22, 1985, the two sides agreed to carry out the exchange of hometown visitors and art troupes as follows in observance of the 40th anniversary of national liberation.

1. Name of Visiting Groups

The name of the visiting groups shall be determined at each side's convenience. The Republic of Korea National Red Cross shall call them "Groups of South-North Dispersed Family Hometown Visitors and Art Troupes."

2. Composition and Size of Visiting Groups

(1) Each group, headed by the highest official of each central Red Cross organization(the president of the Republic of Korea Nationl Red Cross and the chairman of the Central Committee of the Democratic People's Republic of Korea Red Cross), shall be composed of hometown visitors, an art troupe, press members and support personnel.

(2) The size of a visiting group shall be 151 in all, including the highest official of each central Red Cross organization, and shall include :

–Fifty hometown visitors, mostly those hailing from Seoul and Pyongyang.

–Fifty art troupe members (production staff and performers)

–Thirty press members

–Twenty support personnel.

3. Method of Exchange

Visiting groups shall be exchanged simultaneously.

4. Time of Visiting

The time of the visiting shall be September 20–23(three nights and four days.)

5. Places of Visits

The places to be visited shall be Seoul and Pyongyang

6. Arrangement and Scope of Meeting

(1) The two sides shall assist hometown visitors in conveniently locating their families and relatives and in facilitating their meetings under the humanitarian principles of the Red Cross.

(2) The meetings shall be with direct ascendents and descendents of a family at the time of separation and any children they may have. The relatives shall include up to third cousins on the father's side and first cousins on the mother's and wife's side. Depending on the visitors' wishes, other relatives whose fate and whereabouts have been confirmed may be included.

7. Place and Frequency of Performances of Art Troupes

(1) The places of the performances shall be theaters, with complete facilities, which the hosting side offers with good faith.

(2) There shall be two performances for each side.

8. The Nature of Performances

(1) The performances shall be of an artistic nature with emphasis on the nation's traditional songs and dances, and shall not slander, defame irritate the other side.

(2) During performances, moderators may introduce repertoires that are free of political elements and that do not slander or irritate the other side.

9. Exchange of Scripts and Advance Check of Performance Sites.

(1) Scripts shall be provided to the other side three days before the visits.

(2) In order to check in advance matters necessary for the preparation of the performances such as the issues of compositions, change of sets, sound, lighting and other effects, two Red Cross officials and three stage technicians shall visit the other side's performance site September 10–12, 1985.

10. Duration of Performances

Each performance shall last about 120 minutes.

11. Guarantee of Personal Safety

A statement by the relevant authorities guaranteeing the personal safety of the group members, shall be made public seven days before the visits, and the original copy of it shall be delivered to the other side.

12. Transportation and Communications

(1) Members of the visiting groups, equipment and other necessary items entering the hosting side's area by way of Panmunjom shall be transported by the hosting side's vehicles.

(2) During the visits, pouches shall be operated between Seoul and Pyongyang twice a day.

(3) For liaison and press purposes during the visits, the 20 existing direct south-north telephone circuits shall be used and, if necessary, additional circuits shall be installed through mutual agreement.

13. Press Coverage

The hosting side shall guarantee press coverage by the press members of the visiting side at the scene of family reunions, and provide various convenience for press converage.

14. Place of Passage and Passage Procedures

The place of passage shall be Panmunjom, and the passage procedures shall be in accordance with the practice of the South-North Red Cross Conference.

15. Time of Notification of Visitor's List

(1) The lists of hometown visitors shall be notified to the other side 10 days before the visits.

(2) The lists of the members of art troupes, press members and support personnel shall be notified to the other side three days before the visits.

16. Format of Lists of Hometown Visitors

(1) In the lists of hometown visitors, the section for hometown visitors shall be itemized with columns for the name, sex, age, hometown address, relationship with the persons to be visited, and a picture of each

visitor.

(2) In the lists of hometown visitors, the section for the persons to be visited shall be itemized with columns for the name, sex, age, hometown addres, the time of separation, and other information that could be of help in locating the person.

17. Format of Lists of Art Troupe Members, Press Members, and Support Personnel

The lists for the visiting group members other than hometown visitors shall be itemized with columns for the name, sex, position in one's occupation, area of participation and a picture of each member.

18. Insignia and Identification Cards for Visitors

(1) Members of home town visiting groups, art troupes and support personnel shall wear a Red Cross insignia marked with the side to which the wearer belongs.

(2) Press members shall wear armbands in addition to the insignia of visiting groups. Other matters shall be in accordance with the practices of the South-North Red Cross Conference.

(3) Each visitor shall carry an identification card issued by the president (chairman) of the Red Cross of his or her side.

19. Itineraries

The itineraries for the visits shall be delivered to the other side seven days before the visits, which shall then be determined through discussion.

20. Others

(1) Visitors shall follow the guidance and orders of the side they are visiting.

(2) Lodging, boarding, communications and other conveniences shall be provided by the hosting side.

(3) The hosting side shall make provisions so that the visiting troupe can rehearse at the performance site prior to the formal presentations.

(4) Auxiliary workers for setting up the stages, ordinary lighting equipment and other needs related to the performances shall be provided by the hosting side.

261

(5) Performance programs shall be prepared, carried and distributed by the side presenting the performance.

Upon agreeing to exchange groups of hometown visitors and art troupes in September 20-23, 1985, the two Red Cross Societies had four rounds of preliminary liaison contacts on September 8,10, 17 and 19 to discuss overall matters related to the exchange, and to exchange the lists of the 151 visitors and those families and relatives the hometown visitors wished to meet.

At the same time, the government authorities of both sides announced that they would guarantee the personal safety of the 151 visitors during their travel and stay in their respective areas, and exchanged the original copies of the announcement on September 13.

Regarding the exchange of art troupes, each side, based on an agreement reached at the working-level contacts, sent a five-man advance team to the other's area September 10-12 to inspect and check the performance sites in advance.

The stage was thus set for the first hometown visits and consequent reunions between dispersed families and relatives in the 40-year history of national division.

(2) *Realization of the Exchange of Hometown Visitors and Art Troupes*

The groups of south-north hometown visitors and art troupes were exchanged simultaneously at 9 : 30 a.m. September 20, 1985, to set the precious first instance of private-level personnel exchange in the 40 years of national division.

The visiting groups, each comprising 151 members and headed by their respective Red Cross president, reached Seoul and Pyongyang by way of Panmunjom to begin their four-day visits.

Despite the lapse of the 40 long years after national division, 65 of the 100 hometown visitors of the two sides were joyfully reunited with 92 of their family members and relatives in Seoul and Pyongyang. In the family meetings of September 21-22, 35 of ROKNRC visitors met 41 of their families and relatives in Pyongyang and 30 NKRC visitors with 51 in Seoul.

Meanwhile, the visiting art troupes presented two pefromances each September 21-22 : the art troupe from Seoul at the Grand Pyongyang Theater and the Pyongyang troupe at the National Theater in Seoul.

It should be taken into account that the exchange performances barely realized in the midst of protracted disruption and distrust. But while the folk dances of the Seoul troupe's performances drew quite affirmative responses from the north Korean spectators, the reaction of many of the viewers of the north Korean performances was that they reminded them of military-like collective gymnastics and that the Pyongyang performances were far from the traditional arts of Korea as they were heavily patterned after Chinese and Soviet traits.

The four-day exchange of hometown visitors and art troupes, first suggested by the ROKNRC as a pilot project to commemorate the 40th anniversary of national liberation, ended when the 151-member visiting groups returned to their respective areas by way of Panmunjom at noon of September 23, 1985.

Though the hometown visits were limited in terms of the areas visited and the number of people involved and there were some unsatisfactory elements in the course of implementation, the exchange of the visitors was highly significant in that it set the precedent of dispersed families meeting their families and relatives traveling back and forth between the south and the north personally for the first time in the 40-year history of national division. Moreover, as it was the first fruition reaped through the south-north dialogue begun in the 1970, the exchange constituted an epochal milestone that brightened the chances of inter-Korean issues being resolved through dialogue.

f. Inter-Korean Economic Talks

(1) Initiation of Talks

In circumstances where a mood for inter-Korean exchanges and cooperation grew following the delivery and receipt of materials for flood victims, Deputy Prime Minister and Economic Planning Minister Shin Byong-hyon on October 12, 1984, proposed an inter-Korean economic conference to discuss trade and other economic cooperation between south and north Korea. In a message sent to Choe Yong-rim, Deputy Premier of the north's Administrative Council, Shin suggested that an inter-Korean economic meeting be held with the attendance of delegates representing the economic authorities and private economic organizations of the two sides with vice minister-level government officials as chief delegates.

The full text of Deputy Prime Minister Shin's message was as follows :

Recently our government proposed to your side the early implementation of inter-Korean trade and economic cooperation. stressing that south and north Korea should thereby improve relations and pursue common prosperity.

Our proposal is intended to pave the way to mutual economic assistance between the brethren of south and north Korea who have been separated from each other for nearly 40 years, and to use this development to advance at least a little bit the unification of the homeland which all our people crave.

We are positive that if only inter-Korean trade in commodities and economic cooperation can be realized, it will immediately and directly help improve the lives of our south and north Korean brethren, and further contribute to the realization of balanced development, common prosperity and national reconciliation in all areas in the future.

In particular, we believe that in order to safeguard national survival and interests at this time of ever-fiercer international economic competition, south and north Korea should transcend ideologies and systems and join forces instead of continuing to waste national capabilities in antagonism and confrontation.

It is from this standpoint that we hope trade in commodities and economic cooperation between south and north Korea will be realized as soon as possible as our government recently proposed.

Regarding your side's pursuit of new systematic measures to promote economic cooperation with the outside world, we expect that such a step could be conducive to exploring inter-Korean economic exchanges and cooperation in the future. Our gov-

ernment will positively support the participation by our businessmen and industries in inter-Korean trade and economic cooperation.

We believe that to this end, it will be necessary for economic authorities of the south and north Korean governments and representatives of private economic organizations to have an open-hearted dialogue.

If it is determined to be necessary, it would also be good to establish an organization for inter-Korean economic cooperation composed of government authorities of both sides and representatives of economic circles to serve as a permanent body to promote trade and economic cooperation between south and north Korea.

We propose that an inter-Korean economic meeting be held to discuss these questions, attended by delegates representing the authorities of the government and private economic organizations of south and north Korea with vice minister-level government officials as chief delegates.

We hope that such an inter-Korean meeting will be realized soon. We leave it to your side to determine the time and venue of the proposed meeting. We look forward to an affirmative response.

In the meantime, the four economic organizations of the south issued a joint statement on October 13, supporting Deputy Prime Minister Shin's proposal for a south-north economic conference and urging the north to show an affirmative response. The four organizations were the Federation of Korean Industries, Korean Traders' Association, Korea Federation of Small Businesses and the Korean Chamber of Commerce and Industry. By concretely citing the areas where the two sides could engage in joint-venture businesses, the economic organizations said they were willing to participate positively in joint businesses with the north.

On October 16, 1984, north Korea agreed to the south's proposal for economic talks. In a letter to the south, which was signed by Kim Hwan, deputy premier of the Administrative Council, the north suggested that the first meeting be held at Panmunjom on November 15, 1084, with the attendance of five delegates from each side with a vice minister-level government official as chief delegate.

In response, the government of the Republic of Korea, in a radio message signed by Deputy Prime Minister Shin on November 2, welcomed the north's favorable response to the proposal and counter-proposed that the delegations consist of seven members each. He said that to ensure the effective implementation of trade and economic cooperation, "it would be more desirable for the delegations to include members of economic organizations in addition to government officials."

The north agreed to the south's suggestion and the first meeting was to be held at the conference room of the Neutral Nations Supervisory Commission on November 15, 1984.

The lists of the two sides' delegations to the south-north economic conference, which were exchanged over the direct telephone on November 12 and 13, were as follows :

–Delegation of the Republic of Korea–

Chief delegate : Kim Ki-hwan, secretary general of the International Economic Policy Council

Delegate : Cha sang-pil, second assistant minister of Trade and Industry

Delegate : Koo Bon-tae, director of research, National Unification Board

Delegate : Kim In-joon, executive director of the Korea Chamber of Commerce and Industry

Delegate : Shin Bong-shik, executive director of the Federation of Korean Industries

Delegate : Noh Chin-shik, executive managing director of the Korean Traders' Association

Delegate : Lim Byong-suk, managing director of the Korean Federation of Small Businesses

–Delegation of North Korea–

Chief delegate : Li Song-rok, vice minister of Foreign Trade

Delegate :Kye Hyong-myong, director of the Mining Industry Commission

Delegate : Paek Jun-hyok, director of the Foreign Trade Commission

Delegate : Ho Hang-chan, vice president of the External Trade Cooperation Company

Delegate : Li Chin-sik, director general of the Metal Industry Ministry

Delegete : Son Jong-chol, deputy director of the Trade and Economics Institute

Delegate : Kim Hae-ryong, vice president of the Kwangmyong Allied Company

(2) First Meeting

The first south-north economic meeting was opened at 10 a.m. November 5, 1984, at the conference room of the Netural Nations Supervisory Commission to discuss the possible implementation of trade and other economic cooperation between the south and the north.

At the first economic talks ever held since national division, the two sides arrived at a de facto agreement on the operational procedures of the meeting and some tradable items, and also considerably narrowed their differences on the topics of the talks, presaging smooth progress for meeting.

In his first speech, the south's Chief Delegate Kim Ki-hwan stressed that the two sides should do all they could to make the talks a success, stating, "If this meeting could progress well resulting in trade and economic cooperation between the south and the north, it would contribute directly to improving the lives of those of both the south and the north, and contribute immensely to easing tensions, fostering confidence building and promoting national reconciliation between the south and the north."

Chief Delegate Kim then set forth as the topics of the talks 1) the question of implementing trade between the south and the north, and 2) the question of implementing economic cooperation between the south and the north. With respect to Topic No.1, he made a ten-point proposal as follows on such things as tradable items, volume of trade, method of transactions, and currencies for settlement. Kim suggested that the authorities of the two sides conclude a trade agreement and a memorandum for detailed matters based on his ten-point proposal :

First, trade items can be determined through mutual consultation. We can trade beginning with those among the items both sides are interested in whose transactions are relatively easy. For instance, we are interested in purchasing from your side such mineral goods as briquette coal, iron are, pig iron, lead ingot, zinc ingot, silica and scrap ; agricultural and fishery products like pollack, silk cocoons, red beans, corn and castor beans ; and materials for herbal medicines.

Meanwhile, we can sell to your side metalic goods such as steel and steel products, copper and copper products, and aluminum products ; machines like household and industrial sewing machines, power tillers, cars and bicycles ; such electric and electronic goods as watches, color television sets and audio systems ; textiles including yarns, raw materials, fabrics and blankets ; and rubber belts, pianos, potassium sulfate, refined glycerin and medicines.

Second, it would be good to determine the volume of trade on an item-by-item basis in consideration of each side's domestic situation of demand and supply, and its volume of external trade.

Third, it is desirable that prices are set in principle on the basis of objective international prices through negotiations between the trading parties.

Fourth, the subjects of trade can be the specific trading offices or companies designated by each side's government authorities. It will be good to allow a single trading party to do trade in the initial stage with a switch to multiple ones in due course.

Fifth, we think it is most reasonable that trade is implemented based in principle on letters of credit issued by the banks of third countries. At an early stage, compensation trade could be considered, and so could be the method of settlement agreement when trade becomes expanded.

Sixth, settlement can be handled in principle by the banks of third countries. Depending on development, however, the foreign exchange banks of the two sides could be considered.

Seventh, settlement currencies can be selected from among the internationally exchangeable currencies like U.S. dollars, Deutschemarks and British pounds in use by the two sides in common. Creation of a settlement unit applicable only to inter-Korean settlement could be considered in the future.

Eighth, no tariff should be assessed inasmuch as inter-Korean trade is not external trade.

Ninth, it would be convenient to use the ships of the purchasing side in principle when large amounts of cargo are involved. If and when trade becomes expanded, the linking of a railroad between the two sides could be considered to make transportation by rail possible. Small amounts of cargo could be transported by trucks, for which it would be good to create a joint cargo terminal at Panmunjom.

Tenth, other detailed matters incidental to trade, such as issues involving customs, inspection, communications, accident handling and settlement of disputes can be resolved through mutual consultation.

The south Korean delegation also stated that parallel with material trade, the two sides would be able to engage in joint-venture investment in the development of resources like briquette coal and iron ore ; in the production of electric home appliances such as color television sets and audio systems ; in the production of textiles like polyester yarns, medicines and cosmetics ; and in such service areas as tourism and maritime transportation. The southern delegation then proposed that to promote inter-Korean trade and economic cooperation smoothly and steadily, a South-North Economic Cooperation Committee be created among the officials of the government and economic organizations of the two sides.

On the other hand, the north Korean delegation, saying that various difficulties and complexities are foreseen in the realization of economic collaboration and exchanges between the south and the north, stressed that to surmount them, the two sides should adhere to the three major principles of unification, that are, independence, peaceful unification and grand national unity as well as to the principle of respect for mutual opinions and reciprocity. Suggesting that the agenda topic of the economic talks should "concern the realization of collaboration and exchanges in the area of economics between the south and the north", the north's delegation set forth their ideas of economic collaboration and material exchanges as follows :

–North Korean Proposal on Economic Collaboration–

1. Joint Development and Utilization of Underground Resources

Each side should explore mines and minerals in the other's area with its own efforts and facilities.

2. Collaboration in Fishery Area

The south and the north should create joint fishery zones for joint development and use. A joint-venture fisheries company should be established.

3. Collaboration in Farm Area.

Reclamable lands along the west coast of the south should be developed jointly, or the irrigation networks severed by the Military Demarcation Line should be restored.

4. A South-North Economic Cooperation Committee should be created as a joint cooperation body.

–North Korean Proposal on Exchange of Materials–

1. Tradable Items

(1) Items the north is interested in selling to the south : industrial products such as iron ore, coal, magnesia clinker and general machinery ; and such farm and fishery goods as pollack, rice and corn.

(2) Items the north is interested in purchasing from the south: industrial products such as iron materials, tungsten ore, naphtha and petroleum·; and such farm and fishery products as salt and tangerines.

2. Method of Transaction

It is reasonable to conduct the trade of raw materials, finished products and farm goods, with exchanges taking the form of raw materials for raw materials, finished products for finished products and farm goods for farm goods.

3. Transportation

It would be effective to use railroads and harbors. To this end, the Seoul-Shinuiju line should be connected, and the Nampo and Wonsan harbors in the north and the Inchon and Pohang harbors in the south should be opened and used.

At the first meeting, the two sides came near to an accord on such matters as tradable items, the development of natural resources, the creation of Joint South-North Fishery Zones, connection of the Seoul-Shinjiju railroad line and the creation of a South-North Economic Cooperation Committee. In particular, the two sides agreed that the items the south wanted to purchase and the north was interested in sale were briquette coal, iron ore, magnesia clinker, corn and pollack, and those which the north wanted to purchase and the south wanted to sell were iron and steel products and the textiles.

As to the issue of the agenda topics, some differences were apparent because the north insisted on the plan, "concerning the realization of collaboration and exchanges in the area of economics between the south and the north." However, when the south's delegation offered a compromise, "the question of implementing material trade and economic cooperation between the south and the north," the north seemed to respond favorably by changing for instance the expression "collaboration" into "cooperation" as suggested by the south. Yet the north's delegation insisted that the issue should be further discussed at the next meeting. No topic was thus agreed on at the first meeting.

Meanwhile, prior to entering the business talks and again immediately before the adjournment of the meeting, the north Korean delegation proposed contacts between Deputy Prime Minister Shin Byong-hyon and his north Korean counterpart, Deputy Premier Kim Hwan. The north Korean delegation expressed the wish that the proposal be conveyed to Deputy Prime Minister Shin.

Also at the first meeting, the south Korean delegation suggested that future meetings be held behind closed doors to ensure their effective progress, and that one of the direct telephone lines already installed between the two sides be designated exclusively for the economic meetings to facilitate liaison activities and discussions. The north Korean side agreed to the proposal.

(3) Second Meeting

The second south-north economic meeting, originally slated for December 5,1984, was held only on May 17, 1985, six months after the first meeting because the north put it off twice on the grounds of the shooting incident at Panmunjom and the Team Spirit '85 military training exercise.

During the meeting, Im In-taek, second assistant minister of trade and industry, was newly named as a member of the south's delegation in place of Cha Sang-pil, while Han Yong-up, executive member of the Chosun International Trade Promotion Committee, replaced Paek Jun-hyok as a member of the north Korean delegation.

Pointing out that as a matter of course the topics of the meeting should first be determined and then a discussion of the issues entered into, south Korean Chief Delegate Kim Ki-hwan suggested that the topic should be the "question of implementing trade and economic cooperation between the south and the north" as almost agreed on at the first meeting.

Chief Delegate Kim said that to ensure the effective operation and good results of the meeting, the two sides ought to reaffirm the ideas they had in common among their suggestions advanced at the first meeting and then formally agree on such matters through sincere discussions, He then suggested that the two sides enter into trade initially of those items both sides virtually agreed on, which included iron ore, briquette coal, magnesia clinker, corn, pollack, iron and steel products and textiles. The south's chief delegate said that as a measure to advance the realization of trade, the south was willing to purchase immediately from the north 300,000 tons of briquette coal, an item which the north wanted to sell and the south was interested in purchasing.

Also expressing the hope that the Seoul-Shinuiju railroad line would be connected within the year, Chief Delegate Kim proposed that contacts between working-level railroad officials be held within a month to discuss technical issues related to the linking of the railroad.

The contents of the proposal made by Chief Delegate Kim Ki-hwan at the second meeting with respect to the implementation of trade and other forms of economic assistance were as follows :

Of the ideas advanced by both sides at the previous meeting, I shall mention those issues which need to be discussed first today.

First, it would be good to implement trade promptly on those items on which the two sides have reached an accord. Hoping that inter-Korean trade will begin within year, our side, as a measure to advance the realization of trade, proposes to purchase 300,000 tons of briquette coal from your side immediately.

If the two sides were to change mutually their opinions, the tradable items could be increased from those on which we have already reached an accord. For example, of the items your side desires to purchase, we can offer fishery products from the southern coastal sea such as laver, brown seaweed and anchovies ; local specialities like salt and tangerines : and various industrial products. Your side, too, could offer additional raw materials and farm and fishery products to our side.

In this connection, I shall give our side's opinion as to the method of trade.

I would like to know a little further whether the method of trade your side suggested, that is, exchanges in the form of raw materials for raw materials, finished products for finished products and farm and fishery goods for farm and fishery goods, is absolute or there is some room to accommodate other methods of trade.

In our view, if materials were traded under the method your side suggested, it would result in the extreme restriction of tradable items, and would, in the long-run, entail considerable difficulties in expanding trade.

It would be good to implement compensation trade incorporating various items

273

without distinguishing raw materials, finished goods or farm and fishery products. And, depending on the expansion of trade, it could be gradually developed into the method of settlement agreement.

I believe that it would be reasonable to implement the trade of materials by concluding an inter-Korean trade agreement based on the ten-point idea of trade, involving the afore-mentioned issues our side suggested. I would like to know your side's opinion of this.

The issue of linking a railroad, which was raised by both sides, can be considered to have been mutually agreed on. Therefore, it would be good to begin preparing it now so that railroad transport would be available when trade begins between the south and the north.

Hoping that the Seoul-Shinuiju line will be linked within this year, I propose that contacts between working-level railroad officials of the two sides be held within the next month to discuss technical problems related to the linking of the railroad.

And, as to the question of opening ports, we can open Inchon and Pohang to your side, and your side could open Nampo and Wonsan to us when trade is actually initiated.

To ensure economic efficiency in loading and unloading, it is only reasonable that the party doing the selling designate the loading place and the party doing the purchasing the unloading place on a case-by-case basis. Therefore, the two sides could open more harbors in addition to the four if it is considered convenient and agreed on.

Second, there needs to be some adjustment of opinions with regard to the two areas of economic cooperation, of which necessity has already been recognized by both sides. We would need to have concrete discussions about this.

At the previous meeting, your side, while raising the "issue of utilizing each other's coal and other mines with one's own efforts and facilities," suggested that your side provide our side with iron and coal while our side offer tungsten and molybdenum to your side. However, as your side well knows, your side has more tungsten deposits than our side, and the deposits of our side's molybdenum mines are limited and not large enough to be explored jointly with your side. Therefore, our side can offer your side kaoline and silica mines instead, whose quality is outstanding and among the world's best and whose deposits are so abundant that they could be shared with your side. I believe that this issue can be resolved easily if your side accepts this counter-proposal of our side.

Concerning the issue of establishing joint fishery zones for the fishermen of the south and the north, I believe we can expect good results if the two sides come up with some good ideas and discuss them in a positive way. Since this would first require various technical review, it would also be good to discuss this issue through contacts between working-level officials of two sides.

Third, the question of establishing an Inter-Korean Economic Cooperation Committee, too, can be satisfactorily agreed on if the two sides can come up with reasonable ideas and, based thereon, can adjust their opinions.

Last, I shall discuss our side's position regarding the issues of "reclaiming tidal lands along the west coast" and "linking irrigation networks" which your side proposed at the last meeting.

I think that given our side's level of expertise and experience, such projects as the reclamation of tidal lands and linking of irrigation networks are not worth undertaking in joint projects between the south and the north. Our side is quite capable of reclaiming tidal lands with our own ability. We have much experience in the reclamation of tidal lands at home and abroad, and maintain able professional technicians trained to the international standard and lots of equipment.

As your side knows, our side is engaged in civil engineering projects in many countries, earning universal recognition of our technology and ability. Currently we are successfully reclaiming shore land in Singapore and carrying out large-scale irrigation projects in the Middle East and Libya.

Also, concerning the question of linking the irrigation networks cut off by the Military Demarcation Line, we have already resolved the irrigation problem with various irrigation projects.

However, the north Korean delegation, without any utterance on material trade and economic cooperation, insisted only on the creation of a South-North Joint Economic Cooperation Committee headed by a deputy premier-level official from each side as an exclusive body for the discussion and resolution of matters related to economic cooperation and exchanges between the south and the north. They even refused to discuss the issue of agenda topics on which the two sides came near to an accord at the first meeting.

The south's delegation offered a compromising suggestion that since it would review the north Korean offer and disclose its response thereto at the following meeting, the second meeting should discuss the issue of topics and other items the two sides had already raised. Nonetheless, the north refused to enter into business discussion and disclosed the intention to replace the ongoing economic talks with a South-North Joint Economic Cooperation Committee, asserting that "to resolve problems smoothly, it is more efficient and effective in every respect to have a higher-level and authoritative meeting with actual power instead of working-level talks."

Details of the formation and operation of the South-North Joint Economic Cooperation Committee north Korea suggested at the second meeting were as follows :

1. Formation and Organization

(1) One chairman (deputy prime minister-level)and one vice chairman (minister-level)　seven members (minister-or vice minister-level), and a chief secretary (vice minister-level)

(2) Creation of seven sub-committees (each consisting of five members) : resources development, industry-technology, agriculture, fishery, commodity exchanges, transportation-communication, monetary-financing.

2. Function

(1) Discussing and determining the scope and size of economic

cooperation and exchanges, determining the basic form and method of cooperation and exchanges, and discussing uniform plans for cooperation and exchanges.

(2) Guaranteeing the implementation of matters of mutual agreement and determination, and discussing and mediating disputes between the two sides.

(3) Guiding sub-committees and discussing and resolving other matters.

3. Operation

(1) The Joint Committee shall meet every quarter in Pyongyang and Seoul in turns, and sub-committees shall meet at any time of mutual agreement. The first meeting of the Joint Committee shall be held in September in Pyongyang.

(2) Detailed operating procedures of the Joint Committee shall be discussed and adopted separately.

(4) Third Meeting

The inter-Korean economic meeting was held behind closed doors at the conference room of the Neutral Nations Supervisory Commission at 10 a.m. June 20, 1985.

In his first speech, the south's Chief Delegate Kim Ki-hwan, pointing out that there were many items in common among the ideas advanced by the two sides at the first and second meetings, suggested that at the third meeting, the two sides adopt an agreement which puts in order the common ideas aired at the first and second meetings with respect to material trade and economic cooperation and which also incorporates an idea of creating a Joint South-North Economic Cooperation Committee co-chaired by the deputy prime minister-level officials of the two sides as a consultative and implementation organization. He then urged the north to show an affirmative response.

The highlight of the proposal was to affirm the common ideas displayed at the first and second meetings and also to accommodate the creation of an economic cooperation organization headed by deputy prime minister-level officials as suggested by the north, thereby success-fully concluding the economic talks.

The draft agreement on the implementation of trade and economic cooperation and the establishment of the South-North Joint Economic Cooperation Committee put forth by the south Korean delegation was as follows :

−Agreement on the Implementation of Trade and Economic Cooperation and the Establishment of the South-North Joint Economic Cooperation Committee between the South and the North (Draft)−

The two sides,

Desiring to implement direct material trade and programs of eco-nomic cooperation on the basis of reciprocity and equality,

Recognizing that the implementation of direct trade and econo-mic cooperation will contribute to the prosperity and welfare of our peoples, and the peaceful reunification of our nation.

Being assured that trade and economic cooperation shall be im-plemented in good faith and with sincerity,

Have agreed as follows on the implementation of trade and eco-nomic cooperation and the establishment of the South-North Joint Economic Cooperation Committee :

1. The two sides shall take all necessary and appropriate measures to implement and expand trade and economic cooperation effectively be-tween them.

2. The two sides shall designate, for each commodity and project, appropriate trade organizations, corporations, associations, or other au-thorities to participate in commodity trade and economic cooperation projects.

3. Trade between the two sides shall be implemented according to the following guidelines except in cases where the two sides agree on a diffe-rent procedure.

a. The two sides shall start trade with the commodities specified below and may expand trade to other commodities by common consent.

(1) Commodities to be sold by the south : iron products, textiles, salt, tangerines, and such South Sea marine products as green seaweed, brown seaweed, oysters and anchovies.

(2) Commodities to be sold by the north : anthracite coal, iron ore, magnesia clinker, pollack and corn.

b. The amount and volume of trade shall be decided through consultations of the designated parties concerned, considering the supply and demand of the commodity.

c. The price of the commodity shall be decided by the designated parties concerned, considering international market prices.

d. The two sides shall conduct trade by means of Back-to-Back Letters of Credit issued from third country banks. However, in cases where the amount and value of commodities to be traded is the same, the two sides may conduct trade by means of barter trade without the exchange of Letters of Credit or notes.

e. A third country bank, to be agreed upon by the two sides, shall settle the accounts for the Letters of Credit.

f. The currencies for settlement shall be the British Pound and the Swiss Franc.

g. The two sides shall not impose customs or similar charges which they impose on imports from other countries, on the commodities they purchase from the other side.

h. As for customs procedures, inspections, dispute settlements, etc. In connection with commodity trade between the two sides, they shall apply the same regulations which they use for normal external trade.

4. The two sides shall reconnect the Seoul-Shinuiju railway line to facilitate the smooth transport of commodities for trade and economic cooperation.

5. The mode of transportation for commodities shall be determined through consultations between the designated parties, considering the character, weight, etc., of the commodities involved and the costs of

transport. In cases of marine transport, the two sides shall guarantee to extend the most favorable treatment to the transport ships of the other side regarding entry, anchoring, unloading and loading, departure, etc., and to handle all procedures promptly.

6. The two sides shall implement joint economic projects to promote the common prosperity of the peoples of both sides, and shall start joint economic projects in the areas specified below and expand projects into other areas by common consent.

a. The establishment of Joint Fishing Areas.

b. The joint development of natural resources.

7. The scale, method, conditions, timing, etc., for the implementation of the joint projects shall be determined through consultations of the designated parties concerned.

8. The two sides may, if agreed upon, extend exemption or reduction of income taxes, corporation taxes, property taxes, customs, and other taxes for the designated parties concerned of the other side when the designated parties concerned are operating in their territories.

9. The two sides shall open the ports of Inchon and Pohang in the south, and Nampo and Wonsan in the north in order to facilitate marine transport for commodity trade and joint economic projects. In addition, as trade and economic cooperation continue to expand, other ports may be opened as agreed upon.

10. The two sides shall establish communication facilities necessary for trade and joint economic projects, and these facilities may be expanded as agreed upon.

11. The two sides shall permit the designated parties concerned of the other side to visit their territories or territorial waters in order to conduct advance inspections for commodity trade, feasibility studies for joint projects, and related activites.

12. The two sides shall guarantee the visits and safety of the persons concerned with trade and economic cooperation of the other side and assist them as much as possible with traffic, communications, lodging and boarding, medical care, etc.

13. The two sides shall take prompt and effective relief measures for physical injuries incurred by the persons concerned of the other in one's area and notify the other side without delay of the details of the situation.

14. The two sides shall, within thirty days after the signing of the agreement, establish and operate the South-North Joint Economic Cooperation Committ (hereafter referred to as the "Joint Committee"), chaired by deputy prime minister-level officials of the two sides. The Joint Committee shall meet in order to carry out this agreement, to discuss and decide on the methods for developing commodity trade and joint economic projects, and to insure the implementation of all decisions.

15. The organization of the Joint Committee and supporting bodies shall be as follows :

a. The Joint Committee shall consist of seven members from each side: one chairman at the deputy prime minister level ; one vice chairman at the ministerial level ; and five other members at the ministerial or vice ministerial level selected from among the officials of the governement and economic circles.

b. Under the Joint Committee, there shall be the Sub-Committee for Commodity Trade and the Sub-committee for Economic Cooperation and there may be, if necessary, other special Sub-Committees through mutual agreement. To ensure the smooth operation of the Joint Committee and sub-committees, there may be small sub-committees.

c. Each sub-committee shall consist of five persons from each side including the chairman. Sub-committee chairmen shall be appointed by respective Joint Committee chairmen from among Joint Committee members. Sub-committee members shall be at the bureau director level.

d. Under the Joint Committee, there shall be a Joint Secretariat charged with working-level matters. The secretary general of the Joint Secretariat shall be appointed by the chairman of the Joint Committee form among the members of the Joint Committee. At the Secretariat, there shall be clerical officials of a number agreed on by the two sides.

The location of the Secretariat shall be Panmunjom.

16. The Joint Secretariat shall execute the following functions :

a. The faithful implementation of an agreement on commodity trade and economic cooperation projects between the south and the north.

b. Discussion and determination of measures to expand and develop commodity trade and economic cooperation projects between the south and the north. Guaranteeing of its implementation and the conclusion of necessary agreements.

c. Discussion and coordination of the problems arising from the implementation of an agreement on commodity trade and economic cooperation projects between the south and north.

d. Taking of necessary administrative measures to guarantee the safe transport of trading commodities and free travel of people concerned in the implementation of commodity trade and cooperation projects between the south and and the north

e. Promotion and encouragement of the mutual exchanges of persons, trade fairs, shows, information, materials, etc., related to commodity trade and economic cooperation projects between the south and te north.

f. Discussion and determination of other necessary measures to promote commodity trade and economic cooperation projects between the south and the north.

17. Sub-committees shall execute the following functions :

a. Discussion and determination of concrete methods for the implementation of measures agreed to or mandated by the Joint Committee, and insuring their implementation.

b. Preparation of a draft agreement necessary for the concrete realization of commodity trade and economic cooperation projects, and submitting it to the Joint Committee.

c. Discussion and settlement of problems arising in their respective areas and presentation of them, if necessary, to the Joint Committee.

18. The Joint Secretariat shall execute the following functions :

a. Provision of all necessary administrative assistance to the Joint

Committee and Sub-Committees in the form of arranging committee meetings, preparing the place and agenda for meetings, and recording.

b. Establishment and operation of a joint commodity exchange for the exchange of samples, material and letters related to commodity trade and economic cooperation projects.

c. Execution of liaison services and the provision of administrative support necessary for the transport of commodities and travels of people between the two sides.

19. The Joint Committee and sub-committees shall be operated as follows :

a. The meetings of the Joint Committee and the sub-committees shall be held at Panmunjom, and may be held in Seoul and Pyongyang as agreed upon between the two sides.

b. The regular meetings of the Joint Committee shall in principle be held every three months and the meetings of the sub-committees whenever deemed necessary as agreed upon between the two sides.

c. The meetings of the Joint Committee and sub-committees shall be held in principle behind closed doors. However, such meetings may be opened to the public under mutual agreement if necessary.

d. The trading parties and the parties to economic cooperation projects of the two sides and the secretary general and clerical officials of the Joint Secretariat may be allowed to attend the meetings of the Joint Committee and sub-committees.

e. Other matters necessary for the operation of the Joint Committee shall be determined separately through consultations.

20. The Joint Secretariat shall be established as follows :

a. The Joint Secretariat shall be established within thirty days after the signing of this agreement.

b. The Joint Secretariat shall use the House of Peace and Panmun-gak as temporary offices pending the time of the construction of the exclusive office building of the Joint Secretariat at Panmunjom.

c. The expenses necessary for the construction and operation of the exclusive office builiding of the Joint Secretariat shall be borne jointly.

21. This agreement may be amended or supplemented through mutual agreement.

22. This agreement shall be vailid for a period of five years, from the date of its entering into force. Upon the expiration of the said period, its validity shall be automatically extended for another period of five years unless either of the two sides notifies the other side of its intention to terminate this agreement one year prior to its expiration.

23. This agreement shall enter into force on the date when it is signed and authentic texts are exchanged.

In witness whereof, the undersigned, duly authorized by the highest authorities of their respective sides, signed this agreement and exchanged the equally authentic duplicate copies of the agreement done on 1985, 1985 at Panmunjom.

In reaction to this proposal put forth by the south, the north's delegation produced their version of a draft agreement containing only those ideas they offered during the second meeting, thus simply reiterating the stand shown at the second meeting.

The difference shown during the third meeting was that the south proposed to discuss and adopt those items the two sides suggested in common together with the proposed creation of a Joint Committee, while the north wanted only to adopt an agreement on the establishment of the Joint Committee regardless of the results made during the first and second meetings.

However, finding it unable to continue to turn a deaf ear to the accommodative ideas offered by the south, the north agreed in principle to discuss and adopt an Agreement on the Implementation of Trade and Economic Cooperation and the Establishment of a South-North Joint Economic Cooperation Committee. Based on the accord, the two sides decided to review each other's draft agreement and to have concrete discussions of this issue at the fourth meeting.

Meanwhile, as to the south's proposal to purchase 300,000 tons of briquette coal from the north and hold working-level contacts to discuss the linking of the Seoul-Shinuiju railroad line, the north Korean delegation asserted that since these matters were in principle agreed on, they could be resolved by the relevant sub-committees of the Joint Committee to be formed, thus showing no interest in their immediate implementation.

(5) Fourth Meeting

Amidst high public expectations from the inter-Korean economic talks following the decision made in principle between the two sides at the third meeting to adopt an agreement on trade and economic cooperation, the fourth south-north economic meeting was opended at 10 : 00 a.m. September 18, 1985, at the conference room of the Neutral Nations Supervisory Commission at Panmunjom. The meeting was held behind closed doors.

As agreed upon during the third meeting, the two sides produced their respective revised versions of an agreement. However, the north's delegation refused to review the two versions and insisted that the two versions should be referred directly to a working-level meeting.

Kim Ki-hwan, south Korea's chief delegate, laid down his delegation's opinion as follows, reminding the north that during the third meeting the two sides agreed in principle to adopt an Agreement on the Implementation of Trade and Economic Cooperation and the Establishment of the South-North Joint Economic Cooperation Committee :

The first concerns matters related to commodity exchanges.

(1) Tradable Items

The most fundamental and essential step in commodity trade is the selection of tradable items. Both sides have already proposed various items they are interested in purchasing and selling, and there are many items in common. Therefore, it would be appropriate to have these common items indicated in the agreement and, furthermore, to stipulate that commodity trade could be expanded to other items in the future, if agreed upon.

(2) Trade Volume and Customs Clearance and Inspection.

There have been some differences regarding the volume of trade, customs clearance and inspection procedures. But I believe that through discussion and compromise there should be little difficulty in reaching an agreement on these matters.

(3) Method of Trade and Settlement and Bank Procedures.

On this issue, our side accepts in principle your proposal for open accounts and direct settlement. However, until an agreement is concluded between our banks for an open account, commodity trade should be conducted temporarily by means of letters of credit issued from third country banks commonly used by the two sides. In this way, we can begin to implement commodity trade at the earliest possible date.

(4) Trading Parties, Method of Determining Prices, Settlement Currencies, Method of Transport, and Tariffs

Since the two sides are in general of the same view on these issues, details about them can be finalized at a working-level meeting.

The second is the issue of economic cooperation.

(1) Scope of Projects

As for the scope of economic cooperation projects, the areas on which the two sides reached an accord at the first and second meetings, namely, the creation of joint fishing areas and the joint development of natural resources, should be indicated in an agreement. And economic cooperation may be expanded into other areas in the future through mutual agreement.

(2) Scale, Method and form of Projects

These issues should in principle be discussed and determined by the parties involved in economic cooperation projects.

(3) Issue of Tax Favors

Because of the differences in the two sides' respective tax systems, there may be some difficulties in establishing uniform criteria for taxation. However, if an agreement can be reached on this matter, both parties may extend exemption of income taxes, corporate taxes, property taxes and other taxes.

(4) Charges for Using Land, Resources, Etc.

From our point of view, these matters are related to individual property rights, and thus should be determined through the consultations of the parties involoved.

The third is the question of establishing a South-North Joint Economic Cooperation Committee.

In this regard, I am pleased to note that since we have already agreed to establish such a committee at the deputy prime minister-level, I do not find any significant difference of opinion on this matter.

As for the function and operation of the Joint Committee, we can easily come to an agreement since both our proposals are already very similar. Regarding its function, however, it should be especially emphasized that the Joint Committee to be established has the obligation to carry out faithfully the agreed matters contained in an agreement to be adopted.

As for the sub-committes of the Joint Committee, I hope that a sub-committee for commodity trade and a sub-committee for economic cooperation will be established as our side proposed. Furthermore, if necessary, other ad-hoc sub-committees or small sub-committes should be established to support the Joint Committee.

Our side proposed the creation of a joint secretariat under the Joint Committee to take charge of working-level matters while your side suggested the placement of a chief secretary. But I am sure your side will agree that a permanent administrative organization will be needed to prepare for future expansion of commodity trade and economic cooperation.

Based on this basic stand, the south Korean delegation produced a

287

new draft agreement prepared by revising the two versions put forth by the two sides during the third meeting. It then suggested that during the fourth meeting, the two sides narrow their differences on major items through overall discussion and that minor issues could then be ironed out by a working-level meeting to be formed with not more than seven delegates from each said including three delegates to the economic talks and experts in relevant areas. It said the working-level meeting could be convened within a month.

Moreover, the southern delegation expressed the hope that to enliven public trust in and expectations on the agreement and to manifest both sides' determination to promote economic exchanges, the south's offer to purchase 300,000 tons of north Korean anthracite coal and the linking of the Seoul-Shinuiju railroad line, on which both sides had already agreed in principle, could begin to be undertaken withn the year, which happened to be the 40th year of national division. The delegation asked the northern side to show an affirmative response toward the issues.

On the other hand, the north Korean delegation produced a single draft agreement incorporating the three separate ideas they advanced during the third meeting, the three ideas being an Agreement on the Establishment and Operation of a South-North Cooperation Joint Committee, a 16-point proposal for inter-Korean economic collaboration and exchanges, and a plan for the formation of a South-North Commodity Exchange Committee.

Despite the fact that some major issues remained to be resolved, the northern delegation demanded that the draft agreements of both sides be referred directly to a working-level meeting without any debate during the fourth meeting.

The southern side, pointing out that a working-level meeting could only progress smoothly when basic matters were fully discussed at the economic meeting, insisted that the two sides should have substantial discussion of major issues embodied in both sides' draft agreement. But the north refused to enter into an overall debate, insisting that any difference that were found could be presented at the following meeting.

As to the south's offer to purchase anthracite coal and link the Seoul-Shinuiju railroad line within the year, the north made it clear that they would not discuss the issues any further at the economic talks by asserting that the issues could be taken up by a south-north Joint Committee when an overall agreement is adopted and such a committee formed.

Nonetheless, the fourth economic meeting could be taken to have moved the economic talks step forward as two sides produced their respective draft agreements. The two draft agreements showed differences concerning the following nine items.

Major Differences Shown in the Two Sides' Draft Agreements

Classification	The South	The North
Name of Agreement	Agreement on the Implementation of Commodity Exchanges and Economic Cooperation between the South and the North and the Establishment of South-North Joint Economic Cooperation Committee	Agreement on the Realization of Economic Cooperation and Commodity Exchanges between the south and the north and the Formation of South-North Joint Economic Cooperation Committee Chaired by Deputy Prime Minister-Level Officials
Description of Principles	Description of pure economic principles in the preamble of the agreement —Reciprocity, equality	Creation of an independent clause in the first chapter of the agreement, incorporating the three principles for

	and contribution to national prosperity, the promotion of well-being and peaceful unification	national unification (independence, peace and grand national unity)
Exchangeable Items	Items found exchangeable at the 1st and 2nd meetings be described in agreement, exchanges be begun with agreed-on items —Items sellable by the south : steel goods, textiles, salt, tangerines, south coast fishery products (laver, seaweed, oysters, anchovies, etc.) —Items sellable by the North : anthracite coal, iron ore, magnesia clinker, pollack, corn.	A Joint Committee shall discuss and determine exchangeable items in consideration of the items suggested by both sides during the 1st meeting.
Method of Transaction and Bank for Settlement	In principle, open accounts and direct settlement. On a tentative basis pending the conclusion of a settlement agreement, the method of letters of credit issued from third country banks. South and north Korean banks designated by respective sides. Tentatively, third country banks.	Open accounts and direct settlement. South and North Korean banks designated by respective sides.

Scope of Economic Cooperation	Description in the Agreement of the creation of joint fishing areas and joint development of underground resources, on which the two sides reached an accord during the 1st and 2nd meetings.	To begin with the joint development and utilization of natural resources(to be discussed and determined in principle by a Joint Committee).
Function of Joint Committee	Express description in the column on the function of a Joint Committee the duty to carry out agreed matters (exchangeable items, etc.)	Description of the duty to carry out agreed matters not necessary.
Number of Sub-Committees	Initial inauguration of two sub–committees (commodity exchanges, economic cooperation)	Inauguration of six sub-committees (resources development, industry & technology, agriculture & fisheries, commodity exchanges, transporation & communications, monetary & financing)
Description of the Delegation of Authority to Signatories	Description of the fact that the signatories of the Agreement were entrusted with authority by the highest authorities.	Signing of the chief delegates of the two sides would be enough (no need to describe the delegation of authority from the highest authority)

Description of the Name of Country in the Signatory Section	Description of the name of a country in the signatory section of the agreement.	Description in the manner of "delegation of the north" and "delegation of the south" (description of the name of a country not necessary).

(6) Fifth Meeting

At the fifth meeting held on November 20, 1985, the two sides centered their discussions on three items : the question of determining the title of an agreement to be adopted, the question of the principles of inter-Korean projects, and the listing of exchangeable items agreed on between the two sides. The three items were among the nine points of differences shown in the two sides' draft versions of an Agreement on the Implementation of Trade and Economic Cooperation and the Establishment of the South-North Joint Economic Cooperation Committee. which were produced at the earlier fourth meeting.

South Korean Chief Delegate Kim Ki-hwan said that the two sides' draft versions contained a number of points in common or similarity, and expressed the view that some items of difference could be resolved easily if only the two sides exert endeavors to this end. He then presented as follows the results of his delegation's review of seven items – the question of the title of the proposed agreement, principles of the projects to be undertaken, the issue of whether to list the items exchangeable, method of transactions and the question of selecting a bank or banks for settlement, the issue of whether to list the economic projects subject to cooperation, the function of a joint committee, and the number of sub-committees.

The first concerns the title of the agreement. I don't believe there are any differ-

ences here apart from minor ones in the wording. In accordance with what was decided during the thrid round of talks, we believe the title should read : "An Agreement on the Implementation of Commodity Trade and Economic Cooperation and the Establishment of a Joint South-North Economic Cooperation Committee under the Chairmanship at the Deputy Prime Minister Level."

My second point concerns the question of whether to include a clause on the principles of project implementation. Although there are slight differences in wording in the preamble of the two sides' draft versions, both versions expressly describe the basic common spirit and objectives of the south-north economic talks, that are : the restoration of economic relations, increased prosperity for our people, peaceful unification, and so forth. So we believe that it would be redundant to have an additional clause on these issues.

The third issue is about the question of commodity exchanges. Whereas our side's version expressly lists the items on which the two sides reached an accord at the first and second meetings, your side's draft version lacks such a list. We believe that the agreement should identify all the commodities which both sides agreed upon because the agreement should incorporate all the points of agreement reached at the economic talks that lasted more than one year and because these points of agreement should be implemented on a priority basis.

The fourth issue concerns the method of settlement and settlement banks. There seem to be some differences of opinion here but believe there are no major problems. Our delegation is of the opinion that the system of open accounts and direct settlement should be introduced between a bank in the south and bank in the north. However, until a settlement agreement is concluded, trade should be conducted through letters of credit issued by the banks of third countries.

Fifth, our delegation insists that even if the Joint Committee would consider new projects in the future, the economic cooperation projects agreed at the first and second meetings, namely, the establishment of joint fishing areas and the joint development of natural resources, should be specifically listed in the agreement.

Regarding the size, modality, conditions and timing of the projects, our side has suggested that these details should be determined by the parties conducting projects, while your delegation proposed that such matters be discussed and determined by the Joint Committee.

However, even if basic parameters for the projects are to be determined by the Joint Committee, as your side suggests, they would require extensive fine-tuning afterwards in any case by the project parties. Therefore, we believe it proper for your side to accept our opinion.

Seventh, I believe our two sides still differ on the number of the sub-committees to be established under the Joint Committee. Our side's position is that we first inaugurate a sub-committee for commodity exchanges and another for economic cooperation, and that the creation of additional ad hoc or small sub-committees can be discussed later as they are required depending on the expansion of projects.

The south Korean delegation noted that the two sides in effect agreed already a year before on the early implementation of the exchange of materials and on the mutual purchase and sale of items such as briquette coal and steel goods which either of the two sides needs. The south's delegation then proposed to carry out, on a pilot basis, barter trade of goods in conformity with the high public expectations concerning the inter-Korean economic talks. The items should include the 300,000 tons of briquette coal which the south offered to purchase from the north several times.

Meanwhile, the north Korean delegation raised additional disputes on the issue of whether to put the phrase "with authority delegated from the highest official" to the signature line and also on the question of whether to use the title of each country on the signature line. The north even reversed their earlier agreement on the title of an agreement, etc.

Regarding the question of the principles of project implementation, the south's delegation said that the preamble of an agreement could include the principles of national unification as suggested by the north along with the objectives of commodity trade and economic cooperation, namely, the restoration of the economic bond of south and north Korea, national prosperity and peaceful unification. It added, however, that there shouldn't be any overlapping provisions of principles. But the issue couldn't be ironed out as the north's delegation insisted that the principles of the projects should be prescribed in an independent article.

Concerning the question of listing in an agreement those tradable items agreed on between the two sides during the first and second meetings, the south's side suggested that the listing of such items be included in an agreement even as a gesture to conclude the year-long economic talks early and emphasize the importance of the sincere implementation of agreed-on projects. But the northern side rejected even this suggestion.

At the same time, the north Korean delegation kept demanding the prior formation of Joint Committee, thus revealing their intention to scale down the economic talks to the level of working-level contacts and also to delay substantial debates.

As no agreement was seen during the fifth meeting, the two sides shared the view that there was need for a further meeting and agreed to hold the sixth meeting on January 22, 1986.

However, on January 20, 1986, two days before the scheduled sixth meeting, north Korea unilaterally suspended the meeting with the excuse of the "Team Spirit '86" training exercise. On January 22, 1986, the south Korean Chief Delegate made the following comment urging the north to come to the sixth meeting as soon as possible :

I regret deeply that the sixth inter-Korean economic meeting, which the two sides had agreed to hold at Panmunjom today, failed to be held due to north Korea's unilateral suspension.

On January 20, north Korea announced in a radio broadcast a joint statement of their delegations to the inter-Korean dialogue, saying that they would unilaterally suspend the dialogue on which all people had high expectations. Again on January 21, they informed us in a telephone message that they would not attend the sixth inter-Korean economic meeting slated for 10 : 00 a.m. today.

In a joint statement of our chief delegates, our side on January 20 pointed out the unreasonableness of north Korea's suspension of the talks. In a telephone message to the north on January 21, we stressed that agreed matters reached between the two sides should be respected and carried out by all means possible, urging the north to return to the sixth economic meeting at an early date.

Today all the people hope that the inter-Korean economic talks will register

progress as soon as possible so that material exchanges and economic cooperation
can be realized leading to the laying of foundation for reconciliation and mutual
trust.

In keeping with this national wish, north Korea should return to the table of
dialogue at an early date in a modest and sincere posture.

g. Preliminary Contacts for Parliamentarians Conference

(1) Initiation

On April 9, 1985, when the second south-north economic meeting
slated for May 18, 1985, and the eighth full-dress Red Cross talks set to
be held on May 28, 1985, were forthcoming, north Korea from nowhere
proposed to hold a south-north parliamentarians conference to discuss
the question of adopting a "joint declaration on nonaggression." The
overture was made in a message signed by Yang Hyong-sop, chairman
of the Standing Committee of the Supreme People's Assembly, and
addressed to Chae Mun-sik, speaker of the National Assembly. The
message, delivered to the south through Panmunjom on the afternoon of
April 9, was adopted at the fourth session of the seventh-term Supreme
People's Assembly.

In the message, the north claimed that under the circumstance where
no tripartite meeting was realized, the ongoing Red Cross or economic
talks were not enough to resolve such basic issues as the alleviation of
tensions. They then suggested that as a practical means of removing the
danger of war and easing tensions between the south and the north, a
south-north parliamentarians conference be held. The message offered
to hold preliminary contacts at Panmunjom in early May to discuss the
proposal. The north also wanted the copies of the message to be forwarded to the presidents of the Democratic Justice Party, the New
Korea Democratic Party and the the Korea National Party.

In response, Speaker Chae Mun-sik on April 10 called in the heads of
the three parties,-Roh Tae-woo of the Democratic Justice Party, Lee
Min-woo of the New Korea Democratic Party and Lee Man-sop of the
Korea National Party, to hand them the copies of the north Korean
message and discussed the northern offer. It was announced that the

meeting reached the following agreement :

–The attendees shared the view that all political parties should closely consult among themselves in a supra-partisan manner beyond partisan interests so as to deal uniformly and effectively the question of south-north dialogue, thus positively contributing to advancing the time of peaceful unification.

–In line with our consistent policy to move toward the alleviation of tensions and peaceful unification through steady and sincere south-north dialogue, we have decided to send a sincere reply to the north at an early date in consultation between the National Assembly and political parties. Accordingly, the attendees shared the recognition that there needs the creation of a system of the National Assembly to cope with the north Korean offer.

–The attendees agreed that in accordance with the general principles of south-north negotiations, the National Assembly and political parties shall respect the policies of, and cooperate closely with, the authorities concerned with unification issues to make clear the consistent subject of dialogue implementation and elevate the effective results of the dialogue.

–The attendees decided that until the National Assembly is formally inaugurated, the Secretary General of the National Assembly should take charge such matters related to the proposal for a parliamentarians conference as liaison business between the National Assembly and political parties, arrangement of meetings and announcement.

Meanwhile, as preliminary contacts could hardly take place in early May as the north initially proposed because of a delay in the inauguration of the new National Assembly, Secretary General Lee Jin-woo of the National Assembly sent a letter to Kim Bong-ju, chief secretary of the Standing Committee of the north's Supreme People's Assembly on May 8, informing him that the National Assembly would send a reply to the north Korean proposal as soon as the National Assembly is inaugurated.

After the 12th National Assembly was inaugurated in the south, a joint meeting of the speaker, vice speakers and the representatives of the three political parties represented at the Assembly was held on May 16, where it was agreed that the Assembly's Steering Committee would propose a resolution containing a reply to the north Korean offer for deliberation at the plenary Assembly session.

Under the agreement, the Steering Committee formed an ad hoc committee to draft a reply to the north. A draft resolution, thus prepared, was adopted by the Steering Committee before it was introduced to the Assembly plenary session on June 1. The resolution containing a reply to the north over their proposal for a south-north parliamentary conference was unanimously adopted at the 15th meeting of the 125th extraordinary National Assembly session.

In a message which Speaker Lee Chae-hyong sent to Yang Hyong-sop, chairman of the north's Supreme People's Assembly, on June 3, 1985, the National Assembly of the Republic of Korea welcomed the opening of an inter-Korean parliamentary meeting, saying that it could discuss the question of forming a south-north consultative organization to prepare a unified constitution and also matters necessary for laying a foundation for national unification. The Assembly proposed that a preliminary contact attended by five legislators from each side be held at Panmunjom within July to discuss various issues related thereto.

The text of the message the Republic of Korea National Assembly sent to the north was as follows :

Having received a message from your Supreme People's Assembly, the National Assembly of the Republic of Korea is sending this reply which was adopted as a resolution at a plenary session after full consultations and serious debates among political parties and legislators.

We believe that this year, which happens to be the the 40th anniversary of national liberation, should be the very period in which the south and the north should surmount the pains of national division and ease tensions and promote national trust and reconciliation transcending difference in ideologies and systems for the construction of a great homeland, thereby providing a historical turning-point in laying a foundation for peace and unification.

The past 40 years were an era of untold trials and bitterness so far as our nation was concerned, and was a history studded with mutual distrust and confrontation.

Mutual distrust has been the biggest obstacle to the offorts of the nation to put an end to the history of division in a show of brotherly love and united strength and to realize peaceful unification, the ardent wish of the whole compatriots. Such distrust derives from the disruption of dialogue and exchanges.

Herein lies the reason why we call for dialogue in various channels. In this sense, we are truly pleased to see that new inter-Korean contacts were resumed last year, especially the south-north economic meeting and the south-north Red Cross conference. We hope that the suspended south-north sports talks, too, will be resumed at an early date.

Today our compatriots ardently wish that the economic and Red Cross talks will progress successfully so that commodity trade and economic cooperation can be realized between the south and the north and dispersed families and relatives could freely visit their hometowns and meet their blood relatives at an early date. We expect that these will serve as stepping stones toward the alleviation of tensions and toward peaceful unification.

Since long ago, our side has stressed that the alleviation of tensions and consolidation of peace between the south and the north constitute the immediate task which should be resolved exigently through consultations between the responsible authorities of the two sides. And we have made incessant efforts to enable your side to respond favorably for the resolution of the task.

We have proposed a meeting between the highest officials of the two sides' authorities, offering, as a topic of such top leaders' meeting, an idea to take effective steps to ease tensions and prevent the recurrence of a war. We also proposed the conclusion of a provisional agreement on the basic relations between the south and the north as a practical device to reduce tensions and promote national reconciliation.

We believe it is reasonable that the nonaggression declaration issue, too, be discussed at a meeting between the south's and the north's government authorities with

299

the competence and authority to execute it practically.

Therefore, we believe that for your side to discuss sincerely with our side the issue of a nonaggression declaration and other matters to ease tensions and ensure peace between the south and the north and thereby to contribute to national unification, it would be more effective for your Supreme People's Assembly to urge your side's authorities to agree to a meeting between government authorities including the top leaders' meeting our side calls for.

As your side well knows, the inherent function of legislature is to legislate a constitution and various laws and act on agreements on war or peace which government authorities have concluded.

We believe that the most important national task the legislatures of the south and the north should undertake at this moment is to discuss the issue of perparing a unified constitution to facilitate peaceful unification of the homeland. We think that this task represents the ardent wish of the whole people and also their highest expectation from the legislatures of the south and the north.

Therefore the legislatures of the south and the north should exert all efforts to achieve this national task. To this end, there should be sincere dialogue and discussions. The task of preparing a unified constitution for the peaceful unification of the homeland cannot be accomplished with one side's efforts only. It should be discussed at a council formed with the delegates representing the wills of the people of the two sides and achieved in a consensus among the entire people.

The legislatures of the south and the north should not hesitate to promote the preparation of a unified constitution, realizing that this is a historical mission imposed upon us.

Therefore, we welcome the opening of a south-north parliamentary meeting so that we can discuss with your Supreme People's Assembly various issues related to the formation of a consultative organization between the south and the north to prepare a unified constitution and other matters necessary for laying a foundation for unification.

We believe that the proposed south-north parliamentary talks will contribute much to easing tensions and restoring trust between the south and the north and further to laying a foundation for the peaceful unification of the homeland.

From this standpoint, the National Assembly of the Republic of Korea proposes that preliminary contacts attended by five legislators from each side be held at Panmunjom within the month of July to discuss various issues related to the convening of a south-north parliamentary meeting.

I look forward to a reply from your Supreme Peoples's Assembly on our proposal.

North Korea agreed to the south's suggestion on July 5, and the first preliminary contacts were set to be held at the conference room of the Neutral Nations Supervisory Commission at Panmunjom on July 23, 1985, to discuss the proposed inter-Korean parliamentary talks.

–Delegation of the Republic of Korea National Assembly–
Chief Delegate : Kwon Chong-dal, Democratic Justice Party
Delegate : Chong Si-chae, Democratic Justice Party
Dlegate : Shin Sun-bom, New Korea Democratic Pary
Dlegate : Park Kwan-yong, New Korea Kemocratic Party
Delegate : Kang Kyong-sik, Korea National Party

–Delegation of the Supreme People's Assembly of North Korea–
Chief Delegate : Chon Gum-chol, Korean Workers' Party
Deputy Chief Delegate : Chu Chang-jun, Korean Workers' Party
Delegate : Choe Jang-ryong, Korean Workers' Party
Delegate : Ryom Kuk-ryol, Korean Social Democratic Party
Delegate : Wu Dal-ho, Chongdo-gyo Chongwu Party

(2) Progress
At the first preliminany contact held on July 23, 1985, the two sides reached an accord on most of the procedural matters. But they failed to reach any agreement on the most important issue of the topics.

The north's delegation simply repeated their stand contained in their April 9 message, arguing that adopting a "joint declaration on nonaggression" at a south-north parliamentary meeting is the "practical means of realistically resolving the questions of easing tensions and of ensuring peace." The north said that if their proposal were realized, it would have an "encouraging effect on the ongoing Red Cross and economic talks."

The north Korean delegation then disclosed their position toward such procedural matters as the format and topics of the proposed talks, the composition of delegations and the venue of talks were as follows.

–Gist of North Korean Suggestions–

• Format of Talks

Either joint session of the two legislatures or a conference of parliamentary delegates.

• Composition of Delegations

Joint session : About 100 legislators of one side shall attend the plenary session of the other side's legislature.

Delegates Meeting : To be composed of nine to 11 legislators.

Chief delegates : Speakers or vice speakers.

• Venue of Talks

Seoul and Pyongyang

• Agenda of Talks

Concerning the announcement of a joint declaration on nonaggression.

Concerning the discussion of the question of legislating the constitution of a unified state.

• Time of Talks

Within one month after the conclusion of preliminary contacts.

• Direct Telephone Line

A direct telephone line shall be linked between Seoul and Pyongyang for exclusive use during the parliamentary talks.

In response, south Korean Chief Delegate Kwon Chong-dal said it is unreasonable for a south-north parliamentary talks to discuss and resolve the nonaggression question which in nature ought to be resolved through discussions between the government authorities of the two sides. Kwon said legislators talks should instead discuss the legislation of a constitution of a unified state and the formation of a consultative organization to draft such a constitution, the issues which he said befit the competence of legislature.

The south's chief delegate reminded the north that the government of the Republic of Korea has long ago proposed to hold a top leaders' meeting between the south and north to discuss the alleviation of tensions and the prevention of the recurrence of war, and also to conclude Provisional Agreement on Basic Relations between the south and the north, which provided for a cessation of the use of arms and violence of all types, mutual noninterference in each other's internal affairs, and an end to the arms race and the state of military confrontation as practical measures to facilitate peaceful inter-Korean relations.

Chief Delegate Kwon Stressed that if the north Korean legislature is truly interested in adopting a nonaggression issue for the easing of tensions and the consolidation of peace, they had better urge their authorities to respond affirmatively to the south's offer.

Pointing out that no joint objective or charter has ever been prepared to regiment national efforts for peaceful unification in the 40 years since national division, Kwon emphasized that a constitution for a unified state should be legislated if only to present a blueprint of a unified homeland and set forth the direction and path of the future of the nation.

The southern delegation then presented the following suggestions concerning the holding of a parliamentary conference :

First, the two sides shall hold inter-Korean parliamentary talks at an early date in conformity with the Korean people's aspiration for unification. The definite date shall be discussed and decided at the final stage of the preliminary contacts.

Second, the two sides shall hold the inter-Korean parliamentary talks in Seoul and Pyongyang in turns.

Third, each delegation to the talks shall be composed of eleven members. The chief delegates of both sides shall be appointed by their respective speakers.

Fourth, the agenda of the inter-Korean parliamentary talks shall be the "question of organizing a Consultative Conference for National Reunification to draft a constitution of a unified state and related matters necessary for the laying of a groundwork for unification."

Firth, to facilitate communications for the promotion of the inter-Korean parliamentary talks, a direct telephone line shall be installed and operated between the two sides.

Sixth, other procedural matters related to the proceeding of the inter-Korean parliamentarians talks shall be determined through mutual consultation.

Regarding the issue of the agenda, the north said they were not totally opposed to the idea of legislating a constitution for a unified state, but were still adamant to the prior discussion of the the question of making a joint declaration on nonaggression. No accord was thus made on the question of the agenda.

While insisting on the prior handling of their idea at the parliamentary conference, the north's delegation asserted that the parliamentary talks could "recognize the necessity and significance of nonaggression," while the "question of adopting a concrete nonaggression declaration with a binding power" could be left to the government authorities of the two sides, thus showing a logical contradiction in their demand for the debate of the nonaggression issue at a parliamentary meeting.

On procedural matters, however, both sides' ideas were similar, and an accord was thus reached on most of the procedural issues except for the rank of chief delegates to the parliamentary talks and the site of the first meeting.

—Items Agreed on during First Contact—

1. Format of Talks

Meeting of select delegates of both legislatures.

2. Size of Delegations

Eleven members form each side.

3. Place of Conference

Seoul and Pyongyang in turns.

4. Time

First meeting within one month after the end of the preliminary contacts.

5. Reporting and Recording

In ways convenient to each side.

6. Traveling Procedures and Assurance of Conveniences for Delegates

The practice in use for other channels of inter-Korean dialogue shall be applied.

During the second preliminary contact held on September 25, 1985, behind closed doors, the two sides failed to reach an accord on major issues like the topics of the talks. All they could do was to reaffirm their respective stands showed during the first contacts.

In his first speech, Kwon Chong-dal, the south's chief delegate, suggested that during the second contacts both sides should reaffirm what was substantially agreed on during the first contacts, such as the format of the parliamentary talks, the composition of the delegations, the conference sites and the issue of reporting, and then discuss and resolve the issues including those of the agenda, the rank of chief delegates and the venue for the first parliamentary talks – the issues on which the two sides failed to agree during the first contacts.

With respect to the question of the agenda, the south's delegation reiterated that the topic suggested by the south, that is, the "question of organizing a Consultative Conference for National Reunification to draft a constitution of a unified state and related matters necessary for the laying of a groundwork for unification," is very fitting for the parliamentary talks, whereas it is not necessary to put the issue of a "nonaggression declaration" on the agenda of the talks as suggested by the north.

Noting that the question of war and peace is the customary purview of the Executive Branch where the actual power and responsibility belong and that the northern side, too, frankly conceded during the first contacts that the question of nonaggression and that of easing tensions and preventing war are the issues that can be resolved between the government authorities of the two sides, Kwon challenged the north's delegation that if they truly wanted to declare nonaggression together with the south to reduce tensions and consolidate peace, it would be more reasonable for them to urge their government authorities to promptly agree to the talks proposed by the south.

The south's chief delegate further said that given the reality of inter-Korean relations, the issue of easing tensions and promoting confidence-building, including the nonaggression issue, should not end as a mere declaration but must be backed up by concrete measures. He said that to this end, reconciliation, exchanges and cooperation should be translated into action concretely in all areas of the inter-Korean relationship.

On the other hand, the north's delegation set forth a draft agreement containing the substance of their suggestion produced during the first contacts and those procedural matters on which the two sides neared an accord during the first contact, and kept insisting on the discussion of their idea of a joint declaration of nonaggression at the parliamentary talks, arguing that since the question of nonaggression is so important as to affect national survival and destiny, it should be handled by authoritative political organizations like legislatures.

The south's delegation, retorting the north Korean assertion, reasoned that even if a nonaggression declaration was adopted during the proposed talks, it would be no better than a declaration, adding that the question of nonaggression should, therefore, be tackled directly by government authorities with the power to put it into action.

As the north Korean side found it impossible to insist on the nonaggression issue as an agenda topic any longer, they now suggested that the topic should be "concerning the alleviation of tensions between the south and the north, and the acceleration of national unification."

The south's chief delegate said that the new north Korean offer was so broad in definition that it lacked any concreteness and was thus not an agenda item at all. The issue of the agenda thus remained unsettled during the second contacts.

As to the issue of the rank of the chief delegates, the south's delegation showed flexiblity by suggesting that the chief delegates be appointed by respective speakers from among the legislators with the rank of the chairman of a standing committee or higher, while the northern side kept insisting that they should be speakers or vice speakers.

Meanwhile, the two sides agreed to determine over the direct telephone line whether the venue of the third contacts should be the conference room of the Neutral Nations Supervisory Commission, as was the case with the first and second contacts, or "Tongilkak" as the north suggested, and also the time of the next contacts.

However, as north Korea unilaterally suspended all dialogues between the south and the north on January 20, 1986, with the excuse of the Team Spirit '86 Training exercise, the third contacts, which the two sides agreed through a telephone conversation to hold on February 18, 1986, faliled to take place.

h. Lausanne Sports Talks

(1) Background

Ever since the International Olympic Committee(IOC) chose Seoul as the venue of the 24th Olympic Games in its meeting at Baden-Baden, West Germany, in September 1981, North Korea had employed all schemes and machinations to block Seoul from hosting the 1988 Olympics.

North Korea, playing up the tensions on the Korean peninsula, asserted that "Seoul cannot be the proper site of the Olympics" because of the tensions, and that the Olympics in Seoul is the "most vicious expression of a two-Korea policy" and would be an "exploitation for the prolonged grip of power," which, they argues, was "in contravention of the basic ideals of the Olympics, which are to promote understanding and goodwill among peoples, foster an atmosphere conducive to peace, and exchange and promote athletic skills."

Against this backdrop, IOC President Juan Antonio Samaranch suggested a sports meeting betweent the south and the north under the IOC's sponsorship. On February 1, 1985, the IOC Executive Committee formally proposed the talks to the south and north Korean National Olympic committees.

In messages to the heads of the south and north Korea national Olympic committees, the IOC suggested that a meeting between the representives of the two Korean committees be held in Lausanne under the chairmanship of the IOC president, and that the meeting be attended by six delegates from the IOC and six each from the south and north Korean committees. The IOC said that no political remarks would be allowed from either side during the meeting and that the topics would be 1) matters pertaining to sports between the two national Olympic committees and 2) the issue of the 24th Olympics in 1988.

In response, the Republic of Korea Olympic Committee(KOC) accepted the IOC offer on March 31, 1985, on the condition that the IOC decision on the Seoul Olympics should be respected under all circumstances. On the other hand, north Korea, while reiterating their demand that the venue of the 24th Olympics should be changed, had turned a deaf ear to the IOC proposal until July 6, 1985, when they made a sudden about-face and now said they would attend the meeting.

The IOC announced officially on July 24 that an inter-Korean sports meeting would be held in Lausanne under the sponsorship of the IOC. It then notified the south and the north on August 1 that the first meeting would be held October 8–9, 1985. A stage was thus set for sports talks between the two sides of Korea for the first time in one and a half years since inter-Korean sports officials contacts were suspended in May 1984.

The lists of the IOC and south and north Korean delegations to the Lausanne meeting were as follows:

IOC Delegation
Juan Antonio Samaranch, IOC president, Spanish
Alexandru Siperco, IOC 1st vice-president, Romanian
Ashwini Kumar, IOC 2nd vice-president, Indian
Berthold Beitz, IOC 3rd vice-president, West German
Raymond Gafner, IOC interim administrator, Swiss
Sheik Fahad Al-Ahmad Al-Sabah, OCA president, Kuwait,

KOC Delegation
Chief delegate: Kim Chong-ha, KOC president
Deputy chief delegate: Chong Chung-sik, KOC vice-president
Delegate: Choi Man-rip, KOC vice-president
Delegate: Lee Chong-ha, KOC standing member
Delegate: Im Tae-sun, KOC member
Delegate: Nam Chong-mun, KOC member

NKOC Delegation
Chief delegate : Kim Yu-sun, NKOC president
Deputy chief delegate: Chin Chung-kuk, NKOC vice-president
Delegate : Han Jang-un, NKOC member
Delegate : An Bok-man, NKOC member
Delegate : Cho Myong-hwang, NKOC member
Delegate : Chang Wung, NKOC deputy secretary general

(2) First Meeting

The first IOC-hosted inter-Korean sports meeting was held behind the closed doors October 8–9, 1985, in Lausanne, Switzerland, where the IOC main office is. Presided over by IOC President Samaranch, the meeting included two rounds of joint tripartite talks among the IOC and south and north Korean delegates, two rounds of talks between IOC and KOC elegates, and another two between IOC and NKOC delegates. But the meeting failed to register any progress due to the north Koreans' insistence on the co-hosting of the 24th Olympics between the south and the north.

At the first-day meeting on October 8, KOC Chief Delegate Kim Chong-ha said the right to host the 24th Summer Olympics "has been officially granted to the Republic of Korea Olympic Committee and the City of Seoul," pointing out that therefore the "right to hold the 24th Olympics in Seoul has now become an irrevocable fact." He then made it clear that his KOC would fulfill its responsibilities under the rights accorded by the International Olympic Committee.

Stressing that the door to the Seoul Olympics has been thrown wide open so that even north Korean athletes, like those from all other countries, could freely participate in it in accordance with the Olympic Charter, Kim expressed the hope that the question of north Korea's participation would be discussed on the basis of respecting the Olympic Charter and our right to host the Olympic Games.

However, the north Korean delegation, in its first speech, demanded that the 24th Olympics be co-hostcd by the south and the north, a demand that ran counter to the IOC Charter and the basic Olympic spirit.

NKOC Chief Delegate Kim Yu-sun argued that "unless an epochal measure is taken with regard to the venue of the 24th Olympics, a development that may be extremely hazardous to the Korean peoples' great task of unification and to the sound development of the Olympic movement, may occur." Saying that to "save the 24th Olympics" the two sides of Korea should each host half of the 24th Olympic sports, the NKOC chief delegate set forth the details of their demand as follows :

Gist of North Korean Proposal

1. Hosting of the Games

The Games shall be held under the joint sponsorship of the south and the north, which shall field a single delegation to the Games.

2. Title of the Games

The title of the Games shall be either "Korean Olympic Games" or "Korean Pyongyang-Seoul Olympic Games."

3. Allocation of Sports

The Games shall be equally divided between Pyongyang and Seoul.

4. Opening and Closing Ceremonies

The opening and closing ceremonies shall be held in Pyongyang and Seoul for the sports allocated to each side.

5. Question of Free Travel

(1) Athletes, sports officials, press members and tourists shall be allowed to freely travel back and forth between Pyongyang and Seoul by land and sea transportation means and by air.

(2) For free travel, roads and railroads will be linked between Pyongyang and Seoul, and a passenger route will be opened between the Nampo and Inchon ports.

(3) To ensure the maximum convenience of travelers and to ensure the swiftness of travel, only transit certificates will be issued at the points of transit without issuing separate visas.

6. Television Rights and Distribution of Profits

Television rights shall be granted depending on contracts, and profits shall be divided reasonably through discussion.

7. Permanent Organization for Joint Sponsorship

(1) To ensure the joint sponsorship effectively, a joint north-south permanent organization shall be established.

(2) The name of the organization shall be the Korean Olympics Joint Organizing Committee or the Korean Pyongyang-Seoul Olympic Joint Organizing Committee.

Meanwhile, at a separate meeting with the KOC delegation, IOC President Samaranch explained the IOC's basic position that it would respect the IOC's Baden-Baden decision to grant the right to host the 1988 Olympics to Seoul as well as the IOC Charter and the IOC contract with Korea regarding the Seoul Olympics. Samaranch then expressed the hope that the KOC would try to produce ideas that could enable north Korea to take part in the Seoul Olympics more significantly.

In response, the KOC side said that the KOC was willing to consider allotting the preliminaries of a few sports including those of handball to the north and making men's group cycling pass through the north Korean area, the venues and schedule of which have already been fixed concretely.

The KOC side said that it would welcome simultaneous entry of

311

both south and,north Korean delegations into the opening and clos-ing ceremonies and the north's participation in cultural events set to be held during the Olympic period. The KOC delegation stressed that various issues related to these matters, such as those on travels back and forth by sports officials and athletes, transportation of items necessary for matches, installation of communications networks, and guaranteeing personal safety, would have to be concretely discussed and resolved.

At the second-day session held on October 9, the KOC side said that it was prepared to have talks with north Korea at Panmunjom at any time to discuss the questions of inter-Korean sports exchanges and forming single Korean teams for international games. It recalled that inter-Korean contacts were held several times in the past at Pan-munjom to discuss the issue of forming single teams for international games before they were suspended unilaterally by north Korea around the time Pyongyang announced its boycott of the Los Angeles Olympics.

However, the NKOC side insisted on their impracticable idea of "joint sponsorship" and a single inter-Korean team. The first IOC-sponsored inter-Korean sports meeting thus ended without any agree-ment after deciding only to hold the second meeting January 8–9, 1986, in Lausanne.

Meanwhile, IOC President Samaranch announced the results of the meeting in a press conference on the afternoon of October 9. The press meeting was attended by the delegations of both the south and the north. The results of the meeting, which Samaranch announced, were as follows :

> *Upon the IOC's initiatives, the south and north Korean Olympic Committee delegations met with an IOC delegation at the IOC headquarters in Lausanne, Switzerland, October 8-9, 1985. The purpose of the meeting was to explore ways helpful to ensure all the Korean people's participation in the 24th Olympics in Seoul.*

The discussions took place, under the chairmanship of the President of the IOC, in a friendly and truly Olympic atmosphere. The delegations of the two sides of Korea presented their positions and proposals. The IOC thoroughly and carefully studied them, while recalling the necessity of strictly and fully respecting the stipulations of the Olympic Charter as well as the agreements entered into by the IOC pursuant to the awarding of the Games by the 84th session of the IOC in Baden-Baden in 1981.

Although some progress was achieved, the IOC considered that further discussions were necessary before an agreement could be reached. The three parties agreed to meet again in Lausanne January 8–9, 1986.

(3) Second Meeting

The second meeting held January 8-9, 1986, discussed six topics chosen by the IOC on the condition that matters that could contravene the IOC's 1981 decision to award the right to host the 24th Olympics to Seoul cannot be the topic of the meeting any longer.

The six topics which the IOC Executive Committee chose and notified both sides of Korea on October 23, 1985, were as follows :

(1) Greetings from the IOC president.

(2) Discussion of the question of simultaneous entry by the the south and north Korean delegations into the opening ceremony of the 24th Olympics.

(3) Discussion of the sports that may be held in the north Korean area.

(4) Discussion of the sports that may be held in both sides' jurisdictional areas.

(5) Discussion of the question of north Korea's participation in cultural activities.

(6) Follow-up measures and the IOC president's concluding remarks.

But even the second meeting failed to reach any agreement with the north Koreans persisting in their ideas of "joint sponsorship" and

313

a single team for the 24th Olympics.

In his greetings at the first-day session, IOC President Samaranch made it clear that Seoul's hosting of the 24th Summer Olympics cannot disputable any further because he said Seoul has been granted the right to host the 1988 Olympics in a decision made by an IOC meeting held in Baden-Baden in 1981 and because various agrements regarding Seoul's hosting of the Olympics had already been concluded between the IOC and Seoul.

The IOC president went on to say that especially because of some countries' boycott of the 1980 Moscow Olympics and the 1984 Los Angeles Olympics, his IOC was doing its utmost for the development of the Olympic movement. He said that he had arranged the meeting in consideration of the situation of the south and the north being divided countries and in the hope that north Korea would take part in the 24th Summer Olympics.

In his keynote speech, KOC Chief Delegate Kim Chong-ha said that the KOC's right to host the 24th Summer Olympics has now become an irrevocable fait accompli, and that all preparations for the Olympics were nearing completion. He stressed that "since the Olympic movement has begun, the Olympic Charter and decisions of the International Olympic Committee have always been respected and will have to be respected under all circumstances."

Urging north Korea to take part in the Seoul Olympics in conformity with the Olympic Charter and IOC decisions, Kim Chong-ha said that at the second meeting, the KOC was willing to discuss 1) the question of the simultaneous entry of the south and north Korean delegations into the opening ceremony of the Seoul Olympics, 2) the question of allotting the preliminaries of handball and some other ball games to the north Korean area, 3) the question of holding group road cycling through the areas of the south and the north and 4) the question of north Korea's participation in cultural activities during the Seoul Olympics period.

Meanwhile, the north Korean side insisted again that the 24th

Olympics should be co-hosted by the two sides of Korea. While objecting to Topic No. 2, "Question of Simultaneous Entry of the South and North Korean Delegations into the Opening Ceremony of the Olympics," the NKOC also argued that the issue of forming a single inter-Korean team had to be discussed through the good offices of the IOC.

KOC chief delegate Kim Chong-ha, recalling that "since long ago the KOC has endeavored to discuss with the north the issues of inter-Korean sports exchanges and formation of single teams for international games," said that since the question of a single delegation was by no means limited to the 24th Olympics in 1988 nor was the issue included in the topics of the second IOC-sponsored inter-Korean sports meeting, the question could not be discussed at the Lausanne meeting. He added that it would be reasonable for the directly involved two sides of Korea to resolve the issue through direct bilateral talks.

Meanwhile, in his individual contacts at the second-day session, IOC President Samaranch said that though the results of the second Lausanne meeting were not very satisfactory, the position of north Korea had been changing steadily. He then suggested that a third meeting be held in June.

The KOC delegation said that it would agree to hold a third meeting if the north Koreans withdrew their demands for joint sponsorship and the formation of a single team and could be sincere toward topics chosen by the IOC.

Based on the results of such personal contacts, the IOC announced that the third meeting would be held in Lausanne June 10-11, 1986, which the IOC hoped would be the last of such meeting.

KOC chief delegate Kim said that at the second meeting his delegation put forth very realistic and reasonable ideas acceptable by north Korea to the extent the Olympic Charter and spirit permitted and on the basis of the topics chosen by the IOC. He said that if only the Olympic Charter and IOC decisions were respected and discussions were made according to the topics adopted by the IOC, the question of north Korea's participation in the 24th Seoul Olympics would be resolved without difficulty. He said that the KOC would carry on a dialogue sincerely from his approach in the future.

The NKOC, too, said that agreement was reached on some matters at the second meeting, and expressed the view that the remaining issues could be resolved through further studies and debates.

(4) Third Meeting

The 3rd IOC-sponsored south-north sports meeting was held at the IOC headquarters in Lausanne, Switzerland, June 10-11, 1986, behind closed doors. During the meeting, the IOC, in an apparent move to wind up the sports talks early, produced a mediatory plan it worked out based on the results of the first and second sports meetings and its separate contacts with both sides of Korea, asking the south and the north to notify the IOC of whether to accept the plan by the end of June.

North Korea, though it did not repeat their previous demand for "joint sponsorship" and the "formation of a single team," still reiterated their contention with regard to the "split of Olympic Games between the south and the north Korea" and made unreasonable demands with regard to the titles of 1988 Games and its organizing committee, cultural programs related to the Olympics, etc.

At the first-day session on June 10, KOC chief delegate Kim Chong-ha said that the KOC had cooperated positively in the sincere IOC mediatory plan so as to enable the all Korean people to enjoy the honor of hosting the Olympics, and set forth reasonable methods of allowing north Korean athletes to take part in the Seoul Olympics more significantly, endeavoring to realize such methods.

He then said his delegation would make sincere efforts in discussing and resolving the four topics which the IOC produced during the second meeting. Stressing that "if these problems could be resolved, it would serve as historical occasion to facilitate the mutual door-opening between the south and the north through the 24th Seoul Olympics and forge inter-Korean relations based on trust and peace, the KOC chief delegate called for unspared cooperation on the part of the IOC and north Korea, reminding them that the success of the third meeting hinges on whether all the parties respect the Olympic Charter and the decision of the IOC sesson."

On the other hand, the north Korean delegation did not mention their previous demand for "co-hosting" and the "formation of a single delegation." They instead concentrated on obtaining the right to host some sports in the north Korean area.

In his speech, the north's chief delegate Kim Yu-sun said that north Korea disclosed its stand over the question of splitting the 24th Olympics between the south and the north and other issues such as those involving the titles of the 24th Olympics and its organizing committee, cultural activities and other Olympic events during a separate meeting it had in last March with the IOC, suggesting that if the "basic problem" related to organizing the 24th Olympics, namely, the question of allotting some Olympic sports to the north Korean area, were resolved, other concomitant problems could be settled easily.

This attitude by north Korea was believed to have represented not so much a change in their basic position advocating co-hosting as a tactical change aimed at securing the right to hold some Olympic sports in the north Korean area and seeking the resolution of other related problems step by step.

At separate talks that followed a three-party meeting, the IOC and NKOC delegations focused their discussions on the question of allotting some sports to the north Korean area. The IOC asked the KOC if it were willing to transfer several sports including their finals to the north Korean area.

The KOC delegation said that it was "willing to affirmatively review the question of holding two sports including their finals in the north Korean area under the sponsorship of the Seoul Olympic Organizing

Committee" provided that north Korea makes it clear that they would respect the Olympic Charter and the IOC decision made at its Baden-Baden session and unconditionally take part in the 24th Seoul Olympics. He then discussed the KOC's basic position on major pending issues as follows:

1. The Question of Entrance into the Opening Ceremony

The KOC suggested that during the opening ceremony of the Seoul Olympics, south and north Korean officials and athletes enter simultaneously, with south Korean members entering in three rows on the right in their own uniform and carrying the Republic of Korea national flag and the north Korean members also in three rows on the left in their uniform and carrying their flag. The IOC agreed on the idea.

2. The Question of Allotting Specific Sports including Finals to North Korea

(1) No reply from north Korea had been received to the suggestion made at the first and second sports meetings that men's volleyball, men's handball and some preliminaries of soccer be transferred to the north Korean area. The lack of response was regarded as their rejection of the offer.

(2) If north Korea expressly pronounces their respect for the Olympic Charter and IOC decisions and their unconditional participation in the 24th Seoul Olympics, we are willing to hold two sports inclusive of their finals in the north Korean area under the sponsorship of the Seoul Olympic Organizing Committee.

(3) The sports that can be allotted to north Korea are table tennis and fencing including their finals.

(4) If north Korea agrees to the proposal, we will discuss and resolve the questions of checking the facilities of venues, travels back and forth, guarantee of the safety of traveling persons, and communications and the shipping of goods necessary for the operation of the sports.

318

3. The Question of Staging Competition Across the South and the North Korean Areas.

It was suggested during the first and second meetings that group road cycling start in the north Korean area and finish in Seoul.

4. The Question of Participation in Cultural Activities

North Korea's participation in various cultural events to be staged during the 24th Seoul Olympics period will be welcomed.

5. The Question of Title of 24th Seoul Olympics

The Question of the title of the 24th Seoul Olympics does not deserve any discussion.

6. The Question of the Formation of Separate Organization in Case Some Sports Are Allotted to North Korea

The formation of any organization separate from the Seoul Olympic Organizing Committee in connection with the question of allotting some sports to north Korea, runs counter to the Olympic Charter and, therefore, cannot be considered.

During the second-day session on June 11, IOC President Samaranch reiterated the proposal the IOC made during the first-day session, which called for the transfer of table-tennis and archery including their finals to north Korea, holding of a road cycling over the south and the north Korean areas and the transfer of an additional group of soccer preliminaries to north Korea. The IOC president, saying he would formally offer the mediatory plan in messages, asked the two sides to make a reply to the IOC plan by the end of June.

Samaranch said that if the south and the north agree to the mediatory plan, the IOC would discuss various related problems through working-level contacts before the fourth meeting is convened. He called on both sides of Korea to respond to the IOC plan early, noting that everything has to be resolved before the IOC session tentatively scheduled for October so that they can gain the IOC session's approval.

On the afternoon of June 11 following the two-day meeting, Samar-

319

anch held a press conference and discussed the results of the third meeting as follows:

At the initiatives of the International Olympic Committee, south and north Korean Olympic Committee delegations headed by Kim Chong-ha and Kim Yu-sun, respectively, met for the third time at the IOC headquarters in Lausanne, June 10-11, 1986.

In the course of extensive discussion which took place in a cooperative and cordial atmosphere, the differences between the parties were narrowed considerably, both south and north Korean delegations stressing their sincere desire to ensure the success of the 24th Olympic Games in 1988.

The IOC delegation, in the spirit of the Olympic Charter and the decisions taken at the 1981 IOC session in Baden-Baden, proposed to both parties that a number of events on the program of the 24th Olympics be delegated to north Korea. Especially, the organization of two full sports would be entrusted to the north Korean Olympic Committee to be held in its territory.

The IOC has also proposed that certain additional events be partly located in the north Korean area, and that cultural manifestations connected with the Olympic Games be organized in both parts of the Korean peninsula.

The two Korean delegations have undertaken to study this proposal and to communicate to the IOC their willingness to accept it in principle by 30th June 1986 ; they have already confirmed to the IOC that free access of all members of the Olympic Family to the relevant Olympic venues in the north and the south would be ensured. The IOC will then convene a new meeting in order to settle all necessary organizational and operational aspects.

(5) Fourth Meeting

The fourth IOC-sponsored south-north sports meeting was held at the IOC headquarters in Lausanne on July 14-15, 1987, 13 months after the third meeting. The delay of the fourth meeting for more than a year was because of north Korea's de facto objection to the IOC compromise plan.

320

As he stated during the third meeting, IOC president Samaranch delivered to both sides of Korea on June 12, 1986, official messages containing an IOC mediatory plan, in which the IOC suggested that table tennis, archery and part of road cycling and a set of soccer preliminaries be turned over to north Korea, and that Olympics-related cultural activities be staged in both the south and the north.

In response, the KOC on June 30, 1986, accepted the IOC mediatory plan if the north Korean Olympic Committee respects the IOC decisions made at the IOC Baden-Baden session in 1981 and participates unconditionally in the 24th Olympics in Seoul.

On the same day, north Korea, agreeing to the IOC plan, notified the IOC that it would stage table tennis and archery matches in its area. However, in the same notification, the north complained that the two sports allotted to the north were too small in view of the total 24 Olympic sports, asking the IOC to make continued efforts to see to it that the additional sports they requested are granted to the north. They then expressed the hope that during the fourth meeting discussions would be made on such issues as the name, operation and organization of the Games as well as the issue of the number of sports North Korea thus in effect objected to the IOC's mediatory plan.

Thus, the IOC exchanged messages with north Korea four times and had one contact with them in Lausanne in February 1987 to sound out their attitude toward a possible fourth meeting. Thereafter, the IOC suggested to the KOC in April 1987 that the fourth meeting be held to discuss pending issues substantially.

Even at the fourth meeting thus arranged by the IOC, north Korea not only renewed their demand to co-host the Olympics but showed less flexibility than before, demanding, for instance, eight sports or one third of the total, in proportion to the population of the south and the north.

At the first-day session on July 14, KOC chief delegate Kim Chong-ha welcomed the opening of the fourth meeting to "embody and develop the IOC mediatory plan." He recalled that during the three past meetings, his delegation had exerted earnest efforts with broad-mindedness and patience to bring the dialogue to fruition so that the Seoul Olympics would be more successful than any other in history. He then asked the north Koreans to cooperate in the successful conclusion of the meeting by making it clear that they would participate in the 24th Olympics in Seoul, guarantee the free travel of the Olympic Family between the south and the north and willingly take part in the official opening and closing ceremonies in Seoul.

On the other hand, north Korea insisted that eight full sports including the full matches of soccer should be allotted to the north Korean area, a separate organizing committee formed in Pyongyang, and the opening and closing ceremonies held equally in Seoul and Pyongyang.

Meanwhile, in a separate contact with the KOC in the afternoon, the IOC sounded out the KOC's attitude toward a slight modification of its compromise plan that called for the awarding of women's volleyball and men's individual road cycling to north Korea exclusively.

Before presenting its opinion on the modification, the KOC delegation pointed out that despite the fact that the fourth meeting was called to discuss concrete working-level and technical matters related to the compromise plan, north Korea again raised the issue of co-hosting the Games and demanded more sports in proportion to population, thus giving rise to the danger that the sports talks would revert to the starting point in defiance of the IOC compromise plan. The KOC delegation added, however, that if north Korea withdrew the demand to co-host, would participate in the official opening and closing ceremonies in Seoul and would guarantee the free travel of the Olympic Family between the south and the north, it would review IOC President Samaranch's new proposal affirmatively.

At the second-day session on July 15, IOC president Samaranch, pointing out that there was a "slight improvement" in the sports to be allocated to north Korea, asked the south and the north to notify the IOC of whether they acceped the modified plan by the end of August

1987. He then released the following joint statement before concluding the fourth meeting.

— Gist of Joint Statement—

The IOC reaffirms that Seoul was chosen as the venue of the 24th Olympic Games in Baden-Baden on September 30, 1981, in accordance with the IOC Charter.

It is hoped that all relevant people pay attention to the steady efforts the IOC has been making to ensure the success of the 24th Olympics and the participartion of all the national Olympic committees.

As a result of the four rounds of meetings and an IOC delegation's visit to north Korea and on the basis of consultations with the International Federation of Sports and National Olympic Committees, the existing compromise plan has been amended to grant the following sports to the north Korean National Olympic Committee:

—Table tennis, archery (men's and women's), women's volleyball
—A set of soccer preliminaries
—Men's individual road cycling

In consideration of the fact that the IOC will have to send invitations to the 24th Olympics to the national Olympic committees by September 17, 1987, the two sides of Korea should notify the IOC headquarters in Lausanne of their decision concerning the IOC plan as soon as possible.

The IOC stresses that the IOC plan was exceptional and unprecedented in the history of the Olympic movement.

(6) Suspension of Sports Talks by North Korea

On July 16, 1987, IOC President Samaranch officially sent messages containing the new compromise plan produced at the fourth south-north sports meeting to both sides of Korea.

In a message to KOC President Kim Chong-ha, reaffirming again that the honor of hosting the 24th Olympic Games had been granted to the City of Seoul at the IOC Baden-Baden meeting on September 30, 1981, suggested modifying its previous plan and allocate to the north Korean area archery, table tennis and women's volleyball including their finals, one group of soccer preliminaries, and the entire men's road cycling.

The KOC sent a reply to the IOC on August 17, 1987, saying that it would accept the amended IOC compromise plan provided north Korea withdrew its demand to co-host, guaranteed free travel by the Olympic Family between the south and the north and promised their unconditional participation in the opening and closing ceremonies in Seoul.

Meanwhile, in a statement issued by Kim Duk-jun, north Korean Olympic Committee vice-chairman, on August 4, 1987, north Korea responded negatively to the IOC's modified plan. The statement said the new compromise plan produced by the IOC during the fourth meeting was no different from the previous plan and was far from their demand to co-host. On August 11, Jin Chung-kuk, vice-chairman of the north Korean Olympic Committee, made public their official stand toward the modified IOC plan in a press conference.

Jin demanded that 1) five full and one partial sports be held in the area of north Korea, 2) during a fifth meeting, not only the issue of sports to be allocated to the north but such matters as the questions of the title of the games, organization of organizing committee, opening and closing ceremonies and television rights, should be discussed comprehensively, and 3) the fifth meeting be held within the month of August before invitations to the 24th Olympics in Seoul are sent out.

As for the sports to be staged in north Korea, the north demanded all of table tennis, archery, women's volleyball and soccer, including their finals, a full sport to replace road cycling and still another sport, thus rendering the IOC's mediatory efforts meaningless.

When the IOC notified the north on August 24 that it would convene the fifth meeting only when north Korea accepts the modified mediatory plan, Pyongyang sent a reply to IOC President Samaranch on August 31, in which they expressed regret over the IOC stand and called for the opening of the fifth meeting at the earliest possible date. The north asked that if the fifth meeting could not be convened before September 17, then the IOC postpone the mailing of invitations to the 24th Olympics in Seoul until a later date.

Here, the IOC sent another message to the north on Sepember 4, reiterating its stand that "the fifth meeting can be called only when north Korea accepts the mediatory plan." As for the north Korean demand for the postponement of the mailing of Olympic invitations, the IOC turned it down, reasoning that any delay would contravene the IOC Charter that provides for the mailing of invitations one year before an Olympics.

Meanwhile, north Korea, believing that there is a little chance to obtain "co-hosting" through the good offices of the IOC, now sought to have direct talks with the south while shelving the Lausanne meeting for the time being.

In a message addressed to KOC president Kim Chong-ha on September 12, north Korea, in the name of their Olympic Committee Chairman Kim Yu-sun, insisted that the basic way to resolve the question is for the two sides of Korea to first iron out their differences through bilateral talks before holding the fifth Lausanne meeting. They argued that the deadlock of the Lausanne talks was due to a difference in the positions of the south and the north. Kim then proposed that a bilateral south and north Korea meeting be held "within the framework of the tripartite Lausanne meeting."

This maneuver by north Korea stemmed from their scheme to make themselves appear sincere toward the resolution of the Olympic question by proposing a bilateral meeting, to shun worldwide sanction for their refusal to accept the IOC's mediatory plan, and to ultimately shift blame for the breakup of the Lausanne meeting to the south. They knew that they could no longer expect the realization of "co-host" at the Lausanne meeting and that the cause of their demand for "co hosting" would be drastically undermined once Olympic invitations were sent out.

In reaction, the KOC, in a message to the north on September 24, pointed out the unreasonableness of the north Korean proposal for the resolution of the Olympic issue through a bilateral inter-Korean meeting. The south expressed the hope that inasmuch as the deadline for the entry for the Seoul Olympics was only four months away, north Korea would accept the IOC's mediatory plan at an early date so as to conclude the Lausanne talks successfully.

The KOC made it clear in the message that it had agreed to the Lausanne meeting designed to discuss the allotment of some Olympic sports to the north despite the fact that Seoul was given the right to host the 24th Olympics under a decision made by an IOC Baden-Baden meeting in 1981, in a bid to contribute to energizing the international Olympic movement as well as to national harmony and the improvement of the inter-Korean relationship.

The KOC also said that north Korea was trying to distract public attention by proposing bilateral inter-Korean Olympic talks while insisting as if the deadlock of the Lausanne talks were due to the different positions of the south and the north. It said that once an agreeement is reached on basic matters at the Lausanne meeting, the issue of free travel between the south and the north and other procedural matters could naturally be discussed at a meeting between the south and north Korean Olympic Committees.

Despite the KOC's pronouncement of its position, north Korea again sent a message to the south on October 12 reiterating their call for a bilateral south-north meeting. Here, the KOC again emphasized that once a basic agreement can be reached during the Lausanne meeting, the south is prepared to have talks between the south and north Korean Olympic Committees to discuss various matters to ensure the smooth implementation of such an agreement.

Meanwhile, finding it impossible to push through their idea of "co-hosting," north Korea released a statement on October 23 to announce in effect the breakup of the sports talks, arguing that the issue of the Olympic co-host can hardly be realized so long as there exists the incumbent administration of south Korea.

In the statement signed by Kim Yu-sun, the north Korean Olympic Committee chairman, the north asked the IOC to put off the fifth Lausanne meeting unitl after the results of the presidential election in south Korea are known. They asserted that if the "democratic forces" seize power in the December 16 presidential election, the two sides of Korea would be able to form a single team for the Olympics as well as to resolve the issue of "co-hosting" without difficulty.

Despite the fact that it would be practically impossible technically due to time pressure to have talks on issues related to the 24th Olympics after the presidential election in Decmber 1987 in the south, north Korea called for the postponement of the talks until after the election simply to shift blame for the deadlock of the talks to the south and to foment confusion in the south, taking advantage of the election period rather than to seek better results of the talks.

On January 12, 1988, north Korea confirmed their boycott of the Seoul Olympics by officially announcing that they would "not participate in the Olympic Games hosted by the south alone" and that they would make public their position again if the question of the Olympic "co-hosing" is resolved at a joint south-north conference they proposed.

Thus the Lausanne tripartite sports meeting among the IOC, south and north Korea, that lasted two years since October 1985 to discuss the issue of north Korea's participation in the Seoul Olympics, came to a total rupture without any achievement. The south, nevertheless, had kept the Olympic door open toward the north Koreans until immeditately before the opening of the Seoul Games on September 17, 1988, in a policy to make all concessions to an extent the Olympic Charter permits in close cooperation with the IOC so as to facilitate the north's participation. But north Korea refused to join in the efforts to pave the way for a significant momentum to promote national reconciliation.

5. Deadlock of Dialogue and Developments in Inter-Korean Relations

a. Background of Deadlock

On January 20, 1986, barely two days before the sixth south-north economic meeting slated for January 22, north Korea from nowhere announced unilaterally the indefinite postponement of the ongoing dialogue with the excuse of the annual joint Team Spirit '86 Korea-U.S. military exercise.

In a statement made in the form of a "joint statement" by the north's delegations to the economic, Red Cross and preliminary parliamentary meetings, north Korea, branding the Team Spirit exercise as a "nuclear war maneuver aimed" against north Korea, asserted that it would not have talks with the south during the period of the training exercise, trying to shift the blame for the suspension to the side of south Korea and the United States.

Reacting to the north Korean assertions, Republic of Korea delegations to the talks issued a joint statement on the afternoon of the same day, in which they called on the north to carry out all the meetings as scheduled. The joint statement was signed by Kwon Chong-dal, chief delegate to the preliminary parliamentarians contacts : Kim Ki-hwan, chief delegate to the economic meeting and Lee Yung-dug, chief delegate to the Red Cross talks.

The statement stressed that "if the north is really interested in easing tensions and achieving unification, they, instead of rejecting dialogue on the grounds of a routine training exercise, should have dialogue with sincerity and endeavor to build up trust between the south and the north. It then pointed to the unreasonableness of the north's boycott of the scheduled talks with the excuse of a routine military training, as follows in substance :

The Team Spirit exercise is peace-keeping training with a defensive purpose. The annual exercise, held continuously in the past ten years, was foreseen to be held this year too when the two sides agreed on the timing of the three-channeled talks.

As for military training, it is rather a matter of common sense that any country in the world that maintains armed forces takes it for granted that training exercises will be held. If there is any army that does not train, it would be extraordinarily abnormal.

The problem is whether such military exercises are held in secrecy or openly, whether they are offensive or defensive in nature, and whether they serve to strain the existing situation or threaten the other side.

That this training exercise of our side does not pose any threat to north Korea can be proven by the fact that our side formally notified north Korea of the contents and periods of such training many times in the past and even invited the north to send observers to the annual exercise in the south.

Last year alone, north Korea conducted regimental and division-level military exercises all along the Demilitarized Zone and large-scale field maneuvers participated in by all military branches across north Korea. But north Korea has not openly announced such exercises nor has it notified our side thereof.

The very act of north Korea holding military exercises in secrecy and building up offensive weapons along the Demilitarized Zone has made it unavoidalble for our side to hold defensive military exercises in preparation against any eventuality.

Thus seen, north Korea's boycott of the scheduled meetings on the pretext of routine military exercises cannot be justified by any excuse. We cannot but believe that such an act is merely aimed at laying an artificial barrier ahead of the dialogue.

The south and the north held working-level contacts to prepare for a prime ministers meeting and many other talks when military exercises were under way on both sides. As recently as early April 1984, for instance, an inter-Korean sports meeting was held while the Team Spirit exercise was going on. But the north Koreans did not dispute the military exercise in connection with the sports talks.

North Korea, which provoked a shooting spree at Panmunjom on November 23, 1984, tried to distort the fact and shift the blame to the south, putting off a planned inter-Korean economic meeting. Again early last year, they boycotted scheduled economic and Red Cross meetings in protest against our side's annual milit-

ary training.

The tension existing between the south and the north is not attributable to our side's militanry exercises as north Korea argues, but rather is the result of the mutual distrust and hostile relations that have been accumulated in the 40 years of national division.

The most important in the successful implementation of the inter-Korea dialogue is for the two sides to be faithful to each other and to build up mutual trust. This should begin with the maintenance of a posture wherein both sides faithfully carry out and respect what has been agreed upon between them.

However, the north's determination to suspend the talks was firm. On January 21, the north formally notified the south of their unilateral postponement of the 6th economic meeting in a message signed by the north's chief delegate Li Song-rok. In separate telephone messages to the south the following day, January 22, the north said they were suspending the 11th full-dress Red Cross meeting slated for February 25-28, 1986, in Pyongyang, and the third preliminary parliamentary contact set to be held on February 18, 1986, respectively. North Korea thus suspended all the on-going dialogues despite the south's repeated calls for talks.

Examples of Inter-Korea Meetings Held during Periods of Team Spirit Exercise

Exercise Period	Meeting
March 1-27, 1979	Table tennis meeting —Second meeting (March 5, '79) —Third meeting (March 9, '79) —Fourth meeting (March 12, '79) · Contacts between Coordinating Committee Seoul-side delegates and the north's "Front for Fatherland" delegates —Second contacts (March 7, '79) —Third contacts (March 14, '79)

March 1-April 20, 1980	· Working-level contacts for Prime Minis-ters' meeting
	  —Third contacts (March 4, '80)
	  —Fourth contacts (March 18, '80)
	  —Fifth contacts (April 1, '80)
	  —Sixth contacts (April 18, '80)

February1-mid-April, 1984	· First sports meeting (April 9, '84)

b. Efforts of South Korea to Resume Talks

(1) Efforts to Resume Suspended Meetings

After north Korea suspended all the talks such as Red Cross and economic meetings, on which the two sides had agreed, the south had made steady efforts to resume them despite the north Koreans' rejection of the repeated calls.

In their separate telephone messages on March 26, 1986, the south's chief delegates to the Red Cross, economic and preliminary parliamentary talks expressed regrets over the failure to open agreed-on talks due to the north's unilateral suspension, and proposed that the economic meeting be held on April 30 and the third preparatory contact for the parliamentary talks on May 14 at Panmunjom respectively, and the 11th Red Cross meeting on May 27 in Pyongyang. (Vice Economic Planning Minister Moon Hi-gap has replaced Kim Ki-hwan, chief of the International Economic Council, as chief delegate to the inter-Korean economic meeting, which was notified to north Korea on March 24, 1986.)

However, north Korea again turned a deaf ear to the call. In their telephone messages sent to the south on March 31 and April 1, Chon Gum-chol, chief delegate to the preliminary parliamentary meeting, and other of the north's chief delegates to the talks rejected the proposal of the south to resume the dialogue, arguing that the Team Spirit exercise was still going on.

331

Again in a so-called joint statement of the chief north Korean delegates to the dialogue, which was made on April 24 and timed with the end of the Team Spirit military exercise, Pyongyang trying to shift the blame for the suspension of the dialogue to the south, rejected the resumption of the dialogue while denouncing the south in connection with its military training programs and the annual Korea-U.S. Security Council Meeting.

Moreover, north Korea from nowhere proposed a three-way military meeting on June 17, 1986, among the defense ministers of the south and the north and the United Nations commander, and unreasonably made the military meeting a prerequisite to the resumption of the inter-Korean dialogue, asserting that if the tripartite meeting were held and progressed satisfactorily, an "epochal phase" would unfold in the south-north dialogue.

Under these circumstances, the south, in telephone messages to the north on July 11, 1986, called on the north Koreans again to return to the arena of dialogue instead of continuously rejecting the resumption of the talks. In the messages signed by the south's chief delegates to the dialogues, the south proposed that the sixth economic meeting be held on August 6, the third preliminary parliamentary contacts on August 13, both at Panmunjom, and the 11th full-dress Red Cross meeting in Pyongyang on August 28, respectively.

However, north Korea, in separate statements signed by the respective north Korean chief delegates to the talks, rejected such consistent efforts of the Republic of Korea to resume the suspended dialogue.

Because of this intransigency of the north, the public expectation that the inter-Korean dialogue would resume when the Team Spirit exercise would be completed, broke down leading the inter-Korean relations to further deteriorate. It was totally unpredictable when the suspended dialogue could resume.

(2) Proposal for Water Resources Meeting

On October 21, 1986, north Korea formally announced that they began construction on the Kumgangsan power plant in the Kangwon-Province area north of the truce line under the cloak of a "grand reformation of nature."

The south, which carefully studied the impact the projected dam would have on areas south of the truce line, urged, in a statement released by Construction Minister Lee Kyu-ho on October 30 that the north stop the project forthwith, charging that the north Korean project totally ignored international practices governing the utilization of rivers and streams and went against the principle of the peaceful use of national land especially because of the dam's impact on meteorological, ecological, economic and military aspects.

The gist of the statement issued by Construction Minister Lee was as follows :

North Korea has recently launched a project by mobilizing a large number of military troops to build the so-called Kumgangsan power station in the northern area of Kangwon Province. They announced through their news media that all-out efforts are being made to complete the power station at an early date.

Contrary to their allegation, the north Koran project poses various grave problems to the Republic of Korea. According to north Korean announcements, the new power station is goint to be the largest of its kind in the north. Accordingly, it is estimated that the station will have a power generating capacity of at least 800,000KW.

In choosing the site for hydroelectric plant, top priority must be given to both an abundant availability of water and to the height of the drop. In view of such engineering requirements, it is concluded that the Kumgangsan Power Station will be located below where the Pukhan River converges with the Kumgang River just north of the Demilitarized Zone so that the water resources of the Pukhan River can be utilized to the maximum possible extent.

Our analysis shows further that north Korea plans to build a reservoir at Hoeyang and dig a tunnel extending 30 to 60 kilometers northeastward in order to channel the water backward into the Wonsan area. In that way, the water will fall from a height of at least 300 meters to turn the power generators.

One of the grave problems resulting from the power dam construction is that by diverting northeastward the water in the upper stretch of the Pukhan River, which now flows in a southward direction, the north Korean project will inflict on the south an annual loss of about 1.8 billion metric tons of water for industrial, agricultural and household purposes, which would otherwise flow through the Pukhan River system into the Hwachon area. The project is also certain to greatly affect the power generating capabilities of the five dams at Hwachon and further downstream.

In the long term, by reversing the flow of the upper stretch of the Pukhan River, a major source of water for the Han River, the north Korean project will cause terrible disturbances in the ecological system in the east central part of the Korean peninsula including the Kumgang and the Sorak Mountains.

The north Korean dam will have to be built to a height of at least 200 meters in order to maintain the water level in the projected reservoir at 350 meters above sea level so that a natural drop of about 300 meters can be created by diverting the water toward the Wonsan area.

As a result, up to 20 billion metric tons of water will be stored in the reservoir. In the event that the dam, holding back such an enormous quantity of water, collapsed due to natural or artificial causes, there would be a horrible disaster in the Republic.

The dam would begin to pose a potential danger as soon as the volume of water in the reservoir reached about 900 million tons. If the dam breaks at that point, 300,000 tons of water per second would push forth, directly endangering the five dams at Hwachon and further downstream in the south.

Moreover, enormous quantities of water would suddenly pour into the lower stretches of the Han River via the Paltang Dam. This would cause an overflow of water 10 times that recorded during the Han River flood in September 1984 in Seoul and other areas along the entire lower stretch of the Han River, wreaking tremendous havoc.

That disaster could result if the north Korean dam in question only held 900 million tons. Should the mammoth dam collapse after the reservoir filled up with 20 billion tons of water, sudden torrents would pour down the Pukhan River, destroying the five dams downstream one after the other and flooding the entire region along the Han River.

This would completely devastate the central section of the Korean peninsula, including not only Seoul but Kangwon and Kyonggi provinces, inflicting a horrendous disaster.

Under these circumstances, we cannot help but conclude that north Korea's Kumgangsan power plant project totally ignores international practices governing the utilization of rivers and streams and goes against the principle of peaceful use of national land.

We must point out that the safety of the planned dam is a matter of grave concern that will spell life or death for us. We make it clear that the use of a river that runs from the north to the south must not be unilaterally decided on by the north for its own purposes alone.

We believe that the Kumgangsan power station project must be promptly discontinued. North Korea is strongly urged to agree to our rightful position. We make it clear also that the Republic of Korea government is throughly studying appropriate countermeasures to be taken in case north Korea refuses our rightful demand.

North Korea rejected this protest by the south in a statement of their own issued on November 4, 1986, in the name of the director of Resources Development Bureau, Electric Power Industry Commission. In the statement, the north asserted that their Kumgangsan Dam project is a "peaceful undertaking" designed to "develop and reasonable utilize water resources in the area of the Kumgangsan Mountains." They then argued that the project would have a favorable effect on the south, too, such as flood control.

The north maintained that their project cannot be subject to inter-Korean negotiations because, they argued, the project is "an internal issue of the north which therefore cannot be meddled in by a third party."

Even in the circumstances where the north rejected the south's demand and went so far as to rule out any negotiations between the two sides the south continued to urge the north Koreans to discontinue the project, trying to resolve the dispute through dialogue.

In a statement issued by the Minister of National Defense on November 6 and another made by the Minister of Culture and Information on November 21, 1986, the south said that ulterior military motives lurk behind the north's dam project, warning that if north Korea persists in turning a deaf ear to the south's justifiable demand, the south would take all necessary steps to cope with the situation.

And in their joint statement of November 26, the Ministers of National Defense, Construction, Culture and Information, and National Unification made public a government decision to build a dam to counter the north's Kumgangsan Dam.

The four ministers said that the south had decided to build an effective counterdam across the upper reached of the Pukhan River to the south of the Demilitarized Zone as a rightful means of national self-defense against the terrifying threat posed by the north Korean project. They said that if the north ceases the Kumgangsan Dam project, the south is ready to earnestly discuss with them all issues involved in the utilization of the resources of rivers that flow through the territories of both the south and the north.

The substance of the four ministers' joint statement was as follows ;

While clearly pointing out the north's ulterior military intent of securing a horrendous water weapon against the south through the construction of a huge dam allegedly for the Kumgangsan hydroelectric power station, our government strongly urged the north several times to immediately discontinue the dam project from the standpoint of the common good of the Korean people.

Citizens throughout the land are now voicing irate denouncement of north exposed in concrete terms the foolhardy north Korean scheme of aggression incorporated in the dam project and now report daily from major cities around the world on the extent to which the international community is scandalized by the dam project.

North Korea, however, keeps turning a deaf ear to the domestic and international censure and is pressing ahead with the dam project even at this very moment. Keeping a total silence on the project, they are brazenly mounting a campaign of disinformation, alleging that our side is "slandering"them on this matter, and thus attempting to escape censure for the national sin they commit.

Under the circumstances, the government has been awaiting an affirmative response form the north, while at the same time carefully studying various possible countermeasures to be taken to safeguard the survival of the nation.

To that end, intensive efforts have been exerted to work out nationwide measures with the help of in depth research and analyses by experts and on the strength of the entire public's invariously ardent desire to counteract with wisdom the threat to national security.

The government has thus decided to build a sufficiently effective counterdam across the upper reaches of the Pukhan River to the south of the Demilitarized Zone as a rightful means of national self-defense against the terrifying threat posed by the north Korean project. Since the counterproject will require a vast investment, the government has already begun the necessary preparations, including engineering studies and the budgeting of necessary funds.

The government considers it to be of great significance that the countermeasures have been derived from the uniformly strong resolve of all our citizens to protect national security.

We ardently hope that the entire people will continue to extend support and encouragement for the construction of the Peace Dam to neutralize yet another sinister north Korean scheme to communize the south through a water offensive.

At the same time, as the government urges north Korea once again to restore their sense of national conscience, abandon the reckless war of attrition of national energies, and return to a path leading to the common good of the Korean people based on national reconciliation and mutual trust, we want to make it clear that if north Korea ceases the Kumgangsan Dam project, we are ready to earnestly discuss with them all issues involved in the utilization of the water resources of the rivers that flow through the territories of both the south and the north. The north Korean

337

anthorities are strongly urged to respond affirmatively to our manifestation of a deep love of the Korean people.

We have now reached a critical juncture at which we must unite even more firmly than ever to crush the north Korean scheme and plot to breach the peace and bring about national self-injury in order to safeguard our security and survival as a nation.

We believe that in the face of this crisis, the government and the people must be united like one in exerting wisdom and courage to tide over the difficult situation created by the increased menace from the north Korean Communists.

Moreover, on November 28, 1986, Construction Minister Lee Kyu-ho sent a message to his north Korean counterpart, chairman of the Electric Power Industry Comission of the Administrative Council, proposing a south-north water resources meeting to discuss the reasonable exploration and utilization of the rivers that flow through the areas of the two sides.

Meanwhile, in a so-called "White Paper of the Electric Power Industry Commission" issued on December 25, 1986, north Korea rejected the south's demand, reiterating their argument that their dam won't do any harm to the south and rather would bring many advantages to the south such as the "elimination of floods in the Kangwon-do area."

Here, Construction Minister Lee issued a statement on January 16, 1987, in which he renewed the call for a south-north water resources meeting and expressed the willingness to compensate, if the north gives up the dam project, for the loss resulting there form.

Also in the statement, the south pointed out that the north's "White Paper" was full of fabrications intended to cover up their sinister move to use the dam as a water weapon, and proposed that a joint study team be formed of experts from both the south and the north to conduct joint studies to determine such practical engineering questions as the geographical and geological conditions of the Kumgang-san Dam sites, the safety of the dams and their optimum dimensions.

The south also suggested in the statement that if the north sincerely takes part in a dialogue and joint studies concerning the joint use of water resources and as a result abandons the project to reverse the flow of the Pukhan River, the south is willing to supply power to the north to make up sufficiently for the loss of power thus incurred.

The series of these suggestions by the south were part of the effort to forestall by all means heightened tensions and the reckless war of attrition that would inevitably ensue and thereby explore a path leading to national co-prosperity.

Nevertheless, the north rejected the offers, contending that the Kumgangsan power plant project will not have any effect on the south at all. Going a step further, they refused even to receive the south's message of November 28, 1986, in which a south-north water resources meeting was proposed.

Here, finding it impossible to resolve the Kumgangsan Dam issue through dialogue and negotiations, the south came to break ground on February 28, 1987 for the construction of a "Peace dam" as a counter-measure against the north Korean dam project. Tensios thus increased further between the two sides of Korea.

(3) Proposal for South-North Prime Ministers' Meeting

At a time when the north was insisting on the prior convocation of a high-level south-north political and military meeting on the heels of their demand for a tripartite military conference, the south proposed a south-north prime ministers meeting on March 17, 1987. The offer was rimdc in nistessage sent by Prime Minister Lho Shin-yong and Defense Minister Lee Ki-baek to the north's Administrative Council premier and the People's Armed Forces minister. The message was in the form of a reply to the north's call for a high-level south-north political and military meeting, made on March 3, 1987.

In the message, the south, while stressing that "a top leaders meeting would be the most effective and quickest way to reach an epochal turning point leading to improved inter-Korean relations and to resolve the fundamental problem of peaceful unification," proposed that a south-north water resources meeting be held and the suspended dialogues resumed to settle the abnormal inter-Korean relations as soon as possible and foster an elementary and substantial trust between the two sides.

The message also suggested that a south-north prime ministers meeting be held upon the laying of the minimum conditions for mutual trust so as to comprehensively discuss various issues pending between the south and the north.

The text of the message of Prime Minister Lho Shin-yong and Defense Minister Lee Ki-baek sent to the north was as follows:

Your side's letter was received on last March 3.

I believe that the most important step to easing tensions and improving the inter-Korean relations in a circumstances in which the south and the north find themselves today, will be to restore and build up their mutual trust.

I also believe that a top leaders meeting between the south and the north will be the most effective and shortest way to laying an epochal turning point in the improvement of the inter-Korean relations and to resolving the fundamental problem of peaceful unification. There is no change in this position.

Nonetheless, your side showed an insincere attitude in your recent letter. Your side insisted that the existing inter-Korean dialogue could be resumed only when a political and military meeting is held. And even regarding our side's proposal for a top leaders meeting, your side asserted that it could be opend only after a political and military meeting was held and progressed fruitfully, thus in effect shunning a top leaders meeting.

As I am worried that if the present abnormal inter-Korean relations studded with distrust and confrontation as has been the case to date, are left unchecked under the circumstances, it would only aggravate national misfortune and sufferings, I feel that measures should be prepared urgently to surmount it.

To desist from distrust and confrontation and to resolve problems through dialogue, a base of trust should be laid foremost of all.

Your side has unilaterally suspended the south-north Red Cross Conference, inter-Korean econmic meeting, etc., and scrapped agreed matters to which the two sides duly committed themselves. Moreover, by using the issue of military exercise which has nothing to do with the talks as a prerequisite to the resumption of the dialogue, your side laid an obstacle before the talks.

Lately, your side has further fomented tensions between the south and the north by pushing forward the construction of the Kumgangsan Dam, a project that threatens the human lives and properties of the other side.

These series of your side's conducts have led to the deepening of distrust and enmity between the south and the north. Today's reality thus dictates the creation of an atmosphere of trust betweent the two sides on a priority basis.

I am convinced that in order to foster elementary and substantial trust between the south and the north, your side should above all agree to hold an inter-Korean water resources meeting without delay to discuss and resolve issues related to the unitlizaton and development of the water resources of the common rivers of the south and the north in connection with the question of your side's Kumgangsan Dam project which emerges as a new source of tension and distrust. At the same time, I think that the suspended dialogue should be resumed unconditionally.

From this standpoint, I sincerely propose to your side that a south-north prime ministers meeting be held to discuss comprehensively various issues raised by the two sides to improve relations and ease tension between the south and the north·at least under the circumstance in which mutual trust is created by holding a water resources meeting and resuming the suspended dialogue.

I am sure that once a south-north prime ministers meeting is held, it would contribute to creating a more developed and mature atmosphere for the early realization of a south-north top leaders meeting that would provide an epochal and fundamental turning point in the effort to bring about peace and unification on this land.

I believe that if your side does not ignore the nation's wish for improved inter-Korean relations and peaceful unification, your side would affirmatively respond to our side's proposal. I suggest that a first south-north water resources meeting be held at Panmunjom within March and the inter-Korean Red Cross and economic talks in Pyongyang and at Panmunjom, respectively, in April.

The sooner these meetings take place, the better it would be. I leave the concrete times of the meetings to your side.

In a reply to the south on March 30, north Korea agreed to a south-north prime ministers meeting and suggested that a preliminary meeting of minister-level officials be held at Panmunjom on April 23, 1987. While favorably responding to a prime ministers meeting, however, north Korea limited the matters to be discussed at the proposed meeting to those related to the alleviation of tensions. They thus eliminated such issues as mutual supension of slander and defamation and the introduction of many-sided exchanges and "collaboration" which could have eased the state of military confrontation, even though the north had earlier wanted to take up just such issues at the political and military meeting they had proposed.

Moreover, the north become more inflexible. In their March 3, 1987 letter they said that a political and military meeting could take place in parallel with the resumption of the suspended channels of dialogue and that the issue of the Kumgangsan Dam project could be discussed. They now insisted that the existing dialogue could be resumed only after a prime ministers meeting. Furthermore, they called for a preliminary meeting to prepare for a prime ministers meeting although they had not done so when they suggested a political and military meeting.

Their demand for a preliminary meeting seemed to have stemmed from a determination to raise the issues of disarmament and the Team Spirit military exercise, which they had previously suggested for the agenda of the political and miltary meeting, and to use these issues and the south's internal political situation as the basis by which to decide whether to hold a prime ministers meeting or not.

At this point, the south, in a message signed by Prime Minister Lho Shin-yong and addressed to Li Gun-mo, his north Korean counterpart, on April 10, 1987 proposed that a south-north water resources meeting be held at Panmunjom on May 6, 1987, the sixth south-north economic meeting at Panmunjom on May 12, 1987, and the 11th Red Cross meeting in Pyongyang on May 19, 1987. It added that if these meetings were held and progressed satifactorily, preliminary talks for a prime ministers meeting could be held in the foreseeable future.

The text of Prime Minister Lho's message to the north was as follows:

I have received your letter dated March 30. I regard the fact that you showed an interest in our proposal for a south-north prime ministers meeting as a positive thing. We made that proposal in the hope of laying the groundwork for peaceful unification through the improvement of inter-Korean relations, the alleviation of tensions, and the creation of an atmosphere conducive to the early realization of a meeting betwen the top leaders of the south and the north.

If a south-north prime ministers meeeting held and progressed well, it would serve to foster an atmosphere of mutual turst, as you too said in the March 3 letter. This is why we proposed in our previous message that a south-north water resources meeting be held and the suspended Red Cross and economic talks be resumed to create the minimum conditions for the fostering of mutual trust in a prime ministers meeting.

In the recent reply, however, you turned a deaf ear to the proposal for a water resources meeting and the resumption of the existing dialogues, both of which should precede a prime ministers meeting, thus making it difficult in reality to realize a prime ministers meeting.

The deepening tension and confrontation between the south and the north today are due to accumulated distrust and discontinuity over a long period of time.

I firmly believe that in view of our past experiences and the scarcity of any achievement made in the dialogues since the turn of the 1980s, the best way to dissolve such distrust and discontinuity and transform them into trust and cooperative relations is for the south and the north to carry on and develop the dialogues sincerely and without interruption.

I, therefore, think that what is most pressing under the present condition of the suspended dialogues is to revive positively the existing dialogues which your side has unilaterally suspended.

I note that you, too, said in the letter delivered to us on March 3 that "it is our firm stand to resume the suspended multi-pronged dialogues and hold a south-north top-level meeting," thus taking an interest in the resumption of the stalled dialogues.

At the same time, the question of the Kumgangsan Dam project, which is now the source of heightened tension between the south and the north and which will only exact unnecessary waste from both sides, must be urgently discussed and resolved. Inasmuch as your side, too, has already recongnized the need to discuss the issue of the Kumgangsan Dam project and in view of the seriousness and urgency of the issue a south-north water resources meeting ought to be held at an early date.

Once the minimum conditions for mutual trust have been created by the convening of a water resources meeting and the resumption of the suspended dialogues, preparation for a south-north prime ministers meeting would progress smoothly. From this standpoint, we sincerely propose that a south-north water resources meeting be held at Panmunjom on May 6, the sixth inter-Korean economic meeting at Panmunjom on May 12, and the 11th full-dress south-north Red Cross meeting in Pyongyang on May 19. In the near future, when these meetings have been held and have registered progress, a preliminary meeting could be held to prepare for a south-north prime ministers meeting.

I look forward to an affirmative response from you.

In a statement by the spokesman of the Administrative Council on April 24, north Korean rejected the south-north dialogue and tried to shift the blame for the suspension of talks onto the south. In the statement, the north reiterated their previous assertion that "non-political talks cannot resolve the issue of distrust and enmity resulting from the political and military confrontation between the south and the north," and denounced the south's proposal for talks as a "mere time device" designed to shatter all channels of dialogue between the two sides.

They also asserted that "now the south Korean authorities have no right to discuss any further the south-north dialogue and the alleviation of tension. They should be held fundamentally responsible for the consequences of their anti-national act of sealing off even the golden opportunity to resume the south-north dialogue."

(4) Proposal for Foreign Ministers Meeting

At a time when the north called for a "multi-national arms reduction meeting" among the south and the north and the United States, the south proposed to the north on August 3, 1987, that a south-north foreign ministers meeting be held either in New York or in another convenient place during the period of the United Nations General Assembly in September.

In a statement of the Ministry of Foreign Affairs, the south stressed that the arms reduction talks the north suggested could bear concrete results only when systematic security mechanisms were prepared through such steps as the entry of the south and the north into the United Nations and cross recognition by the four neighboring powers and when confidence-building and a durable peace were realized through exchanges and cooperation between the two sides of Korea. It said that the Korean question should be resolved under the principle of national self-determination under all circumstances.

The text of the statement of the Ministry of Foreign Affairs was as follows :

The government of the Republic of Korea has exerted every possible effort to reduce tensions on the Korean peninsula and fulfill the aspirations of the entire Korean people for peaceful reunification through dialogue and negotiation in the spirit on national reconciliation, and such an effort will continue in the future.

We belive that to settle the Korean issues through talks between the parties directly concerned of the south and the north on the basis of the principle of national self-determination is the most appropriate approach reflecting the ardent national aspirations of the Korea people.

The issue of peace and reunification is basically a problem to be settled by the

Korean people themselves, as they are masters of their own country. Accordingly, if north Korea is truly interested in improving relations and relaxing tensions between the south and the north, it must first show sincerity in confidence-building which is the basis for consolidation of peace.

In the meantime, we had the Red Cross talks, the economic talks and preliminary contacts for parliamentary talks in order to reduce tensions and restore trust between the south and the north. In the autumn of 1985, we also had a touching moment of shedding tears over the reunion of members of separated families when they exchanged the home town visiting groups for the first time in the 40 years of division.

Furthermore, the Red Cross talks and the econmoic talks have reached such a stage the concrete projects could have been implemented with only modest concession and cooperation from both sides.

However, north Korea suspended unilaterally all channels of dialogue in January 1986 under the pretext of the Team Spirit exercise and put forward the so-called three-way military authorities talks and politico-military talks. Furthermore, north Korea recently made a proposal to hold armed forces reduction negotiation in Geneva among the three parties, including the United States. Such a proposal runs counter to the principle of self-determination which calls for the settlement of the pending problems by the parties directly concerned, the south and the north.

It is to be reemphasized that the most practical approach to the solution of the pending problems between the south and the north lies in strengthening the foundation for mutual trust by convening water resources talks at an early date while resuming and facilitating the Red Cross and economic talks that the north Korean side has unilaterally suspended.

Talks on armed forces reduction can bear concrete results only when confidence is restored and peace consolidated through exchanges and cooperation between the south and the north on the basis of arrangements for maintaining peace and security such as both Koreas' entry into the United Nations and the cross-recognition by the four neighboring powers.

Under the present circumstances, as far as the issue of armed forces reduction between the south and north is concerned, it is important to make systematic devices for maintaining peace and security as well as avoiding military conflicts.

It is in this perspective that we propose to hold a south-north foreign ministers meeting in order to discuss such issues as conclusion of a nonaggression agreement, U.N. membership, cross-recognition and other matters.

In this meeting, all matters of each other's concern may be discussed, comprising confidence-building measures such as resumption and progress of the suspended dialogue ; consultations and settlement on water resources problem ; various issues including armed forces reduction to relax tensions and establish peace on the Korean peninsula ; and the issue of bringing about successful south-north prime ministers meeting and of realizing eventually a meeting between the highest authorities of the south and the north.

It is desirable that the Foreign Ministers' talks be held either in New York during the period between the opening of the United Nations General Assembly session and the end of September this year when the foreign ministers of the south and the north will be visiting the United Nations or in any other mutually agreeable place during the same period.

We expect that north Korea respond positively to our proposal in full appreciation of our genuine desire for restoring trust and improving relations between the south and the north.

The south's proposal for a foreign ministers meeting stemmed from the recognition that unification should be realized in a peaceful manner through dialogue and that although outsiders were responsible for the division, it is incumbent upon the south and the north themselves to resolve the unification issue.

In particular, to resolve the reality of the problems of the south and the north which maintained the relations of distrust and hostility under mutually conflicting ideologies and systems for more than 40 years, there should be political reconciliation and confidence building beforehand. But the offer that a south-north foreign ministers conference could discuss all matters of mutual concern including armed forces reduction for the sake of the relaxation of tensions and durable peace on the Korean penisnsula, was an overture that took into account even the position of north Korea.

Meanwhile, north Korea issued a statement of the spokesman of their Foreign Ministry on August 6, 1987, to reject in effect the south's proposal by reiterating thier previous call for a three-way meeting. The north insisted that a three-way foreign ministers including the U.S. Secretary of State should be held to discuss the issue of armed forces reduction, etc., on a priority basis.

The north argued in the statement that Seoul's offer to hold an inter-Korean foreign ministers meeting to disuss U.N. membership and cross-recognition was intended to use the south-north dialogue to "perpetuate the division of the nation." It then contended that to relax tensions on the Korean peninsula, the issue of armed forces reduction should first be resolved.

North Korea further asserted that since any settlement of arms reduction would inevitably involve the question of the U.S. forces in Korea, such talks should include the United States. Proposing that a foreign ministers meeting of the south, the north and the United States be held at the soonest possible date in Geneva or any other convenient place, north Korea suggested that to prepare for the meeting, a preliminary meeting of vice-minister-level officials be held at Panmunjom toward the close of August 1987 or at any other mutually agreeable time.

In particular, the north said that if south Korea and the United States regard such a preliminary meeting as awkward, bilateral preliminary contacts could be held between the U.S. and north Korea and between the south and the north. They thus revealed their ulterior motive of using such meeting in preparing an official conduit for contacts with the United States.

On August 13, 1987, the south, pointing out the unreasonableness of a three-way foreign ministers meeting, again urged the north to respond affirmatively to a south-north foreign ministers meeting. In a statement by the spokesman of the Ministry of Foreign Affairs, the south stressed that all pending problems between the south and the north Korea should be discussed and settled by the parties directly concerned, the south and the north on the basis of the principle of national self-determination. It said that talks on armed forces reduction could bear concrete results only when arrangements are made for durable peace such as the conclusion of nonaggression agreement between the south and the north, entry into the United Nations and cross-recognition by the four concerned powers.

However, north Korea on September 24, 1987, rejected the proposal by the south for a south-north foreign ministers meeting. In a statement by the deputy spokesman of the Foreign Ministry, the north insisted that a three-way foreign ministers meeting should be held to discuss the issue of armed forces reduction, demanding again a vice-minister-level preliminary meeting between the south and the north.

c. Dialogue Related North Korean Offers

(1) Three-Way Military Meeting

North Korea, which unilaterally suspend a series of inter-Korean talks such as Red Cross and economic meetings slated for early 1986 on the grounds of the Team Spirit training exercise and has rejected the south's offers to resume the dialogue, proposed (in a message dated June 9) a "three-way military meeting" among the defense ministers of the south, the north and the commander of the United Nations Command in Korea.

In a message addressed to Minister of National Defense Lee Ki-baek and signed by Oh Jin-wu, the north's People's Armed Forces minister, north Korea, contending that the "Korean situation is now at a perilous point where a war may break out due even to a casual cause," suggested that a military authorities meeting be held in July to discuss the questions of "halting military exercises and arms buildup," "respecting the Armistice Agreement," issues which, they argued, constitute the direct causes of tensions and the danger of war. North

Korea proposed that a preliminary contact be held at Panmunjom on June 27 to discuss the proposed military meeting.

North Korea also argued that "if a military meeting were held and substantial measures taken to ease tensions on the Korean peninsula, it would bring about a new breakthrough in the effort to ease tensions and promote peace, unfolding an epochal phase for the inter-Korean dialogue." They thus let it be known that they intend to use the convocation of a three-way military meeting as a prerequisite to the progress of other ongoing inter-Korean talks such as economic and Red Cross meetings.

The gist of the north Korean message was as follows:

The tensions fomented in our country today acutely requieres that our military authorities take responsible measures exigently before the nation and the world to relax tensions. As you, too, realize, there can be nothing more important than to realize peace and peaceful unification of our country before our people who have experienced the misfortune of national division for about 40 years.

To reflect this ardent wish of the nation, the door to dialogue was opened again last year between the north and the south to facilitate multi-pronged talks. And its scope was limited, Red Cross art troupes and hometown visitors were exchanged for the first time since national division to help ease the pains of our people.

Regrettably, however, the inter-Korean relationship reverted to the pre-dialogue state again. As tensions further built up, the south-north dialogues were halted at the same time. Besides, the situation has reached a point where a war may, in fact, break out at any casual factor.

I believe that you, too, will not deny that if a war breaks out in our country, it would devastate the land and drive the entire populace into a nuclear havoc, a development which cannot be of any advantage to either the north or the south. At this important juncture of whether or not we can save the country and people from the danger of a destructive war or of whether or not we can resume the suspended dialogue, the entire Korean populace and the rest of mankind are watching us, the responsible military authorities.

In this respect, in accordance with the peace initiatives taken by the Supreme

Command of the Korean People's Army and in the sincere hope of taking practical and effective measures to relax tensions and remove the danger of war in our country, I courteously propose to you that a military officials meeting be held among the minister of the People's Armed Forces of the Democratic People's Republic of Korea, minister of National Defense of the Republic of Korea and the supreme commander of the United Nations Command in south Korea.

A military officials meeting should in the first place, discuss the most urgent and crucial issues that arise in removing the danger of war and alleviating tensions, which have become a reality before us. These issues can include the question of halting military exercises and arms buildup, the direct causes behind heightening tensions and the danger of war, the question of reducing military manpower and equipment, and the question of abiding by the Military Armistic Agreement as it originally dictates. In addition, issues which you raise to help ease tensions on the Korean peninsula can also be discussed at the meeting.

I believe it is proper to make Panmunjom the venue of the meeting. Any other place considered to be of convenience to both sides can also be used. It would be good to have the meeting within the month of July.

As I regard it as necessary to have a preliminary contact to prepare for a military authorities meeting, I also propose to hold a preliminary contact at Panmunjom on June 27 attended by about three delegates and a proper number of attendants from each side.

If and when a military authorities meeting takes place and substantial measures are taken to relax tension, a new turning-point will be provided for the alleviation of tension and peace on the Korean peninsula and also an epochal phases would unfold in the south-north dialogue.

I express the expectation that you will affirmatively respond to our new initiatives intended to relax tensions and remove the danger of war on the Korean peninsula and accelerate the great task of peaceful unification of the nation.

Meanwhile, north Korea sent an identical message to the commander of the United Nations Command in Korea around the same time they delivered a message to the Defense Minister of the Republic of Korea on June 17.

351

Initially on June 7, north Korea said that they would send a message of the People's Armed Forces minister to the concurrent commander of the Eighth U.S. Army and the Korea-U.S. Combined Forces Command. The United Nations Command, however, pointed out that under the practices of the Military Armistice Commission, messages ought to be exchanged between the commander of the United Nations Command and the Supreme Commander of the North Korea Forces, telling Pyongyang that if north Korea followed the practice, it would accept their message.

Nevertheless, the June 17 message addressed to the United Nations Commander was signed not by the supreme commander of the north Korean forces but by Oh Jin-wu, People's Armed Forces minister or the first deputy of the supreme commander, in violation of the long-held practice of the Military Armistice Commission.

That north Korea suspended the ongoing dialogues unilaterally and proposed a separate three-way military meeting stemmed not from their sincere manner to resolve the Korean question through dialogue but from sinister motives as can be seen in the following :

First, by proposing a three-way military meeting ostensibly to discuss such military issues as a halt to military exercise, north Korea sought to move a step closer to the realization of the so-called tripartite meeting they persistently have demanded since January 1984.

Second, the fact that the north advanced the idea of a military meeting while rejecting the resumption of the existing channels of the dialogue and that they hinted at resuming the suspended dialogue only when the military meeting they proposed is realized, suggests that they made the offer in the hope of escaping censure for their refusal to resume the talks and, at the same time, shifting the blame for the suspension of the dialogue to the south.

Third, with an eye at the Nonaligned Summit Meeting slated for August 26-September 7, 1986, in Zimbabwe and an "international Meeting for Peace on and Non-nuclearization of the Korean Peninsula" set to be held in Pyongyang September 6-8, 1986. North Korea attempts to make it appear as if the basic obstacle to the dialogue and the easing of tensions lies in the Team Spirit training and the presence of the U.S. forces in Korea, thus hoping to enlist international support for their call for the suspension of the Team Spirit exercise and the withdrawal fo U.S. troops from Korea.

Meanwhile, the south, in a reply signed by Defense Minister Lee Ki-baek and sent to the north on June 24, pointed to the unreasonableness of the north Korean proposal for a three-way military meeting and urged the north to agree to resume the existing channels of dialogue such as economic and Red Cross talks in the first place.

The text of Minister Lee's letter to Oh Jin-wu, the north's People's Armed Forces minister, was as follows:

I received your letter of June 17. As your side knows, many-sided talks such as the Red Cross and economic meetings were held between south and north of Korea last year. And dispersed families' hometown visitors and art troupes were exchanged for the first time last year since national division, giving great joy to the whole people and brightening the future of inter-Korean relations.

Since the turn of the year, however, your side regrettably suspended the dialogue one sidedly and rejected our calls for the early resumption of the talks, thus driving the inter-Korean relations into an atmosphere of distrust and tension and disappointing the entire Korean people in the south and the north who crave for peace and unification. It is thus utterly unreasonable to propose a military authorities meeting among the defense ministers of the south, the north and the commander of the United Nations Command on the pretext of discussing the suspension of military exercises and arms reduction at a time when your side has suspended the existing dialogue.

As our side has expressly substantiated through the Military Armistice Commission, tensions and the danger of war on the Korean peninsula are attributed to your side's reckless arms buildup, hostile policy against the south and violations of the Military Armistice Agreement.

Few persons can accept your side proposing a military meeting while covering up such fundamental causes and refusing to take any sincere steps to ease tensions and foster trust.

In this context, I believe that your side should first agree to resume the Red Cross and economic meetings your side has suspended to realize a reunion between dispersed families and undertake economic exchanges at an early date, and thereby show a sincere attitude in easing tensions and restoring trust between the south and the north.

At the same time, instead of proposing a so-called military meeting and indulging in a propaganda campaign, your side should affirmatively respond to discussing the measures to ease military tension our side has already proposed through the existing Military Armistice Commission, which include the "genuine demilitarization of the Demilitarized Zone," "mutual observation of major military exercises" and "introduction of the mutual confirmation system in the Joint Security Area."

Moreover, if your side is truly interested in easing tension and preventing war on the Korean peninsula, your side should agree to holding a meeting between the highest authorities of the south and the north at an early date, aware that such a top leaders meeting would be the shortest way toward achieving peace and unification.

Earlier on June 21, 1986, the United Nations Command in Korea sent a reply to the north's June 17th letter, in which the UN Command said that most of the topics the north suggested for a military meeting should, in nature, be properly discussed between the south and the north, adding, however, that the UN Command is prepared to discuss those matters related to the military armistice at any time at the Military Armistice Commission. The Command noted that it had already produced before the Armistice Commission major ideas to ease tensions.

In the meantime, despite the fact that south Korea and the United Nations Command expressly rejected the north Korean offer for a military meeting because of its unreasonableness, the north notified the south on July 3 of their plan to deliver a second letter in connection with a military meeting. When the south refused to accept the letter, north Korea openly called for the convocation of a three-way military meeting in a radio broadcast on July 11 while stepping up slanderous propaganda against south Korea and the United States.

(2) High-Level Politico-military Meeting

In a policy speech at the first session of the 8th-term Supreme People's Assembly on December 30, 1986, Kim Il-sung proposed a high-level south-north politico-military meeting. Kim Il-sung maintained in the speech that a high-level politico-military meeting should be held to relax the state of political confrontation and foster an atmosphere for genuine trust within the nation. Kim stressed that only when a politico-military comes to fruition can the suspended dialogue be resumed, and only when a politico-military meeting and the existing dialogue are promoted successfully, can a high-level south-north conference be held.

The substance of Kim Il-sung's speech was as follows :

...Under today's circumstances, the key to providing a new breakthrough in the realization of national unification is to relax the acute state of political confrontation and military tensions and foster an atmosphere for genuine trust within the nation at an early date. We recognize that it is necessary to hold a high-level south-north politico-military meeting in order to settle acute problems in the realization of national unification.

The serious distrust existing between the south and the north stems mostly from politial and military confrontation. Dispelling such confrontation and fostering an atmosphere for trust hinge on the efforts of the political and military leaders of the two sides.

At a high-level south-north politico-military meeting, the two sides should discuss measures to dispell the existing political confrontation, such as the suspension of mutual slander and the promotion of national bonds through multi-pronged exchanges and collaboration. In addition, they should discuss ways to ease the existing tensions, such as the reduction of armed forces, a halt to arms race, transformation of the Demilitarized Zone into a peace zone, and the suspension of large-scale military exercises. The high-level south-north politico-military meeting should also discuss the question of strengthening the competence of the Neutral Nations Supervisory Commission and the issue of organizing a neutral nations surveillance force among the military personnel of Czechoslovakia, Poland, Switzerland and Sweden, which are the member nations of the Neutral Nations Supervisory Commission, as an organization designed to watch military activities of both sides in the Demilitarized Zone along the Military Demarcation Line.

We are willing to discuss any proposals suggested by the south Korean side that can be helpful to easing the political and military situation, in addition to these questions.

In order to smoothly resolve various issues raised by both sides at a high-level south-north politico-military meeting, the meeting should be attended by military leaders along with high-level officials of both sides.

Our new proposal for a high-level south-north politico-military meeting is an express of manifestation of the persistent policy of the government of our People's Republic to promote national unity and unification as well as durable peace.

Our new proposal embodies the firm determination and volition of the government of our People's Republic to dispel distrust and confrontation between the same people, promote trust and unity, forestall war and ensure peace on the Korean peninsula, and realize national unification peacefully.

If the south Korean authorities are genuinely interested in surmounting the present tension and marching forward together with us toward peace and peaceful unification, they ought to show a positive response to our sincere proposal. We believe that a high-level south-north politico-military meeting would become an important turning-point in promoting trust between the two sides, in providing a new phase of the alleviation of tensions and the fostering an atmosphere for dialogue.

If a high-level south-north politico-military meeting brings about a good result, it would lead to the dispelling of distrust that had been accumulated over decades, to the arising of the mood of national reconciliation and unity, and to the successful implementation of dialogues in many areas amidst a good atmosphere between the south and the north....

On January 11, 1987, north Korean formally proposed a high-level

356

south-north politico-military meeting in a message signed by the north's Administrative Council Premier Li Gun-mo and People's A-. rmed Forces Minister Oh Jin-wu and addressed to Prime Minister Lho Shin-yong and Defense Minister Lee Ki-baek.

In the open proposal made over a radio broadcast, the north claimed that the convocation of a politico-military meeting will be a "reasonable and realistic nation-saving measure that can dispel the ever-mounting political confrontation and military tensions and that can provide a breakthrough in the realization of durable peace and peaceful unification." North Korea then suggested that its first meeting be held at Panmunjom on January 27, 1987 with the attendance of seven to nine officials and military leaders with a vice-prime-minister-level official as a chief delegate and a military chief-of-staff-level officer as a deputy chief delegate from each side.

North Korea, which earlier suspended the ongoing dialogues unilaterally and then called for a tripartite military meeting, now proposed a high level politico-military meeting, making it a prerequisite to the resumption of the suspended talks. Their latest proposal was intended for them to shun responsibility for the suspension of the dialogues and to launch a deceptive peace offensive with an eye at building up their "peace image" at home and abroad.

In particular, their offer for the discussion of armed forces reduction was motivated not by their genuine intent to ease tensions but by a scheme to engineer the withdrawal of U.S. forces from Korea and contain the buildup of the south Korean forces so as to continue to enjoy a military edge. And their idea of a neutral nations surveillance force was to bolster their demand for the withdrawal of American forces with the excuse of the existence of such a surveillance force.

In reaction to the north Korean proposal for a high-level politico-military meeting, President Chun Doo Hwan, in his policy speech on January 12, 1987, urged the north to agree to resume the suspended talks such as Red Cross and economic meetings and hold a south-north top leaders meeting at an early date. The President said that if and when a top leaders meeting were held, the south would be willing to discuss even the question of a political and military meeting suggested by the north.

Moreover, the south's chief delegates to the Red Cross, economic and preliminary parliamentary contacts issued a joint statement on January 14 to call for the resumption of the suspended dialogues at an early date. The statement pointed out that the north's contention that they cannnot resume the existing channels of dialogue they had suspended unless a three-way military meeting or a high-level politico-military meeting they proposed is held satisfactorily. gives rise to the doubt if the north wasn't using the inter-Korean dialogue for ulterior political objectives. The south's chief delegates stressed that "this is a time when the two sides, most of all, should lay a groundwork for substantial mutual trust by conducting personnel and material exchanges between them."

The statement also urged that if the north is genuinely interested in easing tensions and promotion reconciliation and unification between the south and the north, they should correct the mistaken act of rejecting the existing dialogues with unrealistic excuses and unconditionally agree to resume the suspended talks.

Despite the south's express disclosure of its stand toward the north Korean proposal, north Korea again sent a letter ot the south on January 30, 1987, renewing their call for a politico-military meeting. And as their demand for a "politico-military meeting first and the resumption of the existing talks later" failed to get support at home and abroad, the north sent yet another message on March 3 to the Prime Minister and the Defense Minister, in which they sugested that once a politico-military meeting was held, the question of the Kumgangsan Dam project could be discussed as proposed by the south and the existing dialogues resumed at the same time. The north thus seemed easing their stiff stand a little, but held fast to their demand for a high-level politico-military meeting as a prerequisite to the resumption of the existing dialogue.

(3) Multi-National Arms Reduction Talks

North Korea, which was busy shifting the blame for the suspension of the talks to the south after they had turned down a series of the south's dialogue proposals, again proposed on July 23, 1987, a "multi-national arms reduction talks" to discuss "phased disarmament" on the Korean peninsula.

In an Administration Council statement, the north, contending that "acute military confrontation on the Korean peninsula can be resolved only through effective arms reduction," argued that the military forces of the south and the north should be reduced in three stages from 1988 through 1991 to less than 100,000 for each side, that in parallel with that the U.S. troops in Korea should be withdrawn on a phased basis, so that by the time the south and the north forces are reduced to 100,000 all the U.S. forces in Korea, including their nuclear weapons, would be pulled out and their bases deactivated. The north then proposed that to discuss these issues, a tripartite meeting among the south and north Korean and the United States be held in Geneva in March 1988. They also suggested that observers from the member nations of the Neutral Nations Supervisory Commission attend the meeting.

The part of the north Korean statement related to the arms reduction meeting proposal was as follows :

...The government of the Democratic People's Republic of Korea hereby makes the following proposal to realize a large-scale phased armed forces reduction with a view to providing a decisive phase to relax tension on and accelerate peaceful unification of the Korean peninsula in accordance with the ardent desire of the whole Korean people wishing to live in peace and free of the fear of war and other anxieties forever on a unified land.

First, arms equilibrium between the north and the south on the Korean peninsula should be maintained not in the manner of arms buildup but in the manner of arms reduction. Under this principle, the north and the south shall reduce their armed forces in three stages from 1988 through 1991. Beginning in 1992, they should maintain less than 100,000 troops each.

Second, parallel with the phased reduction of south and north Korean forces, the U.S. forces stationed in south Korea should withdraw step by step. When the troops of the north and the south are reduced to 100,000, the United States should withdraw its entire forces including nuclear weapons from south Korea and their military bases should be deactivated.

Third, the north and the south of Korea should notify each other of the situation of their respective arms reduction and announce it before the world. The United States should notify us of the situation of their military withdrawal and announce it before the world.

In the meantime, the Neutral Nations Supervisory Commission at Panmunjom should carry out a verification program by phase to verify the situation of armed forces reduction in the north and the south and that of U.S. military withdrawal.

Fourth, to prevent the danger of possible armed clashes before and after the reduction of the armed forces of the north and the south, and to continue to maintain peace, the Demilitarized Zone along the Military Demarcation Line shall be made a peace zone, where a neutral nations' surveillance force shall be stationed.

Fifth, a multi-national military reduction meeting shall be held in March 1988 in Geneva to discuss the issues of armed forces reduction on and withdrawal from the Korean peninsula, their verification, transformation of the Demilitarized Zone along the Military Demarcation Line into a peace zone, strengthening of the competence of the Neutral Nations Supervisory Commission. and the organization and deployment of a neutral nations surveillance force, The meeting among the north, the south and the United States shall be attended as observers by the representatives of the member nations of the Neutral Nations Supervisory Commission—Poland, Czechoslovakia, Switzerland and Sweden.

The government of the Democratic People's Republic of Korea shall unilaterally reduce the manpower of the Korean People's Army by 100,000 by the end of 1987 for the purpose of providing a breakthrough in substantial armed forces reduction on the Korean peninsula.

The north Korean proposal for multi-national arms reduction talks was nothing new. It was merely a rehash, with the additional suggestion of substantial topics for discussion, of their earlier proposals for a three-way meeting made in January 1984 and for a three-way military authorities meeting which was put forth in June 1986. In the latter proposal, north Korea suggested as topics for discussion the suspension of military training exercises, a halt to the arms buildup, reduction of military manpower and equipment and respect for the Armistice Agreement.

On the surface, the latest offer represented a return to three-way talks from the direct inter-Korean talks they suggested in December 1986 when Kim Il-sung called for a high-level south-north politico-military meeting. Most of all, their failure to mention, in their most recent proposal, anything about the resumption of the suspended dialogue meant that they had no interest in a dialogue directly with the south.

Moreover, the fact that they set the time of the proposed meeting for March 1988, after a new government was to be installed in the south, showed that they were not really interested in after dialogue, the alleviation of tensions or disarmament, but to obstruct democratization in the south by formenting support for disarmament and the withdrawal of U.S.forces from Korea and thereby splitting public opinion.

In fact, whenever the south went through a political transitition, north Korea made a deceptive peace offer to split public opinion in the south. Immediately after the April 19 Student Uprising in 1960, north Korea proposed a confederation system as a means of unification. Again on the heels of the assassination of President Park Chung Hee on October 26, 1979, they proposed a south-north prime ministers meeting and other bilateral and multilateral contacts between south and north Korean politicians.

Thus seen, the latest north Korean proposal, too, was intended to realize contacts with the United States in connection with the U.S.'s recent policy toward north Korea, and at the same time, to find an excuse to brand the south as a "war-monger" by making a proposal not acceptable to the south, and thus to jeopardize the atmosphere for the Seoul Olympics in 1988. This was evidenced in part by their unusual idea that the talks be held in Geneva and be attended by observers from the member countries of the Neutral Nations Supervisory Commission, an idea aimed at reaping an international propaganda effect.

Meanwhile, the north's unilateral announcement that they were going to reduce their troops by 100,000 by the end of 1987, indicated that they were suffering from excessive military expansion which have become even more acute lately due to serious economic difficulties.

On the other hand, the planned reduction, even if actually carried out, would be meaningless in view of the fact that the reduction would be nothing more than the discharge from active service of part of the 150,000 whom they were using since September 1986 in various construction projects and who would nevertheless remain on the construction projects in a military-like organization.

Part Three

Entry into Age of Inter-Korean Exchanges and Cooperation

1. Pursuit of New Inter-Korean Relations

The pronounced intent of the opening an age of inter-Korean exchanges and cooperation represents a search for new south-north relations, at this time of some 40 years after national division. It now is incumbent upon the two sides of Korea to put an end to their relations of tension and confrontation and together chart an age of co-existence and co-prosperity based on a sense of national community.

In the past, the inter-Korean relationship, begun with an "age of confrontation without dialogue," had gone through the "age of confrontation with dialogue," and has reached an "age of confrontation with exchanges." Thus seen, the unfolding of an "age of exchanges and cooperation" constitutes a highly significant historical fruition achieved on the basis of past progress in south-north relations.

The age of confrontation without dialogue that befell the Koreans at the time of national division defaced much of the edifice of the Koreans' national community. At the same time, it obliged the south and the north to be in a state of extreme confrontation of the Cold War-type. Despite the tragic experience of a fratricidal conflict, the Koreans were thus plagued by the dangers of another Korean War.

Meanwhile, a new change in the surrounding situation since the turn of the 1970s, characterized by detente between the United States and the Soviet Union seeking to end the Cold War, inevitably called for a change in the inter-Korean relationship, providing the momentum for a dialogue between the two sides of Korea. The south-north dialogue of the 1970s, the first of its kind since national division, failed to register any substantial progress due to the north's attempt to use the dialogue for their propaganda, psychological and information purposes. The dialogue, therefore, remained at the limited concept of the age of confrontation with dialogue.

It is true that there were some attempts in the 1970s dialogue to switch the mechanism of hostile confrontation into that of good-intentioned confrontation. But as confrontation was emphasized more than dialogue in the process, the dialogue was far from being anything more than the "age of first-phase dialogue" in the historical sense.

The first-phase dialogue enabled the south to grasp the true picture of the north's posture toward dialogue, that was, dialogue strategy. In fact, it can't be an exaggeration to say that there has been no substantial change in their dialogue attitude from the time of the first-phase dialogue to date. This means that so far as they do not renounce the goal of the "liberation of south Korea," they won't be able to discard the method of "all or nothing" in linkage with their revolutionary goal.

Despite this essential strategy shown during the period of the first-phase dialogue, the north revealed their two-faced strategy – revolutionary attempts on one hand and political propaganda on the other. This is why the ideas the north offered in the dialogue always turned out to be of contradictory and deceptive tactics, which in turn amounted to sowing the seeds of further distrust. Of course, this dialogue strategy or attitude of north Korea cannot but be linked to the traits of communism. In communism, everything but irrevocable revolutionary goals is changeable, and such a change is fully justified and, at the same time, is rated as a strategic tool.

In this sense, any entry into the age of inter-Korean exchanges and cooperation, an age in which the confrontational mechanism is to be overcome or confrontation itself is to be terminated, should be realized on the basis of the full awareness of the nature of the north Korean society or their dialogue strategy. By so doing, north Korea can be induced into a tract toward the creation of a national community even though a substantial change can hardly be engineered overnight in north Korean society.

In fact, the significance of the opening of an age of inter-Korean exchanges and cooperation can be found first in the lesson taught by the first- and second-phase dialogue where the confrontational mechanism could be eliminated altogether. If the 1970s first-phase dialogue can be characterized by the July 4 South-North Joint Communique, the second-phase dialogue refers to the mid-1980s dialogue comprising various channels for talks such as Red Cross, economic, parliamentary and sports talks.

If the south remained in the peripheral zone of reflexionary reaction and security consideration against the north's dialogue strategy in the 1970s dialogue, the south showed a more matured posture in the second-phase dialogue as it managed to induce direct contacts and personnel and material exchanges in a positive reaction toward north Korea's negotiatory dialogue strategy.

In particular, the fact that the south dealt with the inter-Korean relationship with new elasticity despite the north's revolutionary goals and resultant stiff posture toward the dialogue, makes the course of the second-phase dialogue a significant root source behind the advent of the age of south-north exchanges and cooperation.

The second-phase inter-Korean dialogue begun in the autumn of 1984 was the result of the positive and multi-faceted efforts made by the government of the Republic of Korea to promote dialogue. The brisk progress of dialogue in many areas such as Red Cross, economic and parliamentary contacts in 1984, had a significant bearing on the Korean people all the more because the year happened to be the 40th year of national liberation and territorial division. And it was during the second-phase dialogue that the two sides exchanged dispersed family hometown visitors and art troupes for the first time since national division.

The guidelines of the unification policy that engineered the second-phase dialogue, often regarded as an age of confrontation with exchanges, was the Formula for National Reconciliation and Democratic Unification. In the second-phase dialogue, the south concentrated on seeking national reconciliation while trying to work out ways to realize democratic unification. A unification policy prepared to incorporate these efforts was the very Formula for National Reconciliation and Democratic Unification.

National reconciliation cannot but be the most important method of approach toward removing mutual distrust and thereby overcoming the confrontational mechanism. Reconciliation and harmony are meant not to play up mutual differences but to seek new approaches while respecting each other's positions. Herein lay the propellant behind the materialization of more achievement in the second-phase dialogue than in the first-phase.

Based on the spirit of the Formula for National Reconciliation and Democratic Unification, the government of south Korea on February 1, 1982, set forth 20 inter-Korean pilot projects which could be implemented forthwith, including the opening of mutual societies, implementation of exchanges and cooperation and the alleviation of tensions. This was a reasonable overture intended to ease military tensions on the basis of confidence-building achieved through exchanges and cooperation based on the opening of the two societies. The proposal for 20 pilot projects was in effect a measure that foretold and emphasized the need of the entry of south and north Korea into an age of exchanges and cooperation aimed ultimately at restoring the Koreans' national community and laying a foundation for national co-existence and co-prosperity.

On the other hand, north Korea repeated their old-fashioned tactics of putting forth politically-oriented prerequisites or overturning agreed matters, bound by the time-old policy of pursuing a revolution in south Korea. Nonetheless, they showed some changes different from the 1970s. First, north Korea agreed to prepare a basis for personnel exchanges, albeit slightly. A closed society based on Kim Il-sung's monolithic thought, north Korea was most afraid of openness. This was why they tried to shun personnel exchange until as recently as the 1970s. This time, however, they volunteered to increase the number of press members who would accompany the delegations to Red Cross talks, and also agreed to the exchange of dispersed hometown visitors and art troupes. Of course, there were some strategic needs behind such a show of openness. Still, it was true that such a gesture itself helped prompt progress in the inter-Korean relationship.

Another remarkable change was that while accommodating multiple channels of dialogue, they agreed to economic talks, a kind of meeting which the north had in the past tabooed. North Korea showed an allergic negativism toward economic cooperation and commodity trade, an area where the two sides' overall national capacity can be easily compared.

However, during the first economic meeting held in November 1984, north Korea displayed a detailed commodity trade plan which contained many points in common with those produced by the south.

At the second meeting held in May 1985, the north deadlocked the talks by disputing the format of the meeting. They asserted, "We are not here simply to have economic talks." Still, the economic meeting can be taken to have set an important milestone in the history of inter-Korean relations.

These efforts helped facilitate the transformation of the "mechanism of confrontation" into the "mechanism of reconciliation and cooperation." They also represented a significant progress that displayed the ability of the Koreans to engineer the surrounding situation actively.

The phase-two dialogue came to an end when north Korea suspended the dialogue unilaterally in early 1986 with the excuse of the annual Team Spirit military training exercise. It seemed north Korea concluded that the dialogue reached a point where if it progressed any further the opening of their society was unavoidable, which they couldn't stand, and that there no longer was any room for concessions from the south.

All these indicate that the lessons obtained from the first-and second-phase dialogue included the following :

First, both the first-and second-phase dialogue was made possible with the inducement by the south of the passive north to the conference table. The strategic tendency of north Korea is to value the cause of a dialogue more than the dialogue itself and to seek to attain such a cause. And they come to the table of dialogue only when they believe chances are big to achieve such a cause.

Second, north Korea always persisted in the tactics of political negotiations at dialogue. Even the diversified channels of dialogue couldn't offset their attempt to resolve problems in a single political approach. This served to affirm the fact that a workable dialogue can be held when there is a new posture on the part of the north prior to the start of a dialogue rather than when a new attitude is obtained during the course of a dialogue.

Third, both in the first- and second-phase dialogue, north Korea un-ilaterally shifted the blame for the suspension of the dialogue to the south. Moreover, the excuses they produced for their suspension of the talks were not any incidents serious enough to halt the dialogue but only superficial ones they deliberately put up to shun responsibility for the breakoff of the talks. This means that by harming by themselves their trust essential to genuine dialogue, the north rather worked to give rise to the sense of distrust and confrontation. This can be evidenced by the fact that they least care about that their unilateral announcement of the suspension of the dialogue or retraction of agreed matters serve to bring down overnight the bases of mutual respect and trust.

These lessons gained in the course of dialogue shed light on the signifi-cance and limit of both the phases one and two dialogue, and also indi-cate that the unfolding of an age of inter-Korean exchanges and coopera-tion carries a very deep significance in itself. In fact, in order to realize a genuine age of exchanges and cooperation, the mechanism of confronta-tion which lingered on during the past dialogue should be resolutely done away with. To this end, there needs to be a sweeping change in the understanding and recognition of the inter-Korean relationship.

Thus seen, the initiation of the age of exchanges and cooperation can be carried on successfully only when the south and the north regard each other not as rivals in a competition or confrontation but as partners who, under the sense of their being the same people, pursue common prosperity.

The Sixth Republic of south Korea is exerting resolute and positive efforts to establish such a new mode of existence of the south and the north. Of course, such efforts do not disregard the realistic mechanism of confrontation between the two sides, but are intended to lay upon such a mechanism a strong groundwork on which the two sides could exist as a single national community through the restoration of the original shape of the nation by means of a concrete and realistic approach toward unifica-tion.

The efforts also embody the expectation that a positive change in the two sides' recognition of the inter-Korean relationship would lead to the fresh state of the relations, ultimately making unavoidable the initiation of the age of exchanges and cooperation.

The new approach of the Sixth Republic, which would ease or make powerless the restrictive conditions that made the first-and second-phase dialogue break up, will, together with changing conditions for unification, certainly make possible the advent of the age of inter-Korean exchanges and cooperation.

2. Surrounding Situation and Environment for Unification

In the late 1980s, drastic changes have taken place in the international situation, in particular the situation surrounding the Korean peninsula, having a significant effect on the environment for unification.

A closer look at the world situation shows that the East-West relations and the Northeast Asian situation have become related to each other more closely than before and tend to explore a new path.

As a whole, the East-West relations of the late 1980s were of a transitional nature in which they were in the process of being reorganized into the order of openness and detente with the United States and the Soviet Union as the core.

The whirlwind of the change in the international situation in the late 1980s was the rise of Gorbachev in the Soviet Union. Since the birth of the Gorbachev regime in March 1985, there were no fewer than four summit meetings between the United States and the Soviet Union : the Geneva summit in November 1985, barely eight months after Gorbachev's rise to power, the Reykjavik preliminary summit in April 1986, the Washington summit in December 1987, and the Moscow summit in May 1988. Of course, an improved U.S.-USSR relationship has become a significant milestone in the pursuit of East-West stability and reconciliaton regardless of the achievement of such U.S.-USSR summit meetings.

At the U.S.-USSR summit meetings, the interests of the two superpowers were centered on moderating an arms race, culminating in the conclusion of an agreement on the destruction of intermediate nuclear forces (INF).

With the conclusion of the agreement, the two countries were free from the military burden with which they, otherwise, have to maintain nuclear weapons for use in either building up East-West tensions or manipulating East-West relations. This indicates that the East-West relationship has entered a stage of a more solid new detente in the late 1980s than the 1970s detente. In other words, if the 1970s detente was a mere political detente that bypassed military issues, the late 1980s detente can be rated as a comprehensive political detente inclusive of the functional relation of military strength.

What made the changing flow and significance of the new detente expressly evident were Gorbachev's Vladivostok Declaration of July 1986 and his speech made at Krasnoyarsk on September 16, 1988, in which he proposed a seven-point peace plan for the Asian and Pacific area. Ten days later on September 27, Soviet Foreign Minister Shevardnadze in his speech at the United Nations General Assembly announced the de-ideologization of the Soviet foreign policy, giving rise to a possible further change in the international situation as well as the need to pursue a new mode of existence of international society.

In particular, Soviet Foreign Minister Shevardnadze shocked world diplomatic circles by declaring in the speech, "Class struggles have come to an end in the international society and ideology can no longer become the basic principle of international relations." If ideology can no longer be allowed to exercise any influence and hostile competitive relations based on class struggles can be terminated in the world community as Shevardnadze said, international relations would be able to bring about peaceful coexistence and the promotion of partnership and cooperative relationships. As a result, the new detente could expect a more solid fruition.

This declaration, which can be taken as a new change in the Soviet diplomatic pattern, is based on the Soviet reform (*perestroika*) and openness (*glasnost*) policies and a new change in the way of thinking on the part of the Soviets, a change which buttresses such policies. Thus seen, the post-

372

the national security of the USSR but can be linked directly to the danger that it may set off a new search for the balance of power in the Far East.

All in all, the Soviets' move, together with the progress of the East-West relations, is expected to bring about a rapid change in the situation in Northeast Asia. Moreover, if the Sino-USSR relations improve fast after the projected summit between the two countries, the strained inter-Korean relations may rather drive south and north Korea out to the peripheral zone of such a changing situation. In other words, if the south and the north alone remain unaffected by the universal wave of detente, the national ability of Korea cannot but be reduced substantially as seen from a broader point of view.

With respect to the environment for unification, if the south and the north remain in the state of tension even though the Sino-USSR relations have become improved and Japan behaves in keeping pace with such a new development, the subsequent situation may be the repetition of the situation surrounding the Korean peninsula toward the close of the 19th century. Therefore, the policy of the Sixth Republic to launch bold northern programs and improve south-north relations, is highly significant in that it is intended in part to uplift the unification environment to the point of independent variables instead of subjugating it to the international environment.

China, which is in the core of changes in the Northeast Asian situation, has been pursuing a positive open-door policy with an eye at developing itself as an advanced economic country by the mid-21st century. Deng Xiaoping, calling for a four-point modernization policy, declared an independent foreign policy by applying pragmatism even to their external strategy since 1982, and effected full-fledged economic and political reforms beginning in 1984.

In 1984, in particular, China created 14 special economic development areas including the four special districts of Shenyen, Chuhai, Shantou and Shamen. In 1985, China further opened all its coastal cities.

On the other hand, Japan, having emerged as the world's largest economic superpower, seeks to have an international standing and role suitable ure of openness, which resolutely does away with ideological inclination and closed-mindedness, can be known to lead to the pursuit of universal values in the international society and the consolidation of peaceful co-existence. In inter-Korean relations, as well, the base of reconciliation and co-existence can be solidified when north Korea resolutely puts an end to their ideological inclination and closed-mindedness.

Therefore, the trend of the Soviet Union and other Communist-bloc countries toward openness and reform needs to serve as a stimulant to north Korea. A series of measures taken by the south to improve the inter-Korean relationship following President Roh Tae-woo's July 7 Special Declaration would certainly help facilitate the north's accommodation of such a change.

Meanwhile, the situation in Northeast Asia, which determines the external conditions for the unification of the Korean peninsula, has undergone substantial changes comparable to the changes taking place in East-West relations. Gorbachev's Vladivostok declaration manifested the Soviet policy to improve the Sino-USSR relations and also to cope positively with the opening of the age of Asia and the Pacific. The declaration, emphasizing the importance of resources development in the Far East area, calls for joint investment and other forms of economic cooperation among Japan and many other Asian and Pacific-rim countries. In particular, the declaration showed the Soviets' compromisory posture toward improving relations with China, an issue which has long stood in the way to the improvement of the Soviet relations toward Asia.

While the Vladivostok declaration displayed the Soviets' new interest in durable peace in the Asian and Pacific region, it also can be taken to have exhibited their strategic intent to advance positively to this part of the world.

For the declaration is regarded as part of the concrete strategy to embody the "collective security of Asia which they have been calling for since long ago. This means that the declaration has something to do with their strategy to secure a foothold in the Asian and Pacific area in preparation for their more positive Asian policy in the years ahead. This overall Soviet policy does not end merely in the aspects of to their ability.

The sharply expanded economic ability of Japan, along with the improved Sino-USSR relations, is likely to appear as an influential background power in the future change of the Northeast Asian situation.

In view of these changes in East-West relations and the Northeast Asian situation, it can be known that the unification environment on the Korean peninsula is quite fluid and faced with new changes. Therefore, the positive northern policy and the forward-looking unification and foreign policies the government of the Sixth Republic pursues, represent the firm determination to cope with such changes subjectively.

In particular, the July 7 Special Declaration, designed to pursue national self-esteem and co-prosperity through the restoration and development of national community, is highly significant in that it has not only uplifted the inter-Korean relationship to the point of independent variables also made it stand out that the improvement and stability of the inter-Korean relations contribute to stability and detente in the East-West relationship.

In addition, the successful staging of the Seoul Olympics, a grand festival for harmony of all mankind attended by the youths from 160 countries and transcending differences in ideologies, systems, ethnic races and religion for the first time in 12 years, has enhanced the international standing of south Korea, prompting the world community to have a fresh recognition of the role Korea plays in the world community.

Although north Korea failed to participate in the games, the Seoul Olympics served to give the world an added confidence in East-West detente, while proving the inevitability that the abnormal inter-Korean relations characterized by tension and confrontation has to be improved at the initiatives of the direct parties – the south and the north – at an early date. As a result, the Seoul games were an occasion for both the East and the West to realize the need and feasibility of the improvement of the inter Korean relationship, enabling them to understand the substance of Seoul's forward-looking unification and foreign policies.

In fact, all the countries that took part in the Seoul Olympics, including China, the Soviet Union, East European countries and Third World nations, had a first-hand look at the reality of south Korea. And it can't be denied that as a result, the Games served as an occasion for these countries to rectify the prejudice they harbored in the past against the south due to Pyongyang's propaganda allegations.

The northern policy of the south is in line with the efforts to promote the overall reorganization of the world order and proves highly fruitful as the policy is based on the logic of reconciliation and co-existence and is intended not to isolate north Korea from the rest of the world but to make it a responsible member of the world community.

Of course, north Korea may be alarmed at the fast approach between the south and some socialist nations, such as the establishment of trade offices in China and the USSR, and expanding trade with Hungary, Czechoslovakia, Poland and Yugoslavia. But north Korea will have to realize that such economic openness and cross contacts would contribute much to the improvement of the inter-Korean relations as well as to the creation of a more matured environment for unification.

The promotion of an open-door policy and the pursuit of international cooperative relations, beyond the boundary of ideologies and systems, represent the new mode of existence in the international community and are the dictate of the flow of world history. North Korea won't be able to turn a deaf ear to such a flow, and would realize, whether they like it or not, that their rejection of the flow may lead to the shattering of the foundation of their own system.

Thus seen, the announcement by the south of a series of unification and foreign policies starting from the July 7 Special Declaration and ending with the President's address before the United Nations General Assembly on October 18, was the manifestation of the strong will power of the Sixth Republic to bring the unification environment to a more matured dimension and, at the same time, realize the age of south-north reconciliation ahead of time.

The policies also contained a far-reaching vision that the south, along with the powers of the U.S., USSR, China and Japan, would take part in working out a future plan for the 21st century and would assume a proper role based thereon, thereby enhancing the self-esteem of the Korean people.

3. Proposal for South-North High-Level Officials Meeting

As part of the south's positive efforts to resume the stalled dialogue, Prime Minister Lee Hyon-jae on June 3, 1988, proposed to hold a high-level south-north officials meeting either in Seoul or Pyongyang within the month June. In a message addressed to Li Gun-mo, premier of the Administration Council of north Korea, Prime Minister Lee suggested that the delegates be led by Cabinet-member-level officials. The south notified the north over the direct telephone line on May 31, 1988, that it would deliver the message to the north on June 3 at Panmunjom. But north Korea refused to accept the message. The message was subsequently made public by the spokesman of the government.

The full text of Prime Minister Lee Hyon-jae's message to the north was as follows:

It is heartbreaking that although it is nearly half a century since the Korean people were divided into the south and the north, the ordeal of the division has yet to end. We are thus charged with the historic task of achieving peaceful unification at the earliest possible date. Looking back, we have, as the result of the division, lived in an age of pain, sorrow and frustration aggravated by enmity and confrontation, which constitutes a dark spot on the 5,000-year history of the Korean nation.

I believe that we must not put off any further the efforts to bring the unhappy state of affairs to an end to shape a future of Korea as a unified land.

The south and the north have had various forms of dialogue on a number of occasions, producing some limited results. This, however, has been far from satisfactory. I am of the opinion that the reason for this is mutual distrust and a lack of the development of a firm perception of the Korean people as a single national family with one root.

To dispel the mistrust that has grown between the south and the north, it is imperative, above all, to build trust through exchanges and cooperation between the divided halves of the nation. It is self-evident that increasing trust will naturally defuse tensions between the south and the north and restore family bonds, thereby speeding the arrival of the day of unification.

The Games of the 24th Olympiad, due to take place soon in Seoul, will be the first of its kind ever to be staged in our land. Not only the Korean people but all nations of the world are ardently hoping that the Games will serve as a catalyst to bring together not only the East and the West, but also the south and the north.

In response to such domestic and international expectations and wishes, I believe we must make every possible effort to see that the north will participate in the forthcoming Olympics together with us so that it will be a pan-national festival.

For this reason, I courteously propose talks between high-level authorities of the south and the north to speedily dispel the mistrust that is now standing in the way of peaceful unification and thus to lay the groundwork for peaceful unification. The proposed high-level officials talks should be able to discuss the participation of the north with us in the Seoul Olympics, the exchange of people, including politicians, businessmen, journalists, religious leaders, artists, writers, athletes, scholars and students, ways to facilitate the resumption of the existing channels of dialogue, including the Red Cross conference, the economic talks and the inter-parliamentary meetings, all of which used to be concluded and in which the entire Korean people placed high expectations, and other issues raised by both sides.

If both the south and the north adhere just to the view that they are one and the same nation, I believe that such issues can be resolved smoothly and without any difficulty, thus paving the way for unification.

I hope that the proposed talks will become a reality at an early date, preferably within June, with their first round taking place either in Seoul or Pyongyang. I should like each delegation to be composed of about five officials and led by a cabinet minister as the senior delegate.

I look forward to an affirmative response from you.

To conform to the age of national self-esteem and reconciliation at this time, two and a half years after the south-north dialogue was broken off in January 1986, there should be full-fledged efforts at an early date to re-solve the mechanism of division and promote the improvement of the inter-Korean relationship.

In this respect, the proposal for a high-level south-north officials meeting affirmed the mandate that the Seoul Olympics should be developed into a grand festival for national reconciliation and, at the same time, made a decisive occasion to improve the inter-Korean relationship. The overture also reflected a big change in the recognition of north Korea, a change made as a result of successful economic development and democratization in the south.

Prime Minister Lee's proposal to the north can be taken as a first step toward buttressing and realizing the unfolding of an age of south-north cooperation directed toward peaceful unification, which was pronounced by President Roh in his inaugural address early in the year.

At the same time, the proposal reflected the Seoul goverment's positive policy to pool public opinion broadly for use in northward programs at this time when public concern about the unification issue is growing and when there appear varying opinions with respect to the question of north Korea's participation in the Seoul Olympics and the issues of personnel and commodity exchanges between the south and the north including student exchanges.

In particular, the national and worldwide wish and expectations that the 24th Olympiad in Seoul should become an arena for East-West detente, require the authorities of the south and the north with due responsibility and competence to directly consult and work out a solution to the Olympic issue.

The basic purport of the proposal offered against such backdrop was to explore a new way to facilitate north Korea's participation in the Seoul Olympics.

Several rounds of a south-north sports conference were held under the sponsorship of the International Olympic Committee (IOC) to discuss the issue of allotting several sports of the Seoul Games to the north Korean area. But the talks ended in failure because the north refused to accept an IOC mediatory plan. The south Korean government attended the meeting held about 100 or so days before the Seoul Olympics in a bid to do all it could to enable the north to take part in the Games.

Also, the issue of personnel exchanges is one of the vital factors essential to the opening of an age of inter-Korean exchanges and cooperation. Broad exchanges of politicians, businessmen, journalists, religious leaders, writers and artists, scholars, students, etc., would contribute tremendously to removing distrust between the two sides and cementing the bonds of the nation. Such personnel exchanges are not only in keeping with the worldwide trend toward openness but also are in line with the pattern of exchanges taking place between other divided countries of China and Taiwan, and of East and West Germany. This is an issue which the two sides of Korea cannot put off any longer.

The Red Cross, economic and parliamentary talks remain suspended after north Korea unilaterally boycotted them in January 1986. But it was emphasized in the proposal that if only the north showed some sincerity at the proposed high-level officials meeting, the suspended meetings could be resumed at any time.

Therefore, if north Korea is truly interested in normalizing the inter-Korean relations and realizing national unification, they should accept the proposal for a high-level south-north officials meeting if only to provide a momentum for the resumption of the stalled dialogue and thereby join in the efforts to restore national trust and materialize reconciliation.

However, north Korea not only refused to receive the message containing the proposal but also in effect turned the offer down. In a statement released by the so-called Preparatory Committee for Joint South-North Conference on June 6, the north asserted that they could consider the proposed high-level officials meeting only as a preliminary meeting to prepare for a joint south-north conference.

To display their insincerity, the statement was made not by the Administration Council **premier** to whom the south's message containing the proposal was addressed but by a bogus organization named the Preparatory Committee for Joint South-North Conference, **so-called**. Moreover, they were asserting that all issues pending between the two sides should be resolved not at an authorities meeting but at a sort of political rally in the form of a joint conference attended by the representatives of political parties and all layers and strata of the two societies. North Korea seemed trying to exploit the move of some sectors in the south demanding expanded unification talks such as a meeting between political parties and students talks.

While in effect rejecting the proposed high-level officials meeting, north Korea feigned itself to be flexible by arguing that they could favorably consider it as a preliminary meeting to discuss their idea of a joint conference or that "if and when a joint conference is held, it could discuss the questions of Olympic co-hosting, resuming suspended talks and realizing personnel exchanges."

Still, their demand for other forms of dialogue while keeping the well-progressed dialogue suspended, was more than enough to tell that they were not interested in any workable talks with the south. North Korea continued to demand a joint south-north conference or a students' meeting in a series of "letter campaigns" against the south which they launched with the intent of offsetting the international accusation of them following the terrorist bombing of a south Korean passenger plane in November 1987 and also of fomenting a split of opinion and social confusion in the south.

The north Korean rejection of the first proposal made by the Sixth Republic should be understood in this context. At any rate, the forward-looking effort of the south to provide the momentum for inter-Korean confidence-building got nowhere once again.

4. July 7 Special Presidential Declaration for National Self-Esteem, Unification and Prosperity

a. Background and Purport

On July 7, 1988, President Roh Tae-woo announced a special declaration to embody national self-esteem, unification and prosperity, the ideals which the President discussed from the time of the birth of the Sixth Republic. The declaration was significant in that it set forth the basic direction of the unification and foreign policies the new Republic would promote. In particular, it contained a clear determination to seek a new change in the inter-Korean relationship and the government's northern policy, as well as a new vision to create a national community.

In the background of the July 7 declaration were changes in unification environment, which stem from the worldwide trend of reconciliation and detente. The declaration thus pools the fervent national wish to link such changes to seeking a new development of the inter-Korean relationship.

Thanks to the accelerated democratic development and the steady growth of economy following the birth of the Sixth Republic, the Republic of Korea has come to have a firm confidence in national future, which leads to the need of the fresh recognition of, and new ideas in, the promotion of the unification policy.

The approach between the U.S. and the USSR, which has been steadily promoted since the rise of Gorbachev to power, has come to bear solid fruit. Heralding the unveiling of the age of new detente, while the 1988 Seoul Olympics were expected to have served as a mementum to terminate ideological disputed between the East and the West and to unlock the door of a new reconciliation.

Under these circumstances, the south was faced with the need to help north Korea get away from self-imposed international isolation and induce the north to open itself to the world in keeping pace with changing internal and external situations, and thereby enable the nation of Korea to depart from the quagmire of protracted enmity and self-injury and to provide the new momentum for improved inter-Korean relations. The July 7 declaration embodied the policy determination of the Sixth Republic to explore the new age of national self-esteem as a key nation of the Asian and Pacific region and lay a solid groundwork for national unification.

In his first press conference on April 21, 1988, after his inauguration, President **Roh Tae-woo** said that he would make the rest of the term of his office as a period to pave the way for peaceful unification through the promotion of reconciliation and cooperation between the two sides of Korea. Also during his talks with the heads of opposition political parties held at Chong Wa Dae (the presidential residence) about one month later on May 28, 1988, President Roh made it clear that the government would pursue a unification policy in a way that would help create a national community in which all Koreans can live well.

At the same time, the July 7 declaration embodies the intent to explore ways to resolve the Korean question with the nation's own efforts, and to buttress such resolution by forging a national consensus.

Thus seen, the purport of the July 7 declaration can be boiled down to that 1) both the south and the north should cooperate and pave the way to co-prosperity as the same nation instead of regarding each other as rivals in competition or confrontation, 2) the two sides should take a look at the nation's future and determine what can be the way to ensure better lives for the whole Koreans, and 3) the south should now show interest in improving the lives of the north Korean people.

The July 7 declaration made it clear that the south would take a set of measures to embody such purport. Although the inter-Korean relations can be improved only through joint efforts for national reconciliation as was stressed in the declaration that "if the north shows a positive attitude, the south would take more progressive measures one after another," the July 7 declaration contained the will power to one-sidedly take those steps which, with the south's efforts alone, can contribute to the promotion of national reconciliation and cooperation.

b. Significance and Features

The basic significance of the July 7 declaration lies in the fact that it is intended to unfold an age of national self-esteem, unification and prosperity by accommodating positively the new and matured conditions of changes in the unification environment and new developments in the inter-Korean relationship.

The declaration shows that it is the dictate of times for the south to liquidate the age of south-north confrontation and induce the closed north Korean society to open itself up, develop the south-north relations into cooperative and good-intentioned partnership relations, and would have a fresh recognition of both the unification question and the south-north relations.

Thus, the significance of the July 7 declaration can be seen mostly in two aspects : a change in the recognition of north Korea and a switch in the basis of the south's unification and foreign policies.

– Change in the Perception of North Korea –

The July 7 special declaration can be taken to have brought a significant change in the south's view of the north as the south came to accommodate the north as part of the same nation instead of taking it as an adversary in competion, confrontation and hostility. The south has come to recognize north Korea as a member of the national community pursuing co-prosperity based on mutual trust, reconciliation and cooperation.

The south and the north should restore at an early date the sense of their being the same national community sharing the same ethnic blood tree and the same single history and culture. This is so especially because if the two sides persist in self-injurious conduct amidst mutual disruption and distrust, it would lead only to the waste of national energies and a damage to national self-esteem.

The logic behind a change in the recognition of north Korea is based on the fact that the realistic existence of north Korea should be recognized under the premise that there are two systems in the south and the north within a single national community, and thereby national integration should be sought through the promotion of mutual understanding and cooperation.

Such a new recognition starts from the regarding of the inter-Korean relationship as a special one within a national community instead of that of two independent countries in a temporary measure pending the time of unification. This was expressly evident in the fact that inter-Korean trade is regarded not as inter-country trade but as intra-country dealings.

A change in the perception of north Korea is important because it facilitates a realistic and concrete approach toward national unification. In this aspect, the declaration includes the unification idea that the two systems within the same nation should dismantle the barrier of their division, integrate themselves into a community in the areas of social, culture and economy through positive exchanges, openness and cooperation, and based thereon develop this community into a political community to realize unification under a single country in the long run.

– Change in Base for Unification and Foreign Policies –

In addition to a change in recognition of north Korea, the July 7 declaration involved a will power to embody practical policies based on such a change and thereby improve conditions for unification. In other words, the declaration represents a switch in the south's unification and foreign policies by expressing a plan to cooperate in the north's participation in the international community as a responsible member and even support their effort to improve their relations with the U.S., Japan and other allies of the south, in place of pursuing a passive scheme to isolate the north from the rest of the world and thereby prompt a change from within.

The resolute policy switch envisioned in the July 7 declaration is in full conformity with the path of the Korean community required to cope actively with the flow of the openness of the international society since the mid-1980s. The new policy stems from the south's confidence that it would prompt the internal development of and changes in north Korea from an affirmative perception.

This policy suffices the need to form a national community where the quality of every Korean life is elevated a step higher through the balanced development of the south's and the north's societies. Since an excessive economic gap or a power imbalance between the two sides can be detrimental to unification, It would be highly significant for the south to help improve the quality of the north Korean people's lives and play the role of a propellant in the acceleration of a balanced development in the national economy.

The switch in unification and foreign policies, promoted by the July 7 declaration, would serve to accelerate personnel and material exchanges between the two sides of Korea and expand the mood of mutual confidence-building and eased tensions, contributing substantially to the improvement of the inter-Korean relationship and durable peace.

At the same time, the July 7 declaration has marked an important milestone in the history of national unification as it provided the groundwork on which a wasteful diplomacy of competition and confrontation between the two sides could be terminated and the nation's common interests maximized in the international community.

c. Declaration of a Six-Point Policy

The July 7 declaration expresses the basic spirit that the Koreans should unfold the new age of national self-esteem, unification and prosperity by creating a national community in which the entire members of the Korean nation participate based on the principles of independence, peace, democracy and wellbeing.

The substance of the six-point policy to be taken on the basis of the ideas and principles of the July 7 declaration was as follows:

(1) Item 1: Promotion of Exchanges Between the People of South and North Korea and Opening the Door to Free Visits to Both the South and the North by Overseas Koreans

To dispell the distrust accumulated between the two sides and pave the way to national integration, it is important for the two sides to promote mutual understanding and elevate the sense of national bond through exchanges and cooperation as the same people. This is all the more so in view of the fact that the basic reason for the failure to overcome the state of national division for nearly half a century was that the south and the north have built up mutual distrust, unable to solidly develop the sense of their being the single national community standing on the same root.

It was for this reason that the government of the Republic of Korea proposed a south-north high-level officials meeting to discuss the issue of exchanges of people in various sectors, such as politicians, business persons, journalists, religious leaders, writers and artists, athletes, scholars and students. The government said it would positively strive to realize such personnel exchanges through negotiations between government authorities.

The Item 1 of the declaration also includes measures to ensure that overseas Koreans could freely visit the south and the north without any restrictions, so that they could contribute to the elimination of distrust and promotion of mutual understanding between the two sides.

Presently about 2 million Koreans live in Western and Third World countries and another 2.2 million are known to be in the Soviet Union, China and other Communist-bloc countries. It goes without saying that the south, intent of forging the age of south-north reconciliation and cooperation, cannot turn a deaf ear to the pains and misfortune of these overseas Koreans any longer.

The kind of unification and prosperity the Korean nation pursues can be attained only through the creation of a national community in which all those who regard themselves as Koreans participate and lead better lives.

(2) Item 2 : Positive Arrangement of Finding Out of Dispersed Families' Fates and Whereabouts, Exchange of Letters and Mutual Visits

Those who suffer pains and misfortune more than others due to the 43-year-long division are dispersed family members who total about 10 million. Even from the humanitarian point of view, it is the paramount duty of both sides to dispel their pains.

Since the 1970s dialogue, the government of the south has done all it could to resolve the question of separated families through inter-Korean dialogue. One result of the efforts was the exchange of dispersed family hometown visitors and art troupes made in the autumn of 1985

However, the suspension of the dialogue by the north has left the dialogue at a stage where if only the two sides make a little more efforts, a working-level accord could be reached on such issues as finding out of the fate and whereabouts of missing families, exchange of letters and mutual visits.

Item 2 of the declaration was meant in part for the government to express its unswerving intent of arranging the resolution of the dispersed family issue through all available means on a top priority basis.

In the future, the government will provide all assistance through direct or indirect means including the arrangement of travels back and forth between the two sides and creation of a reunion center, so that separated families in the south and the north could find out the fate and whereabouts of their missing families, exchange letters and make mutual visits and meetings.

(3) Item 3 : Opening of Door for South-North Trade

For the south and the north to prosper commonly as a single nation, they should elevate both the size and quality of the national economy a step further by restoring and developing an economic community.

In fact, the two sides have already set a precedent for the practice of mutual assistance through the delivery and receipt of relief materials for flood victims. And at five rounds of the south-north economic meeting, they agreed in principle on the trade of materials and other forms of economic cooperation. The economic meeting itself progressed to a point where the two sides were about to adopt agreed minutes. But the economic talks, too, failed to register any further progress due to the suspension of the overall south-north dialogue.

Item 3 of the declaration premises that in the resolution of the strained inter-Korean relations, it is important for the two sides to open their economic doors to each other and engage in commodity trade. In this regard, one feature is that the south regards the inter-Korean relationship not as that of independent countries but as a "transitory special relationship" oriented toward mutual integration, and accordingly takes inter-Korean trade itself as internal business dealings within the nation. Under the policy, no duties in the form of tariffs would be imposed on goods shipped to the south from the north.

(4) Item 4 : Non-Opposition to Non-Military Trading by Allies

In item 4 of the declaration, it was expressed that the south won't oppose its allies trading with the north if such trade would contribute to stabilizing the livelihood of the north Korean people and enhancing their wellbeing.

It is true that in the past when the south and the north had engaged in a growing competition for national strength in a confrontational approach, the south had asked its allies to refrain from trading with north Korea. However, Item 4 of the declaration stipulates that the south would tolerate the trading of non-military goods other than those controlled by COCOM regulations with north Korea.

Such a measure would serve to prompt north Korea to participate in the international community and accelerate its openness, thereby contributing to the balanced development of the national economy and realizing a national community.

(5) Item 5 : Hope for Free Inter-Korean Contacts and Cooperation in the World Community

The inter-Korean relations should be developed in a way that would not only engineer the development of the internal relations of the nation but also maintain national pride and dignity in the international community.

While noting that in the past the south and the north engaged in a fierce competition and confrontation against each other in international arenas, thus defacing the nation's self-esteem and prestige by themselves and undermining the effort to broaden national interests, Item 5 of the declaration provides that the south, with dauntlessness and maturity, would accommodate the north.

Accordingly, the south would desist from engaging in diplomatic confrontation with the north in such international arenas as the United Nationa and the Non-Aligned Movement, would encourage their entry into world organizations, and would foster conditions in which the two sides' delegates could freely meet and exchange opinions anywhere in the world and together take the lead in directing the world flow of detente and openness.

(6) Item 6 : Willingness to Cooperate in the North's Improvement of Relations With Allies

After the birth of the Sixth Republic, the south positively pursues a northward policy with an eye at improving relations with the northern continental countries with which the south maintains no diplomatic relations.

The special declaration expresses the south's progressive position that based on a confidence in the promotion of the northward policy, it would not only tolerate but also may cooperate in the efforts of north Korea to improve its relations with its allies including the United States and Japan.

The policy would serve to prepare a common foothold to strengthen the nation's independent diplomacy by subjectively accommodating the situation surrounding the Korean peninsula.

d. Relevant Measures

The July special declaration was the expression in the form of declaration of the government's positive will power to chart a new turning point in both the inter-Korean relationship and its northward policy, and realize national integration and prosperity through south-north reconciliation and cooperation.

The basic spirit of the declaration can be sustained through the unconditional and resolute implementation of programs substantially conducive to the improvement of the inter-Korean relations. Accordingly, the government of the south has steadily taken a series of follow-up measures of its own under the spirit of the Special Declaration.

At the same time, for those programs which can work properly only when north Korea joins in, the government has been making many-sided efforts so that the true intent of the July 7 declaration can be understood correctly by the north.

(1) Proposal for a Working-Level Red Cross Meeting

The proposal for a working-level Red Cross meeting was based on Item 2 of the declaration, which said in part, "Even before the successful conclusion of the South-North Red Cross Conference, we will promote and actively support, from a humanitarian viewpoint, all measures which can assist dispersed families in their efforts to find out the fate and whereabouts of their missing families in the other area of the peninsula, and will also promote exchanges of correspondence and visits between them.

Kim Sang-hyop, president of the Republic of Korea National Red Cross (ROKNRC), calling for the early resumption of the suspended South-North Red Cross Conference, proposed on July 13, 1988, that even before the resumption of the talks, a working-level meeting be held between the two Red Crosses to discuss four-point programs to ease the pains of dispersed families, including the second exchange of dispersed family hometown visitors.

The offer was made in a telephone message addressed to Son Song-pil, chairman of the Central Committee of the North Korean Red Cross.

The gist of the proprosal made by the ROKNRC president was as follows :

(1) Exchange of letters of inquiries and replies regarding the finding out of the fate and whereabouts of dispersed families ;

(2) Arrangement of the exchange of letters between those dispersed families whose fate and whereabouts were found out through mutual Red Cross organizations at the time of the exchange of the groups of dispersed family hometown visitors in 1985 ;

(3) Provision of opportunities to overseas dispersed families to find out the fate and whereabouts of their missing families, to exchange letters between them and to realize reunions ;

(4) Promotion of the second exchange of groups of dispersed family hometown visitors before the end of this year ; and

(5) Holding of a working-level Red Cross meeting at Panmunjom on July 30 to discuss these issues.

Also in the message the ROKNRC president assured the north that if north Korean dispersed families wish to visit the area of the south to meet their missing families, the south would guarantee their personal safety and provide all conveniences to them. In addition, he said that under the spirit of the July 7 declaration, his Red Cross was reviewing in earnest various practicable projects to resolve the dispersed family questions on a priority basis.

In response, the north Korean Red Cross's Son Song-pil, in a telephone message of July 16, in effect rejected the idea of holding a working-level meeting, arguing that the "south-north Red Cross talks were suspended due to the south's anti-Communist confrontational policy and war fuss" and insisting that "all elements standing in the way to the resumption of the Red Cross talks should be removed."

Meanwhile, ROKNRC President Kim issued a statement on August 11, 1988, in observance of the 17th anniversary of his Red Cross's proposal for a south-north Red Cross meeting to launch a family search campaign. The statement, calling on north Korea to agree to resume the suspended Red Cross talks, said that the ROKNRC would receive applications from dispersed families for finding out the fate and whereabouts of their missing families and relatives in the north for three months from August 12, the anniversary date of the proposal for the inter-Korean Red Cross talks, through November 12, 1988.

The receipt of such applications is meant in part to prepare beforehand letters of request for search for separated families to be sent to the north, in preparation for a family search project to be undertaken under an agreement between the two Red Crosses.

(2) Proposal for South-North Education Officials Meeting

The proposal for education officials meeting was part of the follow-up measures taken on the basis of Item 1 of the declaration, which provided that the government would positively promote personnel exchanges in all walks of life. On July 15, 1988, Minister of Education Kim Young-sik proposed to the north that a south-north education officials meeting be held at Panmunjom before July 30, 1988, if possible.

In the message addressed to Pyon Yong-rip, chairman of the Education Commission of the north Korean Administration Council, Minister Kim suggested that the proposed meeting could discuss the issues of students grand pilgrimages across the homeland and exchange of student goodwill athletic meets, and matters related to student exchange programs.

The Education Minister proposed that the size of the pilgrimage parties be around 1,000 from each side, and that southern students journey from Panmunjom to Mt. Paekdu, while northern students journey from Panmunjom to Mt. Halla and return. He suggested that the first of such pilgrimages take place within the year. As for the exchange of goodwill sports matches, the minister suggested that each delegation be composed of about 200 persons covering the sporting events of soccer, men's and women's table tennis, and men's and women's volleyball, and that the first meets be held in Pyongyang in October 1988, and the second in Seoul in April of the following year.

Minister Kim said that if the pilot projects were successful, performances and exhibitions could be exchanged in such cultural and art areas as music, arts, concert and dance, and school excursion teams could also be exchanged, in which students could visit scenic and historical sites like Mt. Kumkang and Kyongju.

The proposal, which incorporated even those student opinions raised in connection with south-north student talks, was significant in that it was intended to restore the sense of national trust and integrity among the young generation and to prepare a base for the expanded implementation of multi-pronged personnel exchanges.

At that time, some students in the south raised the issue of south-north student talks by sending an open letter to the students of Kim Il-sung University of the north on March 29, 1988, and two other open letters to the north. North Korea, which sought an opportune time to foment confusion in the south with the Seoul Olympics around the corner, jumped on the student offer. North Korea promptly formed the Northern Preparatory Committee for South-North Student Talks, while instigating southern students by using such slogans as "Fight Relentlessly for the Realization of South-North Student Talks" and "Success of Our Talks will come through Struggles."

Some students in the south held a rally for the student talks and attempted to march to Panmunjom on June 10 to have the talks. But, their attempt failed in the face of public opinion asking the students to restrain themselves from entering talks with a monolithic system on issues unbecoming of students.

After their projected talks on June 10 were thwarted, the students sent the fourth (June 11) and fifth (July 27) letters to the north's declaring that they would now have the south-north student talks on August 15.

In particular, the students argued that they should discuss even political and military issues with north Korean students. The agenda topics they put forth for the talks were 1) the issue of south-north student exchanges, 2) the issue of student efforts to realize meeting between dispersed family members in the south and the north, 3) the issue of student efforts to promote the co-hosting of the 24th Olympic Games, 4) holding of south-north student athletic games (September 15–17), and 5) the issue of dispelling military confrontation between the south and the north.

Moreover, the students disclosed a plan to have the representatives of various political parties, social organizations and all walks of life attend their talks as observers. They thus worked to alter the nature of their projected talks by themselves.

The proposal for a south-north educational officials meeting was to accommodate such unification efforts of students under the circumstances, and, going a step farther, to contribute to the substantial improvement of the south-north relations by enabling students to tour each other's areas instead of their own areas only as they planned.

Meanwhile, despite the notification to the north through the direct south-north telephone line that the Education Minister's message would be delivered to the north on July 15, the north sent to the south a telephone message on July 14 saying that they would not accept the message.

The northern message, signed by Pyon Yong-rip, chairman of the Education Commission, charged the south with "obstructing" the planned student talks, arguing that "we see no reason why government authorities should step in belatedly and interfere in it."

Again on July 17, north Korea formally rejected the southern offer for a south-north education officials meeting. In a statement issued by a spokesman for the Administration Council, the north asserted that "the question of student exchanges is an issue which students themselves should discuss and resolve, and in which government authorities can under no circumstance step in." The north Korean statement further insisted that "the south proposed an education officials meeting not to resolve the question of student exchanges but to block the August 15 student talks, overcome a political crisis and force through their unilateral staging of the Olympics."

The north Korean rejection of an education officials meeting was to agitate students' struggles for the south-north students talks rather than to accommodate and respond favorably to the basic spirit of the July 7 declaration. The north's ulterior motive was to see that a social unrest occures in the south through clashes between radical students trying to force through students talks and the government determined to block it, an unrest which they hoped could lead to the undermining of the Seoul Olympics. In fact, with illusionary expectations from reckless student activities over a south-north student meeting, the north mobilized all propaganda machinery for intensified agitation for students' anti-government struggles in the south.

The north went so far as to send student representatives, press members and an agitation squad to Panmunjom twice on June 10 and August 15, the dates when the student talks were supposed to be held for a series of propaganda activities such as a press conference, shouting of political slogans and singing.

The true objective of the proposal for an education officials meeting was to consolidate the basis of peaceful unification by providing opportunities for south and north Korean students who did not witness the Korean War to personally observe and experience each other's conditions and thus build up the sense of national bond. However, north Korea, which showed an affirmative response to the student talks without any reservation, was negative toward an officials meeting designed to ensure such student exchanges, making objective observers suspect if the north were interested in a genuine dialogue with the south after all.

(3) Forward-Looking Northward and Foreign Policies

On July 16, 1988, Minister of Foreign Affairs Choi Kwang-soo made public a new foreign policy the government of the south would pursue as a follow-up measure of the July 7 Special Presidential Declaration with a view to easing tensions and consolidating peace on the Korean peninsula and developing the inter-Korean relationship as a national community. The substance of the policy was as follows:

(1) We shall not oppose our allies including the United States and Japan trading non-military goods with north Korea under their laws and policies.

(2) Non-military materials here refer to general commodities and technical materials not included in the COCOM(Coordinating Committee for Export to Communist Area) list.

(3) We shall not oppose private people's travels back and forth between our allies and north Korea to make business negotiations or for other purposes to facilitate such trade.

(4) We shall not oppose our allies establishing the branch offices of trading companies in north Korea for such trade.

(5) We shall recognize north Korea's standing in the international community, hoping that north Korea will contribute to world peace and the development of mankind in accordance with the spirit and principle of the United Nations Charter. We shall cooperate in north Korea's participation in the international community as a responsible member.

(6) We shall desist from engaging in a wasteful confrontational diplomacy toward north Korea, and shall not oppose north Korea normalizing its relations with

Non-Aligned and Third World countries.

(7) We urge north Korea to agree that south and north Korea, as the same national community, stop waging unproductive arguments or levelling defamation or slander against each other at diplomatic arenas such as all international organizations and meetings.

(8) We are willing to cooperate in north Korea's participation in all subordinate organizations and specialized agencies of the United Nations and inter-governmental regional cooperation and development organizations.

(9) We welcome north Korea's participation in all cutural, art, academic and sports events anywhere in the world.

(10) At all international meetings ·attended by both south and north Korean delegates, we shall make positive approaches so that mutual contacts and dialogue can be made. Efforts shall also be made at other cultural, art, academic and sports events to have inter-Korean contacts and dialogue.

(11) In countries where both south and north Korea maintain diplomatic missions, we shall endeavor to use all opportunities to promote contacts and talks between south and north Korean diplomats.

(12) We shall not oppose our allies including the United States and Japan making private exchanges with north Korea in the areas of culture, art, academic studies and sports. If necessary, we are willing to cooperate in it.

(13) We shall not oppose U.S. and Japanese diplomats having contacts or dialogue with north Korean diplomats in third countries or at neutral settings.

The new foreign policy announced by Minister Choi was a one-sided action taken by the south to embody the basic spirit of the July 7 declaration. The new policy is expected to result in 1) improvement of the inter-Korean relationship at international diplomatic arenas, 2) improvement of relations between the south's allies and north Korea, and 3) improvement of relations between south Korea and Communist-bloc countries including the Soviet Union, China and East European countries.

In short, the declaration was focused at promoting a durable mechanism for south-north co-prosperity and stability on the Korean peninsula through balanced cross contacts and exchanges.

The new foreign policy contains the meaning that the south would desist from engaging in wasteful confrontational diplomacy and help north Korea become a responsible member of the world society so as to cement the base for national self-esteem.

At the same time, by tolerating contacts and trade with north Korea by the allies of the south including the United States and Japan, the new foreign policy serves to help north Korea improve conditions for contacts and trade with the West. North Korea introduced a joint-venture law in 1984 but their economic exchanges with the West had been sluggish.

In particular, the recent policy provides a base on which the United States could ease its sanctions against north Korea and promote a steady improvement of its relations with the north. Japan, for example, has had sluggish trade exchanges with north Korea, an amount representing only about 2 percent of the trade volume between south Korea and Japan, because largely of the north's defaulted credits and also in consideration of Japan's close relationship with Seoul. In the future, however, Japan would be able to ease financial sanctions against north Korea or expedite Japanese traders' advancement or technology transfer to north Korea.

Again on July 19, 1988, Foreign Minister Choi announced a follow-up measure to facilitate free travels to south and north Korea by overseas Koreans. With the measure, doors to homeland visits by 4,500,000 Korean residents abroad have been completely opened. And reciprocal measures by the north can now be expected.

The new diplomatic policy has laid down conditions for the development of the inter-Korean relationship into that of the same national community in the international society. Depending on the north's response, the policy would serve to expedite the opening of their society and would constitute a clue to turning the situation surrounding the Korean peninsula into the air of peace and reconciliation.

(4) Opening of Informative Materials on North Korea and Other Communist-bloc Countries

On September 3, 1988, Minister of Culture and Information Chung

Han-mo, a government spokesman, announced that the "government has decided to open informative materials on north Korea and other Communist bloc to the public with a view to translate concretely into action the open-door policy toward north Korea based on the July 7 Special Presidential Declaration."

The measure was significant in that it serves to meet the growing demand for communist bloc information caused by stepped-up exchanges with Communist countries, that it helps carry out the north ward policy more effectively, and that it serves to assure the age of inter-Korean exchanges and cooperation more effectively through people's correct understanding of the true conditions of north Korea and the rest of the Communist bloc.

The substance of the policy to open informative materials on north Korea and the rest of the Communist bloc, announced by the government spokesman, was as follows :

(1) All general informative materials on communist-bloc with the exception of those which expressly violate the law of the land such as those issued by north Korea, Chochongryon (the pro-Pyongyang General Association of Korean Residents in Japan), etc., for propaganda purposes, shall be opened.

(2) The Rodong Shinmun and visual materials of north Korea shall be opened to the public on a selective basis.

(3) Even those materials excluded from the list opened to the public, they shall be made available to those who need them for scholarly and other purposes. Procedures for use of such materials will be simplified so as not to cause any inconveniences to their users.

(4) Informative materials in the possession of government offices and public research agencies shall be furnished to various circles to the most possible extent. At the same time, a plan is being promoted to establish and operate a comprehensive material center so that they could be used easily.

(5) Suspension of Slanderous Broadcasts

In accordance with the basic spirit of the July 7 special declaration calling on south and north Korea to pursue a single national community in favor of co-existence and co-prosperity, the government of the Republic of Korea suspended all accusatory broadcasts against north Korea effective July 19, 1988. Accusatory and slanderous broadcasts through the public address system were stopped in the frontline areas, and personal attacks against specific north Korean figures such as Kim Il-sung and Kim Jong-il were suspended in socio-educational programs of the KBS radio.

Accusatory broadcasts by south and north Korea against each other were suspended for about a year in the early 1970s under the provisions of Article 2 of the July 4 South-North Joint Communique of 1972, which stipulated that "the two sides shall not slander each other in order to foster an atmosphere for trust." But the stoppage of slanderous broadcasts could not last long at that time because north Korea one-sidedly breached the agreement.

The one-sided stoppage by the south of slanderous broadcasts against north Korea this time was a prelude to the opening of north Korean materials and contacts with the north such as visits to the north by Korean residents abroad, which are expected to be spurred by the July 7 declaration. Besides this, the prior liquidation of the legacies of the relationship of confrontation and hostility, such as accusatory broadcasts, is a preliminary measure essential to the entry into the age of inter-Korean exchanges and cooperation.

The south intends to go a step farther and take steadily and regardless of response from the north a series of measures to prepare the framework of reconciliation and co-existence, addressing a positive message of peace to north Korea.

(6) Economic Opening to North Korea

The government of the Republic of Korea, in a statement released by Deputy Prime Minister and Economic Planning Minister Rha

Woong-bae, announced a set of measures on Octover 7, 1988, to improve the inter-Korean relations in the economic sector as a follow-up measure of the July 7 special declaration. The measures, designed to translate into action the clause of Item 3 of the declaration, "We shall open our door to south-north trade and shall regard south-north trade as intra-nation dealing," call for economic exchanges between the south and the north even before the resumption of the stalled south-north economic meeting so that the interests of the whole nation could be realized to the most possbile extent.

The substance of the measures, intended to improve both the size and quality of the national economy in preparation for the development of an economic community for the sake of common national prosperity, was as follows :

1. Private companies of the south or foreign trading companies in Korea shall be allowed to import into the country or export to north Korea in the form of indirect trade goods other than military materials. Their re-imports and re-exports shall also be permitted. (Permission to trade north Korean materials by private companies.)

2. Private companies in the south shall be allowed to export north Korean commodities to third countries or relay the exports of the commodities of third countries to north Korea. (Permission to relay north Korean materials by private companies.)

3. When north Korean commodities are taken into the country, the origin or the trade labels of north Korea attached to such commodities shall not be removed. (Allowing the attachment of origin and trade labels to north Korean commodities.)

4. Tariffs and various other duties assessed only on import items shall not be assessed on north Korean materials delivered to the south directly through indirect trade or via a third country; which shall be regarded as intra-country dealings. The shipment of the materials of the south to the north shall be accorded various export-related sys-

tems, with such shipment being regarded as exporting. (Non-imposition of tariffs on direct or indirect trade items.)

5. When private company officials of the south wish to come in contact with north Korean officials or visit north Korea for the purpose of trade negotiations, such contacts or visits shall be permitted. When north Korean business persons wish to visit the south for trade negotiations, such visits shall be welcomed and various conveniences and personal safety shall be guaranteed. (Permission for mutual contacts and visits between south and north Korean business persons.)

6. When north Korean-flag ships carrying trade items from south or north Korea or a third country, request for entry into the ports of south Korea, such entry shall be permitted. (Permission for calls by north Korean-flag merchant ships.)

7. Legal and systematic devices shall be prepared on south-north economic exchanges to back up the realization of the above measures, Pending the preparation of such legal and systematic measures, those regulations covering trade with special areas governed by the External Trade Law shall be applied to indirect trade between the south and the north. (Supplementation of legal measures related to south-north economic exchanges.)

These measures taken by the south represent a leading role it has played to elevate the mutual complementariness of the two sides in the area of economy through expanded economic exchanges so that the two sides could share the profits resulting from an economic community and restore and develop the sense of national community. For if north Korea, which still sticks to self-imposed isolation and closedness, favorably responds to substantial inter-Korean contacts through trade, it would lead to common profits from their mutual economic complementariness and geographical nearness as well as to easing much the state of inter-Korean confrontation and disruption.

For one year beginning November 1984, the south and the north had five rounds of their economic talks, reaching an accord on considerable part of the issues. The measures were ideas the south could take unilaterally to promote inter-Korean trade in whatever possible form based on past experiences and achievements even before economic talks resumed between the south and the north.

In particular, it is noticeable that true to the spirit of the July 7 special declaration, direct and indirect trade between the two sides would be regarded in large part as intra-nation trade dealings and thereby no tariffs, etc., are to be imposed on such trade and various other restrictive factors removed paving the way to substantial economic exchanges between the south and the north.

If and when such direct and indirect trade progresses between the south and the north to·expand mutual contacts and give rise to the need of expanded exchanges, it would serve to ripen an atmosphere and foundation for overall inter-Korean exchanges, constituting a significant momentum for full-fledged inter-Korean economic exchanges, alleviation of tension and the promotion of balanced mutual development.

5. Preparatory Contacts for South-North Parliamentary Talks

a. Background

Following the first and second preliminary contacts held on July 21 and September 25, 1985, for a south-north parliamentary meeting, the third contact slated for February 18, 1986, was called off due to the north's overall suspension of the south-north dialogue.

The renewed preparatory contacts for parliamentary talks began after Kim Jaison, speaker of the Republic of Korea National Assembly, sent to Yang Hyong-sop, chairman of the Standing Committee of the Supreme People's Assembly of the north, on July 18, 1988, a message containing the "Resolution Calling for Participation by North Korea in the Seoul Olympic Games" which the National Assembly unanimously adopted in its 20th plenary meeting of the 142nd Extraordinary Assembly session on July 9. The text of the resolution was as follows :

Resolution Calling for Participation by North Korea in the Seoul Olympic Games

The Republic of Korea National Assembly, noting that the 24th Olympic Games, a festival of all mankind, is scheduled to be held in Seoul of the Republic of Korea with the fervent support from and participation by 161 countries,

In keeping with the yearning of all Koreans for the peaceful unification of the homeland with the expectations of the all the peoples of the world aspiring for a durable peace on the Korean peninsula,

Expressing the firm determination to make the Seoul Olympics a success by all means in the unswerving conviction that if and when the historical, great festival were used to the most possible extent, making it a momentum for national reconciliation and exchanges, it would advance the time of unification,

Strongly calling for north Korea's sincere and positive participation,

Hereby resolves as follows :

–The Republic of Korea National Assembly, hoping that a large number of north Korean athletes will participate in the historical Seoul Olympics opening on September 17, 1988, urges the north Korean authorities to render positive cooperation in line with the lofty spirit and purport of the Olympic Movement and with the recognition that their cooperation would serve as a momentum facilitating grand national reconciliation ;

–The Republic of Korea National Assembly urges the north Korean authorities to render unspared support and efforts so as to develop the Seoul Olympic Games into a proud event where the Korean nation can display before the whole world their homogeneity and superiority, taking note of the fact that the whole world is watching the attitude and relations of the south and the north ;

404

—The Republic of Korea National Assembly hopes that north Korean athletes and compatriots will freely travel back and forth between the south and the north under the guarantee that they would be enabled to visit anywhere in the south for a considerable period around the Olympic period, and will use the occasion as an opportunity to dismantle the barrier of division ; and

—The Republic of Korea National Assembly sincerely proposes that the south and the north will exert their maximum efforts in a mutually positive and forward-looking attitude, positively carrying out exchanges and contacts in all layers and strata and in all walks of life starting with the Seoul Olympics so as to achieve unification, the ultimate wish of the people.

July 9, 1988
Republic of Korea National Assembly

In response to the southern message containing the resolution, north Korea sent a letter to the south on July 21, suggesting that a first joint south-north parliamentary meeting be held in Pyongyang in August. Signed by Yang Hyong-sop, chairman of the Standing Committee of the Supreme People's Assembly, the letter contained a draft Joint Declaration on South-North Nonaggression.

The gist of the north Korean letter was as follows :

Even if exchanges or trade were made, the south and the north, with a demarcation line between them, cannot ever become a harmonious national community unless the issue of easing tensions is resolved.

A joint south-north conference is regarded as a reasonable forum for the alleviation of tensions. But even before such a joint meeting is convened, a south-north parliamentary meeting will be the most ideal talks to discuss a joint declaration on nonaggression our side has proposed.

South-north parliamentary talks can be held in various forms. But the most reasonable one is to convene a joint session between the delegates of our Supreme

405

People's Assembly and the members of the south's National Assembly without going through preliminary contacts.

– Contents of Discussion –

(1) The question of announcing a joint declaration on nonaggression between the south and the north .

(2) Questions raised by the south which can be conducive to easing tension and ensuring peace.

– Method of Operation –

(1) Assembly speakers of the two sides shall serve as co-chairmen.

(2) Chairman of the Supreme People's Assembly shall preside over the meetings taking place in Pyongyang, and the speaker of the National Assembly of the south shall chair the meetings held in Seoul.

(3) At meetings all attendees shall freely discuss the issues introduced.

(4) As for the method of decision, the number of the north's delegates shall be equal to that of the southern delegation, and decisions shall be made with the approval of the majority by a mixture of voting and a show of hands.

– Venue and Time –

(1) Meetings shall be held in Pyongyang and Seoul in turns.

(2) The first meeting shall be held in Pyongyang in August.

– Draft Joint South-North Declaration on Nonaggression –

(1) Non-use of arms against each other and nonaggression against each other by force of arms under any circumstances.

(2) Pending the time of complete unification, mutual differences and disputes shall be peacefully resolved through dialogue and negotiations.

(3) Non-participation or cooperation in alien aggression toward or armed interference with each other.

(4) The boundary line of nonaggression shall be the Military Demarcation Line drawn under the Military Armistice Agreement of July 27, 1953.

(5) Phased mutual reductions in armed forces and a step-by-step withdrawal of foreign forces and nuclear weapons.

(6) The present Demilitarized Zone shall be made a buffer zone, where neutral nations supervisory forces shall be maintained to forestall armed disputes.

(7) A south-north nonaggression declaration shall not be bound by any treaty or agreement concluded by either of the two sides with a foreign country.

At the same time, in a letter sent to Speaker Kim Jaison of the south on July 26, Yang Hyong-sop, chairman of the Standing Committee of the north's Supreme People's Assembly, proposed that the question of inviting north Korea to the Seoul Olympics and the idea of co-hosting the Games be discussed as emergency agenda topics at a joint session of the south and north Korean legislatures.

In response to the north Korean proposal, Speaker Kim Jaison suggested in a message to the north on August 1 that preparatory contacts be held to discuss the materialization of the proposed south-north parliamentary talks within August. In the message, Speaker Kim said that 15 National Assembly members would be sent to Panmunjom on a date of the north's choice in the second week (August 8-13) of August to have a preparatory contact.

However, in their third letter of August 9, the north proposed that working-level contacts attended by three to five legislators from each side be held at 11 a.m. August 17 at Tongilkak in the northern sector of Panmunjom to prepare for a joint south-north parliamentary meeting.

The gist of the third north Korean letter was as follows:

If the south-north parliamentary talks which the south discusses were to be in the form of a meeting between the limited numbers of several persons and exclude the representatives of other political parties and social organizations and individual persons from various strata, then we cannot recognize it as the proper format of talks suitable to the reality.

Since the south did not mention about agenda topics, we cannot but believe that the south has no particular objection to the agenda topics our side set forth in our two earlier letters. In an effort to open a joint south-north parliamentary session and taking note of the fact that the south agreed in principle to a meeting between the south and north Korean legislatures, we plan to attend a meeting with the south to prepare for a joint session as follows :

(1) Time : 11 am. August 17, 1988
(2) Venue : Tongilkak in the northern sector of Panmunjom
(3) Number of delegates : Three to five legislators
(4) Topics :

• The question of holding the first meeting of the joint session of the south and north Korean legislatures in Pyongyang or Seoul for four nights and five days beginning August 26.
• The question of working-level procedures related thereto. (The venue and time of joint session, procedures for passage through Panmunjom, personal safety, guarantee for conveniences, etc.)

We believe that no lengthy time would be required for the discussion of the question of working-level procedures. We regard a single meeting would suffice.

In a message to the north on August 12, the south counter-proposed that the contact be held on August 19. The south notified the north of the list of its delegates to the preparatory contacts for the south-north parliamentary talks in a telephone message on August 17. On August 18, the north notified the south of the list of its delegates. Thus, an official meeting between south and north Korean parliamentarians was set to be held for the first time in two years and 11 months after the second contact for parliamentary talks was held in September 1985.

List of Delegations to Preparatory Contacts

The South

Chief Delegate : Park Jun-kyu, Democratic Justice Party
Delegate : Lee Han-dong, Democratic Justice Party
Delegate : Kim Bong-ho, party for Peace and Democracy
Delegate : Park Kwan-yong, Reunification Democratic Party
Delegate : Kim Yong-hwan, New Democratic Republican Party

The North

Chief Delegate : Chon Gum-chol, Korean Workers' Party
Delegate : An Byong-su, Korean Workers' Party
Delegate : Li Dong-chol, Korean Workers' Party
Delegate : Li Chu-wung, Korean Social Democratic Party
Delegate : Pak Mun-chan, Chondogyo-Chongwu Party

b. Course of Talks

(1) First Preparatory Contacts

The first preparatory contact for the south-north parliamentary talks was held from 11 a.m. August 19, 1988, with the participation of five delegates from each side. The contact, opened to the public, took place at Tongilkak in the northern sector of Panmunjom.

In his keynote speech, north Korean Chief Delegate Chon Gum-chol repeated what were mentioned in their letters to the south and suggested that the proposed south-north parliamentary talks be held in the form of a "joint conference" attended also by the representatives of political parties and social organizations and even individual persons from various layers and strata. He said the agenda topics should be 1) the question of announcing a joint declaration on nonaggression, and 2) the question of

409

the 24th Olympics and other questions raised by the south to ease tensions. The north's chief delegate then produced a draft agreement on the opening and operation of a joint south-north parliamentary conference which they one-sidedly prepared and demanded a review of the draft agreement. The draft agreement of the north was as follows:

Agreement of Opening and Operating Joint South-North Parliamentary Meeting (Draft)

1. Agenda Topics of Joint Meeting

The agenda topics of the joint meeting shall be the question of announcing a joint declaration on south-north nonaggression and the question of the 24th Olympic Games. Besides, the questions raised by the south that can contribute to easing tensions, and guaranteeing peace in the country shall also be made agenda topics.

2. Venue of Joint Meeting

The joint meeting shall be held in Seoul and Pyongyang in turns. The first joint meeting shall be held in Pyongyang.

3. Scope of Attendees

The joint meeting shall be attended by the entire legislators of the two sides plus 50 representatives of those political parties having no floor seats and social organizations and individual persons in various circles from each side.

4. Time and Duration of the First Joint Meeting

The first joint meeting shall be held on August 26, 1988, and its duration shall be four nights and five days.

5. Procedures for Passage through Military Demarcation Line at Panmunjom

(1) The list of participating parliamentarians, representatives of other political parties and social organizations, individual persons, attendants and press members, which contains their names, sex and occupational positions, shall be forwarded to the other side three days before their entry into the other's area.

(2) The persons who travel to the other side's area in connection with the joint meeting shall carry letters of credence or identification cards issued by the legislature or the speaker of their side.

(3) The point of passage along the Military Demarcation Line for both sides'

410

personnel shall be a building on the Military Demarcation Line at Panmunjom which is in the control of the hosting side.

(4) Travellers of both sides shall follow the guidance and order of the hosting side from the time they crossed the Military Demarcation Line to the time of their return to their area.

6. *Guarantee of Personal Safety*

(1) Both sides shall guarantee the personal safety and inviolable rights of the people of the other side during their stay in their areas.

(2) As a guarantee for personal safety and inviolable rights, relevant offices shall issue an official statement, a copy of which shall be furnished to the other side.

7. *Guarantee of Conveniences*

The hosting side shall guarantee all conveniences for the people staying in the other side's area for the joint meeting, such as transportation and communications means and boarding.

8. *Operational Procedures for Joint Parliamentary Meeting*

(1) A joint meeting shall in principle be opened to the public. If necessary, it may be held behind the closed doors.

(2) The qualification of participants in the joint meeting shall be checked by a Joint Qualification Screening Committee consisting of three persons from each side.

(3) A Joint Steering Committee consisting of five persons from each side shall be formed to ensure the smooth operation of the joint meeting.

(4) The meeting shall be proceeded with the Speakers of the southern and northern legislatures as co-chairmen. The north shall take charge of proceedings when the meeting is held in Pyongyang and the south when it is held in Seoul.

(5) A report or a bill may be advanced by either the south or the north or by a political party represented at the legislatures of the two sides.

(6) Debates shall be made freely by any participant in the meeting under the principles of democracy. However, the number of such debators shall be the same

411

between the two sides.

(7) A decision on a bill debated shall be made under the method of majority rule expressed in hand raising or vote.

(8) The number of the legislators participating in decision-taking shall be the same between the south and the north. The chairman of a meeting shall not participate in voting.

(9) To calculate the results of decision-taking, a Joint Calculation Committee shall be formed with five persons from each of the south and the north.

9. The recording of the proceedings of a meeting shall be made in the form of whatever convenient to each side, such as taperecording, videotaping and stenographing. The hosting side shall assure the other side of necessary taperecording cables.

10. Other issues raised shall be determined between working-level officials prior to the opening of a meeting.

The south's Chief Delegate Park Jun-kyu, in his keynote seech, called for the systematic discussion of the format and agenda topics of the proposed talks, composition of delegations, and the time, venue and procedural matters of the talks.

The gist of Chief Delegate Park's keynote speech was as follows :

In the midst of the international trend toward reform and openness, we now should promote a drastic change in our thinking and perceptions about national issues.

Re-examining the historical significance of the fact that the Seoul Games of the 24th Olympiad, a festival of peace and friendship for all mankind, will take place in this land, the Republic of Korea National Assembly came to the conviction that this must be made into an excellent opportunity to promote south-north reconciliation leading to unification. Thereupon, our Assembly unanimously adopted a resolution calling for your athletes to participate in the Olympics.

We, the parliamentarians, should humbly turn an attentive ear to the nation's wish and expectations for national prosperity and peaceful unification, and endeavor to make the south-north parliamentary talks bear rich fruit.

Our side's position with respect to the proposed south-north parliamentary talks is as follows :

1. The format of the south-north parliamentary talks shall be a meeting between selected delegates.

2. Delegations to the south-north parliamentary talks shall each consist of 20 delegates, a 40-member support staff and 50 members of the press. The chief delegate shall be a senior legislator, appointed by the speaker.

3. The agenda of the south-north parliamentary talks shall consist of the following five topics :

(1) The issue of northern athletes' participation in the 24th Seoul Olympics.

(2) The issue of accelerating personnel and commodity exchanges and cooperation between the south and the north.

(3) The issue of recommending a nonaggression agreement between south and north Korean government authorities.

(4) The question of urging the resumption of the south-north Red Cross talks and the south-north economic meeting.

(5) The question of recommending a south-north summit meeting.

4. Accords reached at the south-north parliamentary talks shall be embodied in a joint agreement and shall then be made public. To ensure the effective operation of the talks, an executive panel or a joint steering committee shall be formed with five delegates from each side.

5. The first meeting of the south-north parliamentary talks shall be held within August in Pyongyang and the second meeting in October in Seoul.

6. The period a delegation stays in the other's area shall be three nights and four days.

7. The precedent set in the past travels back and forth between the south and the north shall apply, with appropriate modifications, to all procedural matters such as procedure for passage between the south and the north and the guarantee of personal safety. Detailed matters related to these procedures shall be discussed and decided on by one working-level delegate from each side.

The south-north parliamentary talks are not intended to be an occasion to bring a large number of people together to have them endorse what the two sides have already agreed on, but are designed to focus on, discuss and resolve, in a sincere manner, the question of Olympic participation and many other issues pending between the south and the north. It is obvious that a delegates meeting is the most appropriate for that purpose.

Beginning 1974, the Republic of Korea has proposed the conclusion of a nonaggression agreement between the authorities of the south and the north. At the south-north parliamentary talks, the two sides should affirm the significance of the need for a south-north nonaggression pact, while leaving concrete and practical matters to the government authorities of the two sides, and urge them to conclude such an agreement.

The keynote speeches of the two chief delegates show that though the two sides agree on the holding of the first meeting in Pyongayng in August, they nevertheless differed seriously on the format and agenda topics of the proposed talks.

North Korea unilaterally concluded as if the two sides agreed, through the exchange of letters, on holding the proposed talks in the format of a joint session, and wanted the discussion only of operational and procedural matters, making the format of a joint session a fait accompli.

The south, while reminding the north that the two sides differed on several issues though they agreed in principle on parliamentary talks, made it clear that at preparatory contacts, the two sides should discuss and resolve the format and agenda topics of the proposed talks, composition of delegations, and the time, venue and other procedural matters of the talks – the issues on which differences of opinions existed.

However, as the two sides discussed these matters, the logic behind the north's initial rejection of the need for preparatory talks proved not justified. The first contact ended without any progress as the contact only saw the two sides put forth their respective basic positions.

As to the format of the proposed talks, the south stressed that the form of selected delegates meeting is reasonable in view of the efficiency and productivity such form entails, and also of the nature of the principle of representative politics. It added that the participation by the representatives of political parties and social organizations and individual people in the prosposed talks is not desirable because the meeting is, in nature, parliamentary talks.

On the issue of agenda topics, the south's delegation observed that in view of the function of the legislature, it would be proper for the proposed talks to recommend a nonaggression agreement between the government authorities of the south and the north. The north, on the other hand, didn't show any sign of backing down from their demand for a joint session and the joint announcement of a nonaggression declaration as suggested in their letters and draft agreement.

In light of the importance and urgency of the topics to be discussed at the parliamentary talks, the south proposed that the second preparatory contact be held at 11 a.m. August 20, 1988, to which north Korea agreed.

(2) Second Preparatory Contact

The second preparatory contact was held at the Peace House in the southern sector of Panmunjom from 11 a.m. August 20, 1988, where discussions were centered on the issues of the format and agenda topics of the proposed talks, on which differences were shown between the two sides.

The south offered a compromise plan on the format and agenda topics of the talks, which broadmindedly reflected even north Korean contentions.

As to the format of the talks, the south again stressed that the format should be selected delegates meeting, a method which, it said, conforms to the basic principle of representative politics. The south offered that when agreements are reached at the proposed talks, they may be endorsed unanimously at the two respective legislatures or, if necessary, a joint session of the two legislatures could be held to reaffirm what were agreed on.

Regarding the issue of agenda topics, too, the south set forth the following modified items in consideration of the north Korean position :

(1) The question of the 24th Olympic Games.

(2) The question of personnel and material exchanges between the south and the north.

(3) The question of south-north nonaggression.

(4) The question of resuming the South-North Red Cross Conference and economic meeting.

(5) The question of holding a south-north summit meeting.

In particular, the idea of making the nonaggression issue, the "question of south-north nonaggression" was motivated in part by the effort of the south to explore what could be taken up at both legislatures in consideration of the position of the north.

On the other hand, the north's delegation simply repeated their past position, rejecting the south's compromise plan as "hardly being anything that can be helpful to resolving problems." They insisted that since both the nonaggression and Olympic issues are the exigent questions, they should be taken up at the joint parliamentary session.

With regard to the format of the talks, the north maintained that a joint session of the two legislatures attended by the whole 954 members of both legislatures is the "minimum necessary session." They further demanded the additional participation by the representatives of political parties and social organizations and individual persons in the joint session.

Toward the close of the second contact, the north advanced a new plan of agenda topics, which included 1) the question of joint declaration on nonaggression, 2) question of the 24th Olympics, more specifically the question of the south's invitation of north Korean athletes to the Olympics and the question of co-hosting the Games, and 3) the question of multi-pronged exchanges and cooperation between the south and the north. But, the north asserted that the issue of exchanges and cooperation can be discussed only when the nonaggression and Olympic issues are debated at a joint session.

The south suggested that the nonaggression-related topic be changed to make it a "question of concluding a nonaggression agreement and making joint declaration of nonaggression." But the north rejected even this modified offer, maintaining it could't accept the idea of a nonaggression agreement.

Pointing out that the opening of the Olympics has drawn very near, the south made an emergency proposal that a south-north parliamentary

meeting be held on August 29 in Pyongyang to urgently discuss and resolve the Olympic issue only. The north, while shunning to make any
direct reaction to the new offer, only insisted on the idea of a joint session.
The two sides were thus unable to reach any agreement.

(3) Third Preparatory Contact

The third preparatory contact was held at Tongilkak in the northern
sector of Panmunjom from 11 a.m. August 22, 1988. At the third contact,
the north tended to concentrate on propagandizing on their idea of "joint
session," while trying to check the south from raising the Olympic issue.

The south's delegation stressed that its compromise plan advanced at
the second contact represented the sincere effort of the south to minimize
mutual differences on the format of the talks, while the presentation of the
modified agenda topics, too, was intended to surmount difficulties stemming form mutual differences on the format of the talks and to wind up
the preparatory contacts at an early date.

The south also said that its proposal for a south-north parliamentary
meeting in Pyongayng on August 29 to urgently discuss and settle the
issue of the 24th Olympics only, was meant to facilitate both the south
and the north's participation in the Seoul Olympiad and thereby provide
a sweeping breakthrough in bringing about national reconciliation.

But the north reiterated that the proposed talks should take the form of
a joint session of the two legislatures. On the issue of topics, too, they
insisted that they couldn't agree to the south-suggested "question of
nonaggression" or "question of concluding a nonaggression agreement and
question of the joint declaration of nonaggression." The north's position
was that the "question of advising government authorities to conclude a
nonaggression agreement" should be scrapped and instead the "question
of adopting a joint declaration of nonaggression" alone should be adopted
as an agenda topic.

The north's delegation also rejected the south's emergency suggestion
that a south-north parliamentary meeting be held within the month of
August to discuss and resolve the Olympic issue on a priority basis,
asserting that the proposed talks were to resolve both the Olympic and

nonaggression issues together.

In particular, in a bid not to let the Olympic issue stand out, the north shunned the debate of the agenda issue and instead concentrated on propagandizing on a "joint session," thus showing that they had little interest in realizing the proposed talks before the Olympics.

Here, the south suggested that since the discussion of the Olympic issue cannot be put aside any further because of the imminency of the Games and since there exists the need to prevent open meetings from becoming propaganda-oriented ones, the two chief delegates hold an exclusive meeting first before the two sides determine various issues.

Reacting to this proposal, the north demanded the determination of the time of the fourth contact before they ended the third contact saying that they would let the south know about their response to the idea of chief delegates meeting.

(4) Chief Delegates Exclusive Contact

Toward the south's proposal made at the third contact for an exclusive contact between two chief delegates, the north suggested in a telephone message around 10:20 a.m. the following day, August 23, that the chief delegates contact be held behind the closed doors at 11 a.m. the same day. The north was giving only a 40 minutes' advance notice and while suggesting a closed-door session wanted the presence of a record taker and two attendants.

Here, the south, noting that the notice was too short, counter-proposed that the chief delegates meeting be held at 11 a.m. August 24, and that each chief delegate be accompanied only by an attendant. Through telephone messages, the two sides finally agreed to hold a chief delegates contact at 11 a.m. August 24 at the Peace House of Panmunjom. The contact between the south's Park Jun-kyu and his northern counterpart, Chon Gum-chol, was thus held for two hours from 11 a.m. August 24, 1988. It was attended by a record taker from each side.

During the contact, the south tried to sound the true intention of the north toward the issue of their participation in the Olympic Games. The north, arguing that their basic stand was to prepare for a joint session,

418

demanded that the south present a new plan.

While making express their negativism toward a selected delegates meeting attended by five to six delegates from each side, the north said that a unanimous decision may be obtained at a joint session through discussions made at sub-committees. The north's chief delegate said he would study further the issue of this format of talks.

The south, believing that the chief delegates contact was not productive, decided to have the fourth preparatory contact. In a subsequent telephone message, the south proposed that the fourth contact be held at the Peace House on August 26.

(5) Fourth Preparatory Contact

The fourth preparatory contact was held at 11 a.m. August 26, 1988, at the Peace House. Pointing out that the two sides shared the recognition that the Olympic issue was the most pressing question, the south reiterated the suggestion that a south-north parliamentary meeting be held in Pyongyang on August 29 with the Olympic issue as an emergency question.

Meanwhile, north Korea produced a revised plan which featured the replacement of a "joint session" with a "combined meeting" and the withholding of their demand for the participation of the representatives of political parties and social organizations and individual persons in the proposed talks. However, the north wanted that the issue of these people's participation be discussed once the proposed talks were convened. In substance, however, the north held fast to their idea of a multitude meeting where the 954 legislators of the south and the north would attend and where decisions are to be made under a majority rule.

On the issue of nonaggression, too, the north simply repeated their position that the "question of announcing a joint declaration on nonaggression" alone should be adopted as an agenda topic and that the Olympic issue should be discussed together with the nonaggression question.

The south suggested that since the deadline for final Olympic entries was only a week away, a parliamentary meeting be held as soon as possible to openheartedly discuss the issue of north Korean athletes' participation in the Seoul Olympics. But the north insisted that the Olympic issue should be resolved under the method of a majority rule at a combined meeting where the whole legislators of the two sides attend.

Here, believing that the north was not interested after all in resolving Olympic issue within August, the south proposed that the fifth preparatory contact be held in early October after the Seoul Olympics was over. The south's delegation added that if the north can agree to the offer that a parliamentary meeting be held in Pyongyang on August 29 with the Olympic question as an emergency topic, the south was willing to resume the contacts at any time.

The north suggested that the fifth contact be held on October 13, which the south agreed to. The fifth contact was thus decided to be held on October 13, 1988.

(6) Fifth Preparatory Contact

The fifth preparatory contact was held at 10 a.m. October 13, 1988, at Tongilkak, where the two sides produced revised plans on the issue of the format of the proposed talks.

The north's delegation suggested that the format of the talks should be a combined meeting attended by a sharply reduced number of legislators. Their new idea was that the attendees should be one third (218 persons) of the total delegates to the Supreme People's Assembly of the north and half (150) of the National Assembly of the south.

But the reduction in attendees was made as they pleased without any justifiable ground. They still adhered to the essential elements of a "joint session," insisting on, for instance, the method of a majority rule.

Here, the south's delegation offered a new plan as follows, which could ensure the effectiveness and productivity of talks and which, at the same time, accommodated much of the north's position.

(1) The south-north parliamentary talks shall be held in the order of an opening meeting, a selected delegates meeting to discuss agenda, and a closing meeting.

(2) The opening and closing meetings shall be in the form of joint session where the entire south and north Korean legislators shall attend, while agenda topics shall be discussed at a meeting in the format of a selected delegates meeting.

(3) At an opening meetng, various matters agreed on at preparatory contacts shall be affirmed ; delegates selected for the discussion of agenda topics shall be introudced ; and the speakers of both sides shall deliver opening speeches. The opening meeting shall be held within one month after the end of preparatory contacts in Pyongyang.

(4) At a selected delegates meeting to discuss agenda, introduced agenda topics shall be discussed and a joint resolution including the topics of the parliamentary talks shall be prepared under a mutual agreement. Delegates to a selected delegates meeting shall be in an optimum number agreed on between the two sides, which shall meet in Seoul and Pyongyang in turns. The first selected delegates meeting shall be held immediately after the holding of an opening meeting.

(5) A closing meeting shall affirm and adopt a joint resolution agreed on at the selected delegates meetings, which shall be held in Seoul within one month after the end of the selected delegates meetings to discuss agenda topics.

(6) The opening and closing meetings shall be held under co-chairmanship. A meeting shall be presided over by the speaker of the hosting side.

North Korea even rejected this flexible idea of the south, which called for the travel back and forth between Seoul and Pyongyang by the entire legislators of the south and the north. North Korea simply made remarks not related to the talks, saying, for instance, "A serious situation is being formented on the Korean peninsula." They argued that the opening and closing meetings cannot represent the opinions of the entire legislators.

Meanwhile, with regard to the agenda issue, the south offered new agenda topics, which were 1) the question of personnel and commodity exchanges between the south and the north, including the issue of resuming the Red Cross and economic meetings, 2) the question of south-north

421

nonaggression, and 3) the question of holding a south-north summit meeting.

The south's Chief Delegate Park stressed, "Since the highest officials of the two sides have already recognized the need of a summit meeting and even mentioned about the topics of a summit meeting, the legislators of the south and the north should assist in the realization of a summit meeting."

Regarding the question of nonaggression, the south said that it is beyond the duty of delegations to define the contents and nature of nonaggression at preparatiory contacts, adding that the two sides sould not be bound by such phrases as "agreement," "declaration," "advising" and "delegating."

However, the north made it express that they would eliminate the discussion of a summit issue, and that the "question of announcing a joint declaration on nonaggression" was something they could not back down from. They contended that the seven-point nonaggression declaration they drafted should be the basic substance of a declaration.

Moreover, asserting that there are a "fake nonaggression" and a "genuine nonaggression," the north insisted that a nonaggression declaration which does not reflect their draft version cannot but be a "fake" one.

Even at the fifth contact held immediately after the Seoul Olympics, the two sides failed to iron out their differences. The north showed insincerity toward the realization of the proposed parliamentary talks, stating that there is no need to have next contact in a hurry. At the end, the two sides agreed to hold the sixth preparatory contact on November 17.

(7) Sixth Preparatory Contact

The sixth preparatory contact was held for about three hours and ten minutes including a 30-minute recess beginning 10 a.m. November 17, 1988, at the Peace House in the southern sector of Panmunjom. During the contact, an agreement was reached for the first time since the initiation of the preparatory contacts concerning the format of the proposed parliamentary talks.

The agreement was that the parliamentary talks would be held in the order of an opening meeting, a main meeting to discuss agenda topics and a closing meeting. They agreed that the opening and closing meetings would be attended by the entire south and north Korean legislators and the main meeting by 50 delegates from each side.

With regard to the format of the talks, the south's delegation reiterated the revised six-point proposal suggested at the fifth contact concerning the issue of agenda topics, the south offered to change the topic of the "question of south-north nonaggression" into the "question of south-north nonaggression declaration" in an effort to accommodate the north's position.

The offer of the modified topic by the south was motivated by the fact that the authorities of both sides have already spoken of "nonaggression declaration" as one of the topics of a possible summit meeting, and also by the forward-looking policies of the south to dispel the ground of any dispute over wording and thus to realize the proposed talks at an early date. And the south's basic stand was to have south and north Korean politicians jointly resolve on their determination toward the basic direction of a nonaggression declaration to be adopted between the south and the north, namely, mutual nonaggression, noninterference and the peaceful solution of disputes and have them recommend the government authorities of the two sides to adopt a nonaggression declaration at an early date.

Reacting to these ideas presented by the south, the north's Chief Delegate Chon Gum-chol offered an idea very close to the south's, at least on the surface, by changing their insistence and now suggesting that the proposed talks be divided into an opening meeting, a selected delegates meeting to discuss basic issues and a closing meeting.

The substance of north Korean suggestion was as follows :

– Opening Meeting –

To be held within one month after the completion of the preparatory contacts with the attendance of the entire body of south and north Korean legislators.

Confirmation of matters agreed on at the preparatory contacts, announcement of the list of delegates to a selected delegates meeting, opening speeches by the speakers of the two sides, and congratulatory speeches by the representatives of political parties and individual persons of the two sides.

– Meeting to Discuss Basic Issues –

Shall be held in the form of a selected delegates meeting attended by 100 persons from each side.

The first selected delegates meeting shall be held in Seoul within one month after an opening meeting was held. Afterwards, selected delegates meetings shall be held in Seoul and Pyongyang in turns.

An executive section shall be formed with the representatives of various political parties of the two sides to discuss and adjust differences shown at a selected delegates meeting.

A joint steering committee shall be formed with five delegates from each side to discuss the issue of operational procedures.

Final agreement shall be in the form of a "unanimous agreement," and agreed matters shall be prepared in a written agreement.

– Closing Meeting –

Shall be held within one month after selected delegates meetings were completed, attended by the entire body of south and north Korean legislators.

A written joint agreement shall be affirmed by applause.

In the course of the discussions, the north offered to reduce the number of the delegates to selected delegates meetings from 100 to 50 from each side. It also suggested that an executive section be formed with the same number of delegates from each side, and the proposed talks be operated under the method of mutual agreement.

Despite the superficial nearing of an accord, the north's delegation attached dual logic regarding the selected delegates meetings, showing much difference over basic matters. The north insisted that the selected delegates meetings should be in the form of a meeting by association instead of a bilateral meeting, and operated under the method of "unanimous agreement" based on the principle of majority vote.

They argued that under the "unanimous agreement" system, it would be taken as an "agreement" when an extremely small number of delegates voiced opposition but the absolute majority concurred. This couldn't but be an ambiguous idea.

Ths south's position was that considering the reality and unique conditions of the inter-Korean relationship, agreements should be worked out on all the issues pending between the south and the north through talks taking the form of bilateral meeting. On the other hand, north Korea stuck to their past insistence that each of the delegates to the selected delegates meetings should have a voting right with problems decided on by a majority vote.

On the agenda issue, north Korea showed, at least at that time, an affirmative response to the south's idea of the "question of south-north nonaggression declaration." They argued, however, that in substance the question should contain the issue of the withdrawal of alien forces from Korea.

The sixth preparatory contact thus ended by affirming the differences existing between the south and the north. Yet the two sides could reach a substantial accord on several matters, adding to the expectation for the success of the proposed south-north parliamentary talks.

The two sides agreed to hold the seventh preparatory contact on December 15, 1988.

6. Proposal for a South-North Summit Meeting

In his message on the 43rd anniversary of national liberation on August 15, 1988, President Roh Tae-woo proposed that he and President Kim Il-sung of north Korea meet as soon as possible to discuss ways to promote practically the integration of the Korean nation in response to the yearning of the 60 million Korean people.

President Roh especially stressed that "neither the venue nor the agenda nor the procedures should be an obstacle to the meeting of the top leaders of the south and the north designed to open-heartedly discuss the future of the nation."

His proposal for a south-north summit conference stemmed from his conviction that the question of durable peace and peaceful unification on the Korean peninsula cannot be put off any further and that the overall environment for unification has turned to buttress the feasibility of unification.

At the same time, the offer amounted to the manifestation of the President's strong will to express his genuine intentions to the north and enable them to join in the efforts to form a national community by taking initiatives, from the top leadership level, in putting into action his July 7 special declaration in which he articulated his plan to pursue prosperity for the entire Korean people under the recognition of both the south and the north being the same people and part of the same national community.

Considering the fact that the south and the north have persisted on confrontation and enmity against each other over some 40 years, a meeting between the top leaders of the south and the north itself could constitute a decisive breakthrough in dispelling mutual distrust and paving the way to exchanges and cooperation.

Moreover, as shown in the course of past dialogue, important and complex problems that require the political decision of the top leaders of both sides lie between the south and the north. An open-hearted dialogue between the top leaders of the two sides is a method that can resolve such delicate and conflicting inter-Korean problems most effectively and speedily.

To this proposal, the north's Kim Il-sung made a personal response at a congratulatory reporting session held on September 8, one day before the 40th anniversary of their regime on September 9. In a speech at the session, Kim Il-sung, using the words "south-north coexistence," said that the north would welcome it if (the south Korean president) visits Pyongyang with the intent of adopting a nonaggression declaration and of establishing the confederal government of a unified country or establishing a "peaceful unification committee" to prepare for such a confederal government, at a south-north top leaders meeting. This way, Kim Il-sung mentioned even the topic and site of a proposed summit meeting.

In the same speech, he said that "the south Korean people, carrying high an anti-American and independent banner, are staging a more organized and popular struggle." He then attached a prerequisite to a top leaders meeting by maintaining, "To make ripe the atmosphere for a south-north summit meeting, south Korean authorities should join in a nationwide movement for the independent peaceful unification of the homeland, coming away from their dependence on alien forces."

Kim Il-sung went on to say that "to ensure peace on the Korean peninsula, a peace agreement should be concluded between the north and the United States ; a nonaggression declaration adopted between the south and the north ; American troops and nuclear weapons withdrawn from south Korea ; and the south and the north should drastically reduce their armed forces on a phased basis."

By thus adhering to persistent posture favoring the priority resolution of military issues, Kim Il-sung's speech was suggestive of the fact that there has been no change whatsoever in Pyongyang's basic strategy against the south.

Nonetheless, the south decided to study carefully the north Korean response inasmuch as it was the Seoul government that called for an unconditional south-north summit meeting first and because of its policy to desist from the past practice of coping with such a response from the north rather passively. In a comment on September 10, National Unification Minister Lee Hong-koo said that he noticed that the top north Korean leader himself made the response directly. He said that though it was regrettable that the north reiterated a series of their demands as a prerequisite to a top leaders meeting, the south would carefully study various ways to realize a south-north summit meeting.

Meanwhile, President Roh, in his policy speech at the 144th regular National Assembly session on October 4, 1988, after the Seoul Olympics, once again called for a south-north summit meeting, saying that he was willing to visit Pyongyang personally and that a summit meeting could discuss open-heartedly without any conditions the issue of making a nonaggression declaration and of realizing unification of the homeland and all other questions raised by the two sides.

President Roh thus showed a flexible and accommodative stance that even the topics proposed by the north could be discussed, a posture that was based on the conviction that a south-north summit meeting should be held at an early date so as to provide a turning-point for national reconciliation and unification.

Even toward this renewed call by the President, north Korea, in a statement released by the Committee for the Peaceful Reunification of the Fatherland on October 14, 1988, showed an inflexible stance as ever, advocating the so-called concept of "conditions and atmosphere," in which they demanded that the south should first agree to hold a south-north politico-military meeting and a joint south-north conference, agree to adopt a nonaggression declaration, repeal the National Security Law, etc.

President Roh's will to materialize a south-north summit meeting was reaffirmed in his address made at the United Nations General Assembly on October 18, 1988. In the speech, the President said he expects he would be able to visit Pyongyang at the soonest possible time, stressing that the two sides should explore a joint basis on which to systematize peace on the Korean peninsula and forge a single national community through open-hearted discussions between the two sides.

What was especially noteworthy was that President Roh, going a step farther than the position that the south was willing to discuss a nonaggression declaration issue, proposed in the speech that the two sides agree on nonaggression or non-use of arms and declare such an agreement jointly. In particular, the President declared before the international community that even before a nonaggression declaration is made between the two sides of Korea, the south would not be the first to use arms against the north under any circumstances.

While coping with the north's demand for a "prior resolution of military issues" in such a forward-looking and flexible manner, President Roh, in a bid to make the proposed summit meeting more practicable, said in the speech that a summit meeting could discuss and resolve the issues of preparing a systematic apparatus to facilitate durable peace on the Korean peinsula, realizing national unification, promoting exchanges and coopertion between the south and the north, military issues like an arms reduction and other problems to be raised by the two sides.

The proposal for a south-north summit meeting made under the Sixth Republic was different in its significance from those made in the past. The offer was advanced in consideration of higher feasibility of a summit in view of the new flow of national history.

7. Initiatives for Openness and Reconciliation

a. Pursuit of Age of Democracy, Prosperity and Unification

In a policy address at the 144th regular plenary National

Assembly session on October 4, 1988, President Roh Tae-woo set forth the new national vision of creating an "age of democracy, prosperity and unification" based on the national ability amplified through the successful staging of the Seoul Olympics.

President Roh then laid down as the immediate national goals political and social democratization, promotion of advanced harmonious economy, laying a foundation for unification through national integration, positive promotion of a northern policy, and the inheritance and development of national culture.

In this way, the President expressed the firm determination to develop the achievements the south has made in various sectors in the past 40-odd years into a yet new stage in a bid to pave the way to the realization of an advanced unified country taking advantage of favorable changes in the atmosphere for unification and the successful implementation of a northern policy.

President Roh's policy speech was focused on exploring a path toward achieving a unified national country of a type that can effectively cope with the advent of a new century while calling again for a south-north summit meeting as a positive way of taking the lead in engineering the new wave of openness and reconciliation and bringing the age of south-north exchanges and cooperation onto a full track.

– Plan for a New Unification Idea –

Also in the policy address, President Roh presented a plan to work out a new idea for national unification. The President said, "Our goal is to realize a unified country in which all our people could lead happy lives enjoying freedom and basic human rights and in which our national community can prosper and develop forever. A unification idea should be the kind which both sides could accept and translate into action rather than being based on either side's narrow-minded cold war logic. In this respect, I think we can affirmatively accommodate those from among the varying unification ideas and those advanced by the north which can be considered to be conducive to unification."

The government of the Republic of Korea produced in the July 7 Special Declaration the direction of the basic policy of the Sixth Republic toward the inter-Korean relationship and unification. It also had taken a set of follow-up measures to embody the spirit of the special declaration. These unification efforts exerted by the Sixth Republic were focused on ending a hostile and competitive relationship with north Korea and sharing the new recognition that the south and the north, being parts of the same national community, should be in the state of good-intentioned partnership relations.

In this respect, the President's pronouncement of a plan to prepare a new unification idea was based on the positive government efforts to liberalize debate concerning the unification issue and thereby broadly sample public opinion. The pronouncement also represented the determination of the government to design the future composition of a national community in an age of south-north exchanges and cooperation.

The pronounced plan to prepare a new unification idea was thus significant in that it would duly take into consideration the need to develop the national consensus on the perception of inter-Korean relationship and the process of unification into part of government policies, and would bring the unavoidability for north Korea to come forward to the square of unification.

Therefore, the projected new unification idea would become a great charter that would provide a new breakthrough in the south-north relations as it would fully reflect the opinions of various sectors of the nation and would involve forward-looking and practical elements even accommodating the position of north Korea.

– Call for a Summit Meeting –

In his policy address, President Roh, calling for the early holding of a south-north summit meeting, said that "a meeting between south and north Korean top officials itself would become a turning-point in promoting national reconciliation and unification."

By stating that even the issue of a nonaggression declaration can be discussed in favor of the resolution of more fundamental questions at a summit meeting, the President made it clear that his call for a summit was not for a superficial purpose but for the provision of a genuine turning-point in the materialization of national unification.

– Acceleration of the Northern Policy –

President Roh disclosed a positive and forward-looking policy to improve relations with China, the Soviet Union and East European countries. Since his inauguration, President Roh has consistently stressed that all world countries should maintain normal relations on the principles of reciprocity and equality with one another and pursue common interests and prosperity. It was under this policy that the President positively promoted the establishment of normal relations with Communist-bloc countries including China and the Soviet Union.

This positive northern policy paid off handsomely during the Seoul Olympics in 1988. With the Seoul Olympics as the momentum, socialist countries began to have positive exchanges with the south, sending cultural missions to and establishing permanent trade offices in Seoul, not to mention their participation in the Seoul Games transcending the barrier of ideologies.

In particular, as USSR General Secretary Gorbachev expressly hinted as his policy to improve relations with south Korea in his speech made in Krasnoyarsk, the USSR showed a cooperative stance toward the south's northern policy.

Meanwhile, the south's northern policy has enlisted full concurrence from most of socialist countries especially because it was not intended to isolate north Korea from the rest of the world. In fact, one of the ultimate goals of the northern policy is to prompt north Korea to open itself up, ease tensions between the two sides and promote conditions for national unification from the approach of seeking national co-prosperity. This was made clear when the President stated in his policy address that he hoped socialist countries would maintain better relations with north Korea and help develop the north.

Thus seen, it is express that the northern policy is to restore and develop a national community and thereby broaden the sphere of the Koreans' activities into the whole world, a policy which is closely linked to the effort to realize national unification.

The northern policy of the Republic of Korea is expected to be promoted more broadly and positively than before in the future. And such a policy effort should be understood not from the context of reaping profits through economic exchanges but from the aspect of improving the inter-Korean relationship.

All these indicate that President Roh's policy address put forth a far-reaching plan to construct a new national community and a policy guideline to materialize the construction. This forward-looking unification and foreign policies of the Sixth Republic are expected to help north Korea remove their sense of isolation and crisis, thus contributing to unfolding an age of south-north partnership pursuing co-existence and co-prosperity.

Of course, there need phased preparations for the north's openness. For this reason, in particular, the disclosure in the policy address of a resolute policy to improve the inter-Korean relations and promote a northern policy, would serve to prompt the north to reduce their distrust of and scepticism about the south, contributing much to the laying of a new foundation for the joint entry into the age of south-north reconciliation.

b. Road to Reconciliation and Unification

President Roh Tae Woo delivered an address, "Road to Reconciliation and Unification on the Korean Peninsula" at the 43rd United Nations General Assembly session on October 18, 1988, attended by delegates from 159 UN member countries to become the first Korean president ever to speak at the world organization. The address was significant all the more because it was made in a year that happened to be the 40th anniversary of the founding of the Republic.

President Roh's address is expected to go down in history for long especially since the speech was to address to the whole world the Koreans message of reconciliation and hope against the backdrop of south Korea, a non-UN member nation, enjoying a sharply elevated standing in the world community. The address also took place at a time when the Koreans confidently look forward to the advent of an age of national reconciliation and inter-Korean exchanges and cooperation on the Korean peninsula as well as to world peace and the stability of the power structure in Northeast Asia in the 21st century.

In particular, the Presidential address was significant because in the speech the President, following his July 7 special declaration, made another epochal proposal for a systematic apparatus for durable peace in Northeast Asia as well as for a new turning-point in the realization of independent national integration at a time of a growing trend toward a new East-West detente, openness, exchanges, cooperation and reconciliation.

In short, the address presented a new policy guideline in which the Korean people, who, being victims of the Cold War system and who still suffer from the pains of division, have come to take positive initiatives on their own to liquidate such Cold War legacies and to play a positive role in the worldwide trend toward reconciliation and openness.

The manifestation of the Koreans' confidence in reconciliation and peace and their determination to put an end to the Cold War mechanism has earned the trust and expectations of all the world's people.

President Roh laid down a new and practical method of approach toward altering the confrontation mechanism in Northeast Asia into a system for stability and cooperation, and toward providing a breakthrough in the improvement of the inter-Korean relationship. Above all, the address served to enable all the world's people to better understand the inter-linkage between the world peace and unification atmosphere on the Korean peninsula, thereby contributing to opening a new horizon for the nation's diplomacy.

The background and major features of President Roh's address at the United Nations General Assembly session were as follows.

– Realization of Reconciliation and Unification –

The 43rd General Assembly of the United Nations adopted the Korean question as one of its agenda topics for the first time in 13 years, the topic being titled, "Acceleration of Peace, Reconciliation and Dialogue on the Korean Peninsula." This suggested that the Korean question, while being a task that has to be resolved by the Koreans' own initiatives, cannot but be linked to world peace.

Accordingly, in his address, President Roh clearly reminded the attendees that the tragedy of Korea's division was caused by the joint occupation of Korea by the world powers against the will of the Koreans, thereby enabling the world powers to share the sense of responsibility for the resolution of the Korean question. In this way, the President prompted the world powers to be concerned about the Cold War mechanism that still remains on the Korean peninsula amidst the flow of East-West detente as displayed in the Seoul Olympics while inducing universal concurrence on the need for reconciliation and peace on the Korean peninsula.

At the same time, President Roh conveyed the Seoul Olympic spirit of "Harmony and Progress" to the world community, expressing confidence that such a spirit would spread to every corner and nook of the world becoming the seed of optimism among all mankind.

In addition, President Roh noted that human society has come away from the yoke of the Cold War mechanism and is being guided by the tenets of reason and wisdom into a new order of reconciliation, pointing out that in this context the world should unfold a new horizon of reconciliation, co-existence and co-prosperity and peace through positive openness, exchanges and cooperation.

With the President's address at the United Nations in which he offered the vision of a new future world order, Korea has attained the image of being a peace-oriented country playing a positive role in paving the way to peace in Northeast Asia and the world. Korea has thus become the symbol of courage and hope among other developing countries.

The Presidential address was based on the Koreans' pride and confidence and firm belief in the flow of history moving toward openness and detente, and embodied a strong will to develop such pride and confidence into the momentum for realizing peace and unification on the Korean peninsula.

– Idea of Consultative Conference for Peace in Northeast Aisa –

In his address at the UN General Assembly, President Roh proposed a consultative conference for peace in Northeast Asia to lay a solid · foundation for durable peace and prosperity in Northeast Asia. President Roh especially stressed, "Clearly the problems between the north and south Korean sides must be dealt with and resolved by the independent efforts of the Korean people themselves. But due to Korea's geopolitical situation, the problem of a durable peace on the Korean peninsula cannot be considered in total isolation from its relations with the surrounding nations." He added that in order for durable peace to prevail on the Korean peninsula, both south and north Korea should build and maintain more rational and normal relations with all the nations that have interests in peace on the Korean peninsula.

In other words, President Roh's idea was to seek to ensure durable peace on the Korean peninsula through both strengthened national independent ability and positive international cooperation in order to achieve the dual goals of durable peace and national unification on the Korean peninsula.

The idea of a consultative conference for peace in Northeast Asia was intended to pursue peace and prosperity in the Pacific area by transforming the mechanism of confrontation in the Northeast Asian area into a structure of stability, cooperation and peace, while fostering an international environment conducive to the Koreans' own resolution of the Korean question.

Therefore, the Presidential idea was part of multi-pronged efforts of the nation to plant the universal order of detente in the Northeast Asian zone rather than being a mere effort to prepare a systematic apparatus limited only to the Korean peninsula.

The proposed consultative conference for peace in Northeast Asia differed basically in content and nature from the four-party or a six-party conference, which were proposed in the past in connection with the Korean question. Whereas the past ideas of multilateral conference were limited to the Korean question only and time-limited supplementary devices in nature, the latest idea called for the creation of a permanent consultative organization entrusted with the duty to deal comprehensively issues regarding the whole of Northeast Asia and, at the same time, to promote direct negotiations between south and north Korea.

Moreover, the idea sought to create a regional consultative body beyond the dimension of any bloc organization, as it was designed to discuss regional peace and prosperity among regional countries under the principle of mutual respect and reciprocity and based on a partnership relationship.

The proposal for a consultative conference for peace in Northeast Asia could not but be a highly forward-looking overture in that it sought to pool the basic direction of surrounding countries pursuing openness and cooperation transcending changing situations or ideologies and also in that it intended to provide a way for the north to develop.

– Construction of City of Peace –

President Roh further proposed the construction of a city of peace in the Demilitarized Zone dividing the south and the north of Korea. The President suggested that "in such a city of peace, separated family members could freely reunite, and broad trade and other kinds of exchanges could be facilitated by establishing in the new city of peace such venues as a home for national culture, a center for scholarly exchanges, and a trade center."

One of the ideas to embody reconciliation and unification on the Korean peninsula, the "city of peace" plan was intended to provide a momentum to facilitate personnel and material exchanges between the south and the north. If and when exchanges were materialized briskly through the city of peace, it would constitute a small national community transcending difference in ideologies and systems and headed toward a unified homeland, and could be opened to the rest of the world as a "pilot peace zone."

In this context, a city of peace would be conducive to expanding the sphere of various activities to create a national community and would play a symbolic role as the venue of inter-Korean exchanges, cooperation, dialogue and contacts.

– Determination to Realize Summit Meeting –

In his address at the United Nations General Assembly following his policy speech at the National Assembly on Octover 4, President Roh expressed a firm determination to promote a south-north summit meeting. The Republic of Korea has thereby uplifted the issue of a south-north summit meeting itself to the arena of international politics, and, at the same time, paved the way to laying a "basic frame" in which the state of military confrontation that persisted in the past 30 or so years can be transformed into the relationship of mutual trust and common existence and prosperity on the Korean peninsula.

The President's remarks that all inter-Korean issues including such military matters as arms reduction and nonaggression declaration could be discussed at a summit meeting, indicate that the President accommodated much of north Korean contentions. This was all the more so in view of the fact that in the past the south maintained that military issues could be resolved only on the condition of the full restoration of mutual trust first (See Section 6, Chapter 3).

The address made by President Roh before the UN General Assembly significantly served to produce, as the President of a new-born nation which hosted the 1988 Olympics most successful in history and which proved the superiority of the liberal democratic system, a concrete blueprint of an idea to realize peaceful unification on the Korean peninsula at the arena of world politics.

Appendices

1. President Park's "August 15 Declaration"

(President Park's address delivered on August 15, 1970, commemorating the 25th anniversary of National Liberation)

Exactly a quarter-century ago today, people celebrated our nation's liberation in unparalleled emotion and joy.

Twenty-five years ago today, waving Taegeuk flags decorated every town and village of our land, and resounding cheers of joy for freedom and liberation echoed throughout the country. We rejoiced over the revival of our nation, and pledged to build a new and glorious national history with genuine patriotism and without a trace of selfish interest of motive.

Liberated from oppression and subjugation, and regaining our lost country, we, the Korean people, firmly resolved that we would never repeat what our forefathers had suffered. The elation and burning passion of our people for realization of the lofty dream of a new, prosperous nationhood will forever remain an inextinguishable beacon in our hearts.

Twenty-five years have now passed since that day. This quarter century can be compared to the approach to maturity in a man's life after passing through the stages of infancy, childhood and adolescence. I think a quarter-century also represents a landmark in history, where a serious appraisal has to be made on the growth of a people and a nation.

Once again, we are overwhelmed by profound emotion on this anniversary of national liberation, when the image of a mature Korea is proudly shown to the world.

The history of liberated Korea for the past twenty-five years is, in brief, a period unparalleled for its storms, full of sufferings and tribulations.

Just as the joyful elation over national liberation burst overnight like a bubble in the shock and tragedy of the division of the country, so

443

hope and expectation for prosperity dispersed like a floating cloud in the merciless war started by the north Korean Communists.

Furthermore, the confusion and stagnation which followed the establishment of our Government resulted twice in political convulsions.

For us, who did not then have the capability to understand and cope with all the implications of the fact that the liberation was not won by ourselves, but was brought about by others, these trials and pains may be considered unavoidable.

These sufferings, however, have not been in vain. We have neither faltered in the face of tragedy nor surrendered to tribulation.

The inherent potential of our nation, strong and determined, which had successfully met numerous internal and external challenges with firm resolution throughout our long history, preserving the independence of our fatherland, has gradually begun to re-emerge full blown in the process of overcoming our trials and tribulations.

It was in the past decade of the sixties that the dormant vital and creative power, kindled by a germinating national consciousness, created a historic turning point with an array of advancing columns for national resurrection.

During the past eight or nine years, we have concentrated all our efforts on the task of modernization of our country, and have harvested many achievements.

Thus today, the whole world looks upon our people with respect and admiration, in a new recognition that the war-torn Korea of the 1950's has become an exemplary model of the development of emerging countries.

Rather than the visible accomplishment itself, what I think most valuable and worthy of pride is the re-discovery, in the process of this achievement, of the limitless power of our people, and the newly-won confidence that we can accomplish any great task with our own will and efforts.

We have now entered the 1970's, the decade of our mission to achieve without fail the national resurrection which started in the sixties.

444

At this moment, when a new chapter of history beginning another quarter-century is about to start, we must renew our determination never to repeat past failures, and to strengthen our sense of mission to leave a worthwhile legacy to our posterity.

Dear Brethren!

Today, on this occasion of the twenty-fifth anniversary of liberation, there is one thing over which you and I all share pain and sadness : that is none other that the tragedy of the division of our country.

The national aspiration for unification has never left our thoughts, even for a minute, in the past quarter of century. Yet we still live with the realization that the prospect for unification cannot be said to be bright, that the path is beset with many difficulties and roadblocks.

Why is this? Briefly, it is because a group of national traitors led by Kim Il-sung and his clique have been occupying the northern part of Korea.

This fanatic and militant group of the north Korean Communists has persistently attempted to communize the whole of Korea by force ever since the day of the liberation of our country.

It is this very group of Communists who launched unprovoked aggression against the south on June 25, 1950, committing merciless fratricide. Since the armistice, they have perpetrated more than 7,800 incidents of armed provocation and recently sent a large number of armed agents deep into the south. These facts provide material proof of their sinister intentions.

Doubtlessly, Kim Il-Sung and his clique are war criminals who should be put to the rigorous judgments of history and the nation.

Nevertheless, this clique has repeatedly engaged in unscrupulous stereotyped propaganda campaigns, advocating "peaceful unification," "north-south negotiations," a "federal system," "mutual exchanges," etc.

The intention of the north Korean Communists is as clear as daylight: Obviously, it is the evil design of criminals attempting to place on

445

their intended victims the responsibility for the criminal acts and the heightened tensions which are of their own making. It is nothing less than a wicked maneuver to disguise or conceal their dispatch of armed agents, and to induce an upsurge of sentiment for unification by confusing some naive people. It is, furthermore, a debased calculation aimed at misleading international opinion.

Certainly, no one on earth should believe such deceitful subterfuges of the north Korean Communists.

The political system of communism is a totalitarian dictatorship by a single party that relies on the violation of basic human rights and the iron discipline. North Korea under the Kin Il-sung group, above all, is a closed society where the idolization of one individual prevails, typified by extreme leftist adventurism and the fabrication of history, thus inviting disdain and contempt even among the Communist bloc itself.

The northern part of Korea is now reduced to a military camp, fanatically gripped with war preparations, where despotism and terror predominate.

In the face of this wicked group of armed provocateurs who so want only slight history, the nation, human morals and conscience, we find ourselves in a difficult situation to deal with the question of unification.

Here lies the obstacle impeding the greatest aspiration of our whole nation, the unification of our fatherland.

Even though it is a supreme mandate for our people to achieve unification, we must, however, avoid a war that would exact the wholesale bloodshed of our people.

No matter how tortuous and treacherous the road to unification may be, we must work for a peaceful settlement with unrestrained patience and utmost wisdom.

At the same time, we must keep in mind that we should not be negligent in developing our strength to repel resolutely any armed aggression by the criminal Kim Il-sung and his clique, who refuse to give up their evil scheme for unification and communization of the country by force.

I have said on several occasions, that it might be in the latter part of the 1970's that major efforts could be made for unification.

This is because we hope that, by that time, our strengthened national capacity and the ripening of international conditions could help us unravel the entanglements of the unification question; and especially because we are confident that even the closed social system in the north would also undergo changes from the wave of liberalization, which is the tide of the times, and that the influence of our freedom would overflow into the north.

With this prospect over the coming years, I would like to take this opportunity, on this significant day marking a quarter-century of liberation, to present my thoughts on methods of approach, in the interest of laying the groundwork for peaceful unification.

These are the prerequisite that must be fulfilled. No approach toward unification by peaceful means is feasible without the easing of tensions.

As long as the north Korean Communists persist in the type of aggressive and provocative acts in which they are now engaged, whatever they profess, it is nothing but a disguise, camouflage or fraud.

Therefore, such an approach should be proceded above all by an unequivocal expression of changed attitude by the north Korean Communists, assuring the easing of tensions and followed by its implementation.

Accordingly, the north Korean Communists should desist forthwith from perpetrating all sorts of military provocations, including the dispatch of armed agents into the south, and make a public announcement that they henceforth renounce their policies for communizing the whole of Korea by force and overthrowing the Republic of Korea by means of violent revolution. And they must prove their sincerity by deeds.

If the north Korean Communists accept and comply in deeds with the prerequisites and the United Nations clearly verifies this, I would be prepared to suggest epochal and more advanced measures with a view to removing, step by step, various artificial barriers existing between the south and the north, in the interest of laying the ground-

447

work for unification and on the basis of humanitarian considerations.

Furthermore, if and when the north Korean Communists recognize the United Nations' efforts for the achievement of a unified, democratic and independent Korea and for peace on the Korean peninsula, and accept unepuivocally the competence and authority of the United Nations, we would then not be opposed to the north Korean Communists presence at the United Nations deliberation of the Korean question.

I would like to pose a question : Are the north Korean Communists interested in participating in a competition – a bona fide competition in development, in construction and in creativity – to prove which system, democracy of Communist totalitarianism, can provide better living for the people, and which society is a better place to live in, instead of committing any longer the crime of war preparations at the sacrifice of the welfare of our innocent brethren in the north?

My dear brethren at home and abroad!

This year is close to the centennial anniversary of the time when we opened our doors to the world in the later part of the last century. During the past century, our nation has gone through a series of difficulties, aggravated by retardation, subjugation, war and confusion.

However, our nation has endured such ordeals well and has overcome them, and now before us dawns a morning of national resurrection. It may not be too much to say that this is, indeed, the last opportunity for our national resurrection.

Also, we might well keep in mind that in another twenty-five years or so this century will be close to its end. No one can predict precisely what the world will be like around 2000 A.D., or where the Republic of Korea will stand at that time.

Nevertheless, having achieved unification long before, our country by then ought to have become a strong nation-state, and an affluent and advanced welfare state, with everyone enjoying prosperity; it should have become a respected member of the international community, participating in and contributing to the mainstream of world progress.

Now is the time for steady preparation. Thus the present decade, which links the past with the future in our modern histoty, is a critical period in which the success or failure of national resurrection will be determined. The achievement of national resurrection in this decade will hinge upon whether we can mobilize our resources for productive purposes.

Notional unity and the mobilization of resources – these are certainly the keys to national resurrection.

It is only national unity which will ensure the attainment of our immediate tasks : namely, a self-sustaining national economy and a self-reliant national defense. It is also our strength of unity which will achieve the national aspiration of unification of the country.

On the every day of that national unification which we must achieve by all peaceful means, let us sing together, with overwhelming joy and emotion, even more fervently than we did on August 15, twenty-five years ago. Let us stand united and march forward for that day!

2. Statement by the ROKNRC Proposing South-North Red Cross Talks

(August 12, 1971)

The quarter-century-old barrier between the south and north is the source of all national tragedies; especially, the tragedy of families separated in the South and the North are symbolic of the mankind's tragedy in this century.

In view of our professed mission of humanitarian causes and selfless services for relief work, it is indeed a heart-breaking sorrow to see this situation perpetuated.

The fates of the separated families can of course be terminated when the artificial wall dividing the south and the north is removed. Under the present circumstances, however, it is hard to imagine that this invisible wall will crumble in a short space of time.

In this context, we seek to initiate a "campaign for a search for lost families" to confirm the present condition of the 10 million separated families, arrange exchange of letters between them and realize their reunions.

I, on behalf of the ROKNRC and in accordance with the inherent spirit of the Red Cross, wish to make the following proposal with the purpose of settling the purely humanitarian problem of the Korean people.

First, Red Cross representatives from the south and the north shall hold talks soon with regard to the above-mentioned "campaign for the search for separated families."

Second, a preliminary meeting shall be held in Geneva, Switzerland, before the end of the coming October to discuss procedural matters for the talks.

It is our ardent hope that the above proposals will be met with a due reply from the north Korean Red Cross. The reply may be made through radio broadcasts, communication networks, the International Red Cross or any other means available to them.

We firmly believe that the north Korean Red Cross, with the spirit and the duty of the Red Cross, will respond with good will to this purely humanitarian proposal.

3. President Park's Special Foreign Policy Statement Regarding Peace and Unification

(June 23, 1973)

Dear fifty million fellow countrymen!

Today, I wish to announce the guide-lines of our foreign policy for peace and unification to improve substantially conditions for the attainment of our long-cherished national aspiration – the unification of our fatherland. I make this announcement, taking into account our experiences in the south-north dialogue and the recent developments in international situation.

At the conclusion of World War II, Korea was liberated, but our land was divided and our people were separated against their will.

The 38th Parallel, originally known as a military demarcation line for

450

disarming Japanese forces, turned later into an Iron Curtain. As a result, the south and the north were cut of from each other in political, economic, social, cultural and all other fields.

In the meantime, negotiations were conducted at the meetings of the U.S.-USSR Joint Commission to remove the barrier of the 38th Parallel and to establish a unified democratic government. Yet, these negotiations ended in failure due to basic differences in the positions of the two parties. The Korean question was, then, submitted to the United Nations.

At the second session of the United Nations General Assembly convened in 1947, a resolution was adopted calling for free general elections throughout the whole of Korea. The United Nations Temporary Commission on Korea (UNTCOK) was then dispatched to Korea to facilitate this objective.

However, the general elections were held only in the southern part of Korea because of the negative attitude on the part of north Korea. Thus, the Government of the Republic of Korea was established on 15th August, 1948 and was subsequently recognized by the United Nations as the only lawful goverment in Korea.

On 25th June, 1950, the north Korean Communist forces launched an unprovoked aggression against the Republic of Korea. During the Korean War thus caused, an innumerable number of our brethren lost their lives and the whole country was subjected to destruction by warfare. An armistice was put into effect after three years of war, but the country still remained divided and the prospect of unification of the divided country became even dimmer.

In my commemorative address delivered on the occasion of the 25th anniversary of National Liberation on 15th August, 1970, I called for a relaxation of tension between the south and the north with a view to alleviating the sufferings of our compatriots arising from the division of the country and also to building the foundations for a peaceful unification of the fatherland. On 12th August of the following year our side proposed the South-North Red Cross talks, and on 4th July last year the South-North Joint Communique was issued.

The south-north dialogue was thus started. Yet, the results of these dialogues lasting for almost two years since their beginning have been far from our expectations.

In our talks with the north, we have taken the position that both sides should endeavor to gradually remove the artificial barriers between the south and the north by solving easier and more practical problems first and to phase out feelings of mutual distrust and replace them with those of mutual confidence through concrete results. We further pointed out that such an approach would best serve to make the talks productive and would also serve as a shortcut to the eventual unification of the country by peaceful means.

The north Korean side, in disregard of the existence of deep-rooted feelings of distrust between the south and the north, insisted that military and political problems, which might endanger the security of the Republic of Korea, must first be dealt with, as a package, in the talks. While the very problem of reunification was being discussed at the talks, the north Korean side was continuously engaged in such external activities as would practically perpetuate the division of the country.

In view of the current status of south-north relationship, it is anticipated that not only many difficulties lie in the way of the dialogue, but a considerable length of time also be required before the results of the dialogue originally expected can be attained.

Moreover, if the present state of affairs were to be left as it is, the existing feelings of distrust might be deepened and even the tension between the south and the north might be aggravated.

Now, as for the recent developments in the international situation, it may be said that the era of Cold War after World War II came to an end. We have embarked upon a new era of peaceful coexistence, based on the status quo, through the balance of power among the major powers.

Judging also from a series of events witnessed in this part of the world, it seems unlikely that the unification of our fatherland can be attained within a short period of time.

These international trends give rise to a most serious problem in the

452

history of our nation. The problem is how to pursue the national unification – the supreme aspiration and objective of the entire Korean people – in the face of the stark realities of international situation.

My dear fifty million fellow countrymen!

We must tackle these realities in an active and positive way. We must formulate wise and firm policies for attaining the goal of national unification in the face of internal and external realities. Then, we must assiduously implement such policies.

We should have peace rooted firmly in this land and should achieve, without fail, the ultimate goal of peaceful unification by our own self-reliant efforts.

With these considerations in mind, I now declare the following policies:

1. The peaceful unification of the fatherland is the supreme task of the Korean people. We will continue to exert effort to accomplish this task.
2. Peace must be mantained on the Korean peninsula by all means. The south and the north should neither interfere with each other's internal affairs nor commit aggression against each other.
3. We will continue to make efforts with sincerity and patience to secure concrete results from the south-north dialogue based on the spirit of the South-North Joint Communique dated 4th July, 1972.
4. We shall not oppose north Korea's participation with us in international organizations, if it is conducive to the easing of tension and the furtherance of international cooperation.
5. We shall not object to our admittance into the United Nations together with north Korea if the majority of the member-states of the United Nations so wish, provided that it does not cause hindrance to our national unification. Even before our admittance into the United Nations as a member, we shall not be opposed to north Korea also being invited at the time of the U.N. General Assembly's deliberation of "the Korean question" in which the representative of the Republic of Korea is invited to participate.

6. The Republic of Korea will open its door to all the nations of the world on the basis of the principles of reciprocity and equality. At the same time, we urge those countries whose ideologies and social institutions are different from ours to open their doors likewise to us.
7. Peace and good-neighborliness are the firm basis of the foreign policy of the Republic of Korea. It is reaffirmed that we will continue to further strengthen the ties of friendship existing between friendly nations and our country.

I wish to make it clear that matters concerning north Korea in the policies enumerated above are interim measures during the transition period pending the achievement of our national unification and that the taking of these measures does not signify our recognition of north Korea as a state.

My dear compatriots in the south and the north!

Upon an objective and realistic appraisal of the internal and external situations surrounding our fatherland, I have a firm conviction that these policies are the only short-cut to the achievement of peaceful unification by our own self-reliant efforts amidst international currents of relaxation of tension without impairing the dignity and pride of our nation.

There can-be no despair or frustration for a wise and courageous people. Let us march together, with hope, courage and wisdom, toward the attainment of peace on the Korean peninsula, prosperity of the nation and unification of our fatherland.

4. President Park's Proposal for the South-North Non-Aggression Agreement
(President Park's New Year Press Conference on January 18, 1974.)

Question : North Korea insists on the conclusion of a peace agreement. What do you think of the proposal?

Answer : If my memory is correct, the idea of a peace agreement was first aired by Communist Chinese Premier Chou EnLai in an interview with a correspondent of *the New York Times* during his visit to Peking in August, 1971.

Afterwards, north Korea came forth with the idea time and again. At the meetings of the South-North Coordinating Committee, the Pyongyang side renewed the proposal on many occasions.

The peace agreement proposed by the north sounds tempting because of the word "peace." But the question is whether north Korea proposed the agreement out of any genuine interest in peace.

A look at the contents of the north's proposed peace agreement reveals that it contains several demands including, in the first place, withdrawal of foreign forces from Korea.

In other words, north Korea demands the withdrawal of all American troops now in the south. Another demand is that the two sides reduce the number of their armed forces to 100,000 or less each. In effect, the north insists that the south and the north stop engaging in an arms race and refrain from introducing military equipment and supplies from outside. North Korea says that if and when this agreement is signed, it should replace the existing Armistice Agreement.

The people may be somewhat dazzled by the word "peace" contained in the north Korean proposal, but we should realize the underlying motive.

The proposal, as I have noted already, calls for the commplete pullout of American forces in Korea, reduction of military forces to 100,000 or less, stoppage of introduction of weaponry from outside, and invalidation of the truce agreement.

In a singled word, these demands are mean to undermine our defense capability completely. It is easy to realize that, through this proposition, the north intends to disarm the sough for an invasion and unification of the Korean peninsula under communism at an appropriate time.

If we should accept the north Korean proposal at face value, the result will be more than obvious, It is crystal-clear that it will result in an all-out war like the Korean War in 1950.

The Communists in the north trumpet peace, but we should perceive the extremely dangerous plots, schemes and traps hidden behind the sugar-coated word "peace."

This is why I stress that we cannot be taken in by the north Korean schemes. Had it not been for a bitter experience like the Korean War, we might allow ourselves to be deceived by the Communists. We will never again be fooled by the north Koreans in such a manner.

The north Koreans have lately come up with something like a south-north confederation proposal. This contains just the same contents as the so-called peace agreement. The Communists in the north act one way in front and another behind. They utter sweet words like "peace" on the surface while plotting vicious schemes beneath the surface.

The armistice Agreement concluded in 1953 explicitly contains a provision banning introduction of military equipment from outside. This provision stipulates that from the day of signing of the truce agreement on, no weapons are allowed to be taken in from outside either by the south, the United Nations Forces, or the Communist side.

Nonetheless, the Communists were the first to violate this provision, and introduce weapons from outside. Because the Communist side kept importing weapons despite repeated protests lodged by the United Nations side, this provision of the Armistice Agreement has long since become a dead letter. This instance teaches us the lesson that we must be very careful in the conclusion of any agreement with the communists.

The same thing can be seen in the post-war situation in Vietnam. It is about one year since the ceasefire agreement was signed in Vietnam. But reports indicate that dozens of cases of ceasefire violation take place daily. It is said that scores of battles have been fought since the ceasefire.

Besides, the concept of peace as spoken of by the Communists varies basically from what we think of. Peace in our view eliminates war altogether, ruling out any aggression and forbidding armed conflict in any from.

Quite to the contrary, the Communists bring up peace when they want to gain time and relax the other side's preparedness for the achievement of their own specific objectives.

While calling for peace, the Communists are preparing themselves fully for war. And when they are ready, they stage a provocation. What I am saying is that the so-called peace agreement proposed by the north Koreans is a mere disguised tactic. It is under this tactic that north Korea is lately using the proposal for a peace agreement for political propaganda purposes.

Travelling all over the world, the north Koreans assert that they have proposed to the south the conclusion of a peace agreement, because they do not want war but peace. They say that nevertheless the south rejects the proposal, adding that they want peace but the south does not want it.

If the Communists in the north are truly interested in peace, they don't need anything like a new peace agreement. They can bring about peace and forestall war if only they strictly observe the existing Armistice Agreement.

Likewise, there will be no war here if we faithfully abide by the spirit of the July 4 South-North Joint Communique. I am confident that establishment of lasting peace is possible on the Korean peninsula.

Signing of a sheet of paper for an agreement or such by no means guarantees peace. The question is whether there is a clear-cut willingness to preserve peace and not to provoke war against each other. If there is such a will, no war will ever break out. We would like to ask how faithfully the north Korean Communists have observed the truce agreement in the past.

As far as we know, north Korea violated the Armistice Agreement as many as some 13,000 times during the past 20 years since the signing of the ceasefire. They have not committed these acts because there are no provisions banning them.

Also, let me ask to what extent the north Koreans have respected the South-North Joint Communique. Is it in line with the spirit of the south-north communique that they lately began to claim territorial waters which have hiterto been indisputably under our control, in accordance with an explicit provision of the Armistice Agreement?

If a new agreement is really needed for the establishment of lasting peace between the south and the north, and if north Korea's call for peace actually means what it says, then instead of agreeing with their thinly-veiled deceit in the form of a proposal for a peace agreement, I would rather take this occasion to propose that a nonaggression agreement be concluded between the south and the north.

I can put forth several key provisions of the nonaggression agreement I propose.

The first is that the south and the north pledge before the world that they will not invade each other under whatever circumstances.

Next, we will refrain from meddling in one another's internal affairs.

Another point is that under all circumstances, the existing Military Armistice Agreement should remain in force.

If this proposed nonaggression agreement containing the above-mentioned three basic provisions were concluded and faithfully observed by both sides, I am positive that war can be forestalled and peace maintained on the Korean peninsula.

At the same time I believe that such an agreement, no matter whether there be ten such treaties, would be of little avail if any of the signatories is without the intention to respect it.

Once such an agreement is concluded, the north can coexist peacefully until the time of national unification, during which period they can consolidate the foundations of unification one by one through active dialogue, exchanges and cooperation. This is consonant with the spirit of the June 23 foreign policy statement made by the Government last summer.

We clearly understand that no matter how ardently we long for unification, unification cannot be realized in a day or two. Since this is no time to take up the unification issue forthwith, nor can we expect an atmosphere ripe for national unification, in view of the present relations between the south and the north, we must continue a peaceful coexistence until the time of national unification, during which period we can, as I have already stated, consolidate the foundations for national unification step by step. This is the very spirit of the June 23 statement and, at the same time, is our just proposal.

Peace can never be secured on the Korean peninsula by the north Koreans who, advocating the so-called peace agreement on one hand, work out schemes to subvert it on the other. This is why I am stressing that we must clearly understand what is behind the north Korean proposal for a peace agreement, and remain wary of it.

5. President Chun's Proposal for an Exchange of Visits between the Highest Authorities of South and North Korea

(In his New Year Policy State-
ment on January 12, 1981)

It is now 36 years since Korea was liberated from the yoke of Japanese colonial rule. During this time, yet another major tragedy, another stain, has appeared upon the nation's history with the division of our homeland upon liberation.

A fratricidal war, deepening national heterogeneity, strife in the international arena, and an intermittent dialogue are but a few examples of the many spiritual and material wounds inflicted upon us by the territorial partitioning.

It is the paramount national task to reunify our homeland, characterized by a single people, language and culture, into a unified, independent and democratic nation-state.

Looking back on the past decade, we cannot find any improvement in the relations between the two halves of Korea, in spite of the South-North Joint Communique of July 4, 1972. It must be recognized that both sides have consistently engaged in a war of words and vain expositions of unilateral proposals.

We have no use for empty agreements, which without embodying the will to translate them into action are not worth the paper they are written on. What is truly needed is a firm resolve on both sides to honor even the smallest agreement already reached.

Breaching various agreements contained in the July 4 Joint Communique, the North Korean Communists have continually sent armed agents into the South, demonstrating that they have not given up their scheme to communize the entire Korean peninsula by force of arms. They are intensifying their slander of the Republic of Korea through radio broadcasts of the so-called Voice of the Unification-Revolution Party, as well as through loudspeakers strung along the entire length of the Armistice Line. They also incessantly attempt to subvert the Republic of Korea Government by organizing and funding anti-ROK organizations abroad.

But their scheme to communize the entire Korean peninsula has been totally frustrated by the iron-clad security of the ROK Armed Forces and the firm resolve of the people to defend their country, which is growing steadily stronger.

Can the Korean people who have lived for the past 36 years under two different sets of ideologies, ideals and political systems be unified again? The answer to these questions depends, above all else, on whether a sense of trust can be restored.

Accordingly, I have formulated an epochal proposal to the North Korean authorities, with the aim of finding an avenue to the solution of the unification question that takes into account the prevailing circumstances.

Thus far, a dialogue has been conducted on an on-and-off-again basis at various levels and in various formats. But nothing ever ensued that could contribute to the substantive improvement of relations. The only result has been the wasting of a great deal of time and energy Even the working-level contacts that began last year to pave the way for a South-North Prime Ministers conference were unilaterally suspended by Pyongyang. As we all know, again there is no South-North dialogue.

Once again, I emphasize that the path to unification is not paved by unilateral proposals rich only in rhetoric nor by written promises that are not kept; it is paved by the restoration of trust.

But it is not my intention today to argue over things past. To provide decisive momentum to creating mutual trust between the South and the North of Korea, epochal momentum to preventing a recurrence of tragic, fratricidal war, and historic momentum to paving the way to peaceful unification through unconditional resumption of the suspended dialogue, I hereby solemnly propose that the highest authorities of the South and the North exchange visits.

I invite President Kim Il-sung of North Korea to visit Seoul without any condition attached and free of any burden.

I will ensure that his personal safety is fully guaranteed during his stay in Seoul. I will extend all possible cooperation to him if he wishes to travel to any place of his choice in order to take a first-hand look at the actual situation in Seoul, other cities, or rural areas.

I also want to make it clear that I am prepared, at any time, to visit North Korea if he invites me on the same terms as I offer.

I am convinced that any problems between the South and the North can be resolved if we work strenuously to narrow our differences following the historic exchange of visits between the highest authorities, thus creating mutual trust precluding a fratricidal war and contributing to peaceful unification through a resumption of the dialogue.

The day of reunification, our nation's long-cherished goal, will not be far away, if oly both sides begin reaching agreement on the most amenable matters in the least sensitive areas and progress toward the more difficult ones.

6. Special Presidential Declaration for National Self-Esteem, Unification, and Prosperity

(July 7, 1988)

My dear 60 million compatriots,
Today, I am going to enunciate the policy of the Sixth Republic to

461

achieve the peaceful unification of our homeland, a long-standing goal dear to the hearts of the entire Korean people.

We have been suffering the pain of territorial division for almost half a century. This national division has inflicted numerous ordeals and hardships upon the Korean people, thus hindering national development.

Dismantling the barriers separating the south and the north and building a road to a unified and prosperous homeland is a duty history has imposed on every Korean alive today.

The south and the north, divided by different ideologies and political systems, have gone through a fratricidal war. The divided halves of the single Korean nation have distrusted, denounced, and antagonized each other since the day of territorial partition and this painful state has yet to be remedied.

Even though the division was not brought about by the volition of the Korean people, it is our responsibility to achieve national unification through our independent capabilities.

We must all work together to open a bright era of south-north reconciliation and cooperation. The time has come for all of us to endeavor in concert to promote the well-being and prosperity of the entire Korean people.

Today, the world is entering an age of reconciliation and cooperation transcending ideologies and political systems. A brave new tide of openness and exchange is engulfing peoples of different historical and cultural backgrounds.

I believe we have now come to a historic moment when we should be able to find a breakthrough toward a lasting peace and unification on the Korean peninsula which is still fraught with the danger of war amidst persisting tension and confrontation.

My fellow compatriots,

The fundamental reason that the tragic division is yet to be overcome is because both the south and the north have been regarding the other as an adversary, rather than realizing that both halves of Korea belong to the same national community. As such, inter-Korean enmity has continued to intensify.

Having lived in a single ethnic community, the Korean people have shaped an illustrious history and cultural traditions, while triumphing over almost ceaseless trials and challenges with pooled national strength and wisdom.

Accordingly, developing relations between the south and the north as members of a single nation community to achieve common prosperity is a short cut to realizing a prosperous and unified homeland. This is also the path to national self-esteem and integration.

Now the South and the North must tear down the barrier that divides them and implement exchanges in all fields. Positive step after positive step must be taken to restore mutual trust and strengthen bonds as members of one nations.

With the realization that we both belong to a single community, we must also discontinue confrontation on the international scene. I hope that north Korea will contribute to the community of nations as a responsible member and that this will accelerate the opening and development of the north Korean society.

South and north Korea should recognize each other's place in the international community and cooperate with each other in the best interest of all Koreans.

Sixty million fellow compatriots,

Today, I promise to make efforts to open a new era of national self-esteem, unification, and prosperity by building a social, cultural, economic, and political community in which all Koreans can participate under the principles of independence, peace, democracy, and welfare. To that end, I declare to the nation and to the world that the following policies will be pursued:

1. We will actively promote exchange of visits between the people of south and north Korea, including politicians, businessmen, journal-

ists, religious leaders, cultural leaders, academics and students, and will make necessary arrangements to ensure that Koreans residing overseas can freely visit both Koreas.

2. Even before the successful conclusion of the south-north Red Cross talks, we will promote and actively support, from a humanitarian viewpoint, all measures which can assist dispersed families in their efforts to find out whether their family members in the other part of the peninsula are still alive and their whereabouts, and will also promote exchanges of correspondence and visits between them.

3. We will open doors of trade between south and north Korea, which will be regarded as internal trade within the national community.

4. We hope to achieve a balanced development of the national economy with a view to enhancing the quality of life for all Koreans in both the south and the north, and will not oppose nations friendly with us trading non-miliary goods with North Korea.

5. We hope to bring to end wasteful diplomacy characterized by competition and confrontation between the south and north, and to cooperate in ensuring that north Korea makes a positive contribution to the international community. We also hope that representatives of south and north Korea will contact each other freely in international forums and will cooperate to pursue the common interest of the whole Korean nation.

6. To create an atmosphere conducive to durable peace on the Korean peninsula, we are willing to cooperate with north Korea in its efforts to improve relations with countries friendly to us including the United States and Japan, and in parallel with this, we will continue to seek improved relations with the Soviet Union, China, and other socialist countries.

I trust that north Korea will positively respond to the measures outlined above. If the north shows a positive attitude, I will make it clear that even more progressive measures will be taken one after the other. I hope that this declaration today will serve to open a new chapter in the development of inter-Korean relations and will lead to unification. I believe that if the entire 60 million Korean people pool their wisdom and strength, the south and the north will be integrated into a single social, cultural and economic community before this century is out.

I am confident that on this basis we will accomplish the great task of unifying into a single national entity in the not so very distant future.

7. Proposal for South-North Education Officials Meeting

(July 15, 1988)

To Pyon Yong-nip, chairman of the Education Commission, Administrative Council;

Today, 43 years after the division into south and north, we find ourselves at a juncture where we can no longer ignore the entire nation's craving for national self-esteem, unification, and prosperity.

Especially in the light of the worldwide trend toward reconciliation and co-prosperity despite differences in ideologies and systems, this is a time when we the Korean people, too, should strive together to promote national interest.

For us to uncurtain a new horizon of peace and unification in line with the flow of the times. it is most important to restore and develop the national community as members of the same ethnic group by actively promoting exchanges and corporation in sectors such as politics, economy, social, culture, and sports.

The meeting could discuss the issues of promoting grand pilgrimages across the country and exchanging goodwill sports meets, on which the two sides are of the same opinion, and other problems related to the promotion of student exchanges.

The grand pilgrimages across the country can be managed by a Homeland Pilgrimage Promotion Committee that can be formed in the south and the north, respectively. It would be good for students from the south to journey to Mt. Paektu from Panmunjom while students from the north journey from Panmunjom to Mt. Halla and return. This would eliminate the need for students to travel through

In the past, we set a precedent for mutual assistance by delivering and receiving materials for flood victims, and have seen, thanks to the exchange of dispersed family hometown visitors and art troupes, private citizens traveling between the south and the north for the first time in 40 years.

Such precedent and experience should be cultivated like a valuable bud.

In a message from our Prime Minister on June 3, it was proposed that the two sides discuss the personnel exchange question. Again on June 9, the National Unification Minister expressed the willingness to discuss the issue of student exchanges on a priority basis.

We take note of the fact that the north, too, has recently recognized the need for a many-sided exchange of personnel between the south and the north and in particular, have taken a positive posture toward the question of student exchanges.

I expect that student exchanges at this time when inter-Korean dialogue remains suspended would be highly significant in itself, serving also as a stimulant in realizing exchanges in other areas.

Here, I courteously propose that a south-north education officials meeting be held at an early date to discuss and resolve the issue of promoting exchanges between south and north Korean students.
their own area before meeting at Panmunjom.

The size of the pilgrimage team can be about 1,000 persons from each side. It is desirable that the exchange be made simultaneously as was the case with the exchange of dispersed family hometown visitors and art troupes made in September of 1985.

The time and schedule of the homeland pilgrimages can be determined through consultation between the south and the north. But, we foresee the staging of the first pilgrimage this year and increasing the frequency to about their times a year beginning next year.

The exchange of goodwill sports meets can be managed by the college sports committee of both sides. It would be good if each delegation be formed with about 200 persons and would initially include the sports of soccer, men's and women's table tennis, and men's and women's volleyball. The number of sports can be steadily expanded.

I consider it desirable to hold the good-will exchange meets on a regular basis in the spring and autumn. It is suggested that the first meet be held in Pyongyang in October of this year and the second in Seoul in April of next year, with each meet lasting about five days.

If and when these exchange programs prove to be successful, exchanges could be expanded to include performances and exhibitions between students in the areas of music, art, concert and dance, as well as the exchange of school sojourn teams in which students could tour scenic and historic sites like Mt. Kumkang and Kyongju.

The issues of transit procedures, provisions of various conveniences and guarantee of personal safety necessary for the smooth and orderly implementation of exchange programs, can be easily resolved if we follow past procedures.

Wishing that a south-north education officials meeting to discuss the issue of student exchanges can be held at an early date, I hope that first meeting will take place at Panmunjom on a date of your choosing before July 30, if possible. It would be good if each delegation consist of five officials with a vice ministe-level official as chief delegate.

I am positive that if the proposed meeting were successfully held and south-north student exchanges realized, they would serve as a foothold on which the younger generation responsible for the future of our nation will gain a sense of national trust and integrity. Further, they may provide a basis for the establishment of many additional personnel exchanges between the south and the north in the future.

I look forward to your affirmative response.

8. Proposal for a South-North Summit Meeting.

(August 15, 1988)

...A new horizon is opening in which we will unfold an age of good-will and cooperation together with all other countries of the world.

Rapid changes are taking place even in the world order of the East-West Cold War system, a system which had given us the pains of division without even allowing us time to rejoice over national liberation and which prompted the waging of an appalling fratricidal war on this land.

Stupendous changes are also occurring in the relations among the big powers surrounding the peninsula and in our relations with those countries.

A new wave of openness and cooperation is now sweeping the world community. On the strength of our expanding democratic capabilities and heightening national self-esteem, we shall exploit the domestic and external circumstances on our own to shape a new ara of national integration...

My dear fellow compatriots at home and abroad :

Today, I would like to appeal to all my fellow countrymen, in the south and the north, to join hands to open an epoch of grand reconciliation leading to a unified and prosperous homeland at the earliest possible date.

The time has come for both the south and the north to translate into action the conviction that not through confrontation and conflict but through reconciliation and cooperation will we be able to overcome the pain and ordeal of division and achieve genuine national progress and unification.

Last July 7, I declared that the south and the north must now set about forging relations as members of a single national community designed to seek prosperity for all. The barrier that has been dividing us, who are one and the same people, for over 40 years must now be dismantled through openness, exchanges, and cooperation. In this way, we should be able to create and ripen conditions leading to a breakthrough to unification.

To this end, it is imperative for the top leaders of the south and the north to meet in dialogue. This would be the most effective and quickest way to resolve all issues between the two parts of Korea. The realities both of domestic and international situations and the wishes of our people call for a south-north summit without further delay.

Today, on the occasion of the 43rd anniversary of national liberation, I propose to Kim Il-sung of north Korea to meet with me for talks at the earliest possible date to work out practical ways to bring about national integration in response to the yearning of our 60 million compatriots.

Neither the venue, agenda, nor procedures should be an obstacle to the leaders of the south and the north meeting to discuss the future of the nation in a frank and honest manner. It is my fervent hope that north Korea will make a positive response to my proposal so that a new page can be turned in our national history.

Sixty million compatriots at home and abroad ;

At this juncture as we celebrate the 40th anniversary of the founding of the government, we must firmly open a new epoch of democracy, prosperity, and unification on the strength of the great achievements and confidence we all have made this far and also of the elevated self-esteem of the people who have successfully staged the Olympics with the blessings from the whole world.

This is the road to a new liberation for the present generation. That is the building of an independent nation that our patriotic forbears so courageously pursued even through her darkest hours. Building a prosperous and unified nation is the only way to accomplish in our time the yet-to-be finished task of complete national liberation.

Let us now liquidate with our own self-reliant efforts the history of suffering in which we, as a peripheral country of the world, have had to swallow national division imposed upon us by others.

Let us thereby build a proud country with our own strength, a country which, standing in the center of world history, will play a dignified role for peace and the well-being of mankind.

9. Policy Speech by President Roh Tae-woo

(October 4, 1988)

The Honorable Speaker and esteemed members of the National Assembly,

I consider it very significant for me to discuss with you the basic policies of the new republic in presenting the government's 1989 budget bill for your deliberation.

I join all my fellow citizens in celebrating the fact that the Seoul Olympics, for which the entire nation prepared for seven years, turned out to be the largest Olympiad ever, with the greatest number

470

of nations and athletes in history participating, and, moreover, wound up as the best Games ever, outshining any previous Olympics held in the developed world. Numerous people worked day and night with dedication until the sacred Olympic flame was put out in the Chamsil Main Stadium the night before last. I cannot find words to express my appreciation for all those at home and abroad and in every nook and cranny of our society who did their utmost in the Olympic cause with a spirit of service and patriotism.

I believe that all the Assembly members present here, both from the government party and the opposition, share my deep sense of gratitude to all our fellow citizens for having done everything in their power to make the Seoul Olympics a success. Enthusiastically united, all our citizens managed to make the Seoul Olympics a truly great and splendid festival of the global village. Every citizen was a proud Olympic star.

The Seoul Olympics has thus become a glorious monument to the immense inherent capabilities and spirit of hard work with which our people have pulled ourselves up from the ruins of war and the morass of poverty to achieve a level of development that has astonished the world. I do not think this is an exaggeration. We have never stood before the world as tall as this. Indeed, we have now acquired the confidence that we can do anything to which we put our mind. We are now about to see the end of a painful and dark period in our history characterized by another country's usurpation of our national sovereignty, which took place at the beginning of this century when we were still a small, weak nation, by the division of the land and by a subsequent bloody fratricidal war. Now we are opening a new chapter of history in which Korea should achieve both unification and prosperity and emerge as a major player on the world scene in the 21st century. This will be a great triumph for us who have overcome, on our own, the tribulations and trials history imposed on us.

One achievement should be the stepping stone for another even greater leap forward. Constantly keeping in mind the expectations that my fellow citizens placed in me when they entrusted me with the responsibilities of the presidency, I will do everything in my power to build a more advanced nation on the strength of that breathtaking achievement.

Now, we must forge an era of democracy, prosperity and unification. We are embarking on a new endeavor in response to the call of our time. Together with a great people who have worked a cultural miracle that surprised the world, I will lead our advances in forging that new era, breaking through and leaping over any and all barriers that confront us.

Indeed, the barriers on the world scene that we must leap over before we can join the ranks of advanced nations are tall. There also are tough internal barriers that must be overcome in building a prosperous democratic country. To break through to peaceful unification, we must dismantle the barrier of south-north division that has set us against each other, causing numerous sufferings and tragedies.

Various challenges are facing us at this moment, as we strive to reach out to the world and advance into the future. We must thus jump over all barriers of anxiety and uncertainty and in that way, we should be able to build this country into a prosperous democratic, advanced and unified nation. To do so and thus fulfill our aspirations requires, among other things, the power of national harmony and unity.

I am resolved to dedicate my all to that task. As the one who is ultimately responsible for the affairs of state, I will ensure that we overcome the challenges facing us, while consolidating national stability.

Esteemed members of the Assembly,

A wave of openness and reconciliation is now sweeping the world, ushering in a period of transition. The destiny of the 60 million Korean people must not be left to the mercy of outside forces and influences any longer. The historic mission imposed on us all is to wisely cope, on our own, with the changing international situation and to create, with a spirit of independence, an environment favorable to unification, thus generating a definitive movement toward that goal.

During my tenure, I will endeavor to bring about a spring of reconciliation between the south and the north, which have remained in a deep freeze for 40 years. I will strive to set into motion inter-Korean trade, exchanges and cooperation, including exchanges of people, thus building trust between the two parts of Korea as members of one national community. In cooperation with all nations of the world, I will strive to induce north Korea to open its tightly shut doors and join the international community as a full-fledged member. In that way, I intend to build a solid framework for national integration.

It may be recalled that on July 7, I issued a policy declaration seeking a bold end to south-north confrontation and an antagonism in favor of common prosperity as one national community. On the 43rd Liberation Day, I proposed to meet with President Kim Il-sung of north Korea at any place and at the earliest possible date to discuss any and all issues between the south and the north.

Paying attention to the fact that on September 8, President Kim responded to my proposal, I make it clear that I am willing to visit Pyongyang to meet with him, if the north is agreeable. I believe that at a south-north summit, it will be necessary to conduct, without any restriction, frank discussions on all pending issues raised by both sides, including a joint declaration of nonaggression and the unification of our homeland.

In view of the fact that a single people have been divided and persistently embroiled in mutual antagonism and confrontation, the mere fact of the top leaders of both sides actually meeting together, instead of shunning dialogue under the pretext of one precondition or another, would start a process of national reconciliation leading to unification.

Circumstances affecting unification have changed completely from the past. I believe, therefore, that the time has come to present a new unification formula designed to fulfill the yearning of all our people for a unified nation-state, our long-cherished goal, while at the same time taking advantage of the changed circumstances.

I plan to present to the nation soon the new republic's unification formula which will crystalize the views and opinions of citizens from all walks of life, keeping firmly in mind our yearning to be one people again. Our goal is to build a unified country so that the national community can prosper and develop forever, and every citizen can enjoy freedom, human rights and the happy life to which they are entitled.

A national unification formula should be practicable and acceptable to both sides, rather than wrapped up in Cold War rhetoric or biased in favor of any one party. In this regard, I think that ideas or suggestions helpful to unification can be positively culled not only from the diverse unification debate in the south but also from proposals of the north for incorporation into the contemplated new formula. In developing a progressive and feasible unification formula, I will solicit the active cooperation of the National Assembly as a whole and of your individuallity, who, as esteemed members of the legislature, are the representatives of the people.

Esteemed members of the Assembly,

On the strength of our bonds of friendship and cooperation with countries that have been our friends, I will seet improved relations with all nations of the East and the West, including the socialist world. To promote world peace and the well-being of all mankind, it is vital for all nations on earth to have normal relations with each other on the principle of reciprocity and equality, to resolve dispute through dialogue and to seek common interests and prosperity. I feel the time has come for us to more actively contribute to that end.

It is encouraging that over the past several months since my inauguration, the doors to exchanges and cooperation between our country and socialist nations have been opened much wider. The participation of the Soviet Union, China and major socialist nations in Eastern Europe in the Seoul Olympics will, I think, go a long way toward dismantling East-West barriers, thus ushering in an era of international reconciliation and cooperation. In particular, an agreement has recently been reached with Hungary, a signatory to the Warsaw Pact, to exchange ambassadorial-level permanent missions. This will constitute a historic point of departure for our advances toward a new diplomatic horizon.

I consider it significant that our country and China have broken through a half-century-old barrier of separation and are now progressively boosting bilateral exchanges and cooperation. I also put a positive construction on the fact that Secretary General Gorbachev of the Soviet Union has indicated a progressive attitude toward Korea-Soviet relations. I intend to actively seek improved relations and all manner of cooperation with China, the Soviet Union and Eastern European countries, including personnel and cultural exchanges, the opening of both air routes and shipping lines, trade and economic cooperation and participation in economic development, including the development of Siberia.

At the same time, we will seek to further cement ties with the United States, Japan, Western European nations and other traditional friends. The United States is an ally with whom we have been defending the peace and freedom of the Korean peninsula and who is also our closest partner in economic cooperation and trade.

The importance of external trade to our economy is bound to continue to increase. Paying close attention to the fact that the United States, Japan and the European Community together absorb 70 percent of our total exports, the administration will do everything in its power not only to resolve trade friction with them but also to promote ties of cooperation with them in all fields.

I take this occasion to express my gratitude to the United States, Japan and other friends for their unsparing cooperation in ensuring the safety of the Seoul Olympics.

The administration will also work to intensify cooperation with our Asian-Pacific neighbors. Steps will be taken to promote friendly relations with the many developing countries in the Third World, especially by actively sharing our experience and expertise in economic development.

In pursuing improved relations with our northern neighbors, I will never seek to isolate north Korea. It is hoped that those socialist countries which are developing new cooperative relations with us will maintain even better relations with north Korea so that the development of the north can be accelerated. The improvement of our northern relations should stimulate north Korea into opening itself up and emerging as a responsible member of the international community. This, in turn, should help create conditions favorable to our unification and should also contribute to the stability of Northeast Asia and further to world peace. In that way, I am confident that our national integration and prosperity will be achieved. The Korean peninsula will not only cease to be the powder keg of East Asia but will fulfill an illustrious role in advancing peace and prosperity for all mankind.

If unadulterated, the passion of our young people to pursue ideals in sharp contrast with realities will provide the motive power to shape a tomorrow of national unification and great forward progress. I will make efforts to set up south-north youth exchanges so that young people will be able to travel across the Demilitarized Zone and observe the true state of affairs in the south and the north. I think any form of exchange, including south-north student pilgrimages from one end of the peninsula to the other, joint athletic events held alternately in the south and the north and debates, is desirable.

If the authorities in both the south and the north can agree on arrangements to guarantee personal safety, I believe there need not be any restriction on the size and format for youth exchanges. I am of the opinion that the more south-north youth exchanges, the better. I intend to actively study ways to enable university faculties and students themselves to independently work out exchange programs.

I will also strive for furthur progress in our Northern Policy, so that our young citizens will be able to freely travel to China, the Soviet Union and Eastern Europe also. Such exchanges, of course, should not be limited to young people ; citizens from all works of life should be able to take part. The administration in fact is working toward that goal.

Honorable Speaker, esteemed members of the National Assembly,

Our national abilities and self-confidence have never been greater than they are today, as demonstrated by the fact that we have just staged the Olympics, a global festival, more magnificently than any advanced nation. The world, which used to impose its will on us, is also changing. Owing to a new wave of reconciliation and cooperation, a new frontier is opening up before the nation and challenging us to explore it.

The time has come for us all to unite to forge energetically an era of democracy, prosperity and unification in order to fulfill our national aspirations. It is our glorious duty to pave the way for unification and to build a proud, democratic, advanced, thriving nation so that we can greet the approaching 21st century with hope.

While suffering with my fellow citizens, I am determined to devote my body and soul to accomplishing this historic mission. I solicit the unsparing cooperation of you, the esteemed members of the National Assembly from the governing and opposition parties, and of the citizens from all other walks of life. Without the underpinning of wisdom, harmony and cooperation on the part of the entire public, it will be difficult to accomplish this worthwhile, national task. I thus call on all my fellow citizens to join hands to knock down or leap over the numerous walls on the world scene, between the south and the north and among ourselves.

We are now marching hand in hand, not in the interest of the past but in the interest of the future, not in the interest of any political faction but in the interest of the common good of the nation. I take this opportunity to especially commend the opposition leaders present here for their great contributions to national growth, democratic development and the success of the Seoul Olympics in concert with all citizens. I want to share with you my sense of gratification for all this.

The counterproductive politics that used to pull us apart and the suppression and resistance that used to divide us are now becoming a thing of the past. Let all of us now join forces to practice creative politics that will shape an even more gratifying and brighter future and generate the confidence to spur the nation's forward progress.

Esteemed members of the Assembly,

Let all of us, you, the nation's leaders, and I, strive together to ensure that all our compatriots in the south and the north and all members of the next generation will enjoy the glory of democracy, prosperity and unification. Let all of us who are living today join forces to dismantle and advance beyond every wall standing in our way in order to build an even greater nation, an illustrious era and a world brimming with harmony and peace. Thank you for listening.

10. President Roh's Address to the U.N. General Assembly

(October 18, 1988)

Mr. President, Mr. Secretary-General, distinguished delegates,

Forty-three years ago, as World War II came to an end, the world was taking steps toward the creation of the United Nations with great hope for lasting peace. The new body was to be entrusted with chartering a new international order of peace and stability.

In my country, the end of World War II gave rise to overwhelming jubilation and hope as the Korean people were liberated from the yoke of colonial rule and recovered the land which had been theirs for thousands of years.

The joy of liberation, however, soon turned to despair over the tragic division of our homeland.

As a matter of convenience in the process of disarming the defeated colonial forces, a line of artificial division was drawn through the mid-section of the Korean peninsula along the 38th parallel.

The decision to divide our land was made against the will of the Korean people, dictating the fate of the nation in the decades to come. Overnight, this cruel division turned brother against brother and plunged the Korean peninsula into a violent storm of the Cold War.

On a peaceful Sunday morning in June 1950, war broke out on the Korean peninsula, and soon the whole nation was in flames. Over the next three years, tens of thousands of young people from 20 countries entered the war and eventually over three million lives fell victim to the clash of ideologies. The war also reduced nearly everything on the peninsula to ashes.

Experiencing the battle as a volunteer soldier still wearing my high school uniform, I saw the young and innocent die in the flames of war and came to long for peace and reconciliation. I also came to believe that we must make all possible efforts to end the division and confrontation which were causing such great suffering in our nation.

The conflict ceased in 1953 with the signing of an armistice, but this did not bring about genuine peace. A state of tension and confrontation between the two parts of Korea has persisted ever since.

Even though many seasons have come and gone, and the world has changed dramatically over the decades, this hostile confrontation along the Korean Armistice Line has remained fronzen in time and continues to be a source of danger which could trigger hostilities involving the whole world.

Beyond these political and strategic implications, the human costs of this standoff have been enormous. Millions of family members-fathers and mothers, husbands and wives, brothers and sisters-have remained separated between the north and the south since the war and have been unable to exchange even letters or phone calls. The emotional strains caused by this situation run deep in both the north and the south of Korea.

Is there no way out of this impasse?

I stand here today to answer this question with a message of hope.

We must henceforth do everything possible to hasten the coming of the springtime for peace and reconciliation on the Korean peninsula.

In this connection, I wish to welcome, on behalf of the government and people of the Republic of Korea, the timely decision of the General Assembly to adopt the agenda item entitled "Promotion of Peace, Reconciliation and Dialogue in the Korean Peninsula."

I should also like to congratulate you, Mr. President, on your election as President of the General Assembly. I hope that this session of the General Assembly wil produce fruitful results.

Mr. President,

In the world today, we can see movements toward openness and reconciliation. The Cold War conflicts which dominated the international scene since the end of the Second World War have begun to surrender to the power of human reason and common decency. Mankind's expectations are changing from confrontation to co-existence, from antagonism to reconciliation.

I join all of you in welcoming these trends.

I would also like to express my gratitude and respect the His Excellency the Secretary-General, Mr. Javier Perez de Cuellar, for his insight and leadership which have helped achieve a cease-fire in the eight-year-old Gulf war.

Thanks to the Secretary-General's role, all of us have greater confidence and expectations regarding this bulwark of peace. The Nobel Peace-Prize just awarded to the United Nations Peace keeping Forces is a testimony to this.

In Afghanistan, Cambodia, Namibia and the Western Sahara, steps are being taken toward peaceful resolution of outstanding conflicts.

Furthermore, it is highly encouraging that through their summit meetings, President Reagan and General Secretary Gorbachev have been able to reduce the number of deadly weapons capable of annihilationg mankind.

Mr. President,

I have come here in the spirit of "harmony and progress," the theme for the Seoul Olympiad which ended exactly two weeks ago.

The XXIV Olympic Games were a great festival of cooperation and understanding in which young people from 160 countries gathered together despite differences of ideology, race and religion. Furthermore, the East and the West met in sporting arenas for the first time in twelve years at the Seoul Olympiad.

As one of the most successful Olympiads ever, the Seoul Games instilled in all of us the hope that at last peace and reconciliation are beginning to spread throughout the world.

Still, it is ironic that this wonderful festival of peace should be held in a land where danger of conflict still looms large. But, this also gives us great hope for the future.

In fact, the historical drama I am referring to must be seen as a part of the larger global development that is emerging from man's aspirations for peace and common prosperity.

I would like to take this opportunity to express gratitude to the peoples of all the countries whose participation and support helped make the Seoul Olympiad a successful and safe festival for all mankind.

Only a generation ago, the Korean nation lay in ruins and was shackled with great suffering, hunger and poverty. We have over-come these adversities and made great progress through diligent work mixed with blood and tears.

We are quite proud of our achievements, which we believe have contributed to releasing the wellsprings of harmony among diverse peoples.

It is also our sincere wish that these achievements offer hope and courage to all people in developing nations who are struggling against similar circumstances.

Only three decades ago, we were a poor, agrarian society depen-dent on other nations' help for survival. We were able to transform ourselves into a newly industrializing nation only through our peo-ple's great desire to achieve, together with a passion for education.

We also took advantage of an open and competitive political and economic system which allows individuals to achieve their highest potential. Mankind's inviolate rights and inborn creativity are essential elements for making societal progress.

International trade also has played an important role in our rapid economic growth. As the 12th largest trading nation in the world, we are keenly aware of the fact that the growth of world trade has helped promote the rise in income and employment of trading part-ners. In this, the Republic of Korea has been especially fortunate. So, although the world brought national division and other trials to Korea, it also made it possible for us to grow and make substantial progress.

There are undoubtedly many problems facing mankind today. But it can be discerned nevertheless that progress is being made toward reconciliation, peace and prosperity.

In order for man's hope to survive and progress to be realized, we must spare no effort to promote openness and mutual exchanges, cooperation and reconciliation. There is no other alternative.

Isolation and confrontation will bring only calamity and suffering to every corner of this global village.

As far as the Korean people are concerned, we believe we have been able to progress through international cooperation and openness toward others. That is why we are looking to the future with optimism and confidence that we will eventually achieve democracy, prosperity and national reunification for all Koreans on the peninsula.

There is vitality in every corner of the Republic of Korea today as well as in every individual, thanks to the freedoms protected by our social system.

I am sure that this new vitality will accelerate our progress and bring nearer the springtime of peace and reconciliation on the Korean peninsula.

Mr President,

Today our world stands at an important turning point that delineates one era from another.

It has been said that the only thing that does not change is the inevitability of change itself.

The world of confrontation and conflict is giving way to a world of detente, a trend which is taking place right here at the United Nations. Serious efforts are also commencing to bring peace and the relaxation of tension to the Korean peninsula, one of the last vestiges of the Cold War.

The distrust left behind by the Korean War gave rise to the confrontation between north and south Korea.

During the 35 years since the Armistice Agreement, enormous military forces have continued to confront each other across the Armistice Line.

In order to put an end to this hostile standoff, there is no other alternative but to build mutual trust by engaging in exchange and cooperation, and destroying the wall that separates us.

To achieve this, we need a fresh approach. And that is precisely what I unveiled on July 7th this year.

I have declared that the north and the south of Korea should immediately end all forms of hostile, confrontational relations. For instance, we should immediately cease publicly attacking each other.

I have made clear that we are determined to pursue a relationship of partnership with north Korea. Our cultural and historical unity demands that we devote ourselves to the pursuit of common prosperity and mutual well-being for all Koreans.

In the same declaration, I proposed that we allow not only the reunion of millions of separated family members, but also free exchanges among political, economic and religious leaders as well as ordinary citizens.

Also, I have taken concrete steps to pave the way for free trade between the northern and southern sides of Korea.

We must transform the north-south Korean relationship, so that we can reconnect every roadway, whether a major highway or a little path, linking the two sides which remain disconnected now. Then we could be enabled to go on to develop our common land, by combining our human, technological and financial resourcs.

If there may be any difficulties for north Koreans in opening their doors just now, I believe that we could work together toward this by building a "city of peace" in the Demilitarized Zone. Within such a city, family members who have remained separated for more than three decades could freely reunite. Broad trade and other kinds of exchanges could also be facilitated by establishing in the new "city of peace" such venues as a home for national culture, a center for scholarly exchanges, and a trade center.

Similarly, I stated in the same July 7th declaration that we are determined to end confrontation with north Korea in our external relations.

It is our sincere hope that north Korea participate fully in the international community. Doing so can only benefit the north Korean peo-

484

ple, not harm them.

Within the world community, the north and the south must recognize each other and cooperate to promote the common interest of the entire nation.

It is our wish that our allies and friends will contribute to the progress and opening of north Korea by engaging Pyongyang in expanding relations.

It is also our position that those socialist countries with close ties to north Korea continue to maintain positive relations and cooperate with north Korea even as they improve their relations with us.

The pursuit of mutual respect and prosperity through increasing cooperation, however, is not our ultimate goal.

It is a requisite process we must go through in order to build the relationship of trust necessary for the nation's reunification.

When such a relationship is firmly established, we can look forward to realizing peaceful unificatin.

Mr. President,

On the anniversary of our national liberation last August, I proposed to north Korean President Kim Il-sung that we hold direct talks.

Since the peninsula became divided, both sides have put forth many different proposals concerning peace and reunification.

But what is necessary now is that the leaders of both sides who hold the ultimate responsibilities in their areas meet together without setting any preconditions. We must initiate discussions with a new spirit of openness and explore together possible avenues of compromise acceptable to both sides.

We must find a common ground to build institutions for peace and create a single national community.

Hence I have taken particular notice of the fact that President Kim Il-sung has reacted to my proposal for a north-south Korean summit meeting. I hope I can visit Pyongyang as soon as possible.

when the summit meeting does take place, I would like to propose that we agree to a declaration of nonaggression or nonuse of force in order to better construct a framework for mutual trust and security.

In order to end the military confrontation which has lasted for more than three decades now and build a new relationship dedicated to shared peace and prosperity, we need to create a new basic framework for progress. Creating such a framework, of course, can be accomplished only at the level of direct contact between the leaders of the north and the south.

In this connection, I want to make it absolutely clear that even before a nonaggression declaration is made with the northern side, the Republic of Korea will never use force first against the north.

We cannot expect durable peace on the Korean peninsula without ending the current military confrontation.

I propose that at our summit meeting, we discuss sincerely and resolve all the problems raised by either or both sides with regard to disarmament, arms control and other military matters. We must also explore institutional structures for peaceful relations, mutual contacts and cooperative ventures, and, of course, ways of bringing about reunification.

We can at the same meeting also search for concrete ways to transform the Armistice Agreement into a permanent peace arrangement.

Mr. President,

Clearly, the problems between the northern and southern Korean sides must be dealt with and resolved by the independent efforts of the Korean people themselves.

But due to Korea's geopolitical situation, the problem of durable peace on the Korean peninsula cannot be considered in total isolation from its relations with the surrounding nations.

In order for durable peace to prevail on the Korean peninsula, it is necessary not only for the northern and the southern Korean sides to reach rapprochment, but for both of them to build and maintain more rational and normal relations with all the nations that have interests in peace on the Korean peninsula.

The Republic of Korea will continue to maintain and expand close cooperation with her traditional allies and friends including the United States. In particular, we will continue our consultations and common efforts for the maintenance of peace and stability on the peninsula.

In parallel with such efforts, we are also taking positive steps to improve our relations with countries such as the People's Republic of China, the Union of Soviet Socialist Republics, and many East European nations with which we have had only remote relationships due to our ideological differences.

By conducting normal relations with one another under the principles of equality and mutual respect, all the nations of the world will contribute to mutual prosperity.

This also serves the cause of world peace because, through dialogue and mutual understanding, nations can work to eliminate sources of conflict while cementing friendship and partnership.

It is from this perspective that I welcome as an encouraging development the fact that socialist countries such as China and the Soviet Union are showing a forward-looking attitude in recent months concerning mutual exchanges and cooperation with the Republic of Korea in a number of fields.

I find it significant that China, a nation which traditionally was a good neighbor of Korea, is moving to overcome the wall of separation that has lasted for nearly half a century and is expanding its mutual exchanges and cooperation with the Republic of Korea. I have also taken careful notice of the positive signals being made by General Secretary Gorbachev of the Soviet Union.

At the same time, we will continue to deepen our cooperative relationships with developing countries and, in fact, intend to strengthen our political, economic and cultural ties with many nations of the Third World and the Non-Aligned Movement.

It is our intense desire to do all that we can to share our developmental experience and technical resources with the developing nations. To be able to contribute to the development of the Third World nations would give immense satisfaction to the Korean people who are themselves a developing country.

Mr. President,

The Asia-Pacific region is marching toward a new era of prosperity. This is taking place thanks to the strengthening of international cooperation as well as the strong will of the region's peoples to achieve progress based on their infinite potential and dynamism.

Within the Pacific Rim, Northeast Asia constitutes the seat of age-old Oriental civilization. Yet, this region has challenged world peace as it endured a century of conflicts, namely the Sino-Japanese War, the Russo-Japanese War, the Pacific War and the Korean War.

It is my belief that without peace in Northeast Asia, there cannot be peace in the world, and without cooperation among the area's nations, there cannot commence an era of Pacific prosperity.

Therefore, I take this opportunity to propose a consultative conference for peace among the United States of America, the Union of Soviet Socialist Republics, the People's Republic of China and Japan as well as north and south Korea, in order to lay a solid foundation for durable peace and prosperity in Northeast Asia.

Such a conference can deal with a broad range of issues concerning peace, stability, progress and prosperity within the area.

To be sure, it may not be easy to gather these States together at the same table because of the outstanding differences in ideology, social systems and policies among them.

But, I am sure we can overcome such difficulties if we all acknowledge the fact that we are inseparable partners in the pursuit of peace and prosperity.

The realization to this proposal will certainly create an international environment more conducive to peace in Korea and reunification of the peninsula.

Mr. President,

Looking ahead of the 21st century, I sense a new chapter of human history is unfolding.

Indeed, changes are taking palce in this global village, and mankind is increasingly guided by tenets of reason and wisdom rather than ideological obsessions.

Nonetheless, there is no guarantee that mankind will not someday be plunged into the whirlwind of global conflict.

If we are to avoid this tragedy, openness, peace and cooperation are the only options left to us.

I look forward to this new chapter of history wherein peaceful efforts toward cooperation and progress will be the norm rather than the exception.

Likewise, the time will certainly come on the Korean peninsula when the brotherhood of all Koreans, north and south, will triumph over our differences, leaving the Korean nation free of tension, conflict and the threat of war.

Upon the day when swords are beaten into plowshares on the Korean peninsula, the opportunity for lasting world peace will be strengthened.

Believing that this day will come, I will continue my efforts, together with my sixty million compatriots, in seeking lasting harmony in our nation.

This is the solemn responsibility of my generation and the dream and passion of our younger generations in Korea.

Through concerted efforts, we are determined to overcome whatever difficulties we may encounter.

As the most successful Olympics ever held just concluded in a land once dominated by conflict and poverty, so too the day will come when the wall of separation on the Korean peninsula will fall and harmony will prevail.

Mr. President, Mr. Secretary-General, and distinguished delegates,

Lastly, I earnestly appeal to you all to support and encourage the aspirations of all the Korean people who, as expressed by the theme song of the Seoul Olympics, so strongly desire to go "hand in hand over the walls" and realize the goals of peace and unification.

May I also assure you that the Korean people will demonstrate that they are worthy of your support, as we build a unified, peaceable nation on the peninsula.

I thank you.

Chronology of South-North Dialogue (1970-1988)

August 15 — President Park makes the "August 15 Declaration," proposing a bona fide competition between the south and the north and expressing the willingness to suggest more advanced, epochal measures to remove various artificial barriers existing between the two sides step by step, in the interest of laying the groundwork for unification and on the basis of humanitarian considerations.

«1971«

August 12 — Dr. Choi, president of the Republic of Korea National Red Cross (ROKNRC), proposes a south-north Red Cross conference to discuss a search campaign for dispersed families in the south and the north.

August 14 — The north Korean Red Cross (NKRC) accepts the ROKNRC offer, and suggests that documents related thereto be exchanged by two messengers from each side at 12 noon August 20 at Panmunjom.

August 15 — President Park pledges positive support for the proposed family search campaign.

August 20 — The two sides exchange documents related to the proposed Red Cross talks at the first south-north Red Cross messengers' contact.

— ROKNRC messengers: Lee Chang-yol, Yoon Yo-hun

— NKRC messengers: So Song-chol, Ryom Chong-ryon

August 21 — The ROKNRC suggests that the first preliminary Red Cross meeting be held at 11 a.m. September 28 at the NNSC conference room, that each side be represented by a five-man delegation, that the lists of the two sides' delegates be exchanged at 12 noon September 24 at the NNSC conference room, and that the preliminary meetings discuss the procedural matters of full-dress Red Cross meetings.

August 26 — A message on the ROKNRC proposal for the procedural matters of the preliminary talks is delivered to the NKRC at the second messengers' contact.

491

August 27 — The NKRC counter-proposes that the first preliminary meeting be held at 11 a.m. September 20 and that the lists of the two sides' delegates be exchanged at 12 noon September 16.

August 30 — The ROKNRC receives a message on the NKRC's counter-proposal at the third messengers' contact.

August 31 — The ROKNRC accepts the NKRC's counter-proposal. The first preliminary meeting is thus set to be held at 11 a.m. September 20 at the NNSC conference room at Panmunjom with five delegates attending from each side. The lists of the delegates of the two sides are to be exchanged at 12 noon September 16.

September 3 — A ROKNRC statement on its acceptance of the NKRC's counter-porposal is delivered to the NKRC at the fourth messengers' contact.

September 15 — The ROKNRC makes public the list of its delegates to the full-dress meetings.
— Chief Delegates: Kim Yon-joo (chief of the ROKNRC Health Division and concurrently chief of the Public Relations Division)
— Alternate Chief Delegate: Park Sun-kyoo (chief of the ROKNRC Chungchong-namdo Branch)
— Delegate: Chong Hong-jin (chief of the Conference Management Division, ROKNRC Conference Secretariat)
— Delegate: Mrs. Chong Hee-kyung (ROKNRC Youth Guidance Committee member)
— Delegate: Chong Choo-nyon (spokesman for the ROKNRC Conference Secretariat)

September 15 — The NKRC makes public the list of its delegates to the full-dress meetings.
— Chief of Delegation: Kim Tae-hui (NKRC secretary general)
— Deputy chief of Delegation: Kim Dok -hyon (NKRC Information Division chief)
— Delegate: Cho Myong-il (chief of the NKRC Culture and Information Division)
— Delegate: Lee Chong-hak (NKRC staff member)
— Delegate: So Song-chol (deputy chief of the NKRC Culture and Information Division)

September 16 — The two sides exchange the lists of their delegates to the preliminary meetings at the fifth messengers' contact.

September 16 — The ROKNRC establishes an advance office for the Red Cross talks.

September 20 — The first preliminary meeting of the South-North Red Cross Conference (SNRCC) is held.

Agreement:

— Venue of preliminary meetings: NNSC conference room at Panmunjom.

— Establishment of permanent conference liaison offices and installation of a direct telephone line.

At the meeting, the ROKNRC suggests a seven-point procedure for the full-dress meetings, whereas the NKRC offers the agenda topics of full-dresss meetings in disregard of the preliminary meeting procedures.

September 22 — The south and north Korea Red Cross establish their permanent liaison offices at Panmunjom and install a direct telephone line between the two offices. The ROKNRC liaison office is located at Freedom House and the NKRC liaison office at Panmungak.

September 29 — The second preliminary meeting is held, and the two sides agree on procedural matters for the preliminary meetings. The ROKNRC proposes that full-dress Red Cross meetings be held in Seoul and Pyongyang by turn.

Agreement:

— Eight items on the procedure for preliminary meetings.

— Priority order of the topics of preliminary meetings.

October 6 — The third preliminary meeting is held, and the two sides agree to hold the full-dress Red Cross meetings in Seoul and Pyongyang by turn, and to include in the scope of "other procedural matters" the ROKNRC-proposed 18 additional issues incidental to the selection of Seoul and Pyongyang as sites for the full-dress talks as suggested by the ROKNRC. The two sides' delegations and attendants attend a joint tea party at the NNSC lounge.

October 13 — The fourth preliminary meeting is held to discuss scheduling the full-dress meetings.

— The ROKNRC, maintaining the sooner the full-dress talks could convene the better it would be, suggests that the time be discussed at the final stage of the preliminary meetings.

493

— The NKRC maintains that the first full-dress meeting will be held at 10 a.m. December 10, 1972.

October 20 — The fifth preliminary meeting is held to discuss scheduling the full-dress meetings. The delegates and attendants have a joint luncheon at the NNSC lounge.

October 27 — The sixth preliminary meeting is held. The two sides agree to put off the issue of scheduling until a later date and discuss the question of agenda items for the full-dress meetings.

November 3 — The seventh preliminary meeting is held to discuss the question of agenda items.

— The ROKNRC points out the need for a priority solution to the family search campaign.

— The NKRC insists that friends should be included in the scope of a family search campaign.

— The ROKNRC invites NKRC delegates and attendants to a luncheon.

November 11 — The eighth preliminary meeting is held to discuss the question of agenda items.

— The ROKNRC emphasizes that the proposed family search campaign should be discussed at the full-dress meetings on a priority basis.

— The NKRC insists that separated families, relatives and friends should be allowed to travel in the area of the other side freely.

November 19 — The ninth preliminary meeting is held to discuss the question of agenda items.

— The ROKNRC suggests an extensive definition of separated families.

— The NKRC holds fast to their insistence that the free travel of families, relatives and friends should be guaranteed first.

November 24 — The tenth preliminary meeting is held to discuss the question of agenda items.

— The ROKNRC suggests that part of the relatives north Korea talks about may be included in the definition of families.

— The NKRC sticks to its previous three-point proposition.

December 3 — The 11th preliminary meeting is held to discuss the question of agenda items, and the ROKNRC sets forth a modified six-point proposal.

December 10 — The 12th preliminary meeting is held to discuss the question of agenda items.

— The ROKNRC urges the NKRC to accept the modified proposal laid down at the 11th preliminary meeting.

— The NKRC produces a three-point proposal closely resembling the modified ROKNRC offer.

December 17 — The 13th preliminary meeting is held to discuss the question of agenda items.

— The ROKNRC points out the rationality and fairness of its modified offer.

— The NKRC adheres to the demand for free travel.

«1972»

January 1 — President Park, in his New Year message, pledges positive support for the south-north Red Cross talks.

January 10 — The 14th preliminary meeting is held to discuss the question of determining agenda items for the full-dress meetings.

— The ROKNRC stresses the urgency of a project to eliminate the sufferings of the dispersed families in the south and the north.

— The NKRC continues to demand a guarantee of free travel. The delegates and attendants of the two sides take luncheon together at the NNSC lounge.

January 11 — President Park, in his New Year press conference, vows that the government will extend all available support for the success of the Red Cross talks.

January 19 — The 15th preliminary meeting is held to discuss the question of agenda items.

— The ROKNRC urges the early determination of agenda items for the full-dress talks.

— The NKRC continues demanding the prior guarantee of free travel.

January 28 — The 16th preliminary meeting is held to discuss the question of agenda items.

— The ROKNRC proposes that like items suggested by both sides be worded in a single manner.

— The NKRC agrees to produce a modified proposition of the 17th preliminary meeting.

February 3 — The 17th preliminary meeting is held to discuss the question of agenda items.

— The ROKNRC sets forth a new six-point proposal on the question of determining agenda items for the full-dress talks.

— The NKRC sets forth a new three-point proposal on the question of determining agenda items for the full-dress talks.

February 10 — The 18th preliminary meeting is held to discuss the question of agenda items.

— The ROKNRC emphasizes the need for working-level discussion to adjust the wording of topics on which the two sides basically agree.

— The NKRC objects to the use of the word "arrangement" on the ground that the word carries the implication of "limitedness."

February 17 — The 19th preliminary meeting is held, and the two sides agree to hold a series of working-level meetings to adjust the wording of agenda topics for the full-dress meetings.

February 21 — The first working-level meeting is held to adjust the wording of agenda topics for the full-dress meetings.

— ROKNRC delegate: Chong Hong-jin, Chong Choo-nyun

— NKRC delegate: Cho Myong-il, Lee Chong-hak

February 24 — The second working-level meeting is held.

February 28 — The third working-level meeting is held.

March 6 — The fourth working-level meeting is held.

March 10 — The fifth working-level meeting is held.

March 17 — The sixth working-level meeting is held.

March 24 — The seventh working-level meeting is held.

April 17 — The eighth working-level meeting is held.

May 9 — The ninth working-level meeting is held.

May 12 — The tenth working-level meeting is held.

May 19 — The 11th working-level meeting is held.

May 22 — The 12th working-level meeting is held.

June 5 — The 13th working-level meeting is held.

* Work on the wording of agenda topics for the full-dress meetings is completed.

June 16 — The 20th preliminary meeting is held, and the two sides agree on agenda items for the full-dress meetings.

July 4 — The South-North Joint Communique is announced in Seoul and Pyongyang simultaneously.

July 10 – The 21st preliminary meeting is held to discuss the question of forming delegations to the full-dress meetings.

July 14 — The 22nd preliminary meeting is held to discuss the question of forming delegations to the full-dress meetings.

July 19 — The 23rd preliminary meeting is held, and the two sides agree on the issue of forming delegation to the full-dress meetings. —The two sides also agree in principle to hold the first full-dress meeting on August 5, 1972.

July 26 — The 24th preliminary meeting is held, and the two sides agree to hold working-level meetings to discuss miscellaneous matters for the procedure of the full-dress meetings, as well as convening a working-level communications meeting.

July 27 — The first working-level meeting is held to discuss miscellaneous matters for full-dress meeting procedures.
— ROKNRC delegate: Chong Choo-nyun.
— NKRC delegate: Lee Chong-hak.
— Place: NNSC conference room at Panmunjom.

August 3 — The second working-level meeting is held to discuss miscellaneous matters for full-dress meeting procedures.

August 9 — The third working-level meeting is held to discuss miscellaneous matters for full-dress meeting procedures.

August 11 — The 25th and final preliminary meeting is held, and the two sides agree on the miscellaneous matters for full-dress meeting procedures.
Agreement:
Agreement and confirmation of miscellaneous matters for the full-dress meeting procedures.
— Schedule for the full-dress meetings:
The first full-dress meeting — 10 a.m. August 30, 1972, Pyongyang.
The second full-dress meeting — 10 a.m. September 13, 1972, Seoul.

August 15 — President Park, in his Liberation Day commemorative message, calls upon north Korea to show a sincere posture toward the South-North Red Cross Conference.

August 17 — The ROKNRC makes public the list of its delegates to the full-dress meetings

August 18 — The south and north Korean Red Cross install 20 direct telephone circuits between Seoul and Pyongyang in preparation for the full-dress meetings.

August 22 — Seoul-side SNCC co-chairman Lee issues a statement guaranteeing the personal safety of the members of the north Korean Red Cross delegation.

August 22 — The ROKNRC replaces Kim Hui-jong, one of the advisors, with Ku Bom-mo.

August 23 — The north Korean Ministry of Social Security issues a statement guaranteeing the personal safety of the members of the ROKNRC delegation.

August 24 — The two sides exchange the texts of their statements on the guarantee of personal safety at Panmunjom.

August 25 — The ROKNRC notifies the NKRC of the list of 54 persons set to attend the first full-dress meeting of the Red Cross talks.

August 25 — A direct telephone circuit opens between the central offices of the south and north Korean Red Cross societies.

August 29—September 2 — The first full-dress meeting is held in Pyongyang.

Itinerary:

August 29 — Arrival of the ROKNRC delegation in Pyongyang.

August 30 — The first full-dress meeting is held from 10 a.m. through 12:55 p.m.

August 31 — Tour of Mangyongdae, attendance at a dinner hosted by the SNCC Pyongyang-side co-chairman.

September 1 — Tour of Boys' Palace and a nursery.

September 2 — The ROKNRC delegation leaves Pyongyang and returns to Seoul.

Agreement:

— Confirmation and adoption of the five agenda items for full-dress meetings.

— The two sides pledge to strive to ease the sufferings of dispersed families and to lay a foundation for national unification based on the spirit of the South-North Joint Communique and Red Cross principles.

September 12—16 — The second full-dress meeting is held in Seoul.

Itinerary:

September 12 — Arrival of the NKRC delegation in Seoul.

September 13 — The second full-dress meeting is held from 10:20 a.m. through 12:25 p.m. Tour of the Secret Garden, the Kyung-bok Palace and the National Museum. Attendance at a dinner hosted by the ROKNRC chief delegate.

September 14 — Tour of the Hyonchungsa Shrine. Announcement of the agreement at the second full-dress meeting. Attendance at a dinner hosted by the Seoul-side SNCC co-chairman.

September 15 — Tour of the Octagonal Pavilion at Namsan and of the Seoul Subway. Attendance at a dinner hosted by the Speaker of the National Assembly. The ROKNRC chief delegate meets the press.

September 16 — Chief of the NKRC delegation Kim Tae-hui and advisor Yun Ki-bok call on the Seoul-side SNCC co-chairman. The NKRC delegation leaves Seoul.

Agreement:

— The two sides agree to embody the principles of democracy and freedom, the spirit of the South-North Joint Communique, brotherly love and the Red Cross humanitarian spirit, in solving the agenda items.

— Discussion of the agenda topics will begin at the third full-dress meeting.

— The third full-dress meeting is slated for October 24, 1972 in Pyongyang and the fourth full-dress meeting for November 22, 1972 in Seoul.

October 12 — The first SNCC co-chairmen's meeting held at Freedom House in Panmunjom.

October 23—26 — The third Red Cross full-dress meeting is held in Pyongyang to begin the discussion of Topic No. 1, "Question of tracing, and informing thereof, the fate and whereabouts of the families and relatives dispersed in the south and the north."

Itinerary:

October 23 — Arrival of the ROKNRC delegation in Pyongyang.

October 24 — The third full-dress meeting is held.

Morning session (open) from 10 a.m. to 11:25 a.m.

Afternoon session (closed) from 3 p.m. to 4:10 p.m.

October 25 — Tour of the Korea Revolution Museum, attendance at a dinner hosted by the Pyongyang-side SNCC co-chairman.

October 26 — Departure of the ROKNRC delegation from Pyongyang.

Agreement:

The two sides verbally agree to increase by five the number of pressmen covering the meeting on each side.

November 2—4 — The second SNCC co-chairmen's meeting is held in Pyongyang.

Participants:

— Seoul side: Lee Hu-rak, co-chairman; Chang Key-young, vice prime minister; Choi Kyu-hah, special assistant to the President; Kang In-dock, director of ROKCIA Ninth Bureau; Chong Hong-jin, director of ROKCIA Consultation and Coordination Bureau.

— Pyongyang side: Park Sung-chul, acting co-chairman; Ryu Jang-shik, deputy director of Workers' Party Organization and Guidance Department and concurrently director of External Project Department of the Party: Lee Kyong-sok, a cabinet councilor; Han Ung-shik, an instructor of the Political Committee of the Workers' Party Central Committee; and Kim Dok-hyon, an instructor of the Political Committee of the Workers' Party Central Committee.

Agreement:

— Signing and exchange of the Agreed Minute on Formation & Operation of South-North Coordinating Committee.

— The two sides agree to stop making propaganda broadcasts against each other, using public address systems against each other along the truce line or scattering propaganda leaflets into each other's area effective November 11, 1972.

— Seoul-side delegates meet with Kim Il-sung.

ovember 11 — The two sides make public their agreement on the stoppage of propaganda broadcast against each other, on the use of public address systems against each other along the truce line, and on the scattering of propaganda leaflets into each other's area effective November 11.

November 11 — The SNCC Seoul side asks the Pyongyang side to terminate "Voice of Unification Revolutionary Party" broadcasts against the south.

November 22—24 — The fourth Red Cross full-dress meeting is held in Seoul.

Itinerary.

November 22 — Arrival of the NKRC delegation in Seoul.

Morning session (closed) from 10 a.m. to 11:15 a.m.

Afternoon session (closed) from 3 p.m. to 5:32 p.m.

November 23 — Signing and announcement of an agreement made at the fourth full-dress meeting. Tour of the Sunkyung Chemical Co. textile factory. Attendance at a dinner hosted by the Seoul-side SNCC co-chairman.

November 24 — Departure of the NKRC delegation from Seoul.

Agreement:

— Agreement on the establishment of a south-north Red Cross joint committee and a joint south-north Red Cross project office at Panmunjom.

— Agreement on the discussion and adoption of regulations on the function, operational procedure and composition of the proposed joint committee and project office.

— Agreement on discussion of the establishment of other necessary offices.

November 30 — The third SNCC co-chairmen's meeting is held in Seoul.

November 30—December 2 — The first SNCC meeting is held in Seoul.

— Pyongyang-side delegates call on President Park.

«1973«

March 10 — The first SNCC Executive Council meeting is held at Panmungak, Panmunjom.

March 14—16 — The second SNCC meeting is held in Pyongyang. No agreement is reached at the meeting.

March 20—23 — The fifth Red Cross full-dress meeting is held in Pyongyang.

Itinerary:

March 20 — Arrival of the ROKNRC delegation in Pyongyang.

March 21 — The fifth full-dress meeting (closed) from 10 a.m. to 11:12 a.m. Tour of Mangyongade, and attendance at a dinner hosted by the chairman of the Pyongyang City People's Committee.

March 22 — A session (closed) from 10 a.m. to 12:55 p.m. Tour of a "chicken factory" at Mangyongdae, and viewing of a show at the National Art Theater. Attendance at a dinner hosted by the SNCC Pyongyang-side co-chairman.

March 23 — The ROKNRC delegation leaves Pyongyang. The ROKNRC chief delegate meets the press at Freedom House.

Agreement:

— The two sides agree to hold the sixth full-dress meeting in Seoul May 9-10.

April 16 — Kim Il-sung, in an address at a rally welcoming Norodom Sihanouk's visit to Pyongyang, demands that "representatives of all political parties and social organizations and people from all walks of life in the south and north be allowed to participate in the South-North Coordinating Committee" and that "a political conference attended by the representatives of all political parties and social organizations and people from all walks of life be convened separately from the Coordinating Committee."

April 24 — The second SNCC Executive Council meeting is held at Freedom House.

May 8—11 — The sixth Red Cross full-dress meeting is held in Seoul.

Itinerary:

May 8 — Arrival of the NKRC delegation in Seoul.

May 9 — The sixth full-dress meeting from 10 a.m. to 11:37 a.m. Attendance at a dinner hosted by the ROKNRC chief delegate.

May 10 — A session from 10 a.m. to 11:57 a.m. Tour of Changkyong-won, and attendance at a dinner hosted by the SNCC Seoul-side co-chairman.

May 11 — The NKRC delegation leaves Seoul.

Agreement:

— The two sides agree to hold the seventh full-dress meeting on July 11.

May 23 — The third SNCC Executive Council meeting is held at Panmungak.

June 10 — North Korea resumes making propaganda allegations through public address systems against the south in four areas along the truce line in violation of the agreement reached at the second SNCC co-chairmen's meeting on the stoppage of propaganda activities against each other.

June 11 — North Korea proposes again the stoppage of mutual slanders and defamation. The Seoul-side accepts it.

June 12—14 — The third SNCC meeting is held in Seoul. No agreement

502

is reached.

June 23 — President Park makes public the Special Foreign Policy Statement Regarding Peace and Unification.

June 23 — Kim Il-sung announces his so-called "five-point peaceful unification programme."

June 26 — The SNCC Seoul-side lodges a protest with the Pyongyang side against its continued public address system propaganda along the truce line.

July 5 — The SNCC Seoul-side renews its demand that the Pyongyang-side stop airing "Voice of Unification Revolutinary Party" programs against the south.

July 10—13 — The seventh Red Cross full-dress meeting is held in Pyongyang. The ROKNRC proposes the exchange of groups of tomb visitors on Chusok holiday. The NKRC rejects it.

Itinerary:

July 10 — Arrival of the ROKNRC delegation in Pyongyang.

July 11 — The seventh full-dress meeting from 10 a.m. to 10:48 a.m. Attendance at a dinner hosted by the NKRC Central Committee.

July 12 — A session from 10 a.m. to 11:42 a.m. Tour of the Pyongyang Zoological Garden, and attendance at a dinner hosted by the SNCC Pyongyang-side acting co-chairman.

July 13 — Return of the ROKNRC delegation to Seoul

August 1 — Lee Nak-sun, president of the Korean Volleyball Association, invites, through the SNCC, north Korea to take part in the second Asian Volleyball Coach Training Seminar slated for August 10 in Seoul.

August 2 — North Korea rejects the invitation to the Volleyballl Seminar.

August 28 — Kim Young-joo, SNCC Pyongyang-side co-chairman, declares the unilateral suspension of the inter-Korean dialogue.

August 29 — Lee Hu-rak, SNCC Seoul-side co-chairman, issues a statement refuting the north Korean declaration and calling for its withdrawal.

November 15 — The SNCC Seoul-side calls a meeting of the SNCC Executive Council to discuss the resumption of the stalled dialogue.

November 15 — The ROKNRC proposes that a liaison officers' meeting be held at Panmunjom on November 16 to discuss the opening of the

503

eighth full-dress meeting of the Red Cross talks before the end of the year.

November 16 — Ryu Jang-shik, SNCC Pyongyang-side vice chairman, in a letter addressed to Chang Key-young, Seoul-side vice chairman, contends that north Korea would discuss the question of resuming the talks only if south Korea 1) withdraws the June 23 foreign policy statement and stops "persecuting" the violators of the Anti-Communist Law and the National Security Law, and 2) agrees to include the representatives of various political parties and social organizations in the South-North Coordinating Committee.

November 17 — The NKRC counter-proposes that a liaison officers' meeting be held at 10 a.m. November 21 at Panmunjom. The ROKNRC accepts it.

November 21 — Chang Key-young, SNCC Seoul-side vice chairman, in a message to his north Korean counterpart, Ryu Chang-shik, proposes that the two vice chairmen meet at Panmunjom at 10 a.m. November 27 to discuss the issue of holding the fourth SNCC meeting early as well as the question of reorganizing the SNCC.

November 21 — A south-north Red Cross liaison officers' meeting held from 10 a.m. to 10:50 a.m., where the ROKNRC suggested the eighth full-dress meeting be held in Seoul on December 19, while the NKRC suggested that one of the delegates to the full-dress meetings from each side attend the following liaison officers' meeting.

November 22 — The ROKNRC proposes that the second liaison officers' meeting be held at 10 a.m. November 24.

November 22 — The NKRC counter-proposes that it be held at 10 a.m. November 28.

November 22 — The ROKNRC accepts it.

November 27 — Ryu Jang-shik, SNCC Pyongyang-side vice chairman, in a message to his Seoul-side counterpart, Chang Key-young, agrees to the Seoul-side proposal for vice chairmen's meetings, counter-offering that the first vice chairmen's meeting be held on December 5.

November 27 — The SNCC Seoul-side accepts the Pyongyang-side counter-proposal.

November 28 — The first Red Cross working-level meeting is held from 10 a.m. to 11:30 a.m. at Panmunjom. The NKRC rejects the

ROKNRC suggestion that the eighth full-dress meeting be held in Seoul at an early date.

December 3 — Lee Hu-rak resigns as SNCC Seoul-side co-chairman due to health reasons. Vice Chairman Chang Key-young assumes the duty of acting co-chairman.

December 5 — The first SNCC vice chairmen's meeting is held from 10 a.m. to 12:30 p.m. The Seoul-side suggests that the second vice chairmen's meeting be held on December 12.
— Place: Panmungak at Panmunjom
— Attendees: Seoul-side — Vice chairman Chang Key-young
       Pyongyang-side — Vice chairman Ryu Jang-shik

December 11 — The Pyongyang-side counter-proposes that the second vice chairmen's meeting be held on December 19. The Seoul-side accepts it.

December 13 — The ROKNRC sends a message to the KNRC, urging it to agree to the holding of the eighth full-dress meeting at an early date.

December 19 — The second SNCC vice chairmen's meeting is held at Freedom House at Panmunjom.

December 21 — The NKRC, in a telephone message, insists that the eighth full-dress meeting be held in Pyongyang instead of in Seoul on the grounds of a so-called "environment" problem.

«1974«

January 18 — President Park proposes, in his New Year press conference, a "south-north non-aggression agreement," featuring three component principles; 1) non-aggression, 2) non-interference and 3) maintenance of the Armistice Agreement in force.

January 30 — 3rd SNCC Vice Chairmen's Meeting (Panmungak in Panmunjom.)

On SNCC reorganizations:

Seoul side proposes an increase in the number of Committee members from one side from five to ten, comprising representatives of political parties and social organizations in addition to the authorities.

Pyongyang side makes a fancy proposal that the SNCC be transformed into an obscure mass rally-type body, by organizing it

505

with five, or more, representatives each from some sixty to seventy political parties and social organizations, plus undetermined number of representatives of various classes and strata of people, from each side respectively.

February 25 — 2nd SNRCC delegates' contact (Panmunjom) ROKNRC delegate asks that 1) NKRC assure humanitarian treatment of the fishermen kidnapped to north in the Feb. 15 incident and 2) agree to have the 8th full-dress SNRCC meeting in Seoul Apr. 9-10, 1974. NKRC delegate turns deaf ear to the ROKNRC suggestions.

February 27 — 4th SNCC Vice Chairmen's Meeting (Freedom House in Panmunjom).

On Feb. 15 incident:

Seoul side asks that Pyongyang side:

1) apologize for the incident,
2) return the kidnapped fishing boat and fishermen aboard as well as the remains of the dead fishermen,
3) punish those north Koreans responsible for the incident,
4) compensate for the fishermen drowned dead and damages in property and,
5) guarantee against recurrence of the incident.

Pyongyang side argues that the two fishing boats involved in the Feb. 15 incident were "spyships."

On SNCC reorganization:

Pyongyang side withdraws the fancy proposal of the earlier 3rd Vice Chairmen's Meeting and, instead, says that it would agree to normalize the function of the SNCC, without reorganization, if Seoul side agree to hold a "south-north political conference" in parallel with the SNCC.

March 11 — 3rd SNRCC delegates' contact

NKRC rejects the ROKNRC suggestion that the 8th full-dress SNRCC talks be held Apr. 9-10, 1974, and, instead, proposes that the two sides hold "Panmunjom preliminary meetings," with each side represented there by the alternate chief delegates, "for preliminary discussions on agenda items of the full-dress talks."

March 27 — 5th SNCC Vice Chairmen's Meeting (Panmungak)

Fruitless debates on Feb. 15 incident and SNCC reorganization.

April 3 — 4th SNRCC delegates' contact

ROKNRC proposes that 1) ROKNRC, NKRC and International Committee of the Red Cross (ICRC) form a tripartite fact-finding team for investigation of the conditions of the fishermen detained in north Korea and 2) the two sides hold "temporary Panmunjom meetings of the full-dress talks," wth each side represented by the chief delegate, instead of the "preliminary meeting" proposed by NKRC.

NKRC instantly rejects ROKNRC proposals.

April 24 — 6th SNCC Vice Chairmen's Meeting (Freedom House in Panmunjom)

Fruitless debates on Feb. 15 incident and SNCC reorganization.

April 29 — 5th SNRCC delegates' contact

ROKNRC asks NKRC to offer the latter's good offices for exchange of mails between the Republic of Korea fishermen detained in north Korea and their families. However, NKRC turns a deaf ear to the ROKNRC request.

May 22 — 6th SNRCC delegates' contact

The two sides agree to hold SNRCC "working-level meetings" in Panmunjom, each side represented by the alternate chief delegate, for discussions on 1) agenda items of the full-dress talks on a preliminary basis and 2) the question of holding the 8th full-dress SNRCC talks.

May 29 — 7th SNRCC delegates' contact

The two sides agree to have the first "working-level" meeting held on July 10, 1974, in the conference room of the Neutral Nations Supervisory Commission (NNSC) in Panmunjom, and to have their respective sides represented at the meeting by a three-men delegation each, headed by the alternate chief delegate.

June 28 — 7th SNCC Vice Chairmen's Meeting (Panmungak in Panmunjom)

Seoul-side lodges a strong protest with the authorities of Pyongyang-side over the sinking of a Republic of Korea maritime police patrol boat on high seas off the east coast by north Korean gunships.

Pyongyang-side asserts that the sinking of the Republic of Korea police patrol boat was "exercise of the right of self-defense."

July 10 — 1st SNRCC Working-Level Meeting

ROKNRC proposes that 1) the 8th full-dress SNRCC talks be held on August 30, 1974, in Seoul and 2) the two sides undertake as a pilot project, tracing services for aged parents prior to sweeping implementation of tracing services for separated families and relatives in general.

NKRC rejects the ROKNRC proposals.

July 24 — 2nd SNRCC Working-Level Meeting

NKRC proposes that the two sides adopt a "joint statement" asking the Republic of Korea Government to 1) repeal the Anti-Communist Law and National Security Law. 2) disband all anti-Communist organizations and anti-Communist authorities, 3) illegalize opposition to communism and 4) allow participation by political parties and social organizations in the implementation of the tracing services currently at issue at the SNRCC.

August 15 — President Park declares, in his commemorative speech, three basic principles for peaceful unification of the country; 1) concluding of a "non-aggression agreement" between the two sides of Korea, 2) continuation of the South-North Dialogue and implementation of exchanges and cooperation between the two sides of Korea and 3) holding of a free all-Korea election, under fair election management and supervision, with a representation in direct proportion to the indigenous populace in the two sides of Korea, for achievement of the unification

August 28 — 3rd SNRCC Working-Level Meeting

ROKNRC raises the attempted assassination of the President of the Republic of Korea by north Korean agent of August 15 and demand that north Korea 1) punish those responsible for the murder attempt of August 15, 2) give up the policy blindly pursuing a violent class revolution in the Republic of Korea and 3) show sincerity to have the humanitarian talks of SNRCC normalized at an early date.

September 21 — 8th SNCC Vice Chairmen's Meeting (Freedom House in Panmunjom).

On August 15 incident:

Seoul-side demands that north Korea:

1. Apologize for the incident and punish those north Koreans responsible for the incident.

2. Formally denounce the avowed policy seeking what is called "south Korean revolution."

3. Immediately accept the three basic principles for peaceful unification declared by President Park Chung Hee of the Republic

of Korea in his August 15 speech.

On normalization of SNCC function:

Seoul-side asks that Pyongyang-side:

1. Immediately agree to terminate the Vice Chairmen's Meeting and resume normal operation of the SNCC.

2. Accept the Republic of Korea proposal of a "south-north non-aggression agreement, as well as the Foreign Policy for Peace and Unification of June 23, 1973, and agree to start discussions on the question of concluding the "non-aggression agreement" at the SNCC meetings, as soon as the SNCC has its function normalized.

3. Stop seeking a communist takeover of the southern half of the country by force.

Pyongyang-side refuses to discuss the August 15 incident on the ground that it had "nothing to do" with the incident. On normalization of the SNCC function, Pyongyang-side demands, as preconditions, that Seoul-side:

1. Withdraw the June 23 Foreign Policy for Peace and Unification.

2. Sever Republic of Korea's traditional ties with America and Japan.

3. Prohibit all forms of opposition to communism.

4. Agree to hold what is called a "south-north political conference" in paralled with the SNCC.

September 25 — 4th SNRCC working-level meeting

ROKNRC urges NKRC to accept the ROKNRC offer of "Aged Parents First" program, NKRC again refuses the ROKNRC offer.

November 5 — 5th SNRCC working-level meeting

November 15 — UNC announces discovery of an underground tunnel in the southern sector of DMZ under construction by north Korea.

November 29 — 6th SNRCC working-level meeting

ROKNRC presents a detailed program for implementation of the "Aged Parents First" project.

November 30 — Meeting between SNCC spokesmen of the two sides in Panmunjom. Pyongyang-side proposes a postponement of the 9th SNCC Vice Chairmen's Meeting of December 4.

December 3 — Seoul-side accepts Pyongyang-side's proposal to put off the 9th SNCC Vice Chairmen's Meeting to January 8, 1975, and proposes a meeting of SNCC Executive Council on December 18, 1974.

December 14 — Meeting between SNCC spokesmen in Panmunjom
Pyongyang-side demands reorganization of SNCC Executive Council, as a precondition for holding an Executive Council meeting.

«1975»

January 6 — Pyongyang notifies Seoul, via Seoul-Pyongyang direct
telephone line, that Pyongyang's SNCC Vice Chairman Ryu Jang-
shik has been replaced by Cho Myong-il.

January 8 — 9th SNCC Vice Chairmen's Meeting (Panmungak in
Panmunjom)

January 14 — President Park Chung Hee of the Republic of Korea calls
on north Korea, in a New Year Press Conference to:

1) Accept the offer of a "south-north mutual non-aggression agreement."

2) Immediately resume the South-North Dialogue on both tracks.

3) Either join the United Nations separately or let the Republic
of Korea join the world body alone.

4) Accept preservation of the 1953 Armistice Agreement as a condition for dissolution of the United Nations Command.

January 24 — 7th SNRCC Working-level Meeting is held in NNSC
conference room.

January 24 — SNCC's Seoul-side lodges a protest, via Seoul-Pyongyang
direct telephone line, over north Korea's loudspeaker broadcasts
along DMZ.

January 25 — SNCC's Pyongyang-side replies, via Seoul-Pyongyang
direct telephone line, that north Korea's resumption of loudspeaker
broadcasts along DMZ was a "response" to south Korean side
resuming them first.

January 25 — SNCC's Seoul-side lodges its second protest, via the Seoul-
Pyongyang direct telephone line, over north Korea's resumption of
DMZ loudspeaker broadcasts.

January 28 — SNCC's Seoul-side announces north Korea's discontinu-
ation of the DMZ loudspeaker broadcasts.

February 5 — SNCC's Seoul-side lodges a protest, via Seoul Pyongyang
direct telephone line, over the north Korean electronic operation
jamming Republic of Korea's regular radio and television programs.

February 7 — SNCC's Pyongyang-side denies, via Seoul-Pyongyang
direct telephone line, its complicity in the jamming operation.

February 28 — 8th SNRCC Working-level Meeting is held in NNSC conference room.

March 14 — 10th SNCC Vice Chairmen's Meeting (Freedom House in Panmunjom)

March 24 — The UNC announces discovery of the second underground tunnel found under construction by north Korea within the UNC sector of DMZ some 1.3Km northeast of Chorwon.

March 26 — 9th SNRCC Working-level Meeting is held in NNSC conference room.

May 8 — 10th SNRCC Working-level Meeting is held in NNSC conference room.

May 29 — SNCC's Pyongyang-side unilaterally notifies Seoul, via Seoul-Pyongyang direct telephone line, that the 11th SNCC Vice Chairmen's Meeting, slated for May 30, 1976, is "indefinitely postponed."

May 29 — SNCC's Seoul-side demands, via Seoul-Pyongyang direct telephone line, that the 11th SNCC Vice Chairmen's Meeting be held on May 30 as scheduled.

May 29 — SNCC's Pyongyang-side, via Seoul-Pyongyang direct telephone line, says that it will boycott the 11th SNCC Vice Chairmen's Meeting if Seoul does not consent to its postponement.

June 2 — SNCC's Pyongyang-side issues a statement saying that the 11th SNCC Vice Chairmen's Meeting will "remain indefinitely postponed, pending creation of favorable conditions."

June 9 — NKRC, via direct telephone line between the two Red Cross societies, proposes postponement of the 11th SNRCC Working-level Meeting, slated for June 12, until sometime in July.

June 10 — ROKNRC, via direct telephone line between the two Red Cross societies, asks NKRC to designate a date for the 11th Working-level Meeting proposed to be postoned by NKRC.

June 11 — NKRC, via direct telephone line between the two Red Cross societies, rejects the ROKNRC offer to designate a new date for the 11th Working-level Meeting.

July 3 — SNCC's Pyongyang-side, in a statement issued in the name of its Co-chairman:
  1) Asks ROK to repeal her Foreign Policy for Peace and Unification, terming it a "declaration perpetuating the national division and disrupting the dialogue."
  2) Declares that there is no need for continuation of the dialogue,

511

"so long as south Korea maintains her anti-Communist policies."

3) Asks that the present government of the Republic of Korea be overthrown, to be replaced by a "democratic regime."

4) Suggests that a "grand national congress" be held.

July 4 — President Park Chung Hee of the Republic of Korea issues a statement marking the third anniversary of announcement of the South-North Joint Communique:

1) Asking north Korea to stop all its aggressive war preparations against the Republic of Korea.

2) Urging north Korea to desist from all its covert operations against the Republic of Korea as well as the acts of mud-slinging against the south in overseas activities.

3) Proposes immediate and unconditional normalization of the two-track inter-Korean dialogue both in SNCC and SNRCC.

July 5 — SNCC's Seoul-side, via Seoul-Pyongyang direct telephone line, proposes to Pyongyang that the 11th SNCC Vice Chairmen's Meeting be held on July 15.

July 9 — Seoul's Acting SNCC Co-chairman, in a statement:

1) Suggests that the long-overdue fourth SNCC plenary meeting be held before August 15 in Pyongyang.

2) Assures Seoul-side's willingness to debate, at the resumed SNCC meetings, whatever problems and issues brought up by either of the two sides.

July 10 — ROKNRC, via direct telephone line between the two Red Cross societies, proposes July 25 as the date for the 11th Working-level Meeting.

July 14 — NKRC, via direct telephone line between the two Red Cross societies, counter-proposes July 21 as the date for the 11th Working-level Meeting.

July 14 — SNCC's Pyongyang-side, via Seoul-Pyongyang direct line, rejects Seoul-side's proposal to hold the 11th Vice Chairmen's Meeting on July 15.

July 16 — ROKNRC, via direct telephone line between the two Red Cross societies, accepts the NKRC counterproposal of July 21 as the date for the 11th Working-level Meeting.

July 21 — 11th SNRCC Working-level Meeting is held in NNSC conference room.

August 8 — SNCC's Seoul-side, via Seoul-Pyongyang direct telephone line, proposes August 25 as the date for the 11th Vice Chairmen's Meeting.

August 22 — 12th SNRCC Working-level Meeting is held in NNSC conference room.

August 25 — SNCC's Seoul-side, in a statement, announces that Pyongyang has ignored, even without answering over the telephone, Seoul-side's proposal of August 8, suggesting August 25 as the date for the 11th Vice Chairmen's Meeting.

October 13 — SNCC's Seoul-side, via Seoul-Pyongyang direct telephone line, proposes to Pyongyang that the long-overdue fourth SNCC plenary meeting be held in Panmunjom, instead of Pyongyang, if it suits the conveinence of Pyongyang-side, asking that the 11th Vice Chairmen's Meeting be held on October 20.

October 17 — SNCC's Pyongyang-side, via Seoul-Pyongyang direct telephone line, rejects Seoul-side's proposal of October 13, criticizing Republic of Korea's anti-Communist policies.

October 23 — 13th SNRCC Working-level Meeting is held in NNSC conference room.

November 28 — 14th SNRCC Working-level Meeting is held in NNSC conference room.

«1976«

January 26 — SNCC's Seoul-side in a statement, calls on Pyongyang to come back to the conference table at an early date.

February 10 — SNCC's Seoul-side, via Seoul-Pyongyang direct telephone line, notifies Pyongyang that Lee Yong-hee, a Special Assistant to President Park Chung Hee, has replaced Choi Kyu Hah as one of Seoul-side's SNCC members.

February 12 — 15th SNRCC Working-level Meeting is held in NNSC conference room.

March 9 — ROKNRC, via direct telephone line between the two Red Cross societies, notifies NKRC that Amb. Chi Yeon Tai has replaced Amb. Lee Bum Suk as ROKNRC's chief delegate to SNRCC.

March 31 — ROKNRC, via direct telephone line between the two Red Cross societies, proposes a meeting between the chief delegates of the two sides in SNRCC on ways to break the impasse in the humanitarian talk.

April 7 — NKRC, via direct telephone line between the two Red Cross societies, rejects the ROKNRC's offer of a meeting between chief delegates of the two sides.

April 10 — 16th SNRCC Working-level Meeting is held in NNSC conference room.

April 12 — SNCC's Seoul-side, via Seoul-Pyongyang direct telephone line, proposes to Pyongyang a swap of "old Korean art exhibits" between them and their "joint exhibits" overseas.

April 18 — SNCC's Pyongyang-side issues a statement rejecting the Seoul-side's offer of "art exhibits."

May 13 — ROK Foreign Minister Park Tong–jin issues a statement urging north Korea to consent to resumption of the inter-Korean dialogue between the two sides of Korea, as parties most directly concerned with the problems of divided Korea, warning against the north Korean attempt to terminate the 1953 Armistice Agreement in the absence of a successor arrangement.

May 27 — SNCC's Seoul-side lodges, via Seoul-Pyongyang direct telephone line, a protest with Pyongyang over north Korea's partial resumption of loudspeaker broadcasts along DMZ.

June 9 — 17th SNRCC Working-level Meeting is held in NNSC conference room.

July 3 — SNCC's Seoul-side, in a statement, calls for:
1) Immediate and unconditional normalization of SNCC operation.
2) Settlement of problems in the inter-Korean relations between the two parties most directly concerned through resumption of the inter-Korean dialogue.

July 3 — Radio Pyongyang broadcasts a "joint statement" of SNCC's Pyongyang-side and "Democratic Front for the Reunification of the Fatherland," calling for convocation of a "grand national congress."

August 15 — President Park Chung Hee of the Republic of Korea, in his commemorative speech marking the 31st anniversary of the nation's liberation from Japanese occupation, calls on north Korea to "agree to resume the South-North Dialogue unconditionally and, thereby, normalize the functions of the South-North Coordinating Committee, bearing in mind the fact that there will be no solution to the problems of Korea, unless understanding or agreement is reached to that effect between the parties directly concerned."

August 18 — North Korea commits the axe-wielding murder of two UNC officers in the JSA in Panmunjom.

August 20 — 18th SNRCC Working-level Meeting is held in NNSC conference room.

August 21 — Kim Il-sung conveys to UNC his message of "regret" over the August 18 axe-wielding murder of two U.S. officers in Panmunjom.

August 30 — North Korea discontinues operation of both of the Seoul-Pyongyang direct telephone lines used separately by the SNCC and the two Red Cross societies. North Korea stops answering call signs from Seoul without explanations.

October 19 — 19th SNRCC Working-level Meeting is held in NNSC conference room.

December 10 — 20th SNRCC Working-level Meeting is held in NNSC conference room.

«1977«

January 1 — President Park, in a New Year message, vows steady efforts to normalize the inter-Korean dialogue for peaceful unification, and asks for north Korea's sincerity for peace and dialogue.

January 12 — President Park, in a New Year press conference, expresses the willingness to offer food assistance to north Korea and emphasizes the need for the conclusion of a south-north non-aggression agreement.

January 25 — North Korea renews its demand for a "joint conference of political parties and social organizations" and a "south-north political conference."

January 28 — The SNCC Seoul-side issues a statement calling for the early normalization of the South-North Coordinating Committee and the severed south-north direct telephone line.

January 28 — The SNCC Seoul-side replaces one of its members, Lee Yong Hee, with Kim Dong Jo.

January 31 — The ROKNRC expresses willingness to do all it can to materialize President Park's offer for food to north Korea.

February 11 — The 21st Red Cross working-level meeting is held.

April 28 — The 22nd Red Cross working-level meeting is held.

May 9 — The SNCC Seoul-side appoints Min Kwan-shik as its acting co-chairman.

June 23 — Foreign Minister Park Tong-jin issues a statement on the fourth anniversary of the June 23 special foreign policy, urging north Korea to agree to the conclusion of a non-aggression agreement and to show sincerity toward resumption of the inter-Korean dialogue.

July 4 — The SNCC Seoul-side acting co-chairman issues a statement on the fifth anniversary of the 1972 South-North Joint Communique, in which the Seoul-side:

1) Proposes the discussion of procedure of the conclusion of the proposed south-north non-aggression agreement.

2) Calls for the early resumption of the operation of the Coordinating Committee.

3) Urges the restoration of the direct south-north telephone line.

July 15 — The 23rd Red Cross working-level meeting is held.

July 15 — A spokesman for the Ministry of Foreign Affairs, in a statement, denounces north Korea's establishment of a 200-mile "economic zone."

July 22 — Min Kwan-shik, SNCC Seoul-side acting co-chairman, issues a statement in connection with the establishment of a 200-mile "economic zone," stressing that:

— The issue of 200-mile "economic waters" should be discussed at the Coordinating Committee.

— A vice chairmen's meeting should be held at Panmunjom before the end of July at the latest.

— The direct south-north telephone line should be restored at an early date.

August 1 — The government spokesman (Minister of Culture and Information) issues a statement denouncing north Korea's establishment of a 200-mile "economic zone."

August 10 — A spokesman for the Ministry of Culture and Information issues a statement in connection with the establishment of a 200-mile "economic zone" by north Korea.

August 12 — The ROKNRC issues a statement on the sixth anniversary of the proposal for the south-north Red Cross conference, asking the NKRC to agree to an early normalization of the Red Cross talks.

August 15 — President Park, in a Liberation Day message, declares that the restoration of mutual trust through dialouge and the holding of free general elections are the only way to achieve national unification peacefully.

October 14 — The 24th Red Cross working-level meeting is held.

October 19 — President Park, in an interview with the editor-in-chief of Le Monde of France, reiterates the basic principles for peaceful unification, which are:

1) Conclusion of a mutual non-aggression agreement between south and north Korea;

2) Mutual door-opening, and implementation of many-sided exchanges and cooperation; and

3) Holding of free general elections in proportion to indigenous popuplation.

December 9 — The 25th Red Cross working-level meeting is held.

December 23 — President Park, in an interview with the chairman of Fuji Television of Japan, calls on north Korea to agree to the unconditional resumption of the inter-Korean dialogue, stressing that the exigent tasks facing Korea are to ease tensions and consolidate peace.

«1978«

January 18 — President Park, in a New Year press conference, calls for south-north exchanges and mutual door-opening through dialogue, saying that the basic direction of the government's unification policy is to pursue "peace first and unification later."

February 1 — North Korea's Foreign Ministry makes public a "memorandum" regarding the Korean question.

February 2 — A number of pro-Pyongyang Koreans in Japan visit their homeland on the lunar New Year's day.

March 3 — Min Kwan-shik, SNCC Seoul-side acting co-chairman, issues a statement calling for the unfolding of an age of exchanges and cooperation through the joint exploration of resources, know-how and wisdom between the south and the north, and specifically

517

proposing that:

1) The opeation of the South-North Coordinating Committee be normalized unconditionally at an early date to discuss the question of easing tensions and consolidating peace as well as the issue of economic, socio-cultural and sports exchanges between the two sides.

2) The direct south-north telephone line be restored immediately and a SNCC vice chairmen's meeting be convened to discuss the question of normalizing the operation of the Coordinating Committee.

March 19 — The north Korean Red Cross informs the ROKNRC in a radio broadcast that it would postpone unilaterally the 26th Red Cross working-level meeting slated for March 20.

March 20 — The 26th Red Cross working-level meeting fails to take place due to the NKRC's boycott.

March 20 — The ROKNRC spokesman issues a statement on the NKRC's boycott, calling for the early resumption of the suspended meeting.

June 23 — President Park, in a special statement on the fifth anniversary of the June 23 Special Foreign Policy Statement Regarding Peace and Unification, proposes to north Korea the establishment of a consultative body to expedite economic cooperation between the two sides on a private level.

July 4 — The SNCC Seoul-side, in a statement, urges north Korea to agree to the unconditional resumption of the inter-Korean dialogue as well as to the establishment of the proposed economic cooperation body.

August 12 — The ROKNRC, in a statement on the seventh anniversary of the proposal for the Red Cross talks, suggests that the chiefs of the south and north Korean Red Cross societies hold a meeting either in Panmunjom, Seoul, Pyongyang or a mutually agreeable third place to discuss the resumption of the stalled Red Cross talks.

August 15 — President Park, in a message on the 33rd anniversary of National Liberation, calls for the unconditional resumption of the south-north dialogue and urges north Korea to respond affirmatively to the south's efforts for the promotion of economic cooperation between the south and the north.

September 9 — The Republic of Korea Shooting Federation urges north Korea to take part in the World Shooting Championships taking place in Seoul.

October 27 — The third north Korean invasion tunnel is discovered near Panmunjom.

«1979«

January 19 — President Park proposes in a New Year press conference that authorities of south and north Korea meet at any time, at any place and at any level without preconditions to discuss all issues pending between the two sides.

January 23 — The Central Committee of north Korea's "Democratic Front" issues a statement, proposing that:
— The two sides officially declare their decision to observe the July 4 South-North Joint Communique effective 10:00 hours February 1.
— The two sides stop all hostile activities along the Military Demarcation Line beginning March 1.
— A whole nation conference be held in either Seoul or Pyongyang in early September.
— Working-level preliminary meetings be held in Pyongyang in early June.

January 26 — The government spokesman (Culture and Information Minister), in a statement, calls for a dialogue between the responsible authorities of south and north Korea.

January 27 — Secretariat of the Central Committee of north Korea's "Democratic Front," In a statement, proposes convening of a working-level preliminary meeting in early April to discuss the convocation of a "whole-nation conference."

January 29 — The spokesman of the Ministry of Culture and Information urges the north Korean authorities to make a responsible response.

January 31 — The SNCC's Seoul-side co-chairman issuies a statement calling for :
— Early resumption of the operation of the South-North Coordinating Committee.
— Immediate restoration of the direct Seoul-Pyongyang telephone line.

January 31 — The north Korean Central News Agency issued a statement:

— Announcing that all slanderous activities against the south would be stopped in the entire area of north Korea effective 10:00 hours February 1, 1979.

February 5 — Secretariat of the Central Committee of north Korea's "Democratic Front" proposes the inauguration of a "Preparatory Committee for National Unification" in place of the South-North Coordinating Committee.

February 8 — The Seoul-side of the South-North Coordinating Committee announces the appointment of Hahm Byoung-choon as a Seoul-side member in place of Kim Dong-jo.

February 12 — Secretariat of the Central Committee of north Korea's "Democratic Front" announces:

— The appointment of north Korea-side liaison delegates for the formation of a "Preparatory Committee for National Unification."

— The decision to send the delegates to the NNSC conference room at Panmunjom at 12:00 noon February 20.

February 12 — The government spokesman, in a news conference, says that the "Democratic Front" of north Korea cannot be considered as responsible authorities, adding that there is no change in the stand calling for a "dialogue between authorities."

February 12 — The spokesman of the Seoul-side of the South-North Coordinating Committee, in a statement, proposes a meeting of the vice chairman of the two sides at the Freedom House at Panmunjom at 10:00 a.m. February 17 to discuss the issue of holding the fourth plenary meeting of the Coordinating Committee.

February 13 — Secretariat of the Central Committee of north Korea's "Democratic Front" issues a statement saying that:

— It would send the delegates of the "Democratic Front" to Panmunjom at 10:00 a.m. February 17 to discuss the formation of a "Preparatory Committee for National Unification."

— It would consider whatever delegation of the south under whichever names as the south's liaison delegation for the formation of of a "Preparatory Committee for National Unification."

February 15 — The spokesman of the Seoul-side of the South-North

520

Coordinating Committee announces that the Seoul-side will send its delegation to Panmunjom on February 17.

February 17 — First abnormal contact takes place between the south and the north.

February 20 — In a message co-signed by Kim Yu-soon, chairman of the north Korean Sports Guidance Committee, and Kim Duk-jun, chairman of the north Korean Table Tennis Association, north Korea proposes the formation of a single table tennis team between the south and the north.

February 24 — In responses, the Republic of Korea Amateur Sports Association and the Republic of Korea Table Tennis Association, in a radio message, say they will send a delegation to the NNSC conference room at Panmunjom at 10:00 a.m. February 27 under the authorization by the Seoul-side of the South-North Coordinating Committee.

February 27 — First meeting takes place between the south and north Korean Table Tennis Associations.

February 28 — Spokesman for the People's Armed Forces Ministry of north Korea announces it is withholding a clause of the January 23 statement of the "Democratic Front" concerning the suspension of hostile activities effective 0 hours of March 1, due to a joint Korea-U.S. military training exercise in the south.

March 5 — Second ping-pong meeting takes place.

March 7 — Second abnormal contact held.

March 9 — Third ping-pong meeting takes place.

March 12 — Fourth ping-pong meeting takes place.

March 14 — Third abnormal contact held.

March 24 — North Korea's Sports Guidance Committee and Table Tennis Association propose that the fifth table tennis meeting be held on March 27.

March 26 — Spokesman for the north Korean Table Tennis Association says a north Korean delegation will go to the NNSC conference room at Panmunjom at 10:00 a.m. March 27 as scheduled.

March 26 — The Republic of Korea government spokesman announces:
— A three-men working-level delegation headed by Dong Hoon, Vice Minister of the National Unification Board, will be sent to

Panmunjom at 10:00 a.m. March 28.

— Working-level delegates' contacts may be held in closed-door sessions if necessary.

March 27 — The "liaison delegation of political parties, social organizations and authorites" of north Korea proposes that the fourth liaison delegates' contacts be held at the NNSC conference room at Panmunjom 10:00 hours April 2.

March 27 — A delegation of the north Korean Table Tennis Association appears at Panmunjom, and proposes that a delegates' contact between the two sides' Table Tennis Associations be held at the NNSC conference room at Panmunjom at 10:00 hours April 3.

March 28 — The "working-level delegation of the authorities of the Republic of Korea" issues a statement (following the miscarriage of a working-level delegates' contact):

— Urging north Korea to come to the forum of dialogue between authorities without any further delay.

April 1 — The "liaison delegation of political parties, social organizations and authorities" of north Korea, in a statement, asks the south to inform it whether the south would attend a proposed meeting.

April 2 — The chief delegate of the "working-level delegation of the authorities of the Republic of Korea," in a press conference, makes it clear that it will meet only those delegates of political parties and social organizations appointed by the authorities of Pyongyang.

April 2 — The "liaison delegation of political parties, social organizations and authorities" of north Korea, in a statement, proposes a liaison delegates' contact at the NNSC conference room at Panmunjom at 10:00 a.m. April 10.

April 2 — Spokesman of the north Korean Table Tennis Association, in a statement, suggests the holding of individual contacts to discuss the issue of resuming the south-north ping-pong talks, and announces that to this end, it will send a delegate and an attendant to the NNSC conference room at Panmunjom at 10:00 hours April 3.

April 3 — The president of the Republic of Korea Table Tennis Association, in a press conference, stresses that the issue of a single team is one thing and the question of a south Korean team's participation in the World Championships is another, urging that north Korea should take all necessary steps for a south Korean team's participation.

April 3 — The spokesman of the north Korean Table Tennis Association contends that the ping-pong talks should be resumed so far as there remains the time for the formation of a "unified team."

April 7 — The spokesman of the "working-level delegation of the authorities of the Republic of Korea," in a statement, emphasizes:

— His delegation is interested in substantial talks with a delegation appointed by the responsible authorities of north Korea.

— The doors always remain open to a dialogue between the authorities of the south and the north as well as to the resumption of the operation of the South-North Coordinating Committee.

April 10 — The "liaison delegation of political parties, social organizations and authorities" of north Korea, in a statement, says it has done all available efforts for the progress of liaison delegates' contact, declaring that the question of whether a dialogue would continue to go on or not is how up to the attitude of the south.

May 1 — The Repulbic of Korea National Red Cross announces the appointment of Soh Sang-yong as chief delegate to the South-North Red Cross Conference in place of Chi Yeon-tai.

June 11 — Kim Young-sam, president of the New Democratic Party reveals his willingness to meet north Koreans for himself to discuss unification problems, separate from government authorities.

July 1 — The Presidents of Republic of Korea and the United States issues a joint communique proposing to north Korea holding of a "Meeting of Senior official representatives of the south and north of Korea and the United States" (three authorities meeting).

July 10 — North Korea's Ministry of Foreign Affairs, in a statement, refuses the proposal for the three authorities meeting.

August 12 — The president of ROKNRC issues a statement on the eighth anniversary of the proposal for a South-North Red Cross talks.

August 15 — President Park, in an address marking the thirty-fourth anniversary of National Liberation, urges North Korea to agree to the three authorities meeting.

September 20 — The spokesman for ROKNRC delegation issues a statement urging the northern counterpart to come to the conference table.

December 20 — The north Korean Olympic Committee, in a radio broadcast, proposes to the Republic of Korea Amateur Sports Association (KASA) that a meeting be held on January 17, 1980 to discuss the issue of forming a single team for the Moscow Olympics.

December 24 — KASA president says he has not formally received the north Korean proposal of December 20.

December 26 — The north Korean Olympic Committee, in a radio broadcast, notifies KASA that it would send two liaison officers to Panmunjom at 12 noon on December 27 to deliver a message on the proposal for a single south-north Korean team.

December 27 — The SNCC Seoul side receives a north Korean message at the NNSC conference room at Panmunjom.

«1980«

January 9 — The SNCC Seoul-side spokesman announces that a message from the KASA president addressed to the north Korean Olympic Committee chairman would be delivered at 12 noon on January 11 at Panmunjom.

January 11 — The SNCC Seoul-side delivers the KASA president's message to north Korea, in which the KASA president:

— States the north Korean offer could hardly be implemented, and instead proposed that goodwill sports matches be held between the two sides.

— Welcomes north Korea's participation in international games taking place in Seoul this year.

— Proposes a meeting after the Moscow Olympics to discuss the question of overall sports exchanges between the two sides.

January 11 — North Korea asks for the reopening of the direct south-north telephone line, saying that:

— It unsuccessfully tried to have a telephone conversation with the south.

— It hopes that the Seoul side will receive its call at 6 p.m. on January 11.

January 11 — North Korea announces that it would deliver messages on matters related to unification to the south at 12 noon on January 12 at Panmunjom.

January 12 — The SNCC Seoul-side spokesman, in a statement, states that:
— North Korea rang up on the direct telephone at 8:07 p.m. on January 11, but when the Seoul side demanded that an authorized person use the telephone, north Korea unilaterally suspended the call.
— North Korea announces that it would deliver some letters to the south. The Seoul side inquires who would send them and to whom.

January 12 — North Korea says the letters at issue are signed by Lee Jong-ok and Kim Il and addressed to government authorities and representatives of political parties and social organizations in south Korea.

January 12 — The SNCC Seoul side receives letters of north Korea's Lee Jong-ok and Kim Il.

January 18 — President Choi Kyu-hah announces in his New Year press conference a plan to promote positively the proposed meeting between the prime ministers of the south and the north.

January 19 — The north Korean Olympic Committee announces in a radio broadcast that it would send a second message to the south at 12 noon on January 21.

January 21 — The SNCC Seoul side receives the second message of the north Korean Olympic Committee.

January 22 — North Korea sends letters signed by Kim Il to some anti-Seoul Koreans abroad, proposing a meeting to discuss unification.

January 23 — The SNCC Seoul-side spokesman announces that a message from Prime Minister Shin Hyon-hwack to north Korea's Lee Jong-ok will be delivered to the north at 10 a.m. on January 24 at Panmunjom.

January 24 — The SNCC Seoul side delivers Prime Minister Shin Hyon-hwack's message to the north and makes public its contents. In his message, Prime Minister Shin:
— Proposes a meeting between the prime ministers of the south and the north.
— Proposes that working-level contacts be held to prepare procedural matters for the prime ministers' talks:
Delegates — Three delegates including a vice-minister-level

chief delegate and a few attendants from each side.

Time: 10 a.m. February 6, 1980.

Place: The Freedom House at Panmunjom or another place mutually agreed on.

January 29 — North Korea announces it would deliver Lee Jong-ok's reply to the message of Prime Minister Shin at 10 a.m. on January 30 at Panmunjom.

January 30 — The SNCC Seoul side receives Lee Jong-ok's reply.

January 30 — The SNCC Seoul side announces that north Korea, in Lee Jong-ok's reply, agree to hold working-level contacts as suggested by Prime Minister Shin.

February 1 — The SNCC Seoul side announces that north Korea also stated in Lee Jong-ok's reply that it would send a three man delegation headed by a deputy director of the Central Committee of the Workers' (Communist) Party and concurrently State Council councilor and two technical personnel to the NNSC conference room at Panmunjom at 10 a.m. on February 6.

February 4 — The SNCC Seoul side states that:

— A Republic of Korea working-level delegation consisting of three working-level delegates including a vice-minister-level chief delegate and two attendants would be sent to Panmunjom at 10 a.m. on February 6.

— The delegation would carry credentials signed by Prime Minister Shin. It is expected that the north Korean delegation would carry credentials signed by Lee Jong-ok.

February 5 — The SNCC Seoul side makes public the list of the Republic of Korea working-level delegates:

— **Chief Delegate: Kim Young-choo,** ambassador of the Ministry of Foreign Affairs

Delegate: Chung Chong-shik, director of the Office of Policy Planning, Board of National Unification

Delegate: Lee Dong-bok, director of the South-North Conference Secretariat

— The working-level delegation would be accompanied by two attendants.

526

February 5 — North Korea makes public the list of its working-level delegates:
- **Chief Delegate: Hyon Jun-guk,** deputy director of the Central
  Committe of the Workers' (Communist) Party and concurrently
  State Council councilor
  Delegate: Yim Chun-kil, a State Council director
  Delegate: Paek Jun-hyok, a State Council director

February 6 — The first south-north working-level contact takes place to
prepare for the proposed meeting between the prime ministers of
the south and the north at 10 a.m., at the NNSC conference room.
- Contentions of both sides:
  Republic of Korea: The proposed prime ministers' meeting should
  be held in Geneva, and prior arrangement of agenda is necessary.
  North Korea: The meeting should be held in Seoul and Pyongyang
  by turn, and no prior arrangement of agenda is necessary.
- Matters Agreed on:
  The direct south-north telephone line would be reopened effective
  at 10 a.m. on February 7, 1980.
  Working-level contacts would be held at the Freedom House and
  Panmungak alternately.

February 7 — The direct south-north telephone line reopens.

February 19 — The second working-level contact takes place.
- Matters Agreed on:
  Procedural matters of the prime ministers' talks (whether to open
  meeting, documentation, recording, press briefing, time, facilities,
  marking)
  The third working-level contact is to be held at the Freedom
  House at 10 a.m. on March 4, 1980.

March 3 — The ROKNRC president makes public a radio message addressed
to Son Song-pil, chairman of the north Korean Red Cross, in which
the ROKNRC president asked his north Korean counterpart to
cooperate in securing the early return of the fishermen of the
Haewang-ho Nos. 6 and 7 who had been missing since last January 22.

March 4 — The third working-level contact takes place at the Freedom
House. North Korea counter-proposes on the question of the venue
for the proposed meeting:
- The venue of the contacts between the prime ministers of the

south and the north shall be Panmunjom.

— The first contact shall be held at Panmungak.

— After the first contact, subsequent contacts shall be held in Seoul and Pyongyang by turn through mutual agreement.

March 18 — The fourth working-level contact takes place at Panmungak. Matters Agreed on:

— The meeting between the prime ministers shall be held at the Freedom House and Panmungak by turn.

— If either of the two sides wishes to change the venue, it shall be discussed mutually.

* The venue of the first meeting between the prime ministers shall be determined when the time of the proposed meeting is discussed and settled.

April 1 — The fifth working-level contact takes place at the Freedom House.

April 16 — The ROKNRC spokesman announces that a message would be delivered to NKRC's Son Song-pil the following day.

April 17 — A message from ROKNRC President Lee Ho is delivered to NKRC's Son Song-pil at 12 noon at Panmunjom. In the message, the ROKNRC president calls for early return of the fishermen of the Haewang-ho Nos. 6 and 7 being held in the north.

April 18 — The sixth working-level contact takes place at Panmungak.

April 22 — NKRC sends a radio message to ROKNRC President Lee Ho, expressing willingness to cooperate in the return of the south Korean fishermen held in the north.

April 22 — The ROKNRC president comments on a NKRC radio message.

May 6 — The seventh working-level contact takes place at the Freedom House.

May 6 — NKRC, in a radio message, asks the ROKNRC to provide materials necessary for the return of the fishermen.

May 9 — The ROKNRC announces that a message would be delivered to the NKRC the following day.

May 10 — The ROKNRC delivers the list of fishermen held in the north to the NKRC through Panmunjom.

May 22 — The eighth working-level contact takes place at Panmungak.

June 19 — A building is dedicated in the southern sector of Panmunjom for the south-north prime ministers' meeting.

June 23 — North Korea informs the ROK side over the direct telephone line at 9:35 a.m. that its chief delegate Hyun Jun-guk would not attend the ninth working-level contact for health reasons.

June 24 — The ninth working-level contact is held at Freedom House beginning 10 a.m.

— The ROK side advances two revised agenda topics and a new proposal for the time and place of the first prime ministers' meeting etc.

— The ROK side poses a four-point question to the north regarding north Korea-proposed agenda topics.

— North Korea refuses to discuss the issue of agenda topics on excuse of some internal affairs of the Republic of Korea.

July 4 — SNCC Seoul-side spokesman issues a statement on the 8th anniversary of the July 4 South-North Joint Communique.

August 12 — ROKNRC president issues a statement on the 9th anniversary of the August 12 proposal for south-north Red Cross talks.

August 20 — The 10th working-level contact is held at Panmungak beginning 10 a.m.

— North Korea demands the postponement of the 10th contact on account of some internal affairs of south Korea, attempting to miscarry the contact.

— The ROK side rejects the suggested postponement, asks the north Korean delegation to enter the discussion of the issue of agenda topics, and agrees to hold the next contact at Freedom House on September 26.

September 4 — North Korea resumes slanderous broadcasts against the south by high-power loudspeakers along the truce line beginning 5 p.m.

September 5 — The SNCC Seoul side, in a statement, demands that north Korea stop broadcasts along the truce line and agree to a productive dialogue.

September 8 — North Korea captures the Namjin-ho No. 2 and its 19 fishermen engaged in fishing on the high seas in the East Sea.

September 12 — The ROKNRC sends a message to the NKRC via Panmunjom liaison office, asking that:

— The eighth full-dress Red Cross meeting be held in Seoul October 28-31; and

— North Korea cooperate in the early release of the south Korean fishermen being held in captivity in north Korea.

— A letter of appeal by the representatives of the families of the fishermen held in north Korea is enclosed in the ROKNRC president's message.

September 16 — The ROKNRC president sends messages to ICRC and the League of Red Cross, asking for cooperation in obtaining the return of the captured south Korean fishermen.

September 24 — The north Korean working-level delegation, in a statement broadcast at 7 p.m., announces its intention to boycott the 11th working-level contact slated for September 26, suspending the working-level contacts unilaterally.

September 25 — North Korea suspends the operation of the direct south-north telephone line.

September 26 — The ROK working-level delegation, in a statement, lays down a six-point offer to facilitate early realization of the proposed prime ministers' meeting, and proposes that the 11th working-level contact be held on October 7, 1980.

October 7 — The ROK working-level delegation, in a statement, announces that the 11th working-level contact was miscarried due to north Korea's rejection of the ROK delegation's proposal of September 26.

October 15 — The SNCC Seoul side issues a statement to:

— Expose the fictitiousness of north Korea's idea of "Democratic Confederal Republic of Koryo," and

— Urge north Korea to strive to solve problems through dialogue.

October 27 — Prime Minister Nam Duck-woo, in an address given in observance of the 75th ROKNRC anniversary, urges north Korea to show sincerity toward the resumption of the stalled Red Cross talks.

November 13 — The ROKNRC president issues a statement on the return of the Haewang-ho fishermen, saying:

— North Korea should show an affirmative response to the ROKNRC president's message of September 12 calling for the resumption of the Red Cross talks.

«1981«

January 12 — President Chun Doo Hwan, in his New Year Policy Statement, proposes an Exchange of Visits between Highest Aughorities of the South and the North of Korea.

January 14 — ROK Minister of National Unification proposes to hold a south-north talks to discuss procedural matters for the proposed Exchange of Visits between the Highest Authorities of each sides.

January 19 — North Korea, in a statement by Kim Il, rejects the South's proposal.

June 5 — President Chun Doo Hwan, in an address at the inaugural session of the Advisory Council on Peaceful Unification Policy, proposes to north Korea a Meeting between the Highest Authorities of the south and the north of Korea.

June 19 — The president of the Republic of Korea Amateur Sports Association issues a statement proposing to north Korea for sports exchanges and formation of single teams for international sports events.

July 4 — SNCC Seoul-side issues a statement on the ninth anniversary of the South-North Joint Communique.

August 12 — The president of ROKNRC issues a statement on the tenth anniversary of the proposal for south-north Red Cross talks.

August 20 — Cheon Kwan-wu, chairman of the Central Committee for National Unification of Korea, issues a statement pointing out the unreasonableness of the north Korea's recent call for the "convocation of a conference for acceleration of unfication."

«1982«

January 22 — President Chun Doo-Hwan, in his New Year Policy Statement, announces the Formula for National Reconciliation and Democratic Unification.

January 26 — North Korea, in a statement, rejects President Chun's Unification Fomula.

February 1 — ROK minister of National Unification, in a statement, proposes 20 point projects to implement the proposed Unification Formula.

February 10 — North Korea, in a statement issued in the name of Committee for Peaceful Unification of the Fatherland, proposes a joint meeting between the politicians of the south and the north Korea.

February 25 — ROK Minister of National Unification proposes a "high-level inter-Korean talks."

March 26 — ROK Minister of National Unification urges north Korea to respond affirmatively to his Feb. 25 proposal.

July 4 — The SNCC Seoul-side acting co-chairman issues a statement on the tenth anniversary of the 1972 South-North Joint Communique.

August 6 — The ROKNRC president sends a radio message to North Korea, asking for the early return of the "Masan-ho No. 5" fishing boat and its crewmen hijacked by North Korea.

August 12 — The ROKNRC president issues a statement on the 11th anniversary of the ROKNRC proposal for inter-Korean Red Cross talks.

August 15 — President Chun Doo Hwan states that Korean residents in Communist-bloc countries, including North Korea, can freely visit Korea.

《1983》

January 18 – President Chun Doo Hwan sets forth four tasks to be discussed at a summit meeting.

January 18 – North Korea proposes a joint meeting between the political parties and social organizations of south and north Korea.

February 1 – The National Unification Minister proposes in a statement a meeting between the government authorities and representatives of the political parties and social organizations of South and North Korea.

March 2 – The chairman of the Central Committee for National Unification, in a statement, urges north Korea to accept the proposal for a meeting between the government authorities and representatives of the political parties and social organizations of south and north Korea.

April 1 – The National Unification Minister, in a statement, urges north Korea to accept its earlier proposal for a meeting between the government authorities and representatives of the political parties and social organizations of south and north korea.

June 1 – President Chun Doo Hwan proposes north Korean delegates' participation in the Seoul IPU Congress.

July 4 – The SNCC Seoul-side acting co-charirman issues a statement in observance of the 11th anniversary of the issuance of the South-North Joint Communique.

July 6 – The ROKNRC president calls for the resumption of the South-North Red Cross Conference.

July 24 – The NKRC Central Committee rejects the proposal for the resumption of the Red Cross talks.

August 12 – The ROKNRC president urges the north to agree to resume the Red Cross talks.

《1984》

January 10 – North Korea proposes a tripartite meeting.

January 11 – The National Unification Minister, in a statement, calls for a direct dialogue between south and north Korea.

February 10 – The Prime Minister of the south, in a message to the north, calls for a direct dialogue between south and north Korea.

March 10 – The Prime Minister of the south, in a statement, again urges the north to agree to a direct dialogue between south and north Korea.

March 30 – North Korea proposes a south-north sports meeting.

April 2 – The president of the Korean Amateur Sports Association and the Korean Olympic Committee accepts the proposal for a south-north sports meeting.
- First meeting:10 a.m. April 9 at the conference room of the Neutral Nations Supervisory Commission.
- Composition:Five delegates from each side.
- Topics:The question of forming a single delegation to the 1984 Los Angeles Olympics and other international games, and of conducting south-north sports exchanges.

April 6 – North Korea agrees to the composition of delegates to and the time of a south-north sports meeting.

April 7 – The Korean Olympic Committee makes public the list of its delegates to the south-north sports meeting.
- Chief delegate:Kim Chong-kyu, vice president of the Korean Amateur Sports Association and the Korean Olympic Committee.
- Delegate:Kim Chong-ha, president of the Korean Handball Associa-

tion and standing member of the Korean Olympic Committee.

- Delegate:Lee Chong-ha, member of the Korea University Sports C-
ommittee.
- Delegate:Im Tae-sun, executive member of the Korean Soccer Asso-
ciation and member of the Korean Olympic Committee.
- Delegate:Nam Jong-mun, executive member of the Korean Table
Tennis Association and the Korean Amateur Sports Association.

April 8 – The north Korean Olympic Committee announces the list of its
delegates to the south-north sports meeting.

- Chief delegate:Kim Duk-jun, vice chairman of the north Korean
Olympic Committee.
- Deputy chief delegate:Pak Mu-song, deputy chief secretary of the
north Korean Olympic Committee.
- Delegate:Kim Se-jin, member of the north Korean Olympic Commit-
tee and vice chairman of the north Korean Sports and Arts Guidance
Committee.
- Delegate:So Myong-ho, member of the north Korean Olympic Com-
mittee.
- Delegate:Sok Tae-ho, member of the north Korean Olympic Com-
mittee.

April 9 – First south-north sports meeting held.

April 12 – The president of the Korean Amateur Sports Association and
the Korean Olympic Committee proposes that the second south-north
sports meeting be held on April 18.

April 14 – North Korea rejects the proposal for a second south-north
sports meeting.

April 20 – North Korea proposes that a second south-north sports meeting
be held on April 26.

April 24 – The president of the Korean Amateur Sports Association and
the Korean Olympic Committee counter-proposes that the second
meeting be held on April 30.

April 28 – North Korea agrees to the counter-proposal for the time of the
second meeting.

April 30 – The second south-north sports meeting held.

May 4 – IOC President Samaranch proposes an IOC-proposed south-north sports meeting in Lausanne.

May 9 – The president of the Korean Amateur Sports Association and the Korean Olympic Committee proposes that a third south-north sports meeting be held some day between May 11 and 14.

May 12 – North Korea rejects the proposal for a third sports meeting.

May 18 – The president of the Korean Amateur Sports Association and the Korean Olympic Committee urges the north to agree to hold a third sports meeting on May 23.

May 23 – North Korea counter-proposes that a third south-north sports meeting be held on May 25.

May 24 – North Korea joins in a joint statement issued in Prague by Communist-bloc sports ministers to disclose their boycott of the Los Angeles Olympics.

May 25 – The third south-north sports meeting held.

– The meeting fails even to enter business talks because of the north Korean insistence that the south should admit to and apologize over its "obstruction" of the formation of a single team for the Los Angeles Olympics.

May 29 – The president of the Korean Amateur Sports Association and the Korean Olympic Committee proposes that a fourth sports meeting be held on June 1.

June 1 – North Korea rejects a fourth sports meeting.

June 2 – North Korea announces its boycott of the Los Angeles Olympic Games.

June 2 – The president of the Korean Olympic Committee furnishes the list of the Republic of Korea delegation to the Los Angeles Olympics.

August 17 – The president of the Korean Amateur Sports Association and the Korean Olympic Committee proposes that a fourth sports meeting be held on August 30.

August 20 – President Chun Doo Hwan, in his summer press conference, proposes commodity trade and other forms of economic cooperation between the south and the north, and expresses willingness to offer technology and goods for free of charge to the North.

August 27 – North Korea rejects proposal for a fourth south-north sports meeting.

September 8 – North Korea offers relief goods to flood victims in the south.

September 14 – The ROKNRC president accepts offer for relief goods and proposes working-level contacts.

September 14 – North Korea accepts proposal for working-level south-north Red Cross contacts, and announces a plan to send five delegates to the conference room of the Neutral Nations Supervisory Commission on September 18.

September 15 – The ROKNRC president makes public the list of his delegation to the south-north Red Cross working-level contacts.

– Chief delegate:Lee Young-dug, vice ROKNRC president.

– Delegate:Cho Chol-hwa, ROKNRC secretary general.

– Delegate:Song Young-dae, member of the ROKNRC Disaster Relief Council.

– Delegate:Choi Un-bom, ROKNRC Relief Service Department director.

– Delegate:Lee Jun-hee, ROKNRC advisory member for social services.

September 17 – North Korea announces the list of its delegation to the south-north Red Cross working-level contacts.

– Cheif delegate:Han Wung-sik, NKRC Central Committee vice chairman.

– Delegate:Choi Won-sok, NKRC Central Committee standing member.

– Delegate:Choi Ki-bong, NKRC Central Committee director.

– Delegate:Paek Yong–ho, NKRC Centcal Committee deputy chief delegate.

– Delegate:Li Nam-in, NKRC Nampo Committee vice chairmam.

September 18 – South-north Red Cross working-level contacts held on the issue of the delivery and receipt of flood relief goods.

– North Korean delegates walk out of the conference room one-sidedly after insisting that they would deliver relief goods directly to flood victims.

September 18 – The ROKNRC president calls for the complete delivery of flood relief goods before the close of September.

September 18 – The ROKNRC chief delegate to the working-level contacts tells the north that if it is interested in the delivery of relief goods within September, it should notify the south of a delivery plan in 72 hours.

September 19 – North Korea notifies the south that it would transport relief goods to Panmunjom and the Inchon and Pukpyong harbors.

September 29 – The ROKNRC furnishes a memorandum guaranteeing the personal safety of NKRC workers engaged in the delivery of relief materials.

September 29 – October 4 – Relief materials from the NKRC delivered and received at Panmunjom and the Inchon and Pukpyong harbors.
   – 225,950 bushels of rice, 500,000 meters of fabrics, 100,000 tons of cement, 14 kinds of medicines, etc.

October 4 – The ROKNRC president proposes the resumption of Red Cross talks.

October 4 – The president of the Korean Amateur Sports Association and the Korean Olympic Committee proposes the holding of the fourth south-north sports meeting.

October 12 – Deputy Prime Minister Shin Byong-hyon proposes a south-north economic meeting.

October 13 – The heads of the four economic organizations urge the North to accept the proposal for an economic meeting.

October 16 – The Deputy premier of the north's Administration Council accepts the proposal for a south-north economic meeting.
   – Compostion of delegation:five delegates headed by a vice-minister-level official from each side
   – Time:November 15

October 29 – North Korea proposes a preliaminary meeting to resume the full-dress south-north Red Cross talks
   – Time and place:10 a.m. November 20, conference room of the Neutral Nations Supervisory Commission
   – Delegation:Three persons from each side

November 2 – Deputy Prime Minister Shin Byong-hyon proposes that each side be represented by seven delegates at an ecomomic meeting.

November 10 – Kim Hwan, deputy premier of the north's cabinet, agrees to increase the number of delegates to seven.

November 12 – Deputy Prime Minister Shin Byong-hyon announces the
list of the south's delegates to the economic meeting.
- Chief delegate:Kim Ki-hwan, director of the Council for Internation-
al Economic Cooperation.
- Delegate:Cha sang-pil (Second assistant minister of the Trade and
Industry Ministry.)
- Delegate:Koo Bon-tae, chief research official, National Unification
Board.
- Delegate:Kim In-jun, managing director of the Korean Chamber of
Commerce and Industry
- Delegate:Shin Bong-sik, managing director of the Federation of Ko-
rean Industries.
- Delegate:Noh Jin-sik, managing director of the Korean Traders
Association.
- Delegate:Im Byong-sok, standing director of the Federation of Small
Industrial Cooperatives.
November 13 – North Korea makes public the list of its delegates to the
south-north economic meeting.
- Chief delegate:Li Song-rok, vice trade minister.
- Delegate:Kye Hyong-myon, councilor, Mining Industry Commission.
- Delegate:Paek Jun-hyok, standing member of the north Korean Ex-
ternal Economic Cooperation Company
- Delegate:Ho Hang-chan, vice president of the north Korean Exter-
nal Economic Cooperation Company
- Delegate:Li Jin-sik, bureau director of the Metal Industry Ministry.
- Delegate:Son Jong-chol, deputy director of the Trade Economic In-
stitute.
- Delegate:Kim Hae-ryong, vice president of the north Korean
Kwangmyong Union Co.
November 14 – The ROKNRC president announces the list of delegates to
preliminary contacts for full-dress Red Cross talks.
- Chief delegate:Cho Chol-hwa, ROKNRC secretary general.
- Delegate:Song Young-dae, member of the ROKNRC Disater Relief
Council.
- Delegate: Choi Eun-bom, director of the ROKNRC Relief Service
Department.

November 15 – First south-north economic meeting held.

November 16 – North Korea announces the list of delegates to preliminary contacts for the full-dress Red Cross talks.

– Chief delegate:So Song-chol, standing member of the NKRC Central Committee.

– Delegate:Pak Young-soo, deputy bureau director of the NKRC Central Committee.

– Delegate:Pak Dong-chun, division chief of the NKRC Central Committee.

November 19 – The KOC president calls for the resumption of the fourth south-north sports meeting.

November 20 – A preliminary contact for the full-dress Red Cross talks held.

November 22 – The ROKNRC proposes that the eighth full-dress Red Cross meeting be held on January 22-25, 1985.

November 27 – North Korea postpones the second south-north economic meeting to a later date.

November 28 – The chief southern delegate to the south-north economic meeting counter-proposes that the second economic meeting be held on January 17, 1985.

December 11 – The north Korean foreign minister proposes to the U.S. Secretary of State that a tripartite meeting be held in Beijing.

December 14 – North Korea agrees to the south's counter-proposal for a change in the date of the second economic meeting.

December 14 – North Korea agrees to the south's proposal for the date of the eighth full-dress Red Cross meeting.

December 21 – A test call over a direct telephone line for the south-north economic meeting made.

⟨1985⟩

January 1 – Kim Il-sung hints at the possible opening of a high-level political meeting.

January 7 – The ROKNRC proposes a liaison officials contats to discuss the itinerary of the delegations to the eighth full-dress Red Cross meeting.

– Time and place:10 a.m. January 10, conference room of the Neutral Nations Supervisory Commission.

– Two liaison officials from each side.

January 9 – President Chun Doo Hwan proposes the establishment of permanent missions in Seoul and Pyongyang.

January 9 – The NKRC Central Committee chairman postopones indefinitely the eighth full-dress Red Cross meeting with the excuse of the Team Spirit exercise.

January 9 – The north Korean deputy premier postpones indefinitely the second south-north economic meeting with the excuse of the Team Spirit exercise, and calls for a contact between the deputy prime ministers of the south and the north.

January 10 – The Deputy Prime Minister of the Republic of Korea urges that the second economic meeting should be held on January 17.

January 17 – The chief southern delegate to the economic meeting makes a comment over the failure to open the second economic meeting.

January 23 – The ROKNRC president urges the North to agree to hold the eighth full-dress Red Cross meeting.

February 1 – IOC President Samaranch proposes a south-north sports meeting under the IOC's sponsorship in Lausanne September 11–12.

March 13 – The Korean Olympic Committee agrees to the IOC president's proposal for a Lausanne meeting.

March 25 – The chief southern delegate to the economic meeting proposes that the second economic meeting be held on April 18.

March 25 – The ROKNRC president proposes that the eighth full-dress Red Cross meeting be held on May 14–17.

April 4 – North Korea counter-proposes that the second economic meeting be held on May 17.

April 4 – The NKRC counter-proposes that the eighth full-dress Red Cross meeting be held on May 28.

April 4 – The cheif southern delegate agrees to the north's counterproposal for the date of the second economic meeting.

April 4 – The ROKNRC president agrees to the NKRC's counterproposal for the date of the eighth full-dress Red Cross meeting.

April 9 – The north's Supreme People's Assembly proposes a south-north

540

parliamentary meeting.

April 9 – The north's 7th term Supreme People's Assembly adopts in a fourth session a message to the National Assembly of the Republic of Korea.

– A written proposal for a south-north parliamentary meeting sent to the Speaker and the heads of the three major political parties.

April 30 – Kim Bong-ju, secretary of the standing council of the Supreme People's Assembly, calls for an affirmative response of the south to their proposal for a south-north parliamentary meeting.

May 8 – Lee Jin-woo, secretary general of the National Assembly, notifies the north that the National Assembly would send a reply to the north as soon as the new Assembly is inaugurated.

May 10 – Cha Sang-pil, delegate to the south-north economic meeting, is replaced by Im In-taek, second assistant minister of the Trade and Industry.

May 13 – The ROKNRC president proposes that a liaison officials contact be held on May 15 at the conference room of the Neutral Nations Supervisory Commission in connection with the eighth full-dress Red Cross meeting.

May 14 – The NKRC notifies the ROKNRC that a liaison officials contact be held around May 20 and that it would notify a detailed time later.

May 16 – North Korea replaces Paek Jun-hyok with Han Yong-up, member of the International Trade Promotion Committee, as a delegate to the south-north economic meeting.

May 17 – The second south-north economic meeting held.

May 18 – The south's Home Affairs Minister announces the guarantee of personal safety of the north Korean delegates to the eighth full-dress Red Cross meeting.

May 18 – The ROKNRC announces the list of its delegates to the eighth full-dress Red Cross meeting.

– Chief delegate:Lee Young-dug, ROKNRC vice president

– Delegate:Cho Chol-hwa, ROKNRC secretary general

– Delegate:Song Young-dae, member of the ROKNRC Disaster Relief Committee

– Delegate:Lee Byong-ho, ROKNRC public relations consultant.

–Delegate : Lee Jun-hi, ROKNRC social services consultant.

– Delegate:Chong Yong-sok, ROKNRC consultant for youth affairs.

– Delegate:Lee Byong-wung, ROKNRC chief administrator

May 20 – The NKRC agrees to hold a liaison officials contact on May 20 in connection with the eighth full-dress Red Cross talk.

May 20 – A liaison officials contact held to prepare for the eighth full-dress Red Cross meeting.

May 22 – Yang Hyong-sop, chairman of the Standing Committee, Supreme People's Assembly of the north, asks the south to show a response to his call for a south-north parliamentary meeting at an early date.

May 24 – The NKRC announces the list of its delegates to the eighth full-dress Red Cross meeting

 – Chief delegate:Li Jong-ryul, NKRC Central Committee vice chairman

 – Deputy chief delegate:So Song-chol, NKRC Central Committee standing member

 – Delegate:Han Yon-su, NKRC Central Committee standing member

 – Delegate:Pak Young-su, NKRC Central Committee Compatriots Department director

 – Delegate:Kim Wan-su, NKRC Central Committee Cultural Propaganda Department director

 – Delegate:Pak Dong-chun, NKRC Central Committee International Department deputy director

 – Delegate:Kim Chang-hyon, NKRC Central Committee Organization and Planning Department deputy director

May 27-30 The eighth full-dress Red Cross meeting held in Seoul.

–Agreements–

 – Next meeting:August 26–29 in Pyongyang

 – Exchange of dispersed family hometown visitors and art troupes

June 1 – Speaker Lee Jae-hyong proposes a preliminary contact for the proposed south-north parliamentary meeting within July.

 – Composition of delegations:five legislators from each side.

June 5 – President Chun Doo wan expresses the hope that north Korea would participate in the 1986 Asian Games and the 1988 Olympics both set to be held in Seoul.

June 14 – North Korea proposes that a preliminary contact for the south-north parliamentary meeting be held on July 9.

June 20 – The third south-north economic meeting held.

–Agreements–

– The two sides agreed to adopt an Agreement on the Promotion of Material Exchanges and Economic Cooperation between the South and the North and on the Establishment of a South-North Economic Cooperation Organization Co-Chaired by Deputy-Prime-Minister-Level Officials.

– Fourth meeting:September 18

June 28 – Speaker Lee Jae-hyong counter-proposes that the first preliminary parliamentary contact be held on July 23.

July 5 – North Korea agrees to a change in the date of a preliminary contact.

July 6 – North Korea agrees to an IOC-hosted south-north sports meeting in Lausanne.

July 15 – The first south-north working-level Red Cross contact on the proposed exchange of dispersed family hometown visitors and art troupes held.

– second contact:July 19

July 18 – Speaker Lee Jae-hyong announces the list of delegates to a south-north preliminary parliamentary contact.

– Chief delegate:Kwon Jong-dal, Democratic Justice Party
– Delegate:Chong Si-chae, Democratic Justice Party
– Delegate:Sin Sun-bom, New Korea Democratic Party
– Delegate:Park Kwan-yong, New Korea Democratic Party
– Delegate:Kang Kyong-sik, Korea National Party.

July 19 – The second working-level Red Cross contact on the proposed exchange of dispersed family hometwohn visitors and art troupes held.

– The second contact ended without any agreement on the time of the third contact.

July 19 – North Korea makes public the list of its delegates to the preliminary parliamentary contcts.

- Chief delegate:Chon Gum-chol, Korean Workers' Party
- Deputy chief delegate:Ju Chang-jun, Korean Workers' Party
- Delegate:Choe Jang-ryong, Korean Workers' Party
- Delegate:Ryom Guk-ryol, Korean Socialist Democratic Party
- Delegate:Wu Dal-ho, Chondogyo-Chongwu Party

July 23 – The first south-north preliminary parliamentary contact held.

–Agreements–
- Format of talks: select delegates meeting
- Composition of delegations:11 persons from each side
- Places of talks:Seoul and Pyongyang by turn
- Date of the first parliamentary meeting:Within one month after the end of of the preliminary contacts.
- Second preliminary contact:september 25

July 24 – The IOC announces that a south-north sports meeting would be held in Lausanne within 1985.

July 25– The KOC president again urges North Korea to agree to a direct sports meeting between the south and the north.

July 30 – The deputy north's premier of the Administration Council calls for the co-hosting of the 1988 Olympics between Seoul and Pyongyang and the fielding of a single Korean team to the Olympics.

July 31 – The IOC notifies the both sides of Korea of the date, October 8-9, 1985, of the south-north Lausanne sports meeting.

August 2 – The Sports Minister of the south issues a statement refuting the north Korean demand for Olympic co-host.

August 15 – In his 40th Liberation Day message, President Chun Doo Hwan calls for practical measures to ease tension and consolidate peace.

August 22 – The third south-north working-level Red Cross contact held on the proposed exchange of hometwohn visitors and art troupes.

–Agreements–
- Size of visitors:151 persons – a chief delegate, 50 hometown visitors, 50 art troupe members, 30 press members and 20 support personnel.
- Places to be visited by dispersed families: Seoul and Pyongyang
- Period of visits: September 20-23(three nights and four days)

– Method of exchange: simultaneous exchange

– Number of performances: Two times

August 26-29 – The ninth full-dress Red Cross meeting held in Pyongyang.

– The two sides agreed to hold the 10th meeting Seoul on November 26.

Semptember 6 – The Home Minister of the south announces the guarantee of the personal safety of the five advance visitors of the north Korean art troupe.

September 7 – The north's Public Security Minister announces the guarantee of the personal safety of the advance Art Troupe visitors from the south.

September 10-12 – Advance visitors comprising two Red Cross officials and three stage technicians from each side visit each other's areas.

September 12 – The Home Minister of the south announces the guarantee of the personal safety of the 151 north Korean hometown visitors and art troupe members visiting the south.

September 13 – The Public Security Minister of the north announces the guarantee of the personal safety of the south Korean hometown visitors and Art Troupe members.

September 18 – The fourth south-north economic meeting held.

– The two sides agreed to hold the fifth meeting on November 20.

September 20–23 – South and north Korean hometown visitors and art troupe members simultaneously visit each other's areas.

– Sixty-five dispersed family members meet 92 of their missing families and relatives.

September 25 – The second preliminary parliamentary meeting held.

– The two sides decide to determine the time and place of the third preliminary contact through telephone coversation later.

October 2 – The KOC announces the list of its delegates to the Lausanne south-north sports meeting.

– Chief delegate:Kim Chong-ha, KOC president

– Deputy chief dlegate:Chang Chung-sik, KOC vice president

– Delegate:Choi Man-rip, KOC vice president

– Delegate:Lee Chong-ha, KOC standing member

– Delegate:Im Tae-sun, KOC member
– Delegate:Nam Chong-mun, KOC member

October 6 – The International Association of Track and Field proposes that a relay marathon be held across south and north Korea during the 1987 Seoul World Cup Marathon.

October 8-9 – The first IOC-sponsored Lausanne south-north sports meeting held.

– Delegates:six each from south and north Korea and the IOC
– The second meeting was set to be held on January 8-9, 1986

October 9 – The chief northern delegate to the preliminary parliamentary contacts proposes that the third preliminary contact be held on October 16 at Tongilkak.

October 12 – The chief southern delegate to the preliminary parliamentary contacts tells the north that he notify the north of the time of the third contact at an appropriate time later.

October 18 – Pak Sung-chul, the north's vice president, asserts that "if Korea were to enter the United Nations, it should do so under the same name of the country after realizing a north-south confederation system."

October 25 – The chief northern delegate to the preliminary parliamentary contacts proposes that the third preliminary contact be held on November 1.

October 30 – Kwon Jong-dal, cheif southern delegate to the preliminary parliamentary contacts, informs the north that he would notify the north of the time of the third contact after the regular session (September 20-December 18) of the National Assembly was held.

November 5 – The North Korean Red Cross chairman suggests that an airplane be used in transporting delegates to the 10th full-dress Red Cross meeting.

November 7 – The ROKNRC president expresses his position that the method of transportation should be the way it used to be in the past.

November 15 – The North Korean Red Cross chairman counter-proposes that the time of the tenth full-dress Red Cross be held on December 3.

November 16 – The ROKNRC president agrees to the North's counter-proposal for the time of the·tenth full-dress meeting.

November 18 – Yang Hyong-sop, chairman of the Standing Committee, Supreme People's Assembly, calls for the third preliminary parliamentary contact.

November 20 – The fifth south-north economic meeting held.

– The two sides agreed to hold the sixth meeting on January 22, 1986.

November 25 – The first liaison officials contact for the 10th full-dress Red Cross meeting held.

November 28 – The second liaison officials contact for the 10th full-dress Red Cross meeting held.

November 28 – National Assembly Speaker Lee Jae-hyong gives a reply to the northern call for the third preliminary parliamentary contact.

December 2-5 – The 10th full-dress Red Cross meeting held in Seoul.

– The two sides decide to hold the 11th meeting in Pyongyang on February 26, 1986.

December 20 – Kwohn Jong-dal, chief southern delegate to the preliminary parliamentary contacts, notifies the north of the date (February 18, 1986) of the third preliminary parliamentary contact.

December 24 – North Korea agrees to the time of the third preliminary parliamentary contact.

《1986》

January 1 – In his New Years message, Kim Il-sung hints at the idea of a high-level south-north political conference.

January 2 – The chief northern delegate to the south-north economic meeting supports Kim Il-sung's New Year message.

– Demands the stoppage of the joint Team Spirit military exercise.

January 3 – The chief northern delegate to the south-north Red Cross talks supports Kim Il-sung's New Year message.

– Demands the stoppage of the joint Team Spirit military exercise.

January 4 – The chief northern delegate to the preliminary parliamentary contacts supports Kim Il-sung's New Year message.

– Demands the stoppage of the joint Team Spirit military exercise.

January 8-9 – The second Lausanne south-north sports meeting held.

– The third meeting was set to be held on June 10-11.

January 11 – The North's Foreign Ministry, in a statement, expresses willingness to suspend military exercises in all the area of north Korea, asking the south to take a reciprocal step.

January 18 – The Korea-U.S. Combined Forces Command announces that the Team Spirit 86 would be held from February 10 through mid-April, 1986.

January 20 – The chief northern delegates to south-north talks, in a joint statement, suspends the on-going talks with the excuse of the Team Spirit exercise.

January 20 – The chief southern delegates to the south-north economic, Red Cross and parliamentary talks, in a joint statement, call for the holding of the talks as scheduled.

January 21 – The chief northern delegate to the south-north economic meeting notifies the south of his decision to put off the scheduled sixth economic meeting to a later date.

January 21 – The chief southern delegate to the economic meeting calls for the sixth economic meeting as scheduled.

January 22 – The chief southern delegate to the economic meeting makes a comment on the North's boycott of the sixth economic meeting, asking the north to show a sincere posture toward the dialogue.

Janaury 22 – The chief northern delegate to the Red Cross talks notifies the South of the postponement of the 11th full-dress Red Cross meeting to a later date.

January 22 – The chief northern delegate to the preliminary parliamentary contacts notifies the south of the postponement of the third contact until a later date.

January 23 – Kwon Jong-dal, chief southern delegate to the preliminary parliamentary contacts, calls for the holding of the 3rd contacts as scheduled.

January 23 – Lee Young-dug, chief southern delegate to the south-north Red Cross Conference, calls for the holding of the 11th full-dress meeting as scheduled.

February 10 – The North's Foreign Ministry, in a statement, demands the stoppage of the joint Team Spirit military exercise.

February 18 – Kwon Jong-dal, chief southern delegate to the preliminary parliamentary contacts, calls for the holding of a preliminary contacts as scheduled.

February 26 – Lee Young-dug, chief southern delegate to the Red Cross talks, calls for the holding of the 11th full-dress Red Corss meeting as scheduled.

March 1 – President Chun Doo Hwan, in a Samil Independence Day message, says he expects that a south-north top officials meeting would be held within 1986.

March 4 – Kim Ki-hwan is replaced with Moon Hi-gap as chief southern delegate to the south-north economic meeting.

March 11 – In an address at a rally welcoming the visit of Cuban Premier Fidel Castro to Pyongyang, Kim Il-sung says the 24th Olympics is a political issue before which the North won't sit idly by.

March 26 – Moon Hi-gap, chief southern delegate to the south-north economic meeting, proposes that the sixth economic meeting be held on April 30.

March 26 – Kwon Jong-dal, chief southern delegate to the preliminary parliamentary contacts, proposes the third contact be held on May 14.

March 26 – Lee Young-dug, chief southern delegate to the south-north Red Cross meeting proposes that the 11th full-dress Red Cross meeting be held on May 27.

March 31 – The chief northern delegate to the preliminary parliamentary contacts asserts that the south's call for the resumption of the contacts is an act of ignoring the reality.

April 1 – The chief northern delegate to the south-north economic meeting says efforts should be made to foster conditions ripe for dialogue rather than to try to resume the suspended talks.

April 1 – The chief northern delegate to the Red Cross talks says that the south's proposal for the time of the next Red Cross meeting amounted to an act of ignoring the reality.

April 1 – Moon Hi-gap, chief southern delegate to the south-north economic meeting. calls for the convocation of the sixth economic meeting.

April 1 – Lee Young-dug, chief southern delegate to the Red Cross talks, demands that the north show a sincere stance toward the inter-Korean dialogue.

April 1 – Kwon Jong-dal, chief southern delegate to the preliminary parliamentary contacts, calls for the resumption of the dialogue.

April 3 – The 18th anuual Korea-U.S. Security Consultative Conference says in a joint statement that the Team Spirit exercise would continue to be carried out for the promotion of defense ability.

April 6 - The north's Foreign Ministry, in a statement, claims that the declaration to carry out the Team Spirit training exercise continuously amounts to an act of obstructing the south-north dialogue.

April 9 - The chairman of the north's Supreme People's Assembly issues a statement on the first anniversay of his proposal for a south-north parliamentary meeting.
   – The pronounced intent of carrying out the Team Spirit training exercise continuously was an act of denying and challenging the south-north dialogue.

April 22 – The premier of the north's Administration Council issues a statement :
   – Forcing through of the Seoul Olympics would result in splitting the Olympic movement.
   – The co-host of the Olympics between south and north Korea alone would ensure smooth Olympics.

April 24 – The chief northern delegates to the economic, Red Cross and parliamentary talks issue a joint statement :
   – The south-north dialogue has been suspended and the inter-Korean relationship has deteriorated due to the intensified Team Spririt training exercise.
   – The southern delegates should take appropriate steps to foster an atmosphere ripe for the dialogue.

May 12 – President Chon Doo Hwan addresses the second regional meeting of the Advisory Council on Peaceful Unification Policy.

May 13 – The chairman of the north's Socialist Working Youth League expresses willingness to hold a south-north student meeting.

June 7 – North Korea says it plans to send letters to the south.

June 10-11 – The third Lausanne south-north sports meeting held.
   – The IOC asks both sides of Korea to notify the IOC of whether to accept the IOC mediatory plan by June 30, 1986.

June 11 – The northern side of the Military Armistice Commission calls for an early reply to its June 7 notification.

June 12 – The United Nations Command sector of the Military Armistice Commission says it would give a reply on June 14.

June 14 – The U.N. Command sector of the Military Armistice Commission says it would send a liaison official to Panmunjom on June 17 to receive a north Korean letter.

June 16 – The northern sector of the Military Armistice Commission says it would deliver a letter to the U.N. Command sector on June 17.

June 16 – The U.N. Command secton of the Military Armistice Commission says it wonld receive a north Korean letter on June 17.

June 17 – The people's Armed Forces Minister of the north sends letters to the South one addressed to Defense. Minister Lee Ki-baek and another to General Livsey, Commander of the Korea-U.S. Combined Forces Command :
 – Proposes a three-party military meeting among south and north Korea and the United States.
 – Proposes a preliminary contacts be held on June 27 to prepare for a three-party military meeting.

June 21 – General Livsey, Commander of the Korea-U.S., Combined Forces says that the June 17 north Korean letter was improperly signed, but he had received the letter to review its contents related to the alleviation of tension.

June 21 – Kim Duk-jun, north Korean Olympic Committee vice chairman, issues a statement calling for the co-host of the 1988 Olympics.

June 21 – South Korea notifies the north that it wohd send a message to the north on June 24 in connection with the north-proposed three-way military conference.

June 23 – The chief northern delegate to the preliminary parliamentary contacts issues a statement in support of the proposed three-way military meeting.

June 23 – The north's Administration Council issues a statement proposing negotiations for the creation of a non-nuclear peace zone on the Korean peninsula.

June 24 – Defense Minister Lee Ki-baek sends a message to the north.
 – Expresses the hope that the existing dialogue would be resumed.
 – Expects that the north would favorably respond to the four-point

confidence-building measure proposed at the Military Armisitice Commission.

– Asks the north to agree to a south-north top leaders meeting.

June 26 – The chief northern delegate to the south-north economic meeting issues a statement in support of a three-way military conference.

June 30 – The KOC accepts the IOC mediatory plan.

July 2 – The chief northern delegate to the south-north Red Cross conference issues a statement in support of a three-way military conference.

June 3 – IOC President Samaranch asks the North to let the IOC know whether the North accepts the IOC mediatory plan by July 15.

July 11 – Defense Minister Lee Ki-baek sends a message to the north :

– Asks the north to desist from engaging in propaganda activities by way of the delivery of perfunctory letters.

– Urges the north to agree to resume the suspended dialogue.

– Informs the north he won't accept a north Korean letter.

July 11 – The north's People's Armed Forces minister sends a letter to the south:

– Expects that a favorable resoponse would be given to offer for a three-way military meeting within July.

– Hopes that a preliminary contact would be held at an early date.

– Leaves the time and place of a preliminary contact to the south.

July 11 – The chief northern delegate to the preliminary parliamentary contact proposes that the third preliminary contact be held on August 13.

July 11 – Moon Hi-gap, chief southern delegate to the economic meeting, proposes that the sixth south-north economic meeting be held on August 6.

July 11 – Lee young-dug, chief southern delegate to the south-north Red Cross conference, proposes that the 11th full-dress Red Cross meeting be held on August 28.

July 14 – A spokesman for the north's People's Armed Forces Ministry denounced the south for rejecting a military conference and says the north expects that a military authorities meeting would be realized.

July 15 – The northern delegation to the south-north Red Cross conference, in a statement, says the resumption of the Red Corss talks is not worth any consideration, urging that a military authorities meeting should be held without any delay.

July 16 – The northern delegation to the south-north economic meeting, in a statement, argues it is an impure act for the south to ask for the resumption of the economic talks, stressing that the south should agree to a military authorities meeting without delay.

July 17 – The northen delegation to the south-north parliamentary contacts, in a statement, says the resumption of the parliamentary contacts is not worth any consideration, and urges that a military authorities meeting be held at an early date.

July 19 – The north Kórean Olympic Committee sends a letter to the IOC.

July 28 – IOC President Samaranch sends a letter to the north, telling the north that it should accept the IOC mediatory plan without any condition to ensure a progress of the sports meeting.

August 1 – The north Korean Olympic Committee sends a letter to the IOC calling for a meeting to discuss the issue of increasing the number of sports to be allotted to the north.

August 6 – Moon Hi-gap, chief southern delegate, in a statement, urges the north to agree to hold the sixth economic meeting.

August 10 – Spokesmen for the northern delegations to the economic, Red Cross and parliamentary talk issue a joint statement, calling for the prompt agreement to a military authorities meeting.

August 11 – President Chun Doo Hwan, in a summer press conference, urges the north to agree to a south-north top leaders meeting and the resumption of the suspended dialogue.

August 13 – Kwon Jong-dal, chief southern delegate to the preliminary parliamentary contacts, issues a statement calling for the resumption of the suspended dialogue.

August 15 – In his 41st Liberation Day message, President Chun Doo Hwan calls for the resumption of the suspended existing dialogue.

August 28 – Lee Young-dug, chief southern delegate to the Red Cross talks, issues a statement asking the north to agree to hold the 11th full-dress Red Cross meeting.

October 13 – A spokesman for the 91st IOC meeting holds a press conference, saying that the IOC decided to send an ultimatum to the north asking it to notify the IOC whether it would accept the IOC mediatory plan by September 17, 1987.

October 14 – The vice chairman of the north Korean Olympic Committee, while attending an IOC meeting, demands that eight Olympic sports be transferred to the north.

October 21 – A north Korean raio broadcast says a ceremony marked the ground-breaking for the construction of a Kumgangsan Dam.

October 24 – The northern delegations to the economic, Red Cross and parliamentary talks issue a joint statement, urging the south to renounce its anti-Communist confrontation schemes and anti-communist fascist policies.

October 30 – Construction Minister Lee Kyu-ho, in a statement, urges the north to suspend the Kumgangsan power plant project.

November 4 – The director of Resources Development Bureau of the north's Electric Power Industry Commission issues a statement in connection with the Kumgangsan power plant project.

November 6 – Defense Minister Lee Ki-baek, in a statement, stresses that the south would take a strategic self-defense measure in connection with the Kumgangsan dam project.

November 21 – Minister of Culture and Information Lee Woong-hee, in a statement, urges the north to suspend the Kumgangsan dam project.

November 26 – The four ministers of National Defense, Construction, Culture-Information and Unification issue a joint statement, saying that if the north suspends the Kumgangsan dam project, the south was willing to discuss all issues related to the utilization and development of the water resources of rivers flowing through the areas of the south and the north.

November 27 – Construction Minister Lee Kyu-ho, in a message to the north, informs the north that he would send a liaison official to Panmunjom on November 28 to deliver a message to the north.

November 28 – The north's Electric Power Industry Commission, in a statement, argues that the north would discuss the power plant issue with the south on the condition that the south apologizes for the sin it committed before the nation by building up tension in an anti-

Communist confrontation policy.

November 28 – Construction Minister Lee Kyu-ho, in a message to the north, proposes a south-north water resources meeting.

December 25 – The vice chairman of the north's Electric Power Industry Commission   releases a white paper on the Kumgangsan dam project.

Decmeber 29 – Lee Jae-myong, director of Water Resources Bureau, Ministry of Construction, calls for a south-north authorities meeting on the joint utilization the water resources of rivers flowing through the areas of the south and the north.

December 30 – In a policy speech at the first session of the eighth-term Supreme People's Assmbly, Kim Il-sung hints at a high-level south-north politico-military meeting.

《1987》

January 9 – The premier of the north's Administration Council and the People's Armed Forces minister notify the South they would send liaison officials to Panmunjom on January 10 to deliver their letters to the south.

January 10 – The Prime Minister and the Defense Minister of the south tell the north they would inform them in the foresecable future of the date they would receive north Korean letters.

January 11 – The premier of the Administration Council and the People's Armed Forces minister of the north, in letters to the south, propose a high-level south-north politico-military meeting.

January 12 – President Chun Doo Hwan, in a policy speech, urges the north to agree to a south-north top leaders meeting.

January 14 – The chief southern delegates to the parliamentary, economic and Red Cross talks, in a joint statement, urge the north to unconditionally agree to resume the existing dialogue.

January 15 – The chief northern delegate to the preliminary parliamentary contacts issues a statement in supoprt of a politico-military meeting.

January 16 – Construction Minister Lee Kyu-ho, in a statement, urges the north to suspend the Kumgangsan dam project and agree to a south-north water resources meeting.

555

January 16 – The chief northern delegate to the Red Cross talks issues a statement in support of a politico-military meeting.

January 17 – The chief northern delegate to the south-north economic meeting issues a statement in support of a politico-military meeting.

January 19 – The north's Electric Power Industry Commission, in a statement, suggests that the question of the Kumgangsan power plant project be discussed at a high-level politico-military meeting.

January 21 – The spokesmen of the Administration Council and the People's Armed Foreces Ministry issue a joint statement urging the south to accept their proposal for a politico-military meeting.

January 27 – The premier of the Administration Council and the People's Armed Forces minister of the north notify the south they would send liaison officials to Panmunjom on January 30 to deliver their letters to the south.

January 27 – The Prime Minister and the Defense Minister of the south notify the north they would send liaison officials to Panmunjom on January 30 to receive letters.

January 28 – The premier of the Administration Council and the People's Armed Forces minister of the north nofity the south they would deliver their letters to the south on January 30.

January 28 – The chief northern delegates to the Red Cross, economic and parliamentary talks, in a joint statement, denounce the Team Spirit '87 training exercise and urge the south to agree to a politico-military meeting at an early date.

January 30 – The premier of the Administration Council and the People's Armed Forces minister of the north send their letters to the south.

February 5 – The vice chairman of the north's Electric Power Industry Commission holds a press conference in connection with the Kumgangsan power plant project.

February 11 – The Prime Minister and the Defense Minister of the south notifty the north they would send liaison officials to Panmunjom on February 13 to deliver their messages to the north.

February 12 – The premier of the Administration Council and the

People's Armed Forces minister of the north notify the south they would receive messages from the south on February 13.

February 12 – The chairman of the north Korean Olympic Committee holds a press conference after an official meeting between the IOC and north Korea.

February 13 – The Prime Minister and the Defense Minister of the south notify the north they would send liaison officials to Panmunjom on February 14 to deliver their messages to the north.

February 14 – The Prime Minister and the Defense Minister of the south deliver their messages to the north.

– The message urges the north to agree to resume the suspended dialogue and to agree to hold a south-north top leaders meeting which could discuss the issue of joint exploration and utilization of water resources and even political and military issues.

February 27 – The premier of the Administration Council and the People's Armed Forces minister of the north notify the south they would send liaison officials to Panmunjom on February 28 to deliver letters to the south.

February 27 – The Prime Minister and the Defense Minister of the south notify the north they would receive their letters on March 3.

February 28 – Prime Minister Lho Shin-young, attending a ceremony marking ground-breaking for the construction of Peace Dam, urges the north to suspend the Kumgangsan dam project immediately and agree to a dialogue to discuss the joint utilization of water resources.

March 2 – The premier of the Administration Council and the People's Armed, Forces minister of the north notify the south they would send liaison officials to Panumunjom on March 3 to deliver their letters to the south.

March 3 – The premier of the Administration Council and the People's Armed Forces minister of the north send letters to the south. In the letters, they said that:

– If a politico-military meeting progresses successfully, a top leaders meeting could be held at the soonest possible time.

– The first meeting of a politico-military conference be held on March

26.

March 3 – The vice chairman of the north Korean Olympic Committee, in a press conference, demadns the co-host of the Olympics and the transfer of eight sports to the north.

March 5 – The spokesman of the Electric Power Industry Commission of the north issues a statement in support of a politico-military meeting.

March 5 – The chief northern delegate to the south-north Red Corss talks issues a statement in support of a politico-military meeting.

March 5 – The chief northern delegate to the south-north economic meeting issues a statement in support of a politico-military meeting.

March 8 – The chief northern delegate to the south-north preliminary parliamentary meeting issues a statement in support of a politico-military meeting.

March 12 – The south notifies the north it would send a liaison official to Panmunjom on March 14 to deliver a message from Prime Minister Lho Shin-yong to the north.

March 14 – The premier of the Administration Council and the People's Armed Forces minister of the north nofity the south they would receive the message on March 17.

March 17 – The Prime Minister and the Defense Minister of the south deliver a message to the north, in which they suggested that:

– A south-north prime ministers meeting be held on the condition that a south-north water resources meeting is held and the existing dialogue resumed.

– A south-north water resources meeting be held at Panmnjom within March.

– Red Corss and economic meetings be held in Pyongyang and at Panmunjom, respectively, in April.

– The exact times of the meetings would be left to the north.

March 19 – The north's Foreigh Ministry issues a statement saying that the north is prepared to have contacts and dialogue with official persons of the United States.

March 26 – The premier of the Administration Council and the People's Armed Forces minister of the north notify the south they would send liaison officials to Panmunjom on March 30 to deliver a letter to the south.

March 28 – The Prime Minister and the Defense Minister of the south notify the north they would have liaiosn officials receive the letter from the north on March 30.

March 29 – The north notifies the south that the letter they would send on March 30 would be from only the premier of the Administration Council.

March 30 – The premier of the north's Administration Council sends a letter to the south, in which he proposed a preliminary meeting to prepare for a south-north prime ministers meeting :

– Composition of delegations:A minister-level official appointed by the prime ministers of each side and two attendants.

– Time and place:10 a.m. April 23, Tongilkak, Panmunjom

April 3 – The United States proposes the promotion of trade of a humanitarian nature with north Korea.

April 5 – In an interview with a Cuban news agency, Kim Il-sung argues that more than one third of Olympic sports should be allotted to north Korea for the sake of Olympic co-host.

April 8 – The Prime Minister of the south notifies the north he would send a liaison official to Panmunjom on April 10 to deliver a message to the north.

April 9 – The premier of the north's Administration Council notifies the south he have a liaison official receive the message on April 10.

April 10 – Prime Minister Lho Shin-yong sends a message to the north.

– If and when an atmosphere for mutual trust becomes ripen through the opening of a water resources meeting and the resumption of the suspended dialogue, a preliminary meeting could be held in the foreseeable future to prepare for a south-north prime ministers meeting.

– A south-north water resources meeting be held at Panmunjom on May 6.

– The sixth south-north economic meeting be held at Panmunjom on May 12.

– The 11th full-dress south-north Red Cross meeting be held in Pyongyang on May 19.

April 23 – IOC President Samaranch announces in a press conference that the fourth Lausanne south-north sports meeting would be held on July 14–15.

April 24 – The spokesman of the north's Administration Council rejects a south-north dialogue, trying to shift the blame to the south.

April 26 – The spokesman of the People's Armed Forces Ministry of the north issues a statement in support of the statement by the spokesman of the Administration Council.

April 26 – The spokesman of the Electric Power Industry Commission of the north issues a statement in support of the statement by the spokesman of the Administration Council.

Arpil 27 – The government spokesman of the south, in a statement, urges the north to unconditionally agree to the talks the south had already proposed.

April 27 – The chief northern delegate to the south-north economic meeting issues a statement in support of the statement by the spokesman of the Administration Council.

April 28 – The chief northern delegate to the south-north economic meeting issues a statement in support of the statement by the spokesman of the Administration Council.

Apil 29 – The chief northern delegate to the preliminary parliamentary contacts issues a statement in support of the statement by the spokesman of the Administration Council.

May 7 – The spokesman of the north Korean Olympic Committee, in a statement, demands the co-host of the 1988 Olympics.

May 7 – A joint statement of the Korea-U.S. Security Consultative Meeting says the Team Spirit military exercise would be carried out continuously, and invites north Korea observers to the annual training exercse.

May 11 – SLOOC President Park Seh-jik says in a press conference that the decision to transfer four sports to the north was very magnanimous and there would be no further concession.

May 15 – The northern delegations to the economic, Red Cross and parliamentary talks issue a joint statement to denounce the annual Korea-U.S. Security Consultative Meeting.

May 20 – The north's Committee for the Peaceful Reunification of the Fatherland, in a statement, denounces the south Korean government's views on national unification and poses a seven-point open questionnaire to the south.

May 23 – The northern delegations to the economic, Red Cross and parliamentary talks, in a joint statement, ask the Seoul government to withdraw its unification-related views and give a reply to the open questionnaire.

June 3 – In his openning address at the fourth meeting of the Advisory Council on Peaceful Unification Policy, President Chun calls for the resumption of the existing dialogue and the realization of a south-north top leaders meeting.

June 6 – The north's Committee for the Peaceful Reunification of the Fatherland, in a statement, denounces President Chun's opening address made at the meeting of the Advisory Council on Peaceful Unification Policy and challenges the south to give a reply to its open questionnaire.

July 13 – The north's Foreign Ministry issues a statement pronouncing its position over the idea of a non-nuclear peace zone.

July 14-15 – The fourth Lausanne south-north soports meeting held.
– The IOC offers a revised mediatory plan.

July 23 – The north Korean government issues a statement proposing a multi-national armed forces reduction meeting to discuss phased military reduction on the Korean peninsula.

August 3 – The Foreign Ministry of the south proposes in a statment a south-north foreign ministers meeting.

August 4 – The vice chairman of the north Korean Olympic Committee, in a statement, expresses dissatisfaction at the IOC's revised plan and demands that the fifth Lausanne sports meeting be held before September 17.

August 6 – The spokesman of the north's Foreign Ministry, in a statement, proposes a three-way foreign ministers meeting among south and north Korea and the United States.

August 11 – The vice chairman of the north Korean Olympic Committee, in a press conference, demands that six sports be transferred to the north and that the fifth Lausanne south-north sports meeting be held.

August 13 – The spokesman of the Foreign Ministry of the south issues a statement calling for a south-north foreign ministers meeting again.

August 15 – In his 42nd Liberation Day message, President Chun calls for the resumption of the suspended south-north dialogue and urges the north to take part in the 1988 Seoul Olympic.

August 17 – KOC President Kim Chong-ha sends a message to the IOC, agreeing to the IOC's revised mediatory plan.

August 28 – The spokesman of the north's Foreign Ministry, in a statement, urges the south to agree to preliminary talks for a south-north foreign ministers meeting.

August 31 – The vice chairman of the north Korean Olympic Committee holds a press conference to ask the IOC to postpone the extension of invitations to the Seoul Olympics.

September 8 – The Foreign Ministry of the south makes a comment, asking the north to agree to a south-north foreign ministers meeting.

September 10 – The spokesman of the north's People's Armed Forces Ministry issues a statement urging the south to affirmatively resopond to their call for a armed forces reduction meeting.

September 11 – The north Korean Olympic Committee chairman notifies the south he would deliver a letter to the south.

September 12 – KOC President Kim Chong-ha notifies the north he would have liaison officials receive the letter from the north on September 15.

September 15 – The north Korean Olympic Committee chairman sends a letter to the south, proposing a bilateral south-north meeting before the fifth Lausanne south-north sports meeting.

September 17 – Foreign Minister Choi Kwang-soo of the south, in a press conference, expresses the willingness to have a south-north foreign ministers contact during their attendance at the U.N. General Assembly.

September 21 – The vice chairman of the north Korean Olympic Committee denounces the forwarding to Seoul Olympic invitations to the National Olympic Committees.

September 22 – Kim Chong-ha, KOC president, notifies the north he would send a liaison officail to Panmunjom on September 24 to deliver a message to the notrh.

September 24 – KOC President Kim Chong-ha sends a message to the north, urging the north to agree to the IOC's mediatory plan.

September 24 – The spokesman of the north's Foreign Ministry issues a statement, urging the south to agree to a preliminary meeting for a south-north foreign ministers meeting.

September 26 – Kim Il-sung, in an interview with the chairman of the Japan Socialist Party, expresses the hope for a direct dialogue with the United States.

October 2 – The chairman of the north Korean Olympic Committee notifies the south he would send a liaison official to Panmunjom on October 3 to deliver a letter to the south.

October 2 – KOC President Kim Chong-ha notifies the north he would receive the letter from the north on October 12.

October 5 – In a policy address at the 137th session of the National Assembly, President Chun emphasizes the importance of dialogue between the direct parties involved.

October 6 – The north Korean Olympic Committee chairman agrees to a change in the date of the receipt of a letter the north offered.

October 12 – The north Korean Olympic Committee chairman sends a letter to the south, urging the south to agree to the IOC-proposed second meeting between the south and north Korean Olympic committees.

October 15 – KOC President Kim Chong-ha notifies the north he would send a liaison official to Panmunjom on October 16 to deliver a message to the north.

October 16 – The north Korean Olympic Committee chairman notifies the south he would have a liaison receive the letter on October 20.

October 20 – KOC President Kim Chong-ha sends a message to the north, urging the north to accept the IOC's mediatory plan.

October 23 – The chairman of the north Korean Olympic Committee, in a statement, expresses a plan to postopone negotiations for the co-host of the Olympics.

Novebmer 11 – The Central Committee of the north Korean Democratic

Front for the Reunification Fatherland and the Committee for the Peaceful Reunification of the Fatherland, at a joint meeting, adopt a "message to all political parties, all segaments and the people of all walks of life in the south."

November 20 – The north's foreign Minister sends a message to the United Nations Secretary General, expressing the north's opposition to the simultaneous entry of south and north Korea into the United Nations.

November 26 – KOC President Kim Chong-ha, in a press conference, urges the north to accept the IOC's revised mediatory plan.

《1988》

January 1 – Kim Il-sung proposes a joint south-north conference.

January 12 – The north Korean Olympic Committee issues a statement announcing their boycott of the Seoul Olympics in 1988.

January 13 – The chairman of the north Korean Red Corss Central Committee notifies the south he would send a liaison official to Panmunjom on January 14 to deliver a letter to the south.

January 14 – Kim Sang-hyop, ROKNRC president, says his liaison official would receive letter on January 14.

January 14 – The north Korean letter was from the chairman of the Northern Preparatory Committee for Joint South-North Conference, proposing the convocation of a joint south-north conference.

January 15 – Government spokesman Lee Woong-hee, in a statement, urges the north to apologize over the KAL incident and help foster an atmosphere ripe for dialogue.

January 19 – SLOOC President Park Seh-jik, in a press conference, says the SLOOC would continue to keep the door of the Seoul Olympics open to north Korea.

February 7 – The SLOOC vice preident, in a press conference, urges the north to take part in the Seoul Olympics.

February 9 – The chairman of the north Korean Red Cross Central Committee asks the ROKNRC to let him known whether his January 13 letters were distributed to their recipients.

February 12 – ROKNRC President Kim Sang-hyop informs the north Koran Red Cross that the January 13 letters were distributed to their recipients.

February 20 – The Northern Prepartatory Committee for a Joint South-North Conference, in a statement, urges the south to agree to hold a joint south-north conference.

February 25 – President Roh Tae Woo, in his inaugural address, says the south would continue to keep the door of dialogue open to the north for the sake of peace and grand national reunity on the Korean peninsula.

March 1 – President Roh, in his Samil Independence Day meessage, expresses welcome to the north Korean compatriots participation in the Seoul Olympics.

March 5 – The chairman of the north Korean Red Cross Central Committee notifies the south he would send a liaison official to Panmunjom on March 8 to deliver a letter to the south.

March 7 – ROKNRC President Kim Sang-hyop notifies the north he would have his liaison official receive the letter on March 8.

March 8 – The chairman of the Northern Preparatory Committee for a Joint South-North Conference sends a second letter to the south, proposing again that a preliminary meeting for a joint south-north conference be held on March 28.

March 29 – A candidate chairman of the Student Body of Seoul National University proposes a south-north student meeting in an open message to the students of Kimilsung University of the north.

March 30 – The chief secretary of the Northern Presparatory Committee for a Joint South-North Conference,in a statement, says his committee had decided to leave it to the south to decide on the time of a preliminary meeting for a joint conference.

April 2 – The chairman of the north Korean Red Cross Central Committee notifies the south he would send a liaison official to Panmunjom on April 4 to deliver a letter to the south.

April 4 – ROKNRC President Kim Sang-hyop tells the north that the delivery of letter would not be helpful to the improvement of the inter-Korean relations, urging it to agree to resume the suspended Red Cross talks.

April 4 – The Student Committee of Kimilsung University, in a letter to the Student Body of Seoul National University, says it agreed to a south-north student meeting and suggests that the meeting be held at Panmunjom.

April 7 – The Central Committee of the north's Christians Federation in an appeal to the south Korean Christrians, expresses support to a declaration made by the KNCC and agitates joint struggles in support of the declaration.

April 21 – President Roh, in a press conference, declares the opening of an age of south-north cooperation for peaceful unification.

May 14 – The Council of National Student Representatives proposes detailed measures for a south-north student meeting.

May 17 – The National Student Congress of the north adopts a letter to south Korean college Students in support of a south-north student meeting and organized a northern preparatory committee.

May 18 – The Central Committee of the north Korean Red Cross notifies the south it would send a liaison official to Panmunjom on May 20 to deliver a letter from the Northern Preparatory Committee for a South-North Student Meeting to the south.

May 19 – ROKNRC President Kim Sang-hyop notifies the north he would give a reply to the notification from the north later.

May 20 – The Northern Preparatory Committee for a South-North Student Meeting, in a statement, calls for the realization of a south-north student meeting.

May 24 – ROKNRC President Kim Sang-hyop calls for the resumption of the suspended Red Cross talks.

May 27 – In a speech at a dinner for the visiting General Secretary of the Czechoslovak Communist Party, Kim Il-sung calls for bilateral and multilateral contacts between south and north Korea as well as for the co-host of the Seoul Olympics.

May 31 – Prime Minister Lee Hyon-jae of the south notifies the north he would send a liasion official to Panmunjom on June 3 to deliver a message to the north.

June 2 – The premier of the north's Administration Council refuses to receive message from the Prime Minister of the south.

June 2 – Minister of Culture and Information Chong Han-mo announces a government position over the issue of debate of unification.

June 3 – Prime Minister Lee Hyon-jae, in a message to the north broadcast over radio, proposes a high-level south-north officials meeting.

June 6 – The Northern Preparatory Committee for a Joint South-North Conference, in a statement, says it was willing to accept the idea of a high-level officials meeting in the form of a preliminary conference to prepare for a joint south-north conference.

June 8 – The Northern Preparatory Committee for South-North Student Talks, in a statement, urges the south to guarantee the successful holding of a south-north student meeting.

June 9 – National Unification Minister Lee Hong-koo issues a statement, expressing the government's willingness to discuss student exchanges on a priority basis at the proposed high-level officials meeting.

June 10 – Foreign Minister Choi Kwang-soo, in an address at the third U.N. Special Meeting on Disarmament, offers an idea of theree-stage disarmament on the Korean peninsula.

June 10 – The chief northern delegate to a south-north stduent meeting issues a statement instigating south Korean students to stage struggles to realize the south-north student meeting.

June 11 – Chondaehyop and eight other activist student organizations, in public rally they hosted, propose that the thwarted student meeting be held on August 15.

June 13 – A joint rally of north Korean students, in a message to south Korean students, expresses the intent of sending northern delegates to a south-north student meeting on August 15.

July 2 – The north Korean Red Cross Central Committee notifies the south it would send a liaison official to Panmunjom on July 4 to deliver a letter to the south.

July 4 – ROKNRC President Kim Sang-hyop calls for a dialogue between the authorities of the two sides to realize south-north student exchanges.

July 4 – A letter from the chief northern delegate to a south-north student meeting broadcast over radio.

July 7 – President Roh Tae Woo announces the Special Declaration for National Self-Esteem, Unification and Prosperity.

July 9 – The 20th plenary meeting of the 142nd Extraordinary National Assembly session adopts the Resolution Calling for north Korea's Participation in the Seoul Olympic Games.

July 11 – The Committee for the Peaceful Reunification of the Fatherland, in a statement, denounces the July 7 Special Declaration.

July 13 – ROKNRC President Kim Sang-hyop notifies the north he would send a liaison official to Panmunjom on July 15 to deliver a message from the Education Minister to the north.

July 14 – The chairman of the Education Commission of the north's Administration Council refuses to receive a letter from the south's Education Minister.

July 15 – Education Minister Kim Young-shik, in a statement broadcast over radio, proposes a south-north education officials meeting to discuss the question of realizing south-north student exchanges.

July 16 – Foreign Minister Choi Kwang-soo announces a set of foreign policy measures in connection with the July 7 Special Declaration.

July 16 – The chairman of the north Korean Red Cross Central Committee rejects a proposal for a south-north Red Cross working-level meeting.

July 17 – The spokesman of the north's Administration Council, in a statement, rejects a proposal for a south-north education officials meeting.

July 19 – The ROKNRC spokesman, in a comment, urges the north to agree to resume Red Cross working-level talks.

July 19 – Foreign Minister Choi Kwang-soo of the south proposes a south-north officials meeting to discuss the issue of allowing free visits by Korean residents abroad to south and north Korea and of guaranteeing the personal safety of the overseas Koreans visiting the two sides of Korea.

July 20 – The spokesman of the Education Ministry of the south, in a comment, urges the north to accept the idea of a south-north education officials meeting.

July 21 – Yang Hyong-sop, chairman of the Standing Committee of the north's Supreme People's Assembly, in a "letter to the National Assembly of the Republic of Korea," proposes a joint south-north parliamentary meeting to resolve the question of non-aggression.

July 26 – Yang Hyong-sop, chairman of the Standing Coomittee of the north's Supreme People's Assembly, in a "letter to Speaker Kim Jaison of the National Assembly of the Republic of Korea," suggests that the idea of Olympic co-host be discussed at the proposed joint south-north parliamentary meeting.

August 1 – Speaker Kim Jaison of the south proposes a preparatory contact to realize a south-north parliamentary meeting within the month of August.

August 9 – The chairman of the Standing Committee of the north's Supreme People's Assembly proposes that a working-level contact be held on August 17 to prepare for a joint south-north parliamentary meeting.

August 12 – Speaker Kim Jaison counter-proposes that a preparatory contact be held on August 19 to prepare for a south-north parliamentary meeting.

August 15 – President Roh, in a 43rd Liberation Day message, proposes a south-north top leaders meeting.

August 17 – The chairman of the Standing Committee of the north's Supreme People's Assembly accepts the time of a preparatory contact for a south-north parliamentary meeting.

August 17 – Speaker Kim Jaison of the south notifies the north of the list of its delegates to a preparatory contact for a south-north parliamentary meeting.
  – Chief delegate:Park Jun-kyu, Democratic Justice Party
  – Delegate:Lee Han-dong, Democratic Justrice Party
  – Delgate:Kim Bong-ho,Party for Peace and Democracy
  – Delegate:Park Gwan-Yong, Reunification Democratic Party
  – Delegate:Kim Yong-hwan, New Democratic Republican Party

August 18 – The north notifies the south of the list of its delgates to a preparatory contacts for a south-north parliamentary meeting.
  – Chief delegate:Chon Gum-chol, Korean Wokres' Party
  – Delegate:An Byong-su, Korean Workers' Party
  – Delegate:Li Dong-chol, Korean Workers' Party
  – Delegate:Li Chu-wung, Korean Socialist Democratic Party
  –Delegate: Pak Mun-chan, Chondogyo Chongwu Party

Agust 19 – The first preparatory contact for a south-north parliamentary meeting held.

August 19 – A liaison officials contact held to prepare for the second contact for a south-north parliamentary meeting held.

August 20 – The second preparatory contact for a south-north parliamentary meeting held.

– The third contact set to be held on August 22.

August 22 – The third preparatory contact for a south-north parliamentary meeting held.

– An exclusive chief deleagtes contact proposed.

August 23 – The north suggests that a chief delegates contact be held on August 23.

August 23 – The south counter-proposes that a chief delegates contact be held on August 24.

August 23 – The north agrees to the southern counter-proposal for the time of a chief delegates contact.

August 24 – An exclusive contact between the chief delegates to the preparatory parliamentary contact held.

August 24 – The south proposes that the fourth preparatory contact for a south-north parliamentary meeting be held on August 26.

August 24 – The north agrees to the time of the fourth contact.

August 26 – The fourth preparatory contact for a south-north parliamentary meeting held.

– The fifth preparatory contact set to be held on October 13.

September 3 – Minister of Culture and Information Chong Han-mo announces a decision to make public informative materials on north Korea and the rest of the Communist-bloc.

September 8 – In his "September 9th Day" message, Kim Il-sung says a south-north summit meeting could be held under specific conditions.

October 4 – President Roh, in his policy address, again proposes a south-north top leaders meeting.

October 4 – Deputy Prime Minister and Economic Planning Minister Rha Woong-bae announces a set of follow-up economic measures of the July 7 Special Declaration.

October 13 – The fifth preparatory contact for a south-north parliamentary meeting held.

October 18 – President Roh addresses the United Nations General
　　Assembly :
　　– Proposes the construction of "a city of peace" in the Demilitarized
　　　Zone.
　　– Proposes a south-north top leaders meeting again.
　　– proposes a Consultative Conference for Peace in Northeast Asia.
November 7 – The joint conference of the Central People's Committee, the
　　Standing Committee of the Supreme People's Assembly and the Admi-
　　nistration Council decides to send a "comprehensive peace plan" to
　　south Korea and the Uited State.
November 16 – The premier of the north's Administration Council, in a
　　letter to Prime Minister Lee Hyon-jae, proposes a high-level south-
　　north politico-military meeting.
　　– Delegations:seven to nine high-level political and military representa-
　　　tives headed by a deputy prime minister-level official with an army
　　　chief of staff-level military officer as a deputy chief delegate.
November 17 – The sixth preparatory contact for a south-north par-
　　liamentary meeting held.